CompTIA®
Cloud Essentials+™ Study Guide

Exam CLO-002

Second Edition

Quentin Docter

Cory Fuchs

SYBEX®
A Wiley Brand

Acknowledgments

On a personal note, I need to thank my family. My girls are all incredibly supportive. Unfortunately, writing a book while holding down a full-time job takes up a lot of time. I end up hiding in my office a lot, but they're always there for me, and I couldn't do it without them. Another huge thanks goes to my late grandpa Joe, who got me into computers and taught me so many lessons I will never be able to repay. Finally, thanks to my friends, who keep me relatively sane and laugh at me when I tell them I spent my weekend writing about cloud service models.

Thanks as well to my co-author, Cory Fuchs. I appreciate his technical and business acumen as well as his taste in beverages and BBQ. I also need to give special thanks to our technical editor, Chris Crayton. He was meticulous and thorough and challenged me to always find new and better ways to communicate complex concepts. His entire focus is on providing the best training material possible, and I doubt there's better in the business.

Last but certainly not least is the Wiley publishing team. Kenyon Brown, thank you for bringing me back for another project. Elizabeth Campbell, it's been a few years since we last worked together, but thanks for keeping us on track and making good suggestions. Kathleen Wisor had the fun job of keeping us organized, which is akin to herding cats. Additional tech editor Chris Crayton provided a great set of expert eyes and made excellent suggestions. Copyeditor Kim Wimpsett, reminded me yet again that I am no master of the English language and saved me from butchering it (too badly). Many thanks also go out to proofreader Louise Watson and our indexer, Johnna VanHoose Dinse. Without their great contributions, this book would not have made it into your hands.

—Quentin Docter

As this is my first time writing a book, this acknowledgment is going to be one of the most difficult parts of the book to write. I don't know where to begin. Standard practice would dictate that I thank my wife and children: Jamie, Declan, and Chella. Their patience and understanding during this process has been incalculable and more than I could have hoped for.

I must also thank Quentin Docter for his guidance and help in this opportunity. I would not be writing this without him. He is great friend and mentor in both writing and barbecue.

There are numerous individuals at Wiley whom I need to thank. Many I cannot name because I still have not met them. I do want to thank Ken, Elizabeth, and Chris for working with me on this project.

My parents, Wayne and Adina, have helped and supported me throughout my life. Words cannot begin to express my appreciation for everything they have done for me and my family. They have supported me through trying times and never wavered in their love. Thank you, Mom and Dad, I love you.

—Cory Fuchs

About the Authors

Quentin Docter   (Cloud Essentials+, A+, Network+, IT Fundamentals+, MCSE, CCNA, SCSA) is an IT consultant who started in the industry in 1994. Since then, he's worked as a tech and network support specialist, trainer, consultant, and webmaster. He has written several books for Sybex, including books on A+, IT Fundamentals+, Server+, Windows, and Sun Solaris certifications, as well as PC hardware and maintenance.

Cory Fuchs   (*Fox*) has worked in IT for more than 25 years. He holds several certifications from CompTIA, Microsoft, Cisco, and Red Hat. As a consultant, he was the cloud architect for several Fortune 500 companies working on full migrations and hybrid cloud deployments. As an IT professional Cory has specialized in virtualization, messaging/collaboration, telephony, identity management, automation, security, governance, and compliance. Cory can be reached at coryhfuchs@gmail.com.

Contents at a Glance

Contents

Table of Exercises

Introduction

Shortly after the Internet exploded in popularity, it was common to hear people joke that "maybe this isn't just a fad." Looking back, it's hard to believe that anyone would have ever seriously thought that it was, given its omnipresence in our lives today. The same things can be said about the cloud. What might have seemed like a novelty in the late 2000s is now mainstream. Most of us use cloud-based services every day, whether we realize it or not.

It's safe to say that the cloud has transformed our Internet experience as users. It's also had a massive impact on the way that companies and other organizations conduct business. The cloud has the potential to save organizations money and time, but only if it's implemented properly. Of course, that takes some technical expertise. But it also takes business knowledge. The intersection of business acumen and technical knowledge is where this book focuses.

Why Certify for Cloud Business Skills?

There is a major need in the market today for people who understand both the technical side and the business side of an organization. Indeed, all of the following are reasons to become certified in cloud business skills:

- The largest skills gap in IT workers is business acumen.

- IT employees are now expected to weigh in on business decisions.

- Certification empowers both technical and nontechnical employees to make data-driven cloud recommendations.

- Certification demonstrates readiness for promotional opportunities to management-level positions.

- Certification ensures understanding of personnel working for cloud product and services organizations.

The CompTIA Cloud Essentials+ exam is a great certification for a few reasons. First, it's job-focused and aligned with the needs of employers. Second, it's current with today's cloud environment—the technology and how it's used. Third, it's the only vendor-neutral cloud-specific business certification. It's a great stepping stone for IT and business professionals who want to become certified in specific cloud technologies such as Amazon AWS or Microsoft Azure.

As noted, this certification focuses on the intersection of business and technology. If you're interested in the more technical side of cloud management, consider the CompTIA Cloud+ certification. To help prepare for it, look for *Sybex CompTIA Cloud+ Study Guide, Second Edition*, by Todd Montgomery and Stephen Olson.

Who Should Read This Book?

This book is a great resource as a primer to cloud technologies, with a practical focus. We don't get into too much deep technical theory. We want people who read this book to understand cloud terms and basic technologies and be able to apply that knowledge to business situations.

The Cloud Essentials+ cert, and therefore this book, is for IT and business professionals who:

- Want to move into management and leadership roles
- Work for cloud product and services companies
- Have a strong technical or data background, but do not have a business degree
- Have good general business acumen, but do not have validation of their competency in cloud-specific situations
- Are responsible for providing recommendations on cloud-related decisions
- Wish to understand why their company makes the cloud-related decisions they do
- Want to remain relevant to their employers by demonstrating professional growth, in an area of unmet need

If any of these apply to you, then this book can help you out!

What Does This Book Cover?

This book covers everything you need to know to pass the CompTIA Cloud Essentials+ exam. Official objectives are available here:

https://certification.comptia.org/certifications/cloud-essentials

Chapter 1: Cloud Principles and Design   This chapter introduces basic cloud principles. Included are service models, or what the cloud can deliver, deployment models, or how the cloud can be executed, and several characteristics that make the cloud valuable to a business.

Chapter 2: Cloud Networking and Storage   The cloud is perhaps best known for its storage capabilities, so this chapter covers different features of cloud storage such as compression, deduplication, and capacity on demand, as well as hot versus cold storage, storage types, and software-defined storage and content delivery networks.

Accessing the cloud is also of high importance, so this chapter also discusses cloud connectivity and access types and popular networking tools such as load balancers, DNS, and firewalls.

Chapter 3: Assessing Cloud Needs   Every organization has slightly different cloud needs. This chapter starts with assessing company needs to determine how the cloud will provide benefits. Then, it moves into looking into some specific types of benefits in detail, including access management, data analytics, digital marketing, the Internet of Things, blockchain, and more.

Chapter 4: Engaging Cloud Vendors   After an organization has analyzed the technical side and decided to move to the cloud, it's time to find the right cloud provider. This chapter looks at financial and business aspects of engaging cloud providers. We talk about types of expenditures, licensing models, requests for information, statements of work, service level agreements, evaluations, and contracts and billing.

Chapter 5: Management and Technical Operations   Continuing with some of the technical aspects of operating in the cloud, we discuss data management, availability, disposable resources, monitoring, and visibility. These are a precursor and are used when starting DevOps and a CICD pipeline. Testing and configuration management are critical aspects of DevOps, and we walk through a few examples. Finally, we discuss financials and reporting on usage when using resources in the cloud.

Chapter 6: Governance and Risk   Organizations will have to manage risk whenever they use cloud resources. In this chapter we introduce the concept of risk and the responses. We discuss some risks that are different when using the cloud versus on-premises data centers. We introduce policies and procedures and some of the organization management needed for cloud initiatives. We finish with policies that are specific to security, access, and control.

Chapter 7: Compliance and Security in the Cloud   Cloud security will be a critical piece for any organization wanting to implement resources in the cloud. This chapter looks at regulations and standards that may be required for an organization to use the cloud. We take a deeper dive into data security and processes for securing the data. We give examples of security assessments that any organization should be performing. Finally, we discuss applications and infrastructure security.

What's Included in This Book?

We've included the following study tools throughout the book:

Assessment Test   At the end of this introduction is an assessment test that you can use to check your readiness for the exam. Take this test before you start reading the book; it will help you determine the areas where you might need to brush up. The answers to the assessment test questions appear on a separate page after the last question of the test. Each answer includes an explanation and a note telling you the chapter in which the material appears.

Objective Map and Opening List of Objectives   Just before the assessment test, you'll find a detailed exam objective map, showing you where each of the CompTIA exam objectives is covered in this book. In addition, each chapter opens with a list of the exam objectives it covers. Use these to see exactly where each of the exam topics is covered.

Exam Essentials   Each chapter, just after the summary, includes a number of exam essentials. These are the key topics that you should take from the chapter in terms of areas to focus on when preparing for the exam.

Written Labs   Each chapter includes a written lab to test your knowledge. These labs map to the exam objectives. You can find the answers to those questions in Appendix A.

Chapter Review Questions   To test your knowledge as you progress through the book, there are 20 review questions at the end of each chapter. As you finish each chapter, answer the review questions and then check your answers—the correct answers and explanations are in Appendix B. You can go back to reread the section that deals with each question you got wrong in order to ensure that you answer correctly the next time you're tested on the material.

Interactive Online Learning Environment and Test Bank

Studying the material in the *CompTIA Cloud Essentials+ Study Guide* is an important part of preparing for the Cloud Essentials+ certification exam, but we provide additional tools to help you prepare. The online Test Bank will help you understand the types of questions that will appear on the certification exam.

The sample tests in the Test Bank include all the questions in each chapter as well as the questions from the Assessment test. In addition, there is one more practice exam with 70 questions. You can use these test questions to evaluate your understanding and identify areas that may require additional study.

The flashcards in the Test Bank will push the limits of what you should know for the certification exam. There are more than 100 questions that are provided in digital format. Each flashcard has one question and one correct answer.

The online glossary is a searchable list of key terms introduced in this exam guide that you should know for the Cloud Essentials+ certification exam.

To start using these items to study for the Cloud Essentials+ exam, go to www.wiley .com/go/sybextestprep and register your book to receive your unique PIN. Once you have the PIN, return to www.wiley.com/go/sybextestprep, find your book, and click register or log in and follow the link to register a new account or add this book to an existing account.

How to Contact the Publisher

If you believe you've found a mistake in this book, please bring it to our attention. At John Wiley & Sons, we understand how important it is to provide our customers with accurate content, but even with our best efforts an error may occur.

To submit your possible errata, please email it to our Customer Service Team at wileysupport@wiley.com with the subject line "Possible Book Errata Submission."

Cloud Essentials+ Study Guide Exam Objectives

This table provides the extent, by percentage, to which each domain is represented on the actual examination.

Domain	% of Examination
1.0 Cloud Concepts	24%
2.0 Business Principles of Cloud Environments	28%
3.0 Management and Technical Operations	26%
4.0 Governance, Risk, Compliance, and Security for the Cloud	22%
Total	100%

Exam objectives are subject to change at any time without prior notice and at CompTIA's sole discretion. Please visit CompTIA's website (www.comptia.org) for the most current listing of exam objectives.

Objective Map

Objective	Chapter
Domain 1.0: Cloud Concepts	
1.1 Explain cloud principles.	1
1.2 Identify cloud networking concepts.	2
1.3 Identify cloud storage technologies.	2
1.4 Summarize important aspects of cloud design.	1
Domain 2.0: Business Principles of Cloud Environments	
2.1 Given a scenario, use appropriate cloud assessments.	3
2.2 Summarize the financial aspects of engaging a cloud provider.	4
2.3 Identify the important business aspects of vendor relations in cloud adoptions.	4
2.4 Identify the benefits or solutions of utilizing cloud services.	3
2.5 Compare and contrast cloud migration approaches.	4
Domain 3.0: Management and Technical Operations	
3.1 Explain aspects of operating within the cloud.	5
3.2 Explain DevOps in cloud environments.	5
3.3 Given a scenario, review and report on the financial expenditures related to cloud resources.	5
Domain 4.0: Governance, Risk, Compliance, and Security for the Cloud	
4.1 Recognize risk management concepts related to cloud services.	6
4.2 Explain policies or procedures.	6
4.3 Identify the importance and impacts of compliance in the cloud.	6
4.4 Explain security concerns, measures, or concepts of cloud operations.	7

Assessment Test

1. In the shared responsibility model, who is responsible for the security of compute and storage resources?
   - **A.** CSP
   - **B.** Client
   - **C.** CSP and client
   - **D.** All clients together

2. Gmail is an example of which type of cloud service?
   - **A.** SaaS
   - **B.** IaaS
   - **C.** XaaS
   - **D.** PaaS

3. Microsoft Azure is an example of which type of cloud deployment model?
   - **A.** Commercial
   - **B.** Public
   - **C.** Private
   - **D.** Hybrid

4. Your CTO wants to ensure that company users in Asia, Europe, and South America have access to cloud resources. Which cloud characteristic should be considered to meet the business need?
   - **A.** Self-service
   - **B.** Broad network access
   - **C.** Scalability
   - **D.** Shared responsibility

5. You are negotiating the SLA with a CSP. Which of the following high availability guarantees is likely to cost you the most?
   - **A.** Three nines
   - **B.** Four nines
   - **C.** Five nines
   - **D.** None—they should all be the same price

6. You are negotiating an SLA with a CSP. Who is responsible for defining the RPO and RTO?
   - **A.** The client.
   - **B.** The CSP.
   - **C.** The client defines the RPO, and the CSP defines the RTO.
   - **D.** The client defines the RTO, and the CSP defines the RPO.

7. Which of the following cloud technologies reduces the amount of storage space needed by removing redundant copies of stored files?

   A. Capacity on demand

   B. Compression

   C. Deduplication

   D. Block storage

8. You are setting up a cloud solution for your company, and it needs to be optimized for unstructured data. Which storage type is appropriate?

   A. Block

   B. File

   C. Cold

   D. Object

9. What is SSH used for within the cloud environment?

   A. To remotely manage a Windows server

   B. To remotely manage a Linux server

   C. To remotely access cloud storage

   D. To remotely deliver content to clients

10. You are setting up cloud services and need space to store email archives. Which of the following will be the least expensive solution?

    A. Hot storage

    B. Cold storage

    C. Object storage

    D. Block storage

11. You are obtaining cloud-based networking for your company. The CIO insists that the cloud resources be as safe as possible from potential hackers. Which service will help with this?

    A. Load balancing

    B. DNS

    C. SDN

    D. Firewall

12. Which of the following services within a cloud is responsible for resolving host names to IP addresses?

    A. DNS

    B. SDN

    C. CDN

    D. SDS

13. You are consulting for Company A, and they ask you to run a cloud assessment. In which order should you perform the following tasks as part of this assessment? (List the steps in order.)

    A. Compare benchmarks

    B. Perform a feasibility study

    C. Run a baseline

    D. Gather current and future requirements

14. An engineer on your team says that the company should use new technology to enter a new stream of business. He says that you should sell and monitor linked home appliances and smart thermostats. Which technology is he talking about using?

    A. VDI

    B. IoT

    C. SSO

    D. AI

15. You are beginning a cloud assessment for your company and need to contact key stakeholders. Who in the following list is NOT an example of a key stakeholder for the cloud assessment?

    A. CEO

    B. CISO

    C. CSP

    D. Department manager

16. Which of the following cloud services uses probabilities to make predictions about input?

    A. Artificial intelligence

    B. Autonomous environments

    C. Microservices

    D. Machine learning

17. Which of the following is NOT a key operating principle of blockchain?

    A. Anonymity

    B. Transparency

    C. Immutability

    D. Decentralization

18. You are implementing multiple levels of security for new cloud resources. Which of the following is NOT a method of cloud-based identity access management?

    A. SSO

    B. MFA

    C. VDI

    D. Federation

19. You are searching for the right cloud vendor for your organization. Which of the following should be your first step?

    A. Pilot

    B. RFP

    C. RFQ

    D. RFI

20. Your current cloud contract is expiring, and you need to quickly move to a different provider. Which type of migration is best in this situation?

    A. Rip and replace

    B. Lift and shift

    C. Hybrid

    D. Phased

21. You want to test a solution from a CSP to show that a new technology works properly. Which type of evaluation should you perform?

    A. PoC

    B. PoV

    C. Managed

    D. Pilot

22. Internal IT employees need to learn to use a new cloud-based software interface to manage corporate services. What should you request from the CSP?

    A. Support

    B. Managed services

    C. Training

    D. Professional development

23. The finance department wants you to convert the IT infrastructure capital expenditures to operating expenditures. Which of the following would do this?

    A. Switch to BYOL licensing

    B. Negotiate billing terms for new IT hardware

    C. Switch to a pay-as-you-go model

    D. Depreciate the IT assets on a shorter time horizon

24. A company hires contractors for six-month projects. After six months, a new team of contractors will be brought in. Which type of software licensing allows the licenses to be transferred from the first group to the second group?

    A. Pilot

    B. PoC

    C. Subscription

    D. BYOL

25. You have migrated to the cloud, and users have access to cloud-based productivity software. There are 10 users in the finance group. Each user has a laptop, tablet, and smartphone that can access the productivity software. Using a subscription model, how many software licenses will you need to purchase for the finance department?

    A. 1

    B. 10

    C. 20

    D. 30

26. In the Continuous Integration Continuous Delivery (CI/CD) pipeline the four steps are separated into _____ from each other, and the CI/CD attempts to remove them.

    A. Regions

    B. Zones

    C. Silos

    D. Networks

27. The latency between data and the end user is determined for the most part by the property:

    A. Locality

    B. Provisioned

    C. Replication

    D. Data availability

28. Linux as an operating system utilizes which license type?

    A. Free for use

    B. Pay for use

    C. Rent for use

    D. Lease for use

29. Which replication type keeps data synced between two or more locations in real time?

    A. Asynchronous

    B. Autoscaling

    C. Synchronous

    D. Reserved

30. Copying snapshots of instances to different locations in order to protect against data loss or corruption is an example of:

    A. Geo-redundancy

    B. Replication

    C. Backups

    D. Object storage

31. Immutable infrastructure contains resources that:

   A. Are unchangeable

   B. Are destructable

   C. Are ephemeral

   D. Are changeable

32. Analysis that is dependent on the quality or perceived value of an asset is known as:

   A. Perceptive

   B. Qualititative

   C. Quantitative

   D. Valuative

33. Analysis that is dependent on the monetary value or quantity of an asset is known as:

   A. Qualititative

   B. Perceptive

   C. Valuative

   D. Quantitative

34. The three main components of risk are?

   A. Employees, health, happiness

   B. Servers, network, attack

   C. Assets, threat, probability

   D. Money, stocks, failure

35. ____ and ____ owner are the individuals of an organization who own and manage risk. (Choose two.)

   A. CEO

   B. Risk

   C. President

   D. Asset

36. ____ is a risk response where an organization decides to initiate actions to prevent any risk from taking place.

   A. Transfer

   B. Avoidance

   C. Mitigation

   D. Acceptance

37. _____ are directions, guidance, and provide goals for an organization.

   A. Procedures

   B. Policies

   C. Agendas

   D. Manuals

38. With new advancements in CSP technologies, you don't need to worry about storing sensitive data in the cloud. Without any configuration on your part, a CSP's tools will be sufficient for what?

A. Application scanning

B. Reulatory requirements

C. Confidentiality

D. Integrity

39. An organization that does business internationally needs to take into consideration data sovereignty laws on data stored in: (Choose all that apply.)

A. The nation where the data is stored

B. The nationality of the user the data is about

C. The language that the data is stored in

D. The location of the organization that stores the data

40. In the event of competing local, state, federal, and international regulatory requirements, which regulations should an organization follow?

A. Local

B. State

C. Federal

D. International

41. Your organization is in negotiations with a federal contractor that also deals with sensitive information from the federal government. Which federal regulation will apply in this scenario?

A. FERPA

B. MPAA

C. FISMA

D. NIST

42. You have been tasked with designing an FIPS 140-2 compliant application. Which technology are you most concerned with?

A. User identity and passwords

B. Encryption

C. Mac versus PC

D. Authorization

43. HIPAA, GLBA, PCI DSS, and FINRA are all examples of _____ based standards.

A. Organizational

B. Federal

C. Industry

D. International

Answers to Assessment Test

1. **C.** In the shared responsibility model, the CSP is responsible for security of the cloud, which includes services and infrastructure such as compute and storage resources. Clients are responsible for security in the cloud, such as operating systems, access management, and customer data. See Chapter 1 for more information.

2. **A.** The software as a service (SaaS) model provides software applications, including apps such as Google Docs, Microsoft Office 365, and Gmail. Infrastructure as a service (IaaS) offers hardware for compute, storage, and networking functionality.

    Anything as a service (XaaS) is too broad and can mean a combination of multiple services. Platform as a service (PaaS) provides development platforms for software developers. See Chapter 1 for more information.

3. **B.** Microsoft Azure, Amazon Web Services, and Google Cloud are all examples of public clouds. There is no commercial cloud deployment model. Private clouds are owned and used by one company and not sold to others. A hybrid cloud is both public and private. See Chapter 1 for more information.

4. **C.** Scalability can refer to the ability for cloud services to be scaled geographically. Users from multiple global locations can access resources. Self-service means the ability to add resources without supplier intervention. Broad network access means that various client devices with different operating systems can access resources. Shared responsibility is a model that defines and enhances cloud security. See Chapter 1 for more information.

5. **C.** High availability models are specified in terms of nines. More nines guarantee more uptime but also cost more. Therefore, five nines will cost more than four nines, which will cost more than three nines. See Chapter 1 for more information.

6. **A.** The client is responsible for defining the recovery point objective (RPO), which is the maximum age of files that must be recovered from backups in order to restore normal operations, and the recovery time objective (RTO), which is how long the CSP has to get everything operational, including network access and data restoration, in the event of a disaster. See Chapter 1 for more information.

7. **C.** Deduplication saves storage space by removing redundant copies of files. Compression also saves space but does it by removing redundancy within a file. Capacity on demand is when a client can get more storage space instantaneously. Block storage is a storage type. While it's more efficient than file storage, it doesn't remove redundant files or data. See Chapter 2 for more information.

8. **D.** Object storage is the best option for unstructured data. Block storage is good for databases, storage area networks, and virtual machines. File storage is used on common PC operating systems such as Windows and macOS. Cold storage means the data is offline. See Chapter 2 for more information.

9. **B.** Secure Shell (SSH) is used to remotely manage Linux-based servers. The Remote Desktop Protocol is used to remotely manage Windows-based servers. See Chapter 2 for more information.

10. B. Cold storage will always be less expensive than hot storage. Object and block storage are ways to store files, but either can be hot or cold. See Chapter 2 for more information.

11. D. A firewall is a network- or host-based security device. It can help protect a network or individual computers from malicious network traffic. Load balancing means spreading work across multiple servers. Domain Name System (DNS) resolves host names to IP addresses. Software-defined networking (SDN) makes networks more agile and flexible by separating the forwarding of network packets (the infrastructure layer) from the logical decision-making process (the control layer). See Chapter 2 for more information.

12. A. Domain Name System (DNS) resolves host names to IP addresses. SDN abstracts network hardware in the cloud. A content delivery network does load balancing for websites. Software-defined storage (SDS) allows for the virtualization of cloud storage solutions. See Chapter 2 for more information.

13. D, C, B, A. The first step in a cloud assessment is to determine current and future requirements. Then, run a baseline, followed by a feasibility study, then gap analysis, then use reporting, and then compare to benchmarks. Finally, create documentation and diagrams. See Chapter 3 for more information.

14. B. Linked home appliances and smart thermostats are examples of technologies that rely upon the Internet of Things (IoT). Virtual desktop infrastructure (VDI) creates virtual user desktops. Single sign-on (SSO) is a security mechanism for computer logins. Artificial intelligence is when computers perform complex, human-like tasks. See Chapter 3 for more information.

15. C. Key stakeholders are important people with a vested interest in something. In this case, the chief executive officer (CEO), chief information security officer (CISO), and department manager could all be key stakeholders. The cloud service provider (CSP) is not a key stakeholder who should have input on which cloud services you need. They can make suggestions, but their role is to sell you services. See Chapter 3 for more information.

16. D. Machine learning (ML), which is a general form of artificial intelligence (AI), uses probabilities to make predictions about classifying new input based on previous input it received. Autonomous environments are when machines perform complex, human-like actions without human intervention. Microservices is a way to speed up app development and lower costs. See Chapter 3 for more information.

17. A. Blockchain operates on three key principles: decentralization, transparency, and immutability. No one organization owns the blockchain, and the information is stored on all participating nodes. Therefore, there is decentralization and transparency. The data is also hard to hack, which gives it immutability. While the user IDs are securely hashed in blockchain, there is no anonymity. See Chapter 3 for more information.

18. C. Virtual desktop infrastructure (VDI) is for creating virtual user desktops on a server. It is not related to identity access management (IAM). Single sign-on (SSO), multifactor authentication, and federation are all IAM services. See Chapter 3 for more information.

19. D. The first step is to gather information about a vendor's capabilities, and that is done through a request for information (RFI). After the RFI stage, you might request a bid for standard services with a request for quotation (RFQ) or request for proposal (RFP). A pilot is a small-scale evaluation deployment in the production environment. You would not do that before an RFI. See Chapter 4 for more information.

20. B. Lift and shift, where data and applications are picked up as is and moved to another location, is the quickest and cheapest migration option. In a rip and replace, software needs to be redeveloped to take advantage of cloud services. A hybrid is a combination of the two, or a migration where some items stay in the original location. Phased migrations happen over time. See Chapter 4 for more information.

21. A. A PoC is an evaluation used to prove that a technology works as it should. A proof of value (PoV) is run to see whether cost savings can be realized. Managed services are professional services used to support cloud installations. A pilot is a small-scale initial rollout of a solution into the production environment. See Chapter 4 for more information.

22. C. Training is a short-term activity that focuses on acquiring a specific skillset to perform a job. Support and managed services are professional services that you might buy to help support the cloud. Professional development refers to a long-term educational process focused on employee growth. See Chapter 4 for more information.

23. C. Purchasing IT hardware or other tangible assets is a capital expenditure. Switching to a cloud-based IT infrastructure model with pay-as-you-go pricing means less (or no) need to purchase hardware and therefore no new capital expenditures. BYOL licenses can be permanent or subscription-based. Depreciation timelines are for capital expenditures only. See Chapter 4 for more information.

24. D. Bring your own license (BYOL) is when software can be transferred from one user to another or from one system to another. Subscriptions might or might not qualify as BYOL. Pilots and proof of concepts (PoCs) are types of evaluations. See Chapter 4 for more information.

25. B. Under a subscription-based model, users should have device flexibility, meaning that only one license per user is required. Therefore, you need 10 licenses. See Chapter 4 for more information.

26. C. The four teams involved in the CICD pipeline do not communicate or collaborate with each other. Regions, zones, and networks are terms that are not specific to the CICD pipeline. See Chapter 5 for more information.

27. A. Locality is the measure of the distance between data and the end user. This distance directly impacts the latency between the two. Provisioned is a state of an instance. Replication can affect latency but does not determine it. Data availability is a property of data and the availability. See Chapter 5 for more information.

28. A. The Linux kernel is licensed under the GPL, which is a free-for-use license. Pay for use is a license type, but the Linux kernel is free. C and D are not license types. See Chapter 5 for more information.

29. C. Synchronous replication keeps data synced in real time. Asynchronous replication eventually keeps data consistent. Autoscaling and Reserved are not types of replication. See Chapter 5 for more information.

30. C. Backups are the copying of data to a different location in the event of data loss or corruption. Replication does not copy snapshots. Geo-redundancy does copy data, but the source can still be lost or corrupted. Object storage is where backups are usually copied to. See Chapter 5 for more information.

31. A. Immutable means that the data cannot be modified or changed. B, C, and D are all properties that are changeable. See Chapter 5 for more information.

32. B. Qualitative analysis is the analysis of a value of an asset based on its perceived value. In contrast, quantitative analysis is the analysis of the monetary value of an asset based on monetary value. See Chapter 6 for more information.

33. D. Quantitative analysis is the analysis on of a value of an asset based on monetary value or its quantity. In contrast, qualitative analysis is the analysis of the value of an asset based on its perceived value. See Chapter 6 for more information.

34. C. While the other choices may be assets and potential threats, they are all specific. Risk is the probability or likelihood of a threat against an asset. See Chapter 6 for more information.

35. B, D. While a company's CEO and president maybe the top-level risk owners, they are not all of them. The two identified owners are the risk and asset owners. See Chapter 6 for more information.

36. C. Mitigation is the risk response where an organization lowers or reduces the chance of risk but does not prevent all risk from occurring. Avoidance is the risk response where all risk is removed. See Chapter 6 for more information.

37. B. Policies are general guidelines for an organization. Procedures are specific steps or actions. Agendas and manuals are where the guidelines are either documented or noted. See Chapter 6 for more information.

38. B. CSPs do offer tools that can meet most if not all the regulatory requirements your organization may require. However, compliance is similar to the shared responsibility model. You will need to take some ownership of compliance. See Chapter 7 for more information.

39. A, B, D. Organizations that do business internationally and store data about users and transactions that originate around the globe must consider three criteria: Where the data is physically stored. The nationality of the users for whom the organization is storing data. The location in which the organization is doing business. See Chapter 7 for more information.

40. C. Particularly in the US, federal laws preempt all other regulations. However, most nation states have similar rules due to sovereignty laws. See Chapter 7 for more information.

41. C. The Federal Information Security Management Act (FISMA) is the federal regulation that deals with sensitive information security for federal agencies. FERPA is a federal law that protects the privacy of student education records. Motion Picture Association of America (MPAA) is the association that provides best practices guidance and control frameworks to help major studio partners and vendors design infrastructure and solutions to ensure the security of digital film assets. National Institute of Standards and Technology (NIST) is a part of the US Commerce Department that maintains and promotes guidelines and measurement standards. See Chapter 7 for more information.

42. B. FIPS is a cryptographic standard for encryption. The other answers may use encryption in some fashion, but they are not rated for FIPS compliance. See Chapter 7 for more information.

43. C. All the examples are standards that are industry specific. HIPAA is healthcare, GLBA is financial, PCI DSS is credit care, and FINRA is financial. See Chapter 7 for more information.

Chapter

1

Cloud Principles and Design

THE FOLLOWING COMPTIA CLOUD ESSENTIALS+ EXAM CLO-002 OBJECTIVES ARE COVERED IN THIS CHAPTER:

✓ **1.1 Explain cloud principles.**

- Service models
  - SaaS
  - IaaS
  - PaaS
- Deployment models
  - Public
  - Private
  - Hybrid
- Characteristics
  - Elastic
  - Self-service
  - Scalability
  - Broad network access
  - Pay-as-you-go
  - Availability
- Shared responsibility model

✓ **1.4 Summarize important aspects of cloud design.**

- Redundancy
- High availability
- Disaster recovery
- Recovery objectives
  - RPO
  - RTO

The computer industry is an industry of big, new trends. Every few years, a new technology comes along and becomes popular, until the next wave of newer, faster, and shinier objects comes along to distract everyone from the previous wave. Thinking back over the past few decades, there have been several big waves, including the rise of the Internet, wireless networking, and mobile computing.

The biggest recent wave in the computing world is cloud computing. Its name comes from the fact that the technology is Internet based; in most computer literature, the Internet is represented by a graphic that looks like a cloud. It seems like everyone is jumping on the cloud (pun intended, but doesn't that sound like fun?), and perhaps you or your company have used cloud technologies already. But to many people, the cloud is still nebulous and maybe even a little scary. There's a lot to know about the nuts and bolts of cloud computing.

The CompTIA Cloud Essentials+ certification exam assesses cloud knowledge from the perspective of the business analyst. Business analysts come from a variety of backgrounds, including technophiles who have business-facing roles, those who have business acumen but little technical experience, and anywhere in between. This certification—and this study guide—attempts to balance technical data with practical business information. You'll find some tech-speak here, but we won't get into the hard-core inner workings of cloud management.

If you're interested in the more technical side of cloud management, consider the CompTIA Cloud+ certification. To help prepare for it, look for the *CompTIA Cloud+ Study Guide, Second Edition*, by Todd Montgomery and Stephen Olson (Sybex, 2018).

This chapter starts off by diving into the fundamentals of cloud principles and cloud design. A business analyst (BA) working with cloud providers should understand common service and deployment models, cloud characteristics, and important design aspects such as redundancy, high availability, and disaster recovery.

Understanding Cloud Principles

You hear the term a lot today—*the cloud*. You're probably already using cloud services whether you realize it or not. For example, if you store music in iCloud, use Gmail, or use Microsoft Office 365, you are using cloud-based services. But what exactly is the cloud? The way it's named—and it's probably due to the word *the* at the beginning—makes it sound as if it's one giant, fluffy, magical entity that does everything you could ever want a computer to do. Only it's not quite that big, fluffy, or magical, and it's not even one thing. To help illustrate what the cloud is, let's first consider a pre-cloud example—we'll call it *traditional computing*.

Imagine that you are at a small business in the 1980s—you probably have big hair and make questionable choices in the music you listen to—and need to decide if the company should purchase a computer. This decision might sound silly today, but before the mid-1990s, it was one that required many companies to seriously weigh the pros and cons. Desktop computers were almost a luxury item, and kids' lemonade stands certainly didn't have card readers to accept mobile payments! Perhaps the accounting department could automate payroll, the sales team could make promotional materials, or the boss just wanted to play solitaire. Regardless of the reason, someone went out and priced computers and made the business case to purchase one.

The computer would be traditional in all senses of the word. It would have a collection of hardware such as a processor, memory, and hard drive, an operating system (OS) that interfaced with the hardware, and one or more applications that allowed employees to complete tasks. Figure 1.1 illustrates this traditional computing model. You can see that the hardware is considered the base, and the OS and apps build upon it.

FIGURE 1.1   Traditional computing model

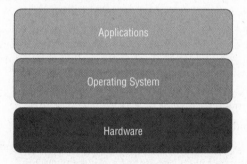

Over the years, the company expands, and more employees need computers. Eventually the computers need to talk to each other, and things like centralized storage and a database are required. So along with computers, you have to buy expensive server hardware, storage devices, and networking equipment such as switches, routers, and a firewall. The costs are adding up, and every year it seems like the IT budget gets squeezed. To top it off, every few years much of the hardware becomes obsolete and really should be replaced. The already tight budgets become even more challenging to manage. To add even another complication, software companies keep producing new versions with features that employees say are critical, so the software needs to be upgraded as well. (The same holds true for OSs.)

The pace of innovation can be staggering, and the cost of keeping up can be overwhelming for many businesses. But in the traditional model of computing, it was just the cost of doing business. Then in the late 2000s, cloud computing started changing everything.

Cloud computing is a method by which you access remote servers that provide software, storage, database, networking, or compute services for you. Instead of your company needing to buy the hardware and software, another company does, and yours essentially rents it from them and accesses it over the Internet. There isn't one cloud but hundreds of commercial clouds in existence today. Many of them are owned by big companies, such as Amazon, Microsoft, Google, HP, and Apple. The three most popular ones for businesses are Amazon Web Services (AWS), Microsoft Azure, and Google Cloud.

One great feature of the cloud is that using it is pretty simple in most cases. If a user can open a web browser and navigate to a website, they can use the cloud. We'll get into more details of different types of cloud access in Chapter 2, "Cloud Networking and Storage."

There are many advantages to cloud computing, and the most important ones revolve around money. Cloud providers get economies of scale by having a big pool of resources available to share among many clients. It may be entirely possible for them to add more clients without needing to add new hardware, which results in greater profit. From a client company's standpoint, the company can pay for only the resources it needs without investing large amounts of capital into hardware and software that will be outdated in a few years. Using the cloud is often cheaper than the alternative.

For clients, there are several other advantages of cloud computing as well, including the following:

- Access to resources from anywhere in the world from multiple types of client computers and devices

- Flexibility and scalability, because additional resources can be quickly added or removed

- Access to newer technologies without someone needing to take a long time to set them up

- Data protection through the use of enterprise-level backups

- Reduced IT staff and administration costs

Plus, if there is a hardware failure within the cloud, the provider handles it. If the cloud is set up right, the client won't even know that a failure occurred.

The biggest disadvantage of the cloud has been security. The client company's data is stored on someone else's server, and company employees are sending it back and forth via the Internet. Cloud providers have dramatically increased their security mechanisms over the last several years, but there can still be issues, especially if the data is highly sensitive material or personally identifiable information (PII). We'll talk more about security in the "Shared Responsibility Model" section later in this chapter. Other disadvantages include potential downtime, either from the service provider being down or from the lack of an Internet connection, and limited control. Some companies don't like the fact that they don't own the assets or have the ability to perform some administrative tasks.

If it seems like there's a lot to learn about the cloud, there is. We'll break it down into manageable sections to help it make more sense. Within this chapter, we will cover the following topics:

- Service models

- Deployment models

- Cloud characteristics

- Shared responsibility model

- Cloud design

Before we get into those topics, though, we're going to take a slight detour into the technology that makes cloud computing possible—virtualization.

Virtualization

Cloud computing is possible thanks to a concept called *virtualization*, which means that there isn't necessarily a one-to-one relationship between a physical server and a logical (or virtual) server or services. In other words, there might be one physical server that virtually hosts cloud services for a dozen companies, or there might be several physical servers working together as one logical server. From the end user's side, the concept of a physical machine versus a virtual machine (VM) doesn't even come into play, because it's all handled behind the scenes.

Virtualization has been around in the computer industry since 1967, but it has only recently exploded in popularity thanks to the flexibility that the Internet offers.

Perhaps the easiest way to understand virtualization is to compare and contrast it to what we called the traditional computing model earlier in this chapter. In the traditional computing model, a computer is identified as being a physical collection of hardware that is running some combination of software, such as an OS and various applications. There's a one-to-one relationship between the hardware and the OS.

For the sake of illustration, imagine that a machine is a file server and now it needs to perform the functions of a web server as well. To make this happen, the administrator would need to ensure that the computer has enough resources to support the service (processor, memory, network bandwidth), install web server software, configure the appropriate files and permissions, and then bring it back online as a file and web server. These would be relatively straightforward administrative tasks.

But now imagine that the machine in question is being asked to run Windows Server and Linux at the same time. Now there's a problem. In the traditional computing model, only one OS can run at one time, because each OS completely controls the hardware resources in the computer. Sure, an administrator can install a second OS and configure the server to dual-boot, meaning which OS to run is chosen during the boot process, but only one OS can run at a time. So if the requirement is to have a Windows-based file server and a Linux-based web server, there's a problem. Two physical computers are needed.

Similarly, imagine that there is a Windows-based workstation being used by an applications programmer. The programmer has been asked to develop an app that works in Linux, macOS, or anything other than Windows. When the programmer needs to test the app to see how well it works, what does she do? She can configure her system to dual-boot, but once again, in the traditional computing model, she's limited to one OS at a time per physical computer. Her company could purchase a second system, but that quickly starts to get expensive when there are multiple users with similar needs.

This is where virtualization comes in. The term *virtualization* is defined as creating virtual (rather than actual) versions of something. In computer jargon, it means creating virtual environments where "computers" can operate. We use quotation marks around the word *computers* because they don't need to be physical computers in the traditional sense. Virtualization is often used to let multiple OSs (or multiple instances of the same OS) run on one physical machine at the same time. Yes, they are often still bound by the physical characteristics of the machine on which they reside, but virtualization breaks down the traditional one-to-one relationship between a physical set of hardware and an OS.

The Hypervisor

The key enabler for virtualization is a piece of software called the *hypervisor*, also known as a *virtual machine manager (VMM)*. The hypervisor software allows multiple OSs to share the same host, and it also manages the physical resource allocation to those virtual OSs. As illustrated in Figure 1.2, there are two types of hypervisors: Type 1 and Type 2.

FIGURE 1.2   Type 1 and Type 2 hypervisors

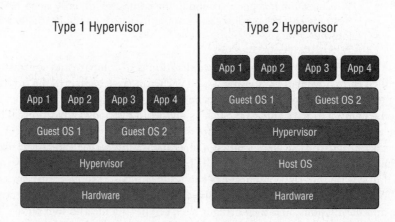

A Type 1 hypervisor sits directly on the hardware, and because of this, it's sometimes referred to as a *bare-metal* hypervisor. In this instance, the hypervisor is basically the OS for the physical machine. This setup is most commonly used for server-side virtualization, because the hypervisor itself typically has very low hardware requirements to support its own functions. Type 1 is generally considered to have better performance than Type 2, simply because there is no host OS involved and the system is dedicated to supporting virtualization. Virtual OSs are run within the hypervisor, and the virtual (guest) OSs are completely independent of each other. Examples of Type 1 hypervisors include Microsoft Hyper-V, VMware ESX, and Citrix XenServer. Figure 1.3 shows an example of the Microsoft Hyper-V interface, running on a Windows 10 workstation. In the "Virtual Machines" pod, you can see that this system is running six VMs, including ones for Linux, Windows clients, and Windows Server. These VMs can be turned on or off at any time and can provide flexibility in production or testing environments.

FIGURE 1.3　Microsoft Hyper-V

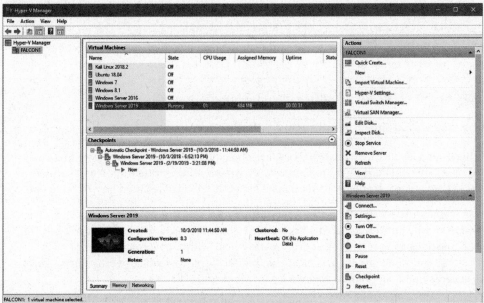

A Type 2 hypervisor sits on top of an existing OS (called the host OS), such as Microsoft Windows. This is most commonly used in client-side virtualization, where multiple OSs are managed on the client machine as opposed to on a server. An example of this would be a Windows user who wants to run Linux at the same time as Windows. The user could install a hypervisor and then install Linux in the hypervisor and run both OSs concurrently and independently. The downsides of Type 2 hypervisors are that the host OS consumes resources, such as processor time and memory, and a host OS failure means that the guest OSs fail as well. Examples of Type 2 hypervisors include Microsoft's Windows Virtual PC and Azure Virtual Server, Oracle VM VirtualBox, VMware Workstation, and Linux KVM.

Linux version 2.6.20 (released in 2007) and newer come with built-in open source virtualization software called the *Kernel-based Virtual Machine (KVM)*. (The CompTIA acronyms list refers to it as *Kernel Virtual Machine*.) The KVM software allows any Linux installation to be turned into a hypervisor and run multiple VMs.

Virtualization Resource Requirements

As you might expect, running multiple OSs on one physical computer can require more resources than running a single OS. There's no rule that says a computer being used for virtualization is required to have more robust hardware than another machine, but for performance reasons, the system should be fairly well equipped. This is especially true for systems running a Type 2 hypervisor, which sits on top of a host OS. The host OS will need resources too, and it will compete with the VMs for those resources.

If you are going to purchase a computer for the purpose of running virtualization, be sure to get a system with plenty of capability; for example, consider a fast multicore processor, lots of memory, a large and fast hard drive (preferably SSD), and a fast network card.

 Real World Scenario

Why Understanding Virtualization Is Important

Virtualization isn't a Cloud Essentials+ exam objective, and it's highly unlikely that you will see exam questions on it. So then why do we talk about virtualization and hypervisors? There are two real-world situations where this knowledge could be helpful to you.

First, if you are working with a cloud service provider (CSP) and asking for services, it's good to know a little about what's happening behind the curtain. It can help you ask the right questions and receive the appropriate services without overpaying for them. In addition, cloud concepts such as elasticity, scalability, and broad network access (which we cover later in this chapter) will make a lot more sense!

Second, you might have users in your company who could benefit from a virtualization workstation. Software developers are a great example. Armed with this knowledge, you can help determine whether a virtualization workstation meets the business needs and understand why you might need to pay for a slightly more powerful machine and additional software to support the user's needs.

Exercise 1.1 walks you through some steps you can take to assess the virtualization needs for a user in your company. Some of the items are more technical. If you're not comfortable with them, enlist someone from the IT department as a partner.

EXERCISE 1.1

Determining a User's Virtualization Needs

1.   Understand why the client needs virtualization.

   For example, do they have a Windows or Mac computer and need to run Linux? Or perhaps they have a Windows computer and want to run macOS at the same time? Determine their needs and then determine what is needed to secure the additional OSs, such as licenses.

2.   Evaluate their computer to ensure that it can support the VM. If not, the user may require a new computer.

   ▪ Does the processor support virtualization?

   ▪ How much RAM does the computer have? Is it enough to meet the minimum requirements of all installed OSs?

- How much free hard drive space is there? It needs to be enough to install the hypervisor and the guest OS as well as to store any files that need to be stored from within the guest OS.

- Does the system have a fast enough network connection if the guest OS needs access to the network?

3. Consider which hypervisor to use. Is there a version of the hypervisor that's compatible with the host OS?

4. Consider security requirements. If the guest OS will be on the Internet, be sure to obtain the proper security software.

5. After all of these have been considered, make the business case for why or why not to proceed. Is the cost required worth the benefits provided?

Service Models

Cloud providers sell everything "as a service." The type of service is named for the highest level of technology provided. For example, if compute and storage are the highest level, the client will purchase infrastructure as a service. If applications are involved, it will be software as a service. Nearly everything that can be digitized can be provided as a service. Figure 1.4 introduces the key differences between the three primary types of services: IaaS, PaaS, and SaaS. We'll define those acronyms and describe each of them in further detail in the following sections, starting from the bottom.

FIGURE 1.4　Cloud service models

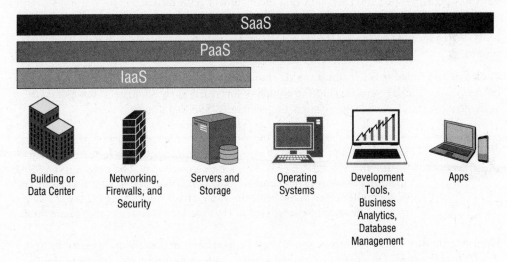

Infrastructure as a Service

Let's say that a company needs extra network capacity, including processing power, storage, and networking services (such as a firewall, which we will discuss in Chapter 2) but doesn't have the money to buy more network hardware. Instead, it can purchase *infrastructure as a service (IaaS)*, which is virtual hardware that replaces physical, on-premises IT infrastructure. The client decides what they need, and the CSP provisions it.

You will hear the term *provisioning* a lot. It just means that the CSP allocates those resources to a client.

IaaS can quickly scale up or down based on client needs. Paying for IaaS is often a lot like paying for utilities—the client pays for what it uses. Common IaaS use cases include the following:

Hosting of Websites and Web Apps   This includes the rapidly growing industry of the Internet of Things (IoT), which we will discuss further in Chapter 3, "Assessing Cloud Needs."

High-Performance Computing   Examples include big data analytics, machine learning, and simulations and modeling. Big temporary projects (sometimes called *batch jobs*) can be run. Once they are finished, the resources are turned off and no longer used or paid for.

Data Storage, Backup, and Recovery   IaaS can replace traditional on-premises data centers in organizations.

Testing and development   IaaS allows a client to quickly scale up an environment to test a new product or service and then shut that environment back down.

Most providers offer features such as self-serve web-based interfaces and management tools. When looking for an IaaS solution, there are three aspects to pay particular attention to.

High Security Standards   If not properly implemented, cloud security can be a major business risk. Check to ensure that the company has third-party security assessments or Statement on Standards for Attestation Engagements (SSAE) 18 audits.

SSAE 18 audits are a set of rigorous auditing standards for CSPs, which ensure that the CSP is providing adequate security. The details of an SSAE 18 audit are beyond the scope of the CompTIA Cloud Essentials+ exam. If you are interested in more information, check out https://ssae-18.org or https://www.aicpa.org/research/standards/auditattest/ssae.html.

High Availability   IaaS resources aren't useful if you can't access them. Seek to understand what the provider has for guaranteed uptime offerings, and work that into the service level agreement (SLA). We'll discuss this more in the "High Availability" section later in this chapter.

Flexible Pricing Arrangements One of the nice features of IaaS is the ability to scale resources up or down as needed. Be sure that the CSP offers pricing at the hourly level or in even shorter increments if that's what you need.

Of the three service models, IaaS requires the most network management expertise from the client. In an IaaS setup, the client provides and manages the software. Examples of IaaS products include AWS, Microsoft Azure, Google Compute Engine (GCE), Rackspace, and Joyent Triton.

Platform as a Service

Companies and individuals developing software typically want to focus on their area of expertise, which is coding. They don't want the extra hassle of managing hardware platforms to slow them down. That's where PaaS comes in.

Platform as a service (PaaS) adds features to IaaS that include OSs and software development tools such as runtime environments. Sometimes you will hear this collection of tools called *cloudware*. The vendor manages the various hardware platforms, freeing up the software developer to focus on building their application and scaling it. Overall, this should speed up the software development process and decrease its cost. Some key features of PaaS include the following:

- The ability to develop and deploy apps in a wide variety of languages, such as Java, JavaScript Object Notation (JSON), .NET, Python, PHP, and Node.js
- Cross-platform support, such as Windows, macOS, iOS, Android, and Linux
- Support for multiple, geographically separated development teams
- Integrated app lifecycle management

Other services that some PaaS providers may offer include help with provisioning, app deployment, load balancing, autoscaling, machine learning, integration with third-party application programming interfaces (APIs), and development operations (DevOps). Finally, some CSPs even have online drag-and-drop tools and templates that make app development possible for nonexperts. Examples of PaaS solutions include Google App Engine, Microsoft Azure, Red Hat OpenShift PaaS, AWS Elastic Beanstalk, Oracle Cloud Platform (OCP), Salesforce aPaaS, and Mendix aPaaS.

Software as a Service

The highest level of the three common cloud services is *software as a service (SaaS)*, which is a software licensing and delivery model where apps are subscribed to and accessed over the Internet. It has the largest market size of the three standard services and is likely the one you are most familiar with.

Clients using SaaS pay a monthly or yearly subscription fee to access software. Providers manage the software, software updates, and patches, as well as all underlying infrastructure needed to run it. Common examples include Google Docs and Microsoft Office 365 as well as email clients such as Gmail. Custom business applications can be built and deployed in a SaaS model as well, such as those for accounting, customer relationship management (CRM), or design.

As with other cloud services, the primary advantages are cost, flexibility, and ease of access. Clients will save money in the long run by not needing to purchase new software every few years, and any user with a web browser can access the software, regardless of the type of device they are using.

The disadvantages are few but can be significant. The biggest worry is generally data security. When working with a cloud, all data is being transmitted over the Internet, and data is stored "somewhere else" other than your on-premises data center. A smaller concern is that there are a relatively limited number of web apps available. This will change as the market matures, but finding the right type of software may be a challenge. Third, an Internet connection is required to use the apps and save data. In the event of a dropped connection, most apps have the ability to temporarily store changed data in the local device's memory, but that's not guaranteed. A lost Internet connection could result in data loss or the inability to access data that's needed.

Even though you may already be familiar with using software online, it never hurts to get hands-on experience to further your learning. Exercise 1.2 gives you some practice using SaaS, in the form of Google Apps.

EXERCISE 1.2

Using Google's Cloud Services

1. Open Google at www.google.com.

    If you do not already have a Google account, you will need to create one. With it, you use Google's online apps and storage as well as a Gmail account.

2. If you are doing this exercise on your own, create a second account to share files and folders with.

3. Once you're logged in, click the Apps icon in the upper-right corner. It's the one that has nine small squares (see Figure 1.5).

FIGURE 1.5 Google icons

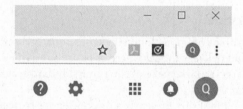

This will open Apps, as shown in Figure 1.6.

FIGURE 1.6   Google Apps

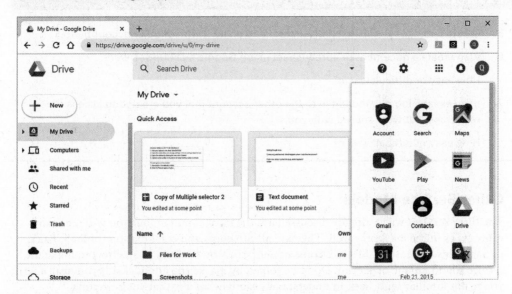

4. In Apps, click Drive. This will open Google Drive, as shown in Figure 1.7.

FIGURE 1.7   Google Drive

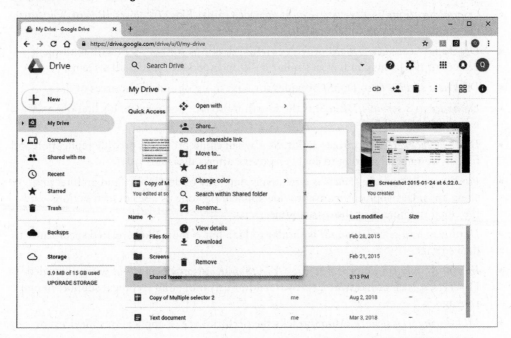

5. Create a folder by clicking New ➤ Folder and share it with another account.

6. Also create a document or spreadsheet using Google's online software.

   How easy or difficult was it?

7. If necessary, log out and log in to the other account that you created to access the resources that were shared with you.

   How easy or difficult was it?

Other Service Models

The three services we've already discussed are the most common, but you will see many other types in the market as well. They are all offshoots and combinations of IaaS, PaaS, or SaaS. In some cases, CSPs will come up with their own names in an effort to make the service sound unique or special. Don't be fooled by marketing gimmicks! If you hear a term you're not familiar with, seek to understand exactly what it is that you're getting.

Here's a list of other service levels that you may see in the real world:

- *Business processes as a service (BPaaS)* provides business processes such as payroll, IT help desk, or other services.

- *Communications as a service (CaaS)* provides things like Voice over IP (VoIP), instant messaging, and video collaboration.

- *Desktop as a service (DaaS)* provides virtual desktops so that users with multiple devices or platforms can have a similar desktop experience across all systems.

- *Data as a service (also DaaS)* provides for a mash-up of multiple sources of data.

- *Database as a service (DBaaS)* is the fourth most common service. It's literally a database hosted by a CSP.

- *Disaster recovery as a service (DRaaS)* is when cloud providers provide replication and full environmental hosting to enable recovery after a disaster.

- *Functions as a service (FaaS)* is a relatively new way of developing and architecting cloud apps. Development teams provide application code as a series of functions, and the cloud provider runs those functions.

- *Hardware as a service (HaaS)* is similar to IaaS but is more likely related specifically to data storage.

- *Information technology as a service (ITaaS)* aims to provide a client with all needed IT services, such as hardware, software, administration, and technical support in one package.

- *Monitoring as a service (MaaS)* tracks the performance of applications, devices, or services within a cloud network.

- *Network as a service (NaaS)* provides network infrastructure similar to IaaS.
- *Anything/everything as a service (XaaS)* is a combination of the services already discussed.

The level of service between the provider and the client is specified in the SLA, which is the contract between the two parties. It should be very clear which party has responsibility for specific elements, such as applications or hardware, should anything go awry. Figure 1.8 wraps up the service models discussion with an overview of how they all fit together. SaaS is the same as the Application layer shown in the figure.

FIGURE 1.8   Reviewing the cloud service models

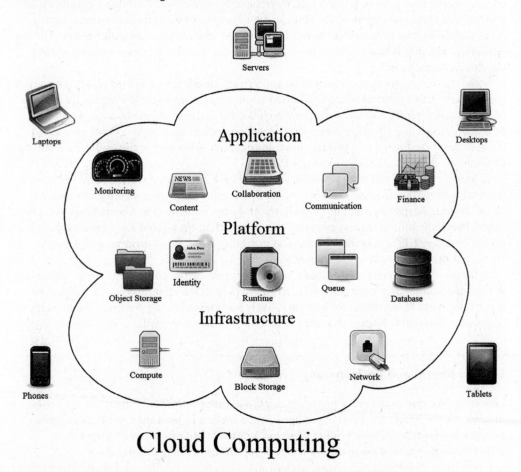

"Cloud computing" by Sam Johnston. Licensed under CC BY-SA 3.0 via Wikimedia Commons.

 As a reminder, the three service models in the exam objectives are SaaS, IaaS, and PaaS.

Deployment Models

The traditional type of cloud that usually comes to mind is a *public cloud*, like the ones operated by the third-party companies we mentioned earlier. These clouds offer the best in scalability, reliability, flexibility, geographical independence, and cost effectiveness. Whatever the client wants, the client gets. For example, if the client needs more resources, it simply scales up and uses more. Of course, the client will also pay more, but that's part of the deal.

Using the cloud is not restricted to big companies offering services over the Internet. Companies can purchase virtualization software to set up individual clouds within their own network. That type of setup is referred to as a *private cloud*. Running a private cloud pretty much eliminates many of the features that companies want from the cloud, such as rapid scalability and eliminating the need to purchase and manage computer assets. The big advantage, though, is that it allows the company to control all of its own security within the cloud environment.

Some clients choose to combine public and private clouds into a *hybrid cloud*. This gives the client the great features of a public cloud while simultaneously allowing for the storage of more sensitive information in the private cloud. It's the best of both worlds. This could be a good model in a situation where the company needs to keep tight control over some data—a database hosted in a private cloud, for example—but also wants to take advantage of productivity software such as Google Docs.

A fourth type of cloud is a *community cloud*. These are created when multiple organizations with common interests, such as schools or merging companies, combine to create a cloud. In a sense, it's like a public cloud but with better security. The clients know who the other clients are and, in theory, can trust them more than they could trust random people on the Internet. The economies of scale and flexibility won't be as great as with a public cloud, but that's the trade-off for better security.

With the exception of private clouds, all cloud types use the concept of *shared resources*. A pool of resources is purchased, and each participant in the cloud pays for a fraction of those resources. Those resources will most likely be external to the company using them, as opposed to internal resources that they would have if they managed a private cloud.

Using a Multicloud Environment

Literature on cloud usage will sometimes refer to a *multicloud environment*. As the name implies, it's the implementation of multiple clouds for one organization. It's not the same thing as a hybrid cloud, which refers to multiple deployment models within the same cloud. Instead, it means using different clouds for different types of services.

For example, a company might use a separate cloud provider for its infrastructure (IaaS) and its software (SaaS). Or, perhaps a company is large enough that it prefers to use multiple providers for IaaS. The IaaS providers might each handle separate infrastructure workloads, or they could be used to load balance the entire workload between them.

An extreme version of multicloud is for a company to have two entirely separate but identical clouds. One cloud can serve as a backup and can spring into action in the event of a primary cloud failure. Of course, a solution such as this is very expensive, but it can be worth it depending on business needs.

Using multiple clouds provides flexibility to customize your network environment to meet the business needs. Downsides can include cost, added complexity for your internal cloud administrators, and occasional interoperability issues between cloud providers.

As a reminder, the three deployment models in the exam objectives are public, private, and hybrid.

If you are interested in learning more about cloud service or deployment models, Amazon has a great reference source at https://aws.amazon.com/types-of-cloud-computing/.

Cloud Characteristics

Within the U.S. Department of Commerce, there is a nonregulatory agency named the National Institute of Standards and Technology (NIST). Its stated mission is to promote innovation and industrial competitiveness. Because it's nonregulatory, though, it doesn't have the power to enforce standards compliance. In 2011, NIST published de facto principles for cloud computing. These principles include three cloud service models and four deployment models, which you have already learned, and an official definition of cloud computing, as follows:

"Cloud computing is a model for enabling ubiquitous, convenient, on-demand network access to a shared pool of configurable computing resources (e.g., networks, servers, storage, applications, and services) that can be rapidly provisioned and released with minimal management effort or service provider interaction."

The definition calls out five key characteristics of cloud computing: on-demand self-service, broad network access, resource pooling, rapid elasticity, and measured service. The CompTIA Cloud Essentials+ exam objectives list six characteristics, using slightly different terms than what NIST put forward. Here, we will examine the six CompTIA cloud characteristics while calling out how they relate to their NIST counterparts.

Elastic   Cloud services must be *elastic*, meaning that they can grow or shrink as the client's needs change. Clouds can do this because, thanks to virtualization, they employ *resource pooling*. The provider's resources are seen as one large pool that can be divided up among clients as needed. Clients should be able to access additional resources as needed, even though the client may not be aware of where the resources are physically located. In most cases, clients can get more resources instantly (or at least very quickly), and that is called *rapid elasticity*. For the client, this is a great feature because they can scale up without needing to purchase, install, and configure new hardware. Elasticity can also work backward; if fewer resources are required, the client may be able to scale down and pay less without needing to sell hardware. Typical pooled resources include network bandwidth, storage, processing power (CPU), and memory (RAM).

Self-Service   From an end user's standpoint, *self-service* (often labeled as *on-demand self-service* by providers) is one of the cloud's best features. This characteristic allows users to access additional resources (such as storage, network, or compute) automatically, 24 hours a day, 7 days a week, 365 days a year, without requiring intervention from the service provider.

Scalability   We've talked about the need for clouds to be elastic and allow clients to use more or fewer resources as needed. The ability to use more or fewer resources is called *scalability*. Most public clouds have a very high degree of scalability—it's highly unlikely that your company will cause AWS to run out of storage space, for example!

Scalability can also refer to location. Public clouds can in theory be accessed from anywhere in the world. They can scale geographically to suit any business situation.

Broad Network Access   Resources need to be accessible over the network by different types of clients, such as workstations, laptops, and mobile phones, using common access software such as web browsers. This also applies to clients using different OSs, such as Windows, macOS, Linux, iOS, or Android, and is called *broad network access*. The ability for users to get the data they want, when they want, and how they want is also sometimes referred to as *ubiquitous access*.

Pay-as-You-Go   Cloud providers track clients' usage and then charge them for services used, much as utility companies charge for electricity, gas, or water used at a residence. In some billing models, clients pay only for the services they use, which is called *pay-as-you-go*. Sometimes you will hear this referred to as *metered service* or *measured service*. This is as opposed to a model where a client signs a contract for a fixed resource and pays regardless of usage. For example, a client might reserve 20 terabytes of storage space, use only 10, but still pay for 20. Regardless of the type of contract, resource usage should be monitored by the provider and reported to the client in a transparent fashion. We'll talk about charging and reporting models more in Chapter 5, "Management and Technical Operations."

Availability   Simply stated, *availability* means that cloud resources are accessible and responsive whenever a client needs them. We'll get into more detail on this concept later in this chapter, in the "High Availability" section.

So Many Organizations and Standards!

In this section we introduced you to NIST, which published de facto standards for cloud computing. In the acronym list for Cloud Essentials+, CompTIA lists other bodies and standards as well, such as ISO and ITIL. You might see even others such as ANSI and

PMI. We don't want to go down too deep a rabbit hole, considering that none of these is an exam objective, but here's a quick explanation of what each acronym stands for and what it means:

American National Standards Institute (ANSI)   ANSI is a private nonprofit institute that helps develop and facilitate the use of voluntary consensus standards in the United States. These are usually referred to as "open" standards because of ANSI's collaborative and consensus-based development and approval process. NIST and ANSI have worked together on creating standards, but ANSI is not specifically involved with cloud technology.

International Organization for Standardization (ISO)   The ISO is an international body that develops international standards, frequently in the technology, workplace safety and health, and environmental arenas. For example, ISO 9001 is an internationally recognized workplace quality management standard. ISO does not have any cloud-specific standards. (And yes, their name and acronym don't really match!)

Information Technology Information Library (ITIL)   ITIL is a framework of best practices for aligning IT services with business needs and delivering those services. It was first developed in the 1980s by the British government's Central Computer and Telecommunications Agency (CCTA) and is periodically revised and updated. ITIL has recommendations on how to best use cloud services but did not participate in standards development.

Project Management Institute (PMI)   PMI is a global nonprofit professional organization for project management. PMI is not focused on cloud standards development.

 The six cloud characteristics found in the exam objectives are elastic, self-service, scalability, broad network access, pay-as-you-go, and availability.

Shared Responsibility Model

An old network technician adage is, "A server is perfectly secure until you install a network card." While this is true, a server without a network connection won't be a very useful server. And since we're talking about cloud services, everything is Internet-based. You're probably well aware of the myriad security challenges the Internet presents. Yet it's a critical piece of infrastructure for most modern businesses.

When business usage of cloud services started to explode in the late 2000s, security was the biggest concern. As with any new technology, there was a lot of ambiguity over who owned what. In this case, most businesses assumed cloud providers would handle all security measures. After all, if a business had servers, infrastructure, and data of its own stored in an on-site data warehouse, it expected to manage all aspects of security. In a new model where a third party managed the services, infrastructure, apps, and data storage, shouldn't that third party also be responsible for all security measures?

Cloud providers had a different perspective. They didn't feel that they should be held responsible for things outside of their control. They agreed that they needed to secure the cloud hardware and infrastructure, but could they really be held responsible for all of their clients' data? What if clients uploaded data with viruses or attempted to hack into data owned by another client?

The ambiguity and assumptions made by both parties unfortunately led to some security holes, and hackers were more than happy to exploit them. Out of this environment rose the concept of the shared responsibility model.

In the *shared responsibility model*, the CSP and the client share security duties, which improves the overall security of the system. The CSP is responsible for security "of" the cloud, while the client is responsible for security "in" the cloud. The CSP takes responsibility for what it can realistically control, and the rest is up to the client. Figure 1.9 shows how the shared responsibility model works.

Don't worry if you're not familiar with some of the cloud terms in Figure 1.9, such as *regions*, *availability zones*, and *edge locations*. You will learn about them in Chapter 5.

FIGURE 1.9   The shared responsibility model

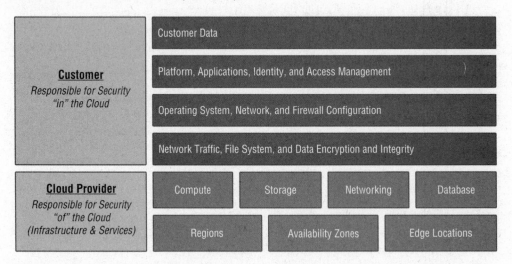

As you can see in Figure 1.9, the security responsibilities are pretty clearly defined. Even as a business client using a cloud, you need to have IT resources that are capable of managing the tasks needed to keep everything in the customer portion of the figure under control.

Breaking the Shared Responsibility Model

New technologies follow a predictable pattern. They are launched, and there's a breaking-in period during which users figure out the best way to apply them. The technology then gains popularity, creating more buzz and interest. Then, enterprising companies and individuals figure out how to expand the technology to make it more powerful or give it additional functionality. The cloud is no exception, and recent enhancements have stretched the shared responsibility model nearly to its breaking point.

Most of the security vectors shown in Figure 1.9 are clear-cut. It's the CSP's responsibility to secure the hardware and infrastructure. Patching an OS, installing a firewall, and securing data on the server falls to the client—easy enough. A few newer cloud implementations, such as containers and serverless (also known as *FaaS*), aren't as easily defined.

The in-the-weeds details of how containers and serverless work isn't too important to your studies at the moment—they are covered in Chapter 5. What is important to know is that each of these models shifts some of the traditional security responsibility from one partner to the other. Most CSPs are aware of situations where they need to take on more responsibility, which they do for FaaS, and have implemented appropriate security procedures. Containers can shift more responsibility to the client, and not all clients fully understand that.

The key takeaway from this story is to think of security holistically from end to end. Have all security needs mapped out, from hardware and infrastructure to software and apps to processes. Then partner closely with your CSP to ensure that all aspects of security are being covered so there are no gaps for hackers to exploit.

 As a reminder, the shared responsibility model is in the exam objectives. Be sure to remember that the CSP is responsible for security of the cloud, and the client is responsible for security in the cloud!

Exploring Cloud Design

A well-designed cloud solution can save a company money in several ways. First, it can eliminate the sunk cost of buying new hardware and software every few years, just to have it go obsolete. Second, it can enable users to have faster and better access to data, freeing their time to build the business. Third, a good cloud solution can help a company quickly recover from what would otherwise be a catastrophic data loss. In this section, you will learn about the last two, in the forms of redundancy and high availability and disaster recovery.

Redundancy and High Availability

If someone at work calls you redundant, that's not typically meant as a compliment. It could mean that your job is not needed or isn't useful, or it could mean that the absence of the role wouldn't result in any loss. If two people have redundant jobs, it doesn't bode well for their employment prospects. Clearly, as employees we do our best to not be redundant!

In computer terms, though, *redundancy* is often a good thing. It means that there is some sort of device, system, or process that can take over in the event of a failure and keep the system running. Data redundancy, for example, can mean that critical data is accessible at any time from any location. Network redundancy can mean that a key server or the Internet is always available. Redundancy plans enable another key feature of clouds—high availability—which means that users have uninterrupted service and good responsiveness from cloud resources.

Redundancy Plans

Building redundancy into your network architecture nearly always means spending more money versus not having redundancy. That negative will always present itself during budget discussions, but if your company will be hurt by a loss of access to resources or data, the positives will outweigh the negative.

> Not all data or infrastructure components need redundancy. If you determine that you can live without a certain resource for a few hours or a few days, then redundancy might be too expensive.

When putting together your cloud needs, build in a redundancy plan that can help eliminate issues caused by a single point of failure. Then, work with your CSP to ensure that proper redundancy is built into the SLA. In most cases, you will need to balance the risk tolerance for a specific failure with the cost of implementing a redundant system. Redundancy plans should cover the following areas:

Hardware   Most network administrators will understand the concept of hardware redundancy, usually referred to as *fault tolerance*. A cloud, of course, uses hardware—all computers do. As a species, humans haven't yet figured out how to create computing devices without a physical component.

Hardware redundancy solutions from a cloud provider should come with an uptime guarantee. That is, what percentage of the time will they guarantee data and services to be available? We'll look at a few examples of this later in the "High Availability" section.

Network   For most companies, the computer network needs to be available at all times. One way to accomplish this is through network redundancy. Network redundancy is closely linked to hardware, but it's just more specific. Whereas hardware redundancy can refer to things such as storage, processors, memory, or network devices, network redundancy is pretty specific. Cloud providers typically differentiate the two by saying that *hardware redundancy* often refers to the servers themselves, whereas *network redundancy* typically refers specifically to network infrastructure such as switches and routers. Network redundancy can also involve guaranteeing a certain amount of network bandwidth.

Geographic   Looking at hardware on an even bigger scale, geographic redundancy means that two or more physical locations have replicas of the same data. Those physical locations should be far enough apart that if one were to suffer a catastrophic natural disaster or failure, the other or others would be spared. Another term for this is *geo-redundancy*, which we'll talk about again in Chapter 5.

> Geographically redundant locations can also help with load balancing for your cloud services. For example, having geo-redundant locations in the United States, Europe, and Asia can help spread the workload, since users from those regions can be directed to their regional site as their primary access point. Users in each region will have significantly better performance than if they accessed one centrally located site.

Process   Business processes are frequently overlooked when it comes to redundancy, but they shouldn't be ignored. If a process fails, it could mean catastrophic results for a business. For example, assume that a company sells products online. The ordering system needs to interface with the billing system, which also interfaces with the fulfillment system. And perhaps the fulfillment system includes several subsystems—one that sends the order to the warehouse, one that contacts the delivery company, and another that emails the client updates on the order status. Most likely, there's an automated process that manages this workflow. If one link in the chain breaks, the entire workflow could be disrupted, and orders won't get filled. That means a loss of sales, which is never a good thing.

Map out critical business processes and understand which require high availability. Then figure out what the single points of failure are—they could be hardware, software, or network infrastructure—and ensure there's a plan in place to avoid issues.

Software   All computers rely upon software, from OSs to applications to drivers that enable communication between the hardware and software. Software redundancy can take one of two forms—redundancy of the program or redundancy within the program.

The concept of redundancy at the program level means that you have a second program that can be run to perform the task in the event that the first one fails. At a very simplistic level, this could mean something like using Google Docs if Microsoft Word fails. Usually word processing isn't critical enough to need a backup, but you get the idea.

Redundancy within the program is a little trickier and is typically an issue only if your company has software developers writing code. It often means placing some sort of failsafe mechanism within the software, so if there's a critical error, the software can recover. It can also mean creating self-adaptive and self-checking programs. Self-adaptive programs are a basic implementation of artificial intelligence.

Data   Last but certainly not least, there is data redundancy. Most often, this takes the form of data backups. Backups come in all shapes and sizes, from ones that are mirrored copies of data and instantly accessible to tapes or other media that needs to be restored before its contents are available.

Data loss can come in a variety of forms. The obvious example is hard drive failure, but that accounts for only a small percentage of overall data loss. Malware such as viruses and ransomware, inadvertent deletion, and malicious acts by hackers, employees, or contractors are much bigger problems.

Implementing some sort of data backup as part of the redundancy plan (or disaster recovery plan) may be legally required for a company, depending on its industry. Even if not, it's the most important thing a company can do. While that might sound like hyperbole, it's absolutely not. Boston Computing has found that 60 percent of companies that experience a data loss without a backup shut down within six months. With cloud computing, data backups and redundancy are incredibly easy to implement and generally not very expensive. It would be foolish to ignore them.

> If you are implementing data backups, be sure to secure the data in those backups via encryption!

High Availability

A great aspect of cloud services is that they provide users with *high availability*, meaning that users have uninterrupted service and responsive access to services. When we say uninterrupted, though, we should probably caveat that by saying it's *mostly* uninterrupted. The level of uptime guaranteed by the CSP will be specified in the SLA.

Service availability is measured in terms of "nines," or how many nines of uptime the provider guarantees. For example, "three nines" means that the service will be available 99.9 percent of the time, whereas "four nines" means it will be up 99.99 percent of the time. More nines means more money, and different aspects of your service contract might require different levels of uptime. For example, a critical medical records database might need more guaranteed uptime than would a word processing application. As we've said before, the level of service you should get depends on how much risk your company is willing to take on and the trade-off with cost. Table 1.1 shows how much downtime is acceptable based on the number of nines of guaranteed uptime.

TABLE 1.1   Availability Downtime

Availability	Downtime per year	Downtime per day
Three nines (99.9%)	8.77 hours	1.44 minutes
Four nines (99.99%)	52.6 minutes	8.64 seconds
Five nines (99.999%)	5.26 minutes	864 milliseconds
Six nines (99.9999%)	31.56 seconds	86.4 milliseconds

Guaranteeing that services will be available with the possible exception of less than one second per day seems pretty impressive, as is the case with five nines. You might see other combinations too, such as "four nines five," which translates into 99.995 percent availability, or no more than 4.32 seconds of downtime per day. The majority of CSPs will provide at least three nines or three nines five.

Disaster Recovery

Having great plans for redundancy and high availability can help avoid service outages and keep your business running smoothly. And with those plans in place, you might think that you've covered your bases in the case of a system failure. That's not true though—unforeseen things can still happen to take out a critical system, application, or data set. There's one more aspect of cloud design to consider, and that's disaster recovery.

Disaster recovery is defined as the ability to become operational after a disaster. The disaster can be catastrophic hardware or software failures, hackers or other cyber criminals, human error, or forces of nature that cripple one or more computer systems. Every organization should have a disaster recovery plan outlining the steps to take to regain operational status in the event of a disaster.

Disaster recovery plans need to account for all aspects of corporate network infrastructure, including hardware, software, network infrastructure, power, and of course data. The plans should also specify what employees should do in the event of a disaster. For example, if a tornado or flood cripples the corporate headquarters overnight, what should employees do the next workday?

The good news is, if you are buying cloud services from a CSP, they can help with disaster planning. And depending on how you set up your SLA, the disaster recovery and response could fall on them, not on you. Policies and procedures for recovery should be clearly agreed to between you and the CSP and spelled out in the SLA—assuming they are going to take care of everything could be a tragic mistake. Two recovery objectives that need to be defined in a disaster recovery plan are the recovery point objective and recovery time objective.

Recovery Point Objective

Imagine a scenario in which your company gets hit by a catastrophic natural disaster. The company is essentially down, and access to critical data is gone. The good news is nobody was hurt, so senior management has shifted to voicing concerns about how they will recover the data. Fortunately, you have a disaster plan with your CSP, and they've been backing up your data per the SLA. Now the question is, how old is the data that they will restore?

This is where the *recovery point objective (RPO)* becomes critical. The RPO defines the maximum age of files that must be recovered from backups in order to restore normal operations. In other words, how old can restored data be and still be useful to use to run the business? The client defines the RPO (and RTO, which we discuss next), and they get added to the SLA.

Different applications and data sets can and should have different RPOs, depending on their criticality and how often they change. OS core files don't change often, and most likely you have the ability to restore an OS and necessary patches from installation media or online. Therefore, an RPO for these types of files isn't needed. If it's a product list that changes once per month, then the RPO should be one month. If it's something like medical data or a financial transactions database, or other high-importance, potentially fast-changing data, the RPO needs to be close to zero.

Catalog the different types of data your company has, and then decide what the maximum age for "good enough" data is. That will help you determine your RPOs.

Recovery Time Objective

Your company has just been hacked and the public website, network infrastructure, and data systems that are hosted in the cloud have effectively been taken down by the attack. Everyone is panicking because every minute of downtime costs the company money. How long will it take to get everything operational again? Never mind the question of how do you prevent that attack from happening again—that's important too!

The maximum amount of time a system can be offline in the event of a disaster is called the *recovery time objective (RTO)*. It defines how long the CSP has to get everything operational, including network access and data restoration.

Much like RPOs, RTOs can and should vary by system. If your company has a website that does not handle any e-commerce transactions, then a failure might be annoying but not essential to business operations. The RTO for that can be a little longer than for a database that hosts the online ordering system, for example.

Assumptions Are Dangerous

Earlier we discussed the shared responsibility model, where both the client and the CSP have responsibility to secure cloud-based systems. Recall that the client is responsible for security *in* the cloud, and the CSP is responsible for security *of* the cloud. Even though there's no official term for it, think of redundancy and disaster recovery in the same way. Don't make assumptions about what the CSP is going to provide in those areas.

CSPs do have redundancy and data recovery services available, but they must be agreed to in the SLA. If they are not specified, then they are not covered. This includes absolutely essential services such as creating and testing data backups. Again, don't assume—that could be a dangerous mistake if you suffer a data loss and have no recovery options!

 There are four aspects of cloud design listed in the exam objectives: redundancy, high availability, disaster recovery, and recovery objectives. The two recovery objectives are RPO and RTO.

Summary

We began this first chapter by introducing you to core cloud concepts. Before getting into cloud concepts, though, you learned about virtualization, which, along with the Internet, enables cloud providers to provide scaled services to multiple clients at the same time. Virtualization is made possible through the use of software called hypervisors. Cloud services benefit client companies by allowing them to forego investing in expensive hardware, and they benefit cloud providers by generating economies of scale.

There are three primary service models in cloud computing: software as a service (SaaS), infrastructure as a service (IaaS), and platform as a service (PaaS). You learned about all three, with IaaS being the lowest level of service, PaaS providing more, and SaaS being the highest level of service. There are also several more types of services that CSPs will offer, such as database as a service (DBaaS) and functions as a service (FaaS), but all are off-shoots of the three we previously mentioned.

Next, we discussed three deployment models: public, private, and hybrid. Public models are quite common, with dozens of providers in the marketplace. The biggest two for businesses are AWS and Microsoft Azure. Google Cloud is also widely used. Each has pros and cons and different pricing and service levels. Private clouds enable more security and control but require the company to buy all of the necessary hardware to support the cloud. Hybrid clouds are an implementation of public and private at the same time.

Clouds have characteristics that make them attractive to client companies. Those are elasticity, self-service, scalability, broad network access, pay-as-you-go models, and high availability. Cloud security is enabled through the shared responsibility model. That means cloud suppliers are responsible for security of the cloud, whereas clients are responsible for security within the cloud.

Finally, the chapter finished with a discussion of important aspects of cloud design, including redundancy, high availability, disaster recovery, and recovery objectives. Redundancy is like fault tolerance, where systems have backups in case something fails. Redundancy is one way to ensure high availability, which means that clients have uninterrupted access to resources. A disaster recovery plan is important for any network, whether it's internal or hosted in the cloud. Two important disaster recovery concepts to understand are the recovery point objective and recovery time objective.

Exam Essentials

Know what SaaS is.   Software as a service means that the CSP provides software for a client as well as the underlying hardware needed to run the software. Popular examples include Microsoft Office 365 and Google Docs.

Know what IaaS is.   In an infrastructure as a service setup, the CSP provides hardware infrastructure. This often means compute, storage, and network capabilities.

Know what PaaS is.   In platform as a service, the CSP provides both hardware and a development platform. That includes software development tools such as runtime environments. This lets the client focus on software development while the CSP manages the hardware and development environment.

Know what the three cloud deployment models are.   The three deployment models are public, private, and hybrid. You might also see literature that refers to multicloud environments. Multicloud refers to having multiple clouds doing the same or specialized tasks, and not to the deployment model.

Be able to list pros and cons for each of the three deployment models.   A public cloud means that the client does not need to invest in hardware that will go obsolete in a few years, but downsides can be lack of control and security. Private clouds allow the company to retain security and resource control but usually cost more because of the hardware replacement life cycle. Hybrid clouds are the best and worst of both worlds, because they combine features of public and private clouds.

Know the six characteristics of clouds.   Clouds are elastic, provide self-service, offer scalability, have broad network access, may offer pay-as-you-go, and have high availability.

Be able to explain what it means for a cloud to be elastic.   Elasticity within a cloud means that the cloud's resources can grow or shrink as the client's needs change. Clouds can do this because they utilize resource pooling. Sometimes you will hear this called rapid elasticity.

Be able to describe what self-service means.   In a cloud environment, much is automated. This includes allowing clients to request or access additional features without requiring intervention from the service provider.

Be able to explain what scalability in the cloud is.   Scalability is closely linked with elasticity. It just means clients have the ability to use more or fewer resources as needed.

Be able to describe what broad network access means.   Cloud clients can access resources regardless of the hardware or OS they run. This can mean access for desktops, laptops, and mobile devices running Windows, macOS, or mobile OSs like iOS or Android.

Be able to explain what pay-as-you-go means.   Cloud providers track client usage and charge them for services used, much as public utilities do. In some payment models, clients only pay for the services they use, which is called pay-as-you-go.

Be able to describe what availability means in the cloud.   It means that resources are available whenever the client needs them. Most commonly, you will hear this referred to as high availability. The goal for the CSP is to provide uninterrupted service.

Understand how the shared responsibility model works.   The shared responsibility model pertains to cloud security. The CSP is responsible for security of the cloud, and the client is responsible for security in the cloud.

Know how redundancy works in a cloud environment.   Cloud providers can provide redundant systems, which is like fault tolerance. That means if one component or system fails, there is no loss of functionality because the redundant system takes over. Redundancy can apply to hardware, software, network infrastructure, geography, processes, or data.

Understand what disaster recovery is.   Disaster recovery is the ability to become operational after a disaster happens. Disasters can include natural disasters, cyberattacks, hardware or software failures, or human error.

Know what an RPO is.   A recovery point objective specifies how old data can be to still be considered current or useful to restore normal operations.

Know what an RTO is.   A recovery time objective defines how long the system or services can be down before being restored, in the event of a disaster or outage.

Written Lab

Fill in the blanks for the questions provided in the written lab. You can find the answers to the written labs in Appendix A.

1. The _____ specifies the oldest that data can be to be acceptable to restore for business use.

2. Microsoft Office 365 is an example of the _____ cloud service model.

3. Cloud security responsibilities are defined by the _____.

4. Cloud users need to access resources from PCs and mobile devices. This is called _____.

5. Cloud clients can get more compute power without CSP intervention based on the _____ characteristic.

6. The _____ cloud deployment model places all security responsibilities on the company that owns it.

7. Thanks to the concept of pooled resources, cloud resources are said to be _____.

8. An SLA that specifies five nines is referring to _____.

9. One month, a cloud client uses twice as many resources as they normally do. The next month, they use their normal amount. They pay for only what they used. This is called _____.

10. The two recovery objectives that should be in a disaster recovery plan are _____ and _____.

Review Questions

The answers to the chapter review questions can be found in Appendix B.

1. The CIO wants to reduce the cost of network ownership for the company, specifically for app licenses. Which service model should you recommend to her?

   A. XaaS

   B. SaaS

   C. PaaS

   D. IaaS

2. Which of the following is a potential outcome of implementing a multicloud environment for your company?

   A. Combined features of public and private clouds

   B. Decreased complexity for internal cloud administrators

   C. Increased security for cloud-based resources

   D. Increased flexibility of using separate SaaS and IaaS vendors

3. You are buying new cloud services. The internal network administration team is worried about cloud access from different OSs, such as Windows, macOS, and Android. What should you tell them?

   A. Resources will be available to only Windows and macOS clients via broad network access.

   B. Resources will be available to only Windows and macOS clients via self-service.

   C. Resources will be available to all client OSs via broad network access.

   D. Cloud services are usable only by Android and iOS mobile devices.

   E. Resources will be available to all client OSs via self-service.

4. The company CIO asks you to ensure that the new cloud solution provides fault tolerance. Which aspect of cloud design does this refer to?

   A. High availability

   B. Shared responsibility

   C. Disaster recovery

   D. Redundancy

5. Which of the following are examples of IaaS that a cloud provider might offer? (Choose two.)

   A. Compute

   B. Applications

   C. Database

   D. Storage

6. Which of the following should you ask for in an SLA if you want to ensure the highest availability of resources for cloud users?

    A. Four nines five

    B. Four nines

    C. Three nines five

    D. Three nines

7. When shopping for public cloud services, the CSP tells you that if your company needs more or fewer resources, the CSP can instantly accommodate that. What cloud characteristic does this refer to?

    A. Elasticity

    B. Self-service

    C. Broad network access

    D. Availability

8. Your CSP makes daily backups of important files and hourly backups of an essential database, which will be used to restore the data if needed. Which aspect of cloud design does this represent?

    A. Redundancy

    B. High availability

    C. Disaster recovery

    D. RTO

9. Which of the following best describes the purpose of the shared responsibility model?

    A. The CSP and client share responsibility for cloud security.

    B. The CSP and client share responsibility for cloud costs.

    C. Clients in a cloud share security responsibility with each other.

    D. Clients in a cloud share costs with each other.

10. Which of the following cloud service models best supports a software development team with members in the United States and Japan?

    A. IaaS

    B. SaaS

    C. DBaaS

    D. PaaS

11. You are negotiating an SLA with a CSP. Which two things need to be included as part of the recovery objectives?

    A. Recovery process objective

    B. Recovery point objective

    C. Recovery time objective

    D. Recovery cost objective

12. In the cloud security model, who is responsible for securing access management and firewall configurations?

 A. CSP

 B. Client

 C. CSP and client

 D. All clients share this responsibility.

13. Which of the following cloud deployment models offers the best scalability and cost effectiveness?

 A. Public

 B. Private

 C. Community

 D. Hybrid

14. Which of the following best describes an RTO?

 A. The oldest that data can be to be useful when it's restored

 B. The amount of time services can be down after a disaster before being restored

 C. The cost associated with restoring services after a disaster

 D. The chain of command for notifications when a disaster occurs within the cloud

15. Which of the following is NOT a common characteristic of public clouds?

 A. Self-service

 B. Pay-as-you-go

 C. Higher cost

 D. Availability

16. Your company uses a financial transactions database that updates frequently. If a natural disaster occurred, any data backup older than one hour would not be useful to the company. To ensure that backups are always more current, what needs to be specified in the disaster recovery plan?

 A. RPO

 B. RTO

 C. TSO

 D. SLA

17. Your network hardware is outdated and needs to be replaced. The CIO suggests using the most cost-effective cloud solution. However, he insists that the company database remain 100 percent controlled by your company. Which solution is the best choice?

 A. Public

 B. Private

 C. Community

 D. Hybrid

18. Your data science team runs complex simulations that require more compute resources. They do about one simulation per month, and it takes one to two days. You want to ensure that the team has available compute resources but that you only pay for the resources when they are in use. Which cloud characteristic do you need?

A. Scalability

B. Availability

C. Pay-as-you-go

D. Elasticity

19. Which of the following is NOT a type of redundancy typically available in public cloud solutions?

A. Process

B. OS

C. Hardware

D. Data

20. Several universities want to band together to get cloud service. They want to share scholarly research but also take advantage of common cloud-based productivity apps. Which solution is the best option for their needs?

A. Public

B. Private

C. Hybrid

D. Community

Chapter 2

Cloud Networking and Storage

THE FOLLOWING COMPTIA CLOUD ESSENTIALS+ EXAM CLO-002 OBJECTIVES ARE COVERED IN THIS CHAPTER:

✓ **1.2 Identify cloud networking concepts.**

- Connectivity types
  - Direct connect
  - VPN
- Common access types
  - RDP
  - SSH
  - HTTPS
- Software-defined networking (SDN)
- Load balancing
- DNS
- Firewall

✓ **1.3 Identify cloud storage technologies.**

- Storage features
  - Compression
  - Deduplication
  - Capacity on demand
- Storage characteristics
  - Performance
  - Hot vs. cold
- Storage types
  - Object storage
  - File storage
  - Block storage
- Software-defined storage
- Content delivery network

Before the Internet was popular, cloud technology foundered in the periphery of computing technology. This is despite the core cloud technology—virtualization—having been in existence for nearly three decades. While cloud concepts were interesting, there was no practical way to implement them and realize their benefits.

The Internet provided the needed environment for cloud usage; as the Internet grew, so too did the number of users who could benefit from cloud services. Clearly, the Internet enabled the cloud. While this relationship is a positive, there's a flip side as well. Not only is the cloud Internet-enabled, it's Internet-dependent. Without Internet access, cloud-based resources are likely to be unavailable. Even private clouds are often accessible via the Internet to allow users in remote locations access to network resources.

From a cloud end-user standpoint, probably nothing is more important than having an Internet connection to access needed resources. Because networking and network connections are so important, we'll spend a lot of time covering those topics in this chapter.

Once connected to the cloud, a majority of users store files for easy sharing, access, and collaboration. Some storage solutions appear quite simple, such as uploading music to iTunes or keeping a few notes in Google Drive. Other cloud storage solutions are incredibly complex, with infrastructure that used to be hosted only in massive on-site data warehouses. Online apps and compute resources are great, but storage was the catalyst for the early growth of cloud services.

In this chapter, we will finish up our discussion of CompTIA Cloud Essentials+ Domain 1.0 Cloud Concepts by covering two key elements—networking and storage. Within the "Understanding Cloud Networking" section, we will cover connectivity and access types, as well as services that enable additional functionality. Our coverage of storage in the "Understanding Cloud Storage Technologies" section includes features, characteristics, and types, along with services such as cloud-defined storage and content delivery networks.

Understanding Cloud Networking Concepts

As you know by now, without networking, the cloud doesn't exist. Networking allows users to access virtualized servers somewhere on the Internet, enabling their company to save money by not needing to purchase hardware or software that will become obsolete in a few years.

One question that might come to mind is, *"How* do cloud users access virtualized cloud resources?" In most use cases, it's pretty simple, but of course there are more complex access methods as well. Before we look at specific methods of cloud access, we're going to do a quick primer on the underlying technology that enables modern networking in the first place. Then we'll provide details on five methods used to connect to the cloud. After that, we will finish this section by covering four networking services that give the cloud more functionality.

Networking: A Quick Primer

You probably use computer networks every day. Maybe you know intricate details of how information gets from point A to point B, but maybe you've never given it a second thought—as long as your email works and you can find the latest cat memes, you're good. Regardless, a basic understanding of how networks work is a good foundation for learning cloud networking concepts. The networking material shared here will most likely not be on the Cloud Essentials+ exam, but it's *really* good to know.

First, let's define a network. Simply enough, a network is two or more computers or devices that can communicate with each other. Those devices need to have software that enables them to talk to each other, called a network client, which is built into every operating system (OS). (Custom software packages are available for specific network communications as well.) From the actual networking side, though, three things are required.

- Network adapter (or network card)
- Transmission method
- Protocol

Practically every computing device today has a built-in network adapter. (It's probably actually every device, but once we claim that, someone will find an exception to the rule.) You'll also hear this hardware component referred to as a *network interface card (NIC).* The NIC's job is to enable the device to communicate on the network. Each NIC has the ability to communicate using one type of networking. For example, some use cellular, others use Bluetooth or Wi-Fi, and some use wired Ethernet. The differences between them isn't important for the moment, but what is important is that for two devices to talk to each other, they need to use NICs using the same technology. Said differently, a cellular-only device can't communicate on a Bluetooth network.

The transmission method is how data travels from device to device. In the old days of computing, this meant copper or fiber-optic cables. While wired connections are still used today, fast wireless networking methods—cellular, Wi-Fi, and Bluetooth—are ubiquitous.

The final component is a networking protocol. This is the language that computers speak to facilitate communication. Protocols are analogous to human languages in many ways, in that they provide the rules and standards for common understanding.

For two devices to talk to each other, they need to speak the same language. To give a human example, let's say that you are fluent in English and Japanese. If someone approaches you speaking Japanese, you can respond in kind. You speak the same protocol.

But if someone approaches you and tries to speak to you in French, the conversation is pretty much over before it begins. It's the same with computers.

Throughout the history of computers, there have been several dozen computer languages developed. Most are obsolete today. The only one you really need to know is Transmission Control Protocol/Internet Protocol (TCP/IP). It's the protocol of the Internet.

Although TCP/IP is often called a protocol, it's actually a modular suite of protocols working together to enable communication. The two namesake protocols are Transmission Control Protocol (TCP) and Internet Protocol (IP), but there are dozens of others, as shown in Figure 2.1. For communication to happen, each device uses one component from each of the four levels. The good news is that all of this happens automatically, so you don't need to think about it!

FIGURE 2.1   TCP/IP protocol suite

DoD Model

| Process/Application | Telnet | RDP | SSH | FTP |
| | DHCP | SMTP | HTTP | HTTPS |

| Host-to-Host | TCP | | UDP | |

| Internet | ICMP | ARP | | RARP |
| | IP | | | |

| Network Access | Ethernet | Fast Ethernet | Gigabit Ethernet | 802.11 (Wi-Fi) |

 TCP/IP structure is based on a U.S. Department of Defense (DoD) networking model; that's why in Figure 2.1 we call the model the DoD model.

Protocols at each layer within the model are responsible for different tasks. For example, one of the things that IP is responsible for is logical addressing, which is why you might be familiar with the term *IP address*. Any device on a TCP/IP network with an IP address, including computers, printers, and router interfaces, is called a *host*. This is a term you'll hear again later in this chapter in the "Domain Name System" section.

You might notice that the majority of protocols are at the Process/Application layer. These are the ones that provide the most customized functionality. You might also notice some exam objective acronyms listed there too, such as RDP, SSH, and HTTPS. There's more to come on each of these in the next section.

Connecting to the Cloud

Depending on how many users need cloud services, connecting to the cloud can take many forms. If it's just one user, the connection method is usually straightforward and requires little training. In most cases, if a user can open an Internet browser, then that user can connect to cloud resources. If an entire organization needs permanent access to cloud resources, then connectivity gets a bit more complicated. In this section, we will explore five different access or connectivity types. We'll start by covering single-client methods and then scale up to full, persistent organizational access.

Using Hypertext Transfer Protocol Secure

Connecting a single client to cloud resources is most often done through a web browser and *Hypertext Transfer Protocol Secure (HTTPS)*. We say single client, but it can also be dozens or hundreds of clients, each of them individually connecting to cloud resources from their own devices. A great thing about this access type is that every client device, including desktops, laptops, tablets, and smartphones, has a built-in web browser. Even better, nearly all users know how to use them! Figure 2.2 shows a connection to Google Drive using HTTPS. You can tell that it's HTTPS by looking in the address bar—the website address starts with https://.

FIGURE 2.2   Connecting to Google Drive with HTTPS

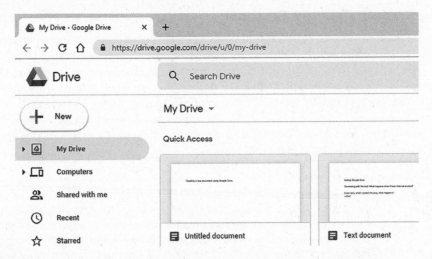

HTTPS is a secure protocol in the Process/Application layer in the TCP/IP suite. It's specifically designed to fetch web pages and encrypt data that is transmitted between a web server and its client. Because HTTPS secures transmissions, you can be confident in typing in usernames, passwords, and other personal information to websites that use it with little fear of it being hacked.

> The alternative web protocol to HTTPS is Hypertext Transfer Protocol (HTTP). It does not encrypt transmissions—anyone scanning network traffic can read HTTP data just as you are reading these words. If the website address in the browser starts with http://, do *not* put in any information that you don't want to be transmitted in plain text without encryption!

HTTPS can be used with any commercial web browser, which is just a specialized piece of software designed to request web pages from web servers. There are several on the market, with the most popular being Google Chrome, Microsoft Edge, Internet Explorer, Safari, and Firefox.

> It's important to point out that HTTPS encrypts data transmissions, but not data on the client or server. Said differently, it encrypts data in transit but not data at rest. Data on clients and servers needs to be encrypted using different methods. We'll look at encryption methods for data at rest in Chapter 7, "Cloud Security."

There are two key takeaways from this section. One, HTTPS is used in conjunction with a web browser and can be used to access cloud resources. Two, HTTPS secures network transmissions between the client and the server.

Using Remote Desktop Protocol

One of the great features of clouds is the ability to create virtual instances of computers. For instance, using the Amazon Web Services (AWS) Elastic Compute Cloud (EC2) interface, a cloud administrator (or anyone with appropriate permissions) can create a virtual Windows server. That server will act like any other Windows server and can host and run apps, provide storage, and do anything else users need a server to do. The process to create a virtual computer takes only a few minutes and doesn't require the client company to purchase any hardware! And of course, once users are done with the virtual computer, they can shut it off, and no physical resources are wasted.

> Throughout the rest of this chapter and elsewhere in the book, we will use AWS to show examples of cloud concepts. The Cloud Essentials+ exam is provider-agnostic, and we are not advocating for the use of one provider over another. AWS does allow for the creation of free accounts, though, which makes it convenient for us when we want to show examples. Other CSPs will generally have options similar to those that we show in this book.

Virtual machines have a number of uses, including the following:

- Providing extra server capacity, almost instantaneously

- Allowing developers to test software on multiple OS platforms

- Creating a test environment for network administrators to install and configure changes before rolling them out to a production environment

Once a virtual computer is created, someone will probably need to log in to that computer. For example, an administrator might need to start services for clients, or a developer might need to log in to install and test his app. *Remote Desktop Protocol (RDP)* is used to log into an online Windows instance. Once a user is logged in, they can use it just as they would use a computer sitting front of them.

To use RDP, you must install an RDP client onto the device that will be logging in to the virtual instance. Windows includes an RDP client called Remote Desktop Connection, which is shown in Figure 2.3. Linux users can use the rdesktop command, and macOS users can download the Microsoft Remote Desktop app from the Mac App Store. Android and iOS users will find RDP clients in their respective app stores as well. Some are free, and others will charge for their services.

FIGURE 2.3   Windows Remote Desktop Connection

Upon opening the RDP client, a user will be required to supply several pieces of information to connect. That includes the ID or address of the instance (or computer name as shown in Figure 2.3), a username and password, and the location of the private security key. Like HTTPS, RDP uses encryption to secure communications between the client and the virtual instance.

Using Security Key Pairs

RDP requires the use of a public/private key pair to authenticate users seeking to log in to remote instances. This is far more secure than requiring just a username and password.

The premise is that a private, encrypted security key is created for a specific user. In practice, it's a security code encrypted in a file stored on the user's device. (For RDP, the private key will have a .pem file extension.) When the user presents that private key to another device holding the corresponding public key, the public key is used to decipher the private key and validate the holder's identity. For security purposes, the user clearly needs to not let anyone else have access to their private key! The public key can be sent to anyone who needs to verify the identity of the private key holder.

The public/private key pairs are generated by a security server known as a *certificate authority (CA)*. Several commercial CA services are available on the Internet. If you are using a CSP, odds are they have their own CA that will generate keys as needed. For example, in AWS, security keys are created in the EC2 dashboard.

Figure 2.4 shows an example of a remote instance of Windows Server 2019. Looking at Figure 2.4, you might think, "Big deal, it looks just like a Windows Server desktop." That *is* a big deal, and the fact that it looks and acts just like Windows Server 2019 is the point. This screenshot was taken from a desktop computer running Windows 10, and the virtual machine is somewhere else in the world. But anyone sitting at the Windows 10 computer could manage the server, just as if they were sitting in front of it.

FIGURE 2.4 Using RDP to manage Windows Server 2019

It may be too small to read in the printed Figure 2.4, but the host name, instance ID, public IP address, private IP address, and other information are in the upper-right corner of the desktop.

As mentioned previously, you can also manage remote instances from mobile devices. Figure 2.5 shows a screenshot of managing the same server using the iOS free Microsoft RD client. Again, the picture might not seem impressive, but remember it's taken from an iPhone. Managing a server from an iPhone isn't the most convenient thing in the world, but know that with RDP, it's an option.

FIGURE 2.5   Managing a Windows server from an iPhone

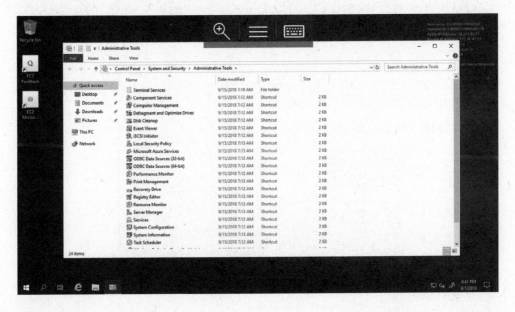

Only one RDP client connection can be made to a virtual instance at one time.

Using Secure Shell

Secure shell (SSH) is to Linux instances what RDP is to Windows Server instances. It allows clients to remotely connect to a virtual Linux machine, securely, and act as if the user were sitting at the virtual computer.

In its most basic form, SSH is run as a text command from a command prompt. For example, if you open a Windows command prompt to run the SSH command, specify the name of the security key file, and provide a username and the address of a virtual Ubuntu Linux server hosted on AWS, the command wlll look like this:

```
ssh -i "QDt1.pem" ubuntu@ec2-13-58-100-31.us-east-2.compute.amazonaws.com
```

> Ubuntu is one of the many versions of Linux. Linux is an open source OS, meaning that people and companies can create their own versions as they want.

In the sample SSH command, the -i option tells the computer that the next input will be the security file—in this case it's QDt1.pem. Next is the username, Ubuntu, followed by the instance's Internet address. It's highly unlikely that you will need to know SSH syntax for the Cloud Essentials+ exam, but this gives you a taste of how it could be used.

If your computer doesn't have an SSH client and you'd rather use something besides a command prompt, there are plenty of options in the marketplace. Doing a Google search of the app store will reveal several for every common OS. For example, a free open source SSH client is called PuTTY. It can be used in Windows and many other OSs. Figure 2.6 shows the PuTTY for Windows connection screen.

FIGURE 2.6   Windows PuTTY SSH client

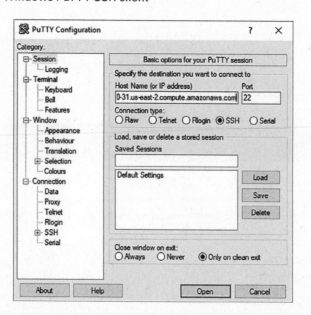

To log in, provide the host name of the server and the location of the security key file (in the Connection ➤ SSH menu on the left) and click Open. The PuTTY client will open, and then you can log in. Once logged in, you will have a text-based command prompt from which you can manage your Linux server. It's the last line shown in Figure 2.7.

FIGURE 2.7   Logged into the Ubuntu Linux server

```
ubuntu@ip-172-31-34-254: ~                                       —    □    ×
login as: ubuntu
Authenticating with public key "imported-openssh-key"
Welcome to Ubuntu 18.04.2 LTS (GNU/Linux 4.15.0-1032-aws x86_64)

* Documentation:  https://help.ubuntu.com
* Management:     https://landscape.canonical.com
* Support:        https://ubuntu.com/advantage

 System information as of Fri Jun 14 20:12:26 UTC 2019

 System load:  0.0               Processes:            84
 Usage of /:   13.7% of 7.69GB   Users logged in:      0
 Memory usage: 13%               IP address for eth0: 172.31.34.254
 Swap usage:   0%

* Ubuntu's Kubernetes 1.14 distributions can bypass Docker and use containerd
  directly, see https://bit.ly/ubuntu-containerd or try it now with

    snap install microk8s --classic

 Get cloud support with Ubuntu Advantage Cloud Guest:
    http://www.ubuntu.com/business/services/cloud

0 packages can be updated.
0 updates are security updates.


Last login: Fri Jun 14 20:06:22 2019 from 50.5.137.235
To run a command as administrator (user "root"), use "sudo <command>".
See "man sudo_root" for details.

ubuntu@ip-172-31-34-254:~$
```

Windows historically has not come with an SSH client, so users had to download something such as PuTTY. Another option is OpenSSH. With the release of Windows 10 build 1089 and Windows Server 2019, OpenSSH is included as an optional feature. To install it, go to Start ➢ Settings ➢ Apps ➢ Apps And Features ➢ Manage Optional Features.

Using a Virtual Private Network

The Internet is a public network. Data sent from point A bounces through several routers and eventually ends up at point B, but during that time, it can be read by the right people with the right equipment. Protocols such as HTTPS encrypt the data, making it considerably harder to read. Still, with enough time and dedication, that data can be decrypted and read.

Realistically, the odds of someone hacking your personal data sent through HTTPS are incredibly small, so don't waste too much mental energy worrying about it. Professional hackers rarely go after individual people anyway—winning small prizes is too inefficient. They'd rather go after bigger organizations.

Another way to secure Internet traffic is to use a *virtual private network (VPN)*. A VPN is a secure (private) network connection that occurs through a public network. VPNs can be used to connect individual users to a corporate network or server or to connect company networks or clouds together across the Internet or other public networks. For an individual user, this might look like sending HTTPS data through a VPN—two layers of encryption are more secure than one! VPNs can secure more than just HTTPS traffic, though. For example, a company with a geo-redundant cloud might use a VPN to secure traffic between the physical cloud sites. Figure 2.8 illustrates how a VPN works.

FIGURE 2.8   A VPN

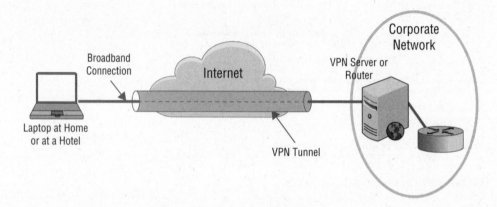

A VPN is a point-to-point secure tunnel through the Internet. The tunneled private network connection provides security over an otherwise unsecure connection. In Figure 2.8, one point is an end user, but it could be another corporate VPN server as well. All traffic going from one network to the other would have to flow through the VPN servers. In some cases, that can be a considerable amount of network traffic, so the VPN device needs to be configured appropriately.

A VPN connection is a great option for users who work from home or travel for work. When using a VPN, the remote end appears to be connected to the network as if it were connected locally. From the server side, a VPN requires dedicated hardware or a software package running on a server or router. Clients use specialized VPN client software to connect, most often over a broadband Internet link. Windows 10 comes with its own VPN client software accessible through Start ➢ Settings ➢ Network & Internet ➢ VPN, as do some other OSs. Many third-party options are also available. Some may be free for individual users, but most corporately used VPN clients cost money. Figure 2.9 shows an example of Pulse Secure VPN client on an iPhone.

FIGURE 2.9   Pulse Secure VPN client

 Don't get VPNs confused with virtual local area networks (VLANs). VPN connections are made over the Internet. A VLAN is configured on a network switch and simply puts several computers together on their own local network segment.

Using Direct Connect

The final connectivity method is called *direct connect*. It's used to provide a physical connection between your company's on-site network and the CSP's network. If a large number of users need persistent access to cloud services or there is a large amount of data transferred between the cloud and the on-site network, direct connect is likely going to be the fastest and most cost-effective option. Most CSPs offer connections that support 100Gbps data transfers. Lower-bandwidth plans can be as cheap as about $50 per month. Faster plans with unlimited data transfers can cost more than $50,000 per month.

With direct connect, you are literally connecting a router from your network directly to the CSP's router. Direct connections often come with uptime guarantees such as three nines or four nines—you'll recall we introduced these high availability standards in Chapter 1, "Cloud Principles and Design." Examples of direct connect services are Azure ExpressRoute, AWS Direct Connect, and Google Cloud Interconnect.

Cloud Networking Services

The basic cloud services are compute, storage, networking, and database. Beyond that, cloud providers can provide extra networking services, for a charge, of course. In this section, we will look at four of those options: software-defined networking, load balancing, DNS, and firewall. Software-defined networking is the only one that's cloud-specific. The other three are networking services that can be provided outside of cloud environments as well.

Software-Defined Networking

To help illustrate what software-defined networking is, let's first look at a relatively simple network layout, such as the one shown in Figure 2.10.

FIGURE 2.10   A sample network

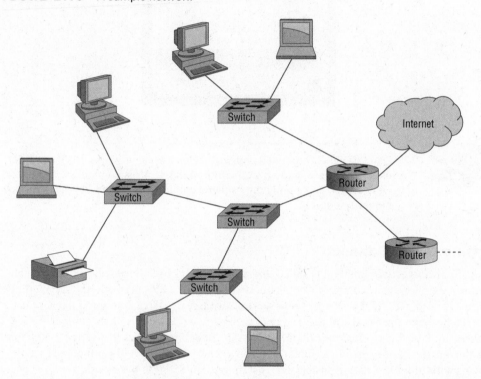

The network in Figure 2.10 has two routers, including one that connects the corporate network to the Internet. Four switches manage internal network traffic, and client devices connect to the switches. New network clients can attach to existing switches, and if the switches run out of ports, more can be added. Of course, in today's environment, we should draw in wireless access points and their clients as well. The wireless access points will connect to a switch or router with a network cable. Adding additional switches, routers, or other network control devices requires purchasing and installing the device and some configuration, but it's nothing that a good net admin can't handle.

Large enterprise networks are significantly more complex, and include more routers and perhaps load balancers, firewalls, and other network appliances. Adding to the network becomes more complicated. In particular, adding more routers requires a lot of reconfiguration so the routers know how to talk to each other.

Routers play a critical role in intra-network communications. The router's job is to take incoming data packets, read the destination address, and send the packet on to the next network that gets the data closer to delivery. There are two critical pieces to the router's job. One is the physical connections and internal circuitry that makes routing happen. The other is a logical component—each router has its own database, called a routing table, which it uses to determine where to send the packets. In a traditional networking environment, each router is responsible for maintaining its own table. While almost all routers have the ability to talk to their neighbor routers for route updates, the whole setup is still pretty complicated for administrators to manage. The complexity can really become a problem when troubleshooting data delivery problems.

Enter *software-defined networking (SDN)*. The goal of SDN is to make networks more agile and flexible by separating the forwarding of network packets (the infrastructure layer) from the logical decision-making process (the control layer). The control layer consists of one or more devices that make the decisions on where to send packets—they're the brains of the operation. The physical devices then just forward packets based on what the control layer tells them. Figure 2.11 illustrates the logical SDN structure.

FIGURE 2.11   Software-defined networking

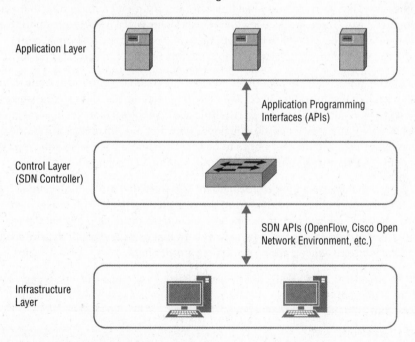

In addition to agility and flexibility, a third advantage to using SDN is centralized network monitoring. Instead of running monitoring apps for each individual piece of network hardware, the SDN software can monitor all devices in one app.

The SDN controller acts as an abstraction layer. Applications that need to use the network actually interface with the SDN controller, thinking that they are working directly with the networking hardware. In the end, data still gets from point A to point B, so the distinction between how that happens isn't important. Because the abstraction layer exists, though, the underlying network hardware and configuration can change, and it won't affect how the applications work. It's the job of the SDN controller to understand how to talk to the infrastructure.

 Real World Scenario

That's Abstract

Database systems make use of abstraction layers all the time. They act as translators between apps and the database itself, reducing the cost and complexity of reconfiguring data systems. They can also act as a security mechanism of sorts, blocking data from those who don't need to see it.

For example, say that your company has four different front-end applications that access a common database. There is a website where customers place orders, an app for the accounts receivable department to bill customers, an app for the warehouse to pull orders and check inventory, and a dashboard so management can see sales performance.

Because of a change in data management policies, the database structure needs to be changed. If each of the apps interfaced directly with the database, then all four apps would need to be recoded to work properly. This could require a significant investment of time and money and may jeopardize business performance. Instead, if an abstraction layer exists, it's the only thing that needs to be recoded before you can use the new database structure. As far as the apps are concerned, nothing has changed.

In addition, say that the management dashboard has sales and profit information. The customers certainly shouldn't see that from the website, but the customers do need to be able to see if something is in stock. The abstraction layer can help protect the sensitive information, acting as a security layer to ensure that sales and profit data doesn't get passed to the web app, while passing through inventory data.

So while an abstraction layer might seem like it increases complexity—and it can—know that there are good reasons to use one. It can help increase system agility, provide a layer of security, and ultimately keep costs down.

To make things even more fun, SDN can be used to create virtual networks without any hardware at all. In Chapter 1, we introduced the concept of a virtual machine—a computer that exists without a specific one-to-one hardware relationship. SDN can accomplish the same idea with networking.

Imagine having five logical servers running in a cloud, all using the same hardware. If they want to talk to each other, they will send data like they know how to—that is, to their network cards for delivery on the network, likely through a switch or router. But if they are using the same hardware, then they all have the same network adapter. That makes things weird, right? Well, not really, because SDN manages the communications between the servers. Each server will be assigned a logical NIC and communicate to the others via their logical NICs. SDN manages it all, and there are no communication issues.

For many years, SDN was commonly associated with the OpenFlow protocol, because OpenFlow was the dominant technology in the marketplace. In more recent years, OpenFlow has run into issues, with some experts calling it inefficient at best. Other competitors have entered the market, including Cisco's Open Network Environment (ONE) and VMware's NSX.

Load Balancing

Imagine you want to do some online shopping. You open your browser, type amazon.com into the address bar, and the site appears. You've made a connection to the Amazon server, right? But is there only one Amazon server? Considering the millions of transactions Amazon completes each day, that seems highly unlikely. In fact, it's not the case. Amazon has dozens if not hundreds of web servers, each of them capable of fulfilling the same tasks to make your shopping experience as easy as possible. Each server helps balance out the work for the website, which is called *load balancing.*

Load balancing technology predates its usage in the cloud. Hardware devices, conveniently named load balancers, would essentially act like the web server to the outside world. Then when a user visited the website, the load balancer would send the request to one of many real web servers to fulfill the request. Cloud implementations have made load balancing easier to configure, since the servers can be virtual instead of physical. While hardware load balancers still exist, many CSPs' load balancer as a service (LBaaS) offerings are cheaper and more convenient to set up and manage.

Common Load Balancing Configurations

We already shared one example of load balancing with an online retailer. In that example, all servers are identical (or very close to identical) and perform the same tasks. Two other common load-balancing configurations are cross-region and content-based.

In a cross-region setup, all servers likely provide access to the same types of content, much like in our Amazon example. The big feature with this setup is that there are servers local to each region—proximity to the users will help speed up network performance. For example, say that a company has a geo-redundant cloud and users in North America, Asia, and Europe. When a request comes in, the load balancer senses the incoming IP address and routes the request to a server in that region. This is illustrated in Figure 2.12. If all servers in that region are too busy with other requests, then it might be sent to another region for processing.

FIGURE 2.12   Cross-region load balancing

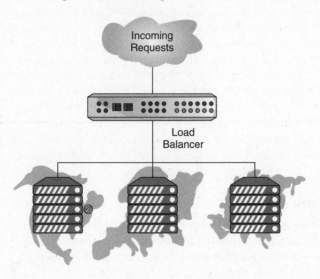

Another common way to load balance is to split up banks of servers to handle specific types of requests. For example, one group of servers could handle web requests, while a second set hosts streaming video and a third set manages downloads. This type of load balancing is called content-based load balancing and is shown in Figure 2.13.

FIGURE 2.13   Content-based load balancing

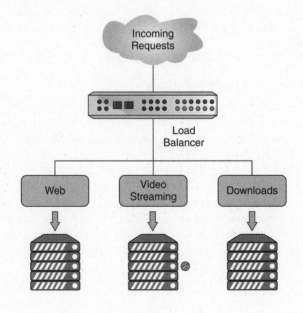

Load Balancing Benefits

Cloud-based load balancing has performance benefits for high-traffic networks and heavily used applications. Scalability and reliability are important benefits as well. Let's give a few examples of each.

Performance   The Amazon example we used earlier is probably the best example of this, but not all companies provide massive online shopping services. Smaller companies can benefit from performance enhancements as well. Servers that are specialized to handle a specific content type are often more efficient than multipurpose ones. And, the global load balancing example can be applied to distributed sites within a country as well.

Scalability   We know that the cloud is scalable, and so is load balancing within the cloud. For example, let's say that your company does sell products online and has two servers dedicated to that task. For the vast majority of the year, the two servers can handle the traffic without a problem. On the busiest shopping day of the year—Cyber Monday—those servers are overwhelmed. With cloud-based load balancing, traffic spikes can be handled by quickly provisioning additional virtual servers to handle the traffic. When the capacity is no longer required, the servers are turned off.

Cloud-based load balancing can also be scaled to function across a multicloud environment.

Reliability   Imagine a company that uses a business-critical application for remote salespeople. What happens if the server hosting that application crashes? It wouldn't be good.

With cloud-based load balancing, different servers can host the application, even in different regions. Perhaps a hurricane wipes out the data center in Florida. The load balancer can direct users to other data centers in different regions, and the business can continue to generate revenue.

Domain Name System

For one host on a TCP/IP network to communicate with another, it must know the remote host's IP address. Think about the implications of this when using the Internet. You open your browser, and in the address bar you type the *uniform resource locator (URL)* of your favorite website, something like www.google.com, and press Enter. The first question your computer asks is, "Who is that?" The website name means nothing to it—your device requires an IP address to connect to the website. The *Domain Name System (DNS)* server provides the answer, "That is 72.14.205.104." Now that your computer knows the address of the website you want, it's able to traverse the Internet to connect to it.

DNS has one function on the network, and that is to resolve hostnames (or URLs) to IP addresses. This sounds simple enough, but it has profound implications for our everyday lives.

Each DNS server has a database where it stores hostname-to-IP-address pairs, called a *zone file*. If the DNS server does not know the address of the host you are seeking, it has the ability to query other DNS servers to help answer the request.

We all probably use Google several times a day, but in all honesty how many of us know its IP address? It's certainly not something that we are likely to have memorized. Much less, how could you possibly memorize the IP addresses of all of the websites you visit? Because of DNS, it's easy to find resources. Whether you want to find Coca-Cola, Toyota, Amazon, or thousands of other companies, it's usually pretty easy to figure out how. Type in the name with a .com on the end of it and you're usually right. The only reason why this is successful is that DNS is there to perform resolution of that name to the corresponding IP address.

DNS works the same way on an intranet (a local network not attached to the Internet) as it does on the Internet. The only difference is that instead of helping you find www.google.com, it may help you find Jenny's print server or Joe's file server. From a client-side perspective, the host just needs to be configured with the address of one or two legitimate DNS servers and it should be good to go.

 Any company hosting a website is required to maintain its own DNS. In fact, the company is required to have two DNS servers for fault tolerance.

Protocols and Ports

We introduced several TCP/IP protocols in the last few sections. To help keep network traffic organized across an IP-based network, each Process/Application layer protocol uses what's called a *port number*. The port number is combined with the IP address to form a *socket*. Using cable television as an analogy, think of the IP address as the home address where the cable television is delivered, and the port number is the channel that's being watched.

Port numbers aren't specifically called out in the CompTIA Cloud Essentials+ exam objectives. However, we'd hate for you to be unprepared if one of them pops up on the test. Table 2.1 lists the protocols we've discussed and their associated port numbers. For a full list (and there are a lot!), you can visit https://www.iana.org/assignments/service-names-port-numbers/service-names-port-numbers.xhtml.

TABLE 2.1 Protocols and port numbers

Protocol	Port number
DNS	53
HTTP	80
HTTPS	443
RDP	3389
SSH	22

Firewalls

A *firewall* is a hardware or software solution that serves as a network's security guard. They're probably the most important devices on networks connected to the Internet. Firewalls can protect network resources from hackers lurking in the dark corners of the Internet, and they can simultaneously prevent computers on your network from accessing undesirable content on the Internet. At a basic level, firewalls filter network traffic based on rules defined by the network administrator.

Anti-malware software examines individual files for threats. Firewalls protect you from streams of network traffic that could be harmful to your computer.

Firewalls can be stand-alone "black boxes," software installed on a server or router, or some combination of hardware and software. In addition to the categorizations of hardware and software, there are two types of firewalls: network-based and host-based. A network-based firewall is designed to protect a whole network of computers and almost always is a hardware solution with software on it. Host-based firewalls protect only one computer and are almost always software solutions.

How Firewalls Work

Most network-based firewalls have at least two network connections: one to the Internet, or *public side*, and one to the internal network, or *private side*. Some firewalls have a third network port for a second semi-internal network. This port is used to connect servers that can be considered both public and private, such as web and email servers. This intermediary network is known as a *demilitarized zone (DMZ)*. A DMZ can also be configured as a space between two firewalls. Figure 2.14 shows examples of DMZs.

A firewall is configured to allow only packets (network data) that pass specific security restrictions to get through. By default, most firewalls are configured as default deny, which means that all traffic is blocked unless specifically authorized by the administrator. The basic method of configuring firewalls is to use an *access control list (ACL)*. The ACL is the set of rules that determines which traffic gets through the firewall and which traffic is blocked. There will be different ACLs for inbound and outbound network traffic. ACLs are typically configured to block traffic by IP address, protocol (such as HTTPS or RDP), domain name, or some combination of characteristics. Packets that meet the criteria in the ACL are passed through the firewall to their destination.

FIGURE 2.14   Two ways to configure a DMZ

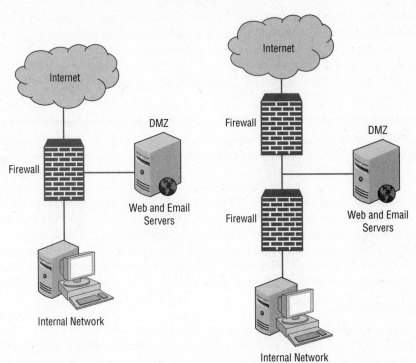

Obtaining a Firewall

Windows comes with its own software firewall called Windows Defender Firewall. There are also numerous firewalls on the market—Barracuda and Zscaler are popular ones—and of course AWS and Azure provide firewall services as well. Some third-party security software, such as Norton Internet Security, comes with its own software firewall. In cases where you have those types of programs installed, they will turn off Windows Defender Firewall automatically.

Regardless of which firewall is used, the key principle is to use one. Combined with anti-malware software, they are critical security features for any network.

As a reminder, for the Cloud Essentials+ Exam, you need to know about direct connect, VPN, RDP, SSH, and HTTP cloud access. You also should be able to identify and understand what software-defined networking (SDN), load balancing, DNS, and firewalls do.

Understanding Cloud Storage Technologies

The cloud offers companies and users a large number of services, and it seems like more service types are being added every day. Fundamentally, though, what the cloud really provides is compute, network, and storage services without the need to invest in the underlying hardware. Of these three, storage is the most tangible and understandable. It's also the most widely used and the one that catapulted the cloud to popularity.

It's easy to see why cloud storage is so popular. Among its benefits are convenient file access, easy sharing and collaboration, and automated redundancy. Users can access files from anywhere in the world, nearly instantaneously. Those same users can collaborate on a document or project, which wouldn't be nearly as easy or even possible if files had to be stored on someone's local hard drive. And the cloud has systems to back up all those files without users needing to intervene. To top it all off, cloud storage is cheap!

In this section, we will look at cloud storage technologies. We'll start with a high-level overview of how cloud storage works and how providers set it up. Then we'll get into storage characteristics, types, and features. Finally, we'll end by looking at a specific type of cloud storage—a content delivery network.

How Cloud Storage Works

Most computing devices come with some sort of long-term persistent storage media. By persistent, we mean that once the power is turned off, the device retains the information stored on it. Usually this device is called a *hard drive*. A hard drive is either a set of spinning metal-coated platters or electronic circuitry that stores long stretches of binary data—literally 0s and 1s—for later retrieval. It's up to the device's OS and apps to make sense of those 0s and 1s to know where relevant information starts and stops. If the device runs low on free storage space, performance can suffer. If the device runs out of storage space, no new data can be stored.

Storage in the cloud looks and acts a lot like storage on a local device. There's a physical hard drive—more like hundreds or thousands of them—sitting somewhere storing data, controlled by one or more servers. Data is stored persistently and can be retrieved by a user who has the appropriate access. Of course, just like accessing any other cloud service, the user needs a network connection.

Even though there are a lot of similarities between how traditional and cloud storage work, there's one major difference. On a traditional computing device, the number of storage devices, and consequently the maximum storage space, is limited by the number of drive connections the computer has. For example, if a computer's motherboard has only four hard drive connectors, then that computer can manage a maximum of four hard drives.

Cloud storage runs on a technology called *software-defined storage (SDS)*. In SDS, the physical storage of data is separated from the logical control over drive configuration, independent from the underlying hardware. If this sounds a lot like SDN, that's because it is. It's the same idea, just applied to storage instead of networking. Figure 2.15 shows an example.

FIGURE 2.15   Software-defined storage

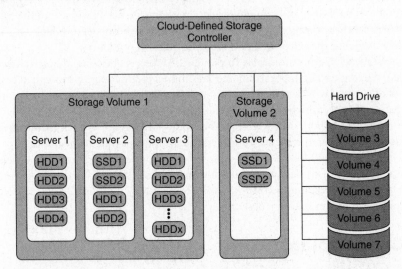

In SDS, one logical unit of storage can be composed of an innumerable number of physical hard drives, enabling virtually unlimited storage. At the same time, one physical hard drive can be separated into a large number of logical storage units. Those two extremes and every combination in between are possible. The user doesn't know what the underlying hardware is, and quite frankly it doesn't matter as long as the files are safe, secure, and easily accessible.

Finally, a good SDS solution will have the following features:

Scalability   Both the amount of storage offered to clients and the underlying hardware should be scalable without any performance issues or downtime. Scalability for clients should be automated.

Transparency   Administrators and clients should know how much storage is available and what the cost of storage is.

A Standard Interface   Management and maintenance of SDS should be easy for administrators and clients.

Storage Type Support   The SDS should support applications written for object, file, or block storage. (We will review these concepts in more detail in the "Storage Types" section later in this chapter.)

Cloud-Based Storage Providers

There is no shortage of cloud-based storage providers on the market today. They come in a variety of sizes, from the big Cloud Service Providers (CSPs) that deliver a full range of services, such as AWS, Azure, and Google Cloud, to niche players that offer storage solutions only. Each one offers slightly different features, and most of them will offer limited storage for free and premium services for more data-heavy users. Table 2.2 shows you a comparison of some personal plans from the more well-known storage providers. Please note that this table is for illustrative purposes only, since the data storage limits and costs can change. Most of these providers offer business plans with very high or unlimited storage for an additional fee.

TABLE 2.2   Cloud-based storage providers and features

Service	Free	Premium	Cost per Year
Dropbox	2GB	1TB	$99
Apple iCloud	5GB	50GB, 200GB, or 2TB	$12, $36, or $120
Box	10GB	100GB	$120
Microsoft OneDrive	5GB	50GB or 1TB	$24 or $70
Google Drive	15GB	100GB, 1TB, or 10TB	$24, $120, or $1200

Which one should you choose? If you want extra features such as web-based applications, then Google or Microsoft is probably the best choice. If you just need data storage, then Box or Dropbox might be a better option.

Nearly all client OSs will work with any of the cloud-based storage providers, with the exception of Linux, which natively works only with Dropbox.

Most cloud storage providers offer synchronization to the desktop, which makes it so that you have a folder on your computer, just as if it were on your hard drive. And importantly, that folder will always have the most current edition of the files stored in the cloud.

Cloud Storage Terminology

When working with a CSP to set up cloud storage, you will be presented with a plethora of features. Having a solid understanding of the terms that will be thrown in your direction will make it easier to determine which solutions are best for your business. In this section, we'll look at storage characteristics, types, and features.

Storage Characteristics

The first thing your company needs to decide is what the cloud storage will be used for. Some want cloud storage to be instantly accessible, like a replacement for local hard drive space. Others need long-term archival storage, and of course, there could be any combination in between. Once you understand the purpose for the storage, you can focus on performance and price of available solutions.

Taking a high-level view of cloud storage, there are two major categories of performance— hot and cold. *Hot storage* refers to data that is readily available at all times. *Cold storage* refers to data that isn't needed very often, such as archived data. It might take from several minutes to several days to make cold data available to access. Table 2.3 shows an overview of hot versus cold storage performance characteristics.

TABLE 2.3   Hot versus cold storage performance

Trait	Hot	Cold
Access frequency	Frequent	Infrequent
Access speed	Fast	Slow
Media type	Fast hard drives such as solid-state drives (SSDs)	Slower hard drives such as conventional hard disk drives (HDDs), tape drives, offline
Cost per GB	Higher	Lower

Cloud storage would be pretty easy to navigate if there were only two options to consider. In the real world, CSPs offer a wide range of storage solutions with varying performance and cost. For example, Microsoft Azure offers premium, hot, cool, and archive tiers. Google has two hot options—multiregional storage and regional storage—along with nearline and coldline options. AWS has two primary designations, which are its Simple Storage Service (S3) for hot data and S3 Glacier for archives. Within S3 and S3 Glacier, there are multiple options to choose from.

You might have noticed in the previous paragraph that there are a few types of service not covered in Table 2.3. It's common for providers to have a level of service between hot and cold, sometimes called warm or cool. Maybe they will even have both. Google calls its in-between service *nearline*, to indicate it's not quite as fast as online but not as slow as a traditional archive.

Understanding Storage Containers

When a client uploads data to the cloud, that data is placed into a storage container. CSPs call their containers by different names. For example, AWS and Google Cloud use the term *bucket*, whereas Azure uses *blob*. This leads to the use of some unintentionally funny phrases—making archived Azure data readable again is called *rehydrating the blob*.

CSPs allow clients to have multiple containers to meet their storage needs. For example, many companies will have several hot containers for different offices or departments, and more cold containers to archive data. The end result is a flexible infrastructure that can be customized to meet any client's needs.

Regardless of what the CSP chooses to call its storage offering, focus on the performance characteristics and cost. As you might expect, the hotter the service and the more features it has, the more you will pay per gigabyte. Here are some key performance characteristics and parameters to pay attention to:

- Cost per gigabyte
- Storage capacity limits
- The maximum number of containers allowed
- Data encryption
- Storage compression and/or deduplication
- If intelligent analysis of storage usage and/or automated optimization is provided
- Dynamic container resizing (e.g., capacity on demand)
- Data read/write speed
- Number of data reads/writes allowed, or cost per thousand reads/writes
- Data latency for reads/writes
- Data retrieval time for archives
- Archived data retrieval cost

Most companies tend to overestimate the amount of data they need to store, as well as capacity needed for other cloud services. It's possibly cheaper to pay for less capacity and then pay for peak overage charges than it is to pay for more capacity all the time. Do the due diligence to price out options, knowing that if you really need more capacity later, you can almost always add it dynamically.

Storage Types

At the hardware level, data is stored as long strings of 1s and 0s on its storage media. This includes everything from critical OS files to databases to pictures of your last vacation to that inappropriate video clip of the last company holiday party. It's up to the device's OS or software to interpret the data and know where a relevant piece of information starts and stops.

There are multiple ways in which data can be stored and retrieved by a computer. The underlying 1s and 0s don't change, but how they are logically organized into groups and accessed can make a big performance difference. The three storage types you need to know are file storage, block storage, and object storage.

File Storage

For anyone who has used a Windows-based or Mac computer, *file storage* is instantly recognizable. It's based on the concept of a filing cabinet. Inside the filing cabinet are folders, and files are stored within the folders. Each file has a unique name when you include the folders and subfolders it's stored in. For example, `c:\files\doc1.txt` is different than `c:\papers\doc1.txt`. Figure 2.16 shows an example of file storage, as seen through Windows Explorer.

FIGURE 2.16   File storage

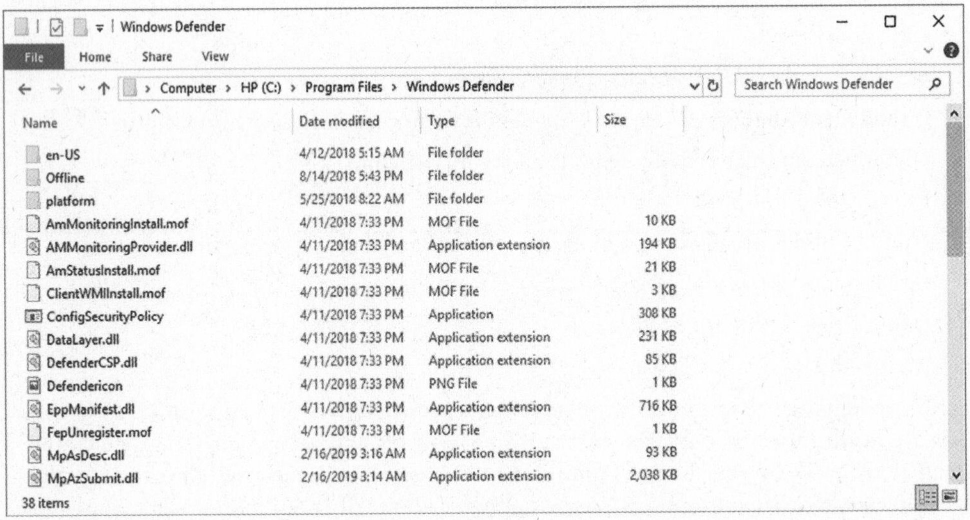

The hierarchical folder structure and naming scheme of file storage makes it relatively easy for humans to navigate. Larger data sets and multiple embedded folders can make it trickier—who here *hasn't* spent 10 minutes trying to figure out which folder they put that file in—but it's still pretty straightforward.

OSs have built-in file systems that manage files. Windows uses the New Technology File System (NTFS), Macs use Apple File System (APFS), and Linux uses the fourth extended file system (ext4), among others. Although they all function in slightly different ways, each file system maintains a table that tracks all files and includes a pointer to where each file resides. (Folders are just specialized files that can contain pointers to other folders or files.) Because of the pointer system and the way that files are written to hard drives, it's entirely possible (and in fact likely) that c:\files\doc1.txt and c:\files\doc2.txt are in completely different locations on the hard drive. On top of it all, most file systems are specific to an OS. A Windows-based computer, for example, can't natively read an APFS- or ext4-formatted hard drive.

File systems will experience performance problems when they are responsible for storing large numbers of files or very large files, such as databases. Their structure makes them highly inefficient. They work great in an office environment where users need to store some data on their PC, share files with co-workers, and make small backups. Large-scale data environments require a different solution.

Block Storage

With file storage, each file is treated as its own singular entity, regardless of how small or large it is. With *block storage*, files are split into chunks of data of equal size, assigned a unique identifier, and then stored on the hard drive. Because each piece of data has a unique address, a file structure is not needed. Figure 2.17 illustrates what this looks like.

FIGURE 2.17   Block storage

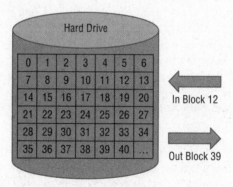

Block storage allows files to be broken into more manageable chunks rather than being stored as one entity. This allows the OS to modify one portion of a file without needing to open the entire file. In addition, since data reads and writes are always of the same block size, data transfers are more efficient and therefore faster. Latency with block storage is lower than with other types of storage.

One of the first common use cases for block storage was for databases, and it remains the best choice for large, structured databases today. Block storage is also used for storage area networks (SANs) that are found in large data centers, and many email server applications natively support block storage because of its efficiency over file storage. Finally, virtualization software uses block storage as well. Essentially, the VMM creates block storage containers for guest OSs, which function as the storage system for the guest OSs.

While block storage is great for large, structured data sets that need to be accessed and updated frequently, it's not perfect. One thing it doesn't handle well is metadata, which is needed to make sense of unstructured data. For unstructured data, the best choice is object storage.

When data is referred to as *structured*, that means it conforms to defined parameters. The best examples to think of are spreadsheets and relational databases, which have columns and rows to provide the structure. On the flip side, unstructured data is information that is not organized in a predefined way. Unstructured information is often text-heavy, such as a novel stored as a long string of words with no punctuation or chapter breaks. Data such as dates, numbers, and facts can be unstructured too, if they're not stored in a relational way. Images and videos are other great examples of unstructured data.

Object Storage

Not all data fits into easily defined or standard parameters. Think about pictures or videos stored on a hard drive, for example. How would a user easily search a folder containing 1,000 pictures for people wearing green shirts? With file or even block storage, this is next to impossible without opening every file and examining it. Contrast that to searching 1,000 text files for the word *green*, which is a much simpler task.

Pictures and videos are two examples of unstructured data—they don't have a predefined data model, and they can't be organized in a predefined structure. (To be fair, they could be organized into a predefined structure, but it would require tedious manual labor and be inflexible. For example, say you create a folder and put any picture with someone wearing a green shirt into it. Now how do you easily search that folder for people with blue shirts as well? You don't.)

A term that's thrown around a lot today is *big data*. It seems that every company wants to find an edge by analyzing big data, but most people in positions of power don't even really know what that means. Big data doesn't necessarily refer to the size of the data set, even though it can. Really, big data refers to a collection of unstructured data that, if properly analyzed, can yield new insights.

By using *object storage*, a company can make the organization and retrieval of unstructured data easier. In object storage, every unit of storage is called an object. There's no predefined size or structure for each object—it could be a small text file, a two-hour long movie, a song, or a copy of *War and Peace*. An object can be literally anything that anyone wants to store. If you've posted a picture in social media, you've used object storage. Each object has four characteristics, which are shown in Figure 2.18.

The Data   This is the data for the object itself—literally the bits that make up the file or image or whatever it is that's being stored.

Metadata Describing the Object   Metadata is optional information about the object. It can describe the object, what it's used for, or anything else that will be relevant for people trying to find the object. In the green shirt example we used earlier, a metadata tag could say *green shirt*, for example. Metadata could also describe the type of shirt, words or logo on the shirt, who is wearing the shirt, where the picture was taken, the wearer's favorite food, or anything else. Metadata is completely customizable and can be entered in by the creator or others who access the file.

Object Attributes   These are classifications of metadata, such as color, person, or other relevant characteristics. They're optional but can make it easier to compare different unstructured data sets.

A Unique Identifying ID   Each object needs a unique ID within the system in which it resides. As with block storage, there is no hierarchical folder structure.

FIGURE 2.18   Object storage

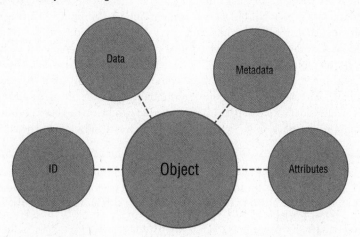

In direct contrast to block storage, which makes every storage unit the same size, object storage sets no restrictions on object size. Similarly, there is no limit to how much metadata can be created for any object. The result is a completely flexible and customizable data storage solution.

One downside compared to block storage is that in object storage, the entire object must be opened to modify any part of it. This can result in slower performance for large objects that are frequently modified. Because of this, object storage is inferior to block storage for things like databases.

As for use cases, we already mentioned the storage of unstructured data such as pictures and videos. The other big use case for object storage is for backup archives. By nature, backup archives are often massive but rarely if ever need to be modified. That's a great combination to take advantage of the features of object storage.

Storage Features

Cloud storage solutions offer two features to help save space—compression and deduplication. They also allow you to obtain additional services at any time, which is called *capacity on demand*. We'll look at each one in more detail next.

Compression

The purpose of *compression* is to make files smaller so they take up less storage space. Compression works by looking for repeated information within a file and then replacing that information with a shorter string. Therefore, fewer bits are required to store the same amount of information.

For example, let's imagine you want to apply compression to the rules manual for the National Football League (NFL). You can probably think of a lot of words that will be repeated, such as *football*, *player*, *touchdown*, *pass*, *run*, *kick*, *tackle*, and so on. A compression utility can replace the word *football* with a 1, *player* with a 2, *touchdown* with a 3, and so forth. Every time the word *football* is mentioned, a 1 is used instead, saving seven characters of space. Every time *player* is used, you save five characters. Interestingly (maybe only to us), the word *football* appears only 25 times in the 2018 NFL official playing rules, so only 168 characters are saved. But *player* is mentioned a whopping 812 times in 89 pages. Compressing that to a single character saves 4,060 characters. Repeating this process for all files in a storage unit can save a lot of capacity. A dictionary file is maintained to keep track of all the replacements.

Of course, real-life compression is bit more complicated than this, but this example illustrates the principle. The process is to remove redundant words or phrases and replace them with a shorter placeholder to save space. Before the file can be opened or modified by a user, it must be decompressed back to its original form, which will slow down the computer.

Almost all OSs allow for folder and file compression. In most versions of Windows, right-click the folder or file, go to Properties, and click the Advanced button. You will see a screen similar to the one shown in Figure 2.19.

FIGURE 2.19   Advanced attributes folder compression

Deduplication

On the surface, compression and deduplication might seem like the same thing, but they're not. Data *deduplication* works at the file level or block level to eliminate duplicate data.

As an example of this, imagine a backup of an email server that stores email for 2,000 corporate users. The users collaborate a lot, so there are a lot of emails that go back and forth with Word or Excel attachments in them. It's easy to conceive that there might be dozens or even hundreds of backed-up emails that contain the same attached Excel file. With deduplication, only one copy of that Excel file will be stored. For the other instances, a small pointer file is created, pointing to the original. In this way, deduplication saves storage space. When used in large data sets, compression and deduplication can save companies thousands of dollars per year in storage costs.

To save money, compress or deduplicate files before uploading them to the CSP. If you upload 100GB of data and the CSP is able to compress or dedupe it down to 10GB, you will still be charged for 100GB of storage. Most of the time, you won't know that the CSP has compressed or deduped the data. But if you do it yourself and upload that 10GB, you will be charged for only 10GB.

Capacity on Demand

We've already hit on the concept of *capacity on demand* in both Chapter 1 and earlier in this chapter. The idea is straightforward—if you need extra storage capacity, it is instantaneously available. You just pay extra for the extra capacity that you use.

Capacity on demand can be great, but it poses some risks as well. Just because you *can* have the capacity doesn't mean you *should* use the capacity. Many times, excessive capacity can be obtained unintentionally.

For example, take a company that has a 100GB cloud-hosted customer service database. Clearly, it will pay for the 100GB of storage. In addition, an admin set up the database to be replicated, just in case of failure. So now it's paying for 200GB. A perfectly well-meaning network administrator doesn't know that the database is replicated and decides to set up a backup for the same database. Now the company is paying for 300GB or even 400GB, depending on what the admin did. The CSP isn't going to ping you to be sure your company really wants to buy 400GB of storage; they will be happy to just send you the bill.

This is a good time to remind you to conduct frequent capacity planning and usage analysis and adjust your purchase accordingly. Also remember that organizations tend to overestimate the capacity they will need. If you can, pay for only what you absolutely need and use!

Content Delivery Networks

A *content delivery network (CDN)* is a specialized type of load balancing used with web servers. Its primary use is to speed up access to web resources for users in geographically distributed locations. CDNs allow users in remote locations to access web data on servers that are closer to them than the original web server is. An example is shown in Figure 2.20.

FIGURE 2.20 A content delivery network

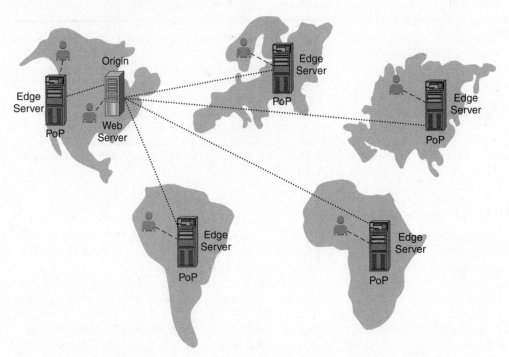

In Figure 2.20, you can see that the company's web server is based in the eastern United States. In CDN terms, this server is the *origin* because it's the primary content server. If users across the globe needed to access this one server, there could be some potential issues. Latency (delay) can be a problem, because users in Asia or Africa are quite some distance away. The number of users can also be a problem, because more users equates to slower response times.

The CDN creates a *point of presence (PoP)* in each remote location. Within each PoP will be one or more edge servers. The job of the *edge server* is to cache the content of the origin and serve it to users who are located nearby. If everything is configured properly, the edge server will have the same information that the origin does. The cached content is typically a website but can include data such as plain text, images, videos, audio, PDFs, or scripting files for programmers.

From the end user's standpoint, the location of the server is transparent. All they have to do is open their browser and type in the website's address. They won't know where the server that responds is located, nor does it really matter as long as they get their content and get it quickly. It's estimated that more than 75 percent of large multinational corporations use CDNs to distribute web content.

Some key benefits of using a CDN are as follows:

- Increased website performance via faster load times
- Increased reliability, thanks to greater availability and redundancy
- Decreased bandwidth costs
- Greater scalability for web resources
- Increased security

The first four benefits probably make a lot of intuitive sense, but increased security might not be so apparent. Take the instance of a *distributed denial-of-service (DDoS) attack*, where the attacker attempts to overwhelm a web server and make it unable to respond to legitimate requests. For an example, assume this attack comes from Europe. If the CDN is configured properly, the attack may temporarily disable the European edge server, but it won't affect the other locations. Users making requests of the website can be directed to other edge servers to fulfill the request.

As a reminder, the objectives you need to know from this section for the exam are the following:

- Storage features
    - Compression
    - Deduplication
    - Capacity on demand
- Storage characteristics
    - Performance
    - Hot vs. cold
- Storage types
    - Object storage
    - File storage
    - Block storage
- Software-defined storage
- Content delivery network

If you don't feel comfortable with all of these concepts, go back through them before answering the end-of-chapter review questions!

Summary

This chapter covered two major cloud concepts: networking and storage. First, we started with a quick networking primer to make sure that the other cloud networking concepts make sense within a framework. Once you learned more than you might have wanted to about TCP/IP, we looked at the ways to connect to a cloud. Common approaches for single clients include HTTPS, RDP, SSH, and a VPN. For multiple clients or an entire site, VPNs and direct connect are the two connectivity types to remember.

We finished our discussion of cloud networking by reviewing four services that you can get from cloud service providers. The first is software-defined networking. It's a service where the physical networking hardware is abstracted and logically controlled through a single interface. It's great for network flexibility and scalability. Load balancing spreads out the work that servers need to do to efficiently increase network performance. DNS resolves host names to IP addresses. Without it, the Internet might kind of suck—or at least it would be very different from what we're used to today. The final service was a firewall, which is a security device for computers or a network.

To kick off our discussion of cloud storage technologies, we first looked at how cloud storage works. One of the primary technologies behind cloud storage is software-defined storage. After that, we talked about some popular cloud storage providers and gave examples of different plans.

The main part of learning about cloud storage was around characteristics, types, and features. Characteristics are hot and cold and performance profiles for each. The storage types we discussed are file, block, and object storage. Features you need to know are compression, deduplication, and capacity on demand. We ended the chapter by talking about how a content delivery network can help load balance web services.

Exam Essentials

Know how to connect to a cloud with HTTPS.   Hypertext Transfer Protocol Secure is used by a web browser such as Google Chrome, Microsoft Edge, or Apple Safari to connect to a URL for the cloud resource.

Know what RDP is used for.   Remote Desktop Protocol is used to connect to a remote Windows-based server.

Know what SSH is used for.   Secure Shell is used to connect to a remote Linux-based server.

Understand how VPNs are used.   A virtual private network is a secure tunnel through an unsecured network, such as the Internet. VPNs can be used to connect an individual user to a cloud server, and they can also be used to connect one corporate site to another.

Know when a direct connect should be used.   If a company needs to make extensive use of cloud services and have very little delay, a direct connect between that company's network and a CSP's network might be the best option.

Know which connectivity methods are secure.   HTTPS, RDP, SSH, and VPNs all have built-in encryption. A direct connection should be secure as well, provided it's configured properly.

Understand what SDN is.   In software-defined networking, the physical routing of packets is separated from the logical control of where the packets should be routed to. SDN provides flexibility and scalability for corporate networks in the cloud.

Know what a load balancer does.   Load balancing is a set of servers configured to perform the same task. They can speed up network performance by sending tasks to the server that has the most capacity.

Understand what DNS does.   Domain Name System resolves host names to IP addresses.

Understand what a firewall does.   A firewall is a security device that protects computers or networks from malicious network traffic.

Know what file compression is.   File compression makes files smaller to take up less room when they are stored. It works by looking for repeated words or phrases within a file and replacing them with a shortened version.

Understand the difference between file compression and deduplication.   File compression works within a file. Deduplication works between files. For example, if there are 10 copies of a Word document, a deduplicated file system will store only one copy of it and replace the others with pointers to the original file.

Know what capacity on demand is.   With capacity on demand, clients can get more storage space from their CSP nearly instantly.

Understand hot versus cold storage and the performance implications of each.   Hot storage is online and always accessible. Cold storage may be offline or on tapes. Hot is more expensive per gigabyte, but the performance is much faster.

Understand when to use file, block, or object storage.   File storage is used on personal computers and many servers and works best for smaller storage solutions. Block storage is best suited for databases and large-scale, frequently accessed storage solutions such as those found in a SAN. Object storage is great for unstructured ("big") data and for large computer or network data backups.

Know what SDS is.   With software-defined storage, the physical storage medium is abstracted from the user and controlled by a central server. This allows storage volumes to span physical devices or many storage volumes to be held within one physical device.

Understand what a CDN is.   A content delivery network is a load balancer for web-based content. Edge servers in remote locations service users who are in closer proximity to them than they are to the original web server.

Written Lab

Fill in the blanks for the questions provided in the written lab. You can find the answers to the written labs in Appendix A.

1. A user wanting to log in and remotely manage a virtual instance of Windows Server 2019 would use the _____ access type.

2. The two methods used to securely connect many users at once to a cloud resource are _____ and _____.

3. A DNS server is responsible for what?

4. Which cloud networking server functions as a security gateway?

5. Google Chrome connects to the cloud using _____.

6. _____ storage is the best type for large data backups.

7. _____ storage is less expensive per gigabyte than _____ storage.

8. To save space on a cloud storage volume, _____ is used to remove multiple copies of the same file.

9. _____ use a point of presence to locate servers nearer to potential users.

10. Windows 10 natively uses the _____ storage type.

Review Questions

The answers to the chapter review questions can be found in Appendix B.

1. Your company needs to upload a large, offline backup archive to the new cloud service. What type of storage is best for this archive in the cloud?

   A. Object

   B. File

   C. Block

   D. Hot

2. A CSP is configuring access to your cloud-hosted web server. Which of the following services will help users locate your web server on the Internet?

   A. SDN

   B. DNS

   C. SDS

   D. CDN

3. Which of the following protocols is used with a web browser to securely access cloud storage?

   A. RDP

   B. SSH

   C. HTTP

   D. HTTPS

4. A network administrator needs to remotely log into a cloud-based Linux server to perform some administrative tasks. Which access method should she use?

   A. RDP

   B. SSH

   C. Direct connect

   D. HTTPS

5. Which of the following cloud storage types is designed to provide the fastest access to data and will be more expensive per gigabyte than other options?

   A. Block

   B. Object

   C. Hot

   D. Cold

6. You are migrating to the cloud. Which solution should you use to handle spikes in the need for compute resources?

    A. DNS

    B. Firewall

    C. SDN

    D. Load balancing

7. Which of the following technologies is used to create a secure point-to-point tunneled connection over the Internet?

    A. VPN

    B. RDP

    C. SSH

    D. HTTPS

8. The global sales team needs to ensure that all regional teams have quick access to the same selling materials, including sizzle videos and PDFs with pricing. Which of the following should be implemented to enable this?

    A. SDS

    B. CDN

    C. DNS

    D. SDN

9. Your company is migrating its network storage to a cloud-based solution. Which of the following are most likely to be the least expensive storage options? (Choose two.)

    A. Cold

    B. Hot

    C. Tape

    D. Warm

10. The cost for your cloud storage keeps growing, and you need to find ways to reduce those costs. Which of the following can help you do that? (Choose two.)

    A. Compression

    B. Deduplication

    C. Capacity on demand

    D. Object storage

    E. Block storage

11. Which cloud concept makes networks more agile by separating the forwarding of network packets from the logical decision-making process?

    A. SDS

    B. DNS

    C. SDN

    D. CDN

12. Your company just signed up with a new CSP and needs to upload a large customer information database to the cloud. Once it's uploaded, employees will continue to access and update the database. Which storage type is recommended?

    A. Object

    B. File

    C. Block

    D. Cold

13. You are negotiating cloud services with a CSP. You need to ensure that your organization can get more storage space without CSP intervention. Which service do you need?

    A. Software-defined storage

    B. Software-defined networking

    C. Content delivery network

    D. Capacity on demand

14. Which of the following technologies lets a cloud provider create one logical storage volume from multiple physical storage devices?

    A. SDS

    B. DNS

    C. SDN

    D. CDN

15. Which cloud technology makes use of an edge server?

    A. SDS

    B. DNS

    C. SDN

    D. CDN

16. Your company has 500 users who need access to cloud resources during all working hours. Due to the nature of their work, there can be little to no latency. Which connectivity type is the best choice?

    A. Direct connect

    B. VPN

    C. HTTPS

    D. RDP

17. You need to have multiple users connect simultaneously to cloud resources through a single connection. Which two options allow this type of configuration? (Choose two.)

    A. RDP

    B. SSH

    C. HTTPS

    D. VPN

    E. Direct connect

18. A network administrator tells you that he needs to create a DMZ in the cloud. Which of the following cloud-based services will help him do this?

    A. SDN

    B. Load balancer

    C. DNS

    D. Firewall

19. Your company's in-house data center has a small storage area network that will be migrated to the cloud. Which of the following cloud storage types is most likely to resemble the way data is stored in the SAN?

    A. Load balanced

    B. Block storage

    C. File storage

    D. Object storage

20. You are moving your company's network to the cloud. Network administrators want to know if they can still manage Linux- and Windows-based servers. Which of the following are designed specifically for these tasks? (Choose two.)

    A. HTTPS

    B. VPN

    C. SSH

    D. RDP

Chapter

3

Assessing Cloud Needs

THE FOLLOWING COMPTIA CLOUD ESSENTIALS+ EXAM CLO-002 OBJECTIVES ARE COVERED IN THIS CHAPTER:

✓ **2.1 Given a scenario, use appropriate cloud assessments.**

- Current and future requirements
- Baseline
- Feasibility study
- Gap analysis
    - Business
    - Technical
- Reporting
    - Compute
    - Network
    - Storage
- Benchmarks
- Documentation and diagrams
- Key stakeholders
- Point of contact

✓ **2.4 Identify the benefits or solutions of utilizing cloud services.**

- Identity access management
    - Single sign-on
    - Multifactor authentication
    - Federation

- Cloud-native applications
  - Microservices
  - Containerization
- Data analytics
  - Machine learning
  - Artificial intelligence
  - Big Data
- Digital marketing
  - Email campaigns
  - Social media
- Autonomous environments
- IoT
- Blockchain
- Subscription services
- Collaboration
- VDI
- Self-service

In the first two chapters of this book, we talked about cloud concepts and characteristics. The material definitely had a technical slant—that's kind of hard to avoid when you're talking about networking and data storage—but the implicit assumption was that your business *needs* cloud services. Let's challenge that assumption for a minute. Does your business really need the cloud? If you're not sure, how do you determine the answer? To help figure it out, run a cloud assessment.

Cloud assessments can also help in situations where you have cloud services but want to understand if you are paying for too many bells and whistles or maybe you need more. You should run periodic assessments of current services to understand what you have and what your business needs to optimize success.

Part of running a cloud assessment is to understand what clouds can do for your business. From Chapters 1 and 2, you already learned that clouds can provide compute, network, storage, and database capacity. Paying less for those services in a cloud rather than in an on-premises data center certainly helps make the business case for cloud usage. But clouds can benefit your business in so many other ways too, from providing streamlined security to enabling big data analytics to empowering efficient digital marketing campaigns.

In this chapter, we will start with a discussion of using cloud assessments. The knowledge you gain here can be applied whether or not your business already has cloud services. Then, we will finish by looking at specific benefits and solutions clouds can provide for your business. Armed with this information, you will be able to confidently engage a cloud service provider (CSP) and obtain the services you need.

Using Cloud Assessments

If your business isn't using the cloud today, it's entirely possible that someone high up in the management chain will pop over to your desk one day and declare, "We need the cloud. Make it happen!" More likely, though, your company will be under pressure to cut costs and increase productivity—at the same time, so do more with less—and it will be up to you or a small team of people to figure out how to hit those productivity goals. A popular strategy in the last few years (and of course the reason you're reading this book) is for companies to move some or all of their computing needs to the cloud.

But one doesn't just snap her fingers and move a corporate network—even pieces of a small one—to the cloud. If you were planning a physical on-premises network, you would spend weeks or months laying out plans, making sure all needs were covered, and going back to revise those plans some more. Planning cloud services should be no different. Improper assessment and planning can result in anything from minor annoyances, such as paying too much, to major catastrophes, like the company being unable to make money.

If you search the Internet, you'll find dozens of different frameworks for cloud assessment and migration. Each major CSP and cloud consulting agency seems to have their own framework, and at first it can be overwhelming. All of the frameworks can basically be broken down into five steps, as illustrated in Figure 3.1.

FIGURE 3.1   Cloud implementation framework

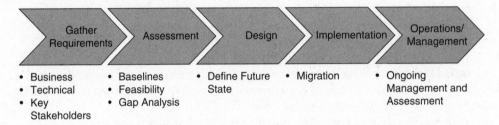

- Business
- Technical
- Key Stakeholders

- Baselines
- Feasibility
- Gap Analysis

- Define Future State

- Migration

- Ongoing Management and Assessment

In this section, we will focus mostly on the first two categories: gathering requirements and making assessments. To do that, we'll take you through seven different types of assessment activities that will help determine your company's cloud needs. Along the way, we'll present several scenarios to help illustrate when and how to use various aspects of cloud assessments.

In Chapter 4, "Engaging Cloud Vendors," we will get into more details on the design and implementation steps. Operations and management are covered in Chapter 5, "Management and Technical Operations."

Gathering Current and Future Requirements

Going back to a question we asked earlier, does your business even need the cloud? Somehow you've arrived at the point where you need to figure out the answer to that question. It could have been a directive from management, or perhaps you're just looking for ways to save the company money or improve productivity. Or, maybe your company already has cloud services, and you need to figure out if they're the best ones for the current business environment. Whether or not you have cloud services, the first question to ask is, "What do we need?" It's time to gather some requirements. It's the first step and also the most important one to ensure a good end result.

Gathering requirements is easiest when you know the right questions to ask and who to ask them of. We're going to hold off on the questions to ask for now and focus on who we need to talk to. Those are the key stakeholders. Then we'll get into what we need to talk to them about.

Key Stakeholders

A stakeholder is someone with a vested interest or concern in something. Therefore, a *key stakeholder* is an important person with a vested interest or concern in something. There may be only one key stakeholder at your company, or there may be more than 100, depending on the size and scope of your organization. If it's the latter, we feel sorry for you! Taking a systematic approach to identifying and contacting the stakeholders will help you get the input you need for this critical assessment phase.

Here's a list of some people who could be key stakeholders when it comes to cloud requirements:

- Chief executive officer (CEO)
- Chief financial officer (CFO)
- Chief information officer (CIO)
- Chief technology officer (CTO)
- Chief information security officer (CISO)
- Department managers or supervisors
- Key network and application users

There are quite a few people on that list, especially when you start to consider department managers and network users. If you have a smaller company, you might not have more than one or two "C-suite" executives you need to talk to. Even in many big companies, there are not separate CIO, CTO, and CISO roles. One person handles all information technology, though they might have people reporting to them who handle specific aspects such as information security.

One of the things you will find out during an assessment like this is that almost everyone in the company *thinks* that they are a key stakeholder. To help make the key stakeholders list manageable, find the most senior person in the organization to be the approver of the list. Ask that person who they think should have input and then work with those people. If employees who are not on that list think they should have input, then they can work that out separately with the list approver.

Another strategy that can help is to have a *single point of contact (SPOC)* for every department that needs to have input. For instance, maybe you know that the engineering and accounting departments have very different computing needs, but you aren't an expert in either one. Work with the department manager to identify a SPOC and then have that SPOC gather departmental needs and share the consolidated list with you. It's far easier to work with one person than to try to work with 20.

Real World Scenario

A Point about Contacts

Not only is it easier to work with one person than with 20, it's a lot easier to keep projects organized and on track if one person is taking the lead. This is why you should use a SPOC—CompTIA Cloud Essentials+ exam objectives refer to it simply as a *point of contact (POC)*—for multiple aspects of the cloud assessment and migration process.

For example, there should be one person designated as the overall leader of the cloud assessment process. This person should be high enough in the organization to make decisions without worry of being overridden by other people. This could be the CEO, CIO, CTO, or this role could be delegated to someone else with decision-making authority.

In addition, we already discussed having a SPOC for each department to gather cloud needs for that department. There should also be a SPOC from your company that the cloud provider interacts with. Perhaps there needs to be a technical leader and a business leader, so two points of contact, but those two people then need to be in constant communication about cloud needs and performance.

Having a designated POC can also help avoid problems with vendors. For example, some CSPs may be overly aggressive about selling additional services. If they don't get the sale from the person they're talking to, they might contact someone else to try to get the sale instead. If departmental employees all know that one person is the SPOC who makes the arrangements with the CSP, they can simply refer the CSP back to the original person and avoid any issues.

Identify who the points of contact are, and ensure that everyone involved with the project knows who those people are.

Asking the Right Questions

Now that you've figured out who to talk to, it's time to define current and future requirements. What benefits does the company want to get from the cloud?

From a timeframe standpoint, identifying current requirements is fairly straightforward. What are the company's needs right now? The future is quite ambiguous, though. How far in the future should you try to look? One month? One year? Five years? The further out you look, the foggier the crystal ball becomes. There's not one right answer to the question—it really depends on your business, its needs, and normal planning cycles.

For example, most companies will depreciate large-scale investments over a three- or five-year window. So, if your company does that, perhaps future requirements should attempt to define what will be needed in three or five years. Or, because your company strictly adheres to a yearly budgeting process, all you need to identify are the needs for the next 12 months. Or maybe the company is expanding so rapidly that the only timeframe you can realistically forecast is about six months out. You know your company best and can set the appropriate horizon for when the "future" is.

Even if you are forced into planning in short-term windows, create a long-term (three- to five-year) technology road map. Review it every year to assess the current situation and changing needs and update it as necessary.

Once you've established the future timeframe, develop the framework for assessing current and future requirements. Most CSPs have frameworks you can use to help with this process. For example, Amazon has the AWS Cloud Adoption Framework (CAF), which can be found at https://d1.awsstatic.com/whitepapers/aws_cloud_adoption_framework.pdf. The AWS CAF outlines six perspectives you should consider when assessing cloud needs, as shown in Figure 3.2.

FIGURE 3.2   An adaptation of the AWS CAF

Usually, the business, platform, and security perspectives are top of mind. We're used to thinking in terms of delivering business results, having the right technology to enable users, and securing data. People, governance, and operations quite often get neglected. Is there staffing to handle a cloud transition, and are those people trained to perform those tasks? And once the cloud is in place, who will be responsible for governance and making sure everything is working properly? All of those perspectives should be considered when assessing current and future requirements.

Microsoft has its own CAF as well, located at `https://docs.microsoft.com/en-us/azure/architecture/cloud-adoption/`. Within this trove of information is a downloadable cloud adoption framework strategy and plan template that you can use to help gather requirements. The document has places to list business priorities, organized by priority, and areas to document the stakeholders, desired outcome, business drivers, *key performance indicators* (KPIs), and necessary capabilities. An example from that document is shown in Figure 3.3.

FIGURE 3.3   Microsoft's cloud adoption framework strategy and plan template

Business outcomes

What are the expected <u>business outcomes</u> from adopting the cloud? Collect them in the corresponding table below, organized by priority.

High Priority

Stakeholder:		Outcome:		
Business Drivers		**KPI**		**Capabilities**
List any business drivers		List success metrics		List necessary capabilities

KPIs are success metrics for the project. They are often financial (save *X* amount of dollars) or technical (speed up development time by 20 percent). They should be specific and measurable and directly reflective of the success of that project.

To summarize, when determining current and future business requirements, get clear on who the key stakeholders are and when the "future" is. Then, create a systemic approach to gathering those requirements. Don't feel like you need to reinvent the wheel for that approach—plenty of frameworks exist online and can be adapted to meet your business needs.

We referenced CAFs from Amazon and Microsoft, which may imply we are endorsing their products. We're not recommending any specific cloud provider, but using these as examples from major CSPs. There are dozens of third-party, vendor-agnostic assessment tools available on the Internet—find the one that works for you.

Using Baselines

Your company is currently managing an on-premises network, using cloud services, or running some combination of the two. How well is the current environment performing? While you might hear feedback from disgruntled employees—"the network is terrible!"—quantitative data is likely going to be more helpful. To understand current performance, you need to run a baseline.

A *baseline* is a test that captures performance data for a system. For example, network administrators often establish baselines for a server's central processing unit (CPU) usage, random access memory (RAM) usage, network throughput, and hard disk data transfer speed and storage utilization.

Determining what to baseline is important, but *when* to run the baseline is also critical. For example, Amazon's web servers are likely to be busier during Cyber Monday than they are on some random Wednesday in May. Similarly, a network's security servers might have more latency (delay) around 8 a.m. when everyone is logging in versus 7:30 p.m. Running baselines at different times during the day is helpful to understand what normal performance and peak performance look like.

Sometimes when getting baselines, you don't necessarily know if the reading is good or bad. For example, let's say your network administrator tells you that the server's CPU is, on average, utilized 30 percent of the time. Is that good or bad? (Generally speaking, it's pretty good.) In isolation, that reading is just a number. If the server seems to be responding to user requests in a timely fashion, then things are fine. But if a year later the same server has an average CPU utilization of 70 percent, then that 30 percent reading gives you important context. What changed? Are users complaining about response times? Are other services impacted? If so, then an intervention is warranted. If not, then things are probably still fine, but more frequent monitoring of the CPU might be needed. In the upcoming "Understanding Benchmarks" section, we'll talk about the usage of benchmarks as context for baseline reads.

From a cloud assessment perspective, the baseline will give you an indicator of current performance. It will help determine how many cloud resources are needed. If your on-premises network is out of storage space, then more cloud storage space is most likely warranted. If local servers' CPUs are sitting idle, then perhaps fewer virtual servers are needed. The baseline will also be helpful to have at some point in the future, when someone in management asks how much better the network is after you migrated to the cloud.

So, first understand current and future requirements for your company's information technology needs. Then, make sure you have baselines for current performance.

Running a Feasibility Study

The first step in cloud assessment is to understand current and future requirements. Once the future requirements are understood, there are a few new questions to ask.

- Do the future requirements require the cloud?
- Does the company have the ability to migrate to the cloud?

These questions should be part of a *feasibility study*, which is used to determine the practicality of the proposed move to the cloud. In other words, we're back to a question we've already asked a few times, which is "Do we need the cloud?" And if so, can we make it happen?

Not all companies need the cloud, and not all IT services should be migrated to a cloud. The first part of the feasibility study should be to determine which services, if any, should be moved. It's better to figure out that you don't need the cloud *before* you sign a contract and begin to migrate! Most CSPs will be happy to help you run a feasibility study for free. Unless your company has internal cloud experts to do it, outsourcing it is a good way to go.

A feasibility study will generally help determine the following things:

- Which capabilities can and should be offloaded to the cloud
- The level of availability your company needs (e.g., three nines, four nines, etc.)
- Compliance, security, and privacy guidelines
- Support services needed, either internal or from the CSP
- A migration path to the cloud

Keep in mind that a cloud migration is not an all-or-nothing solution. For example, your company might decide to migrate only its email services to the cloud and adopt Gmail. Or, maybe your company needs extra storage space for data archives, so a cloud-based backup solution could save the company money. After the feasibility study, you should have a good idea if a cloud solution makes sense for your company and what might be required to complete a migration.

Conducting a Gap Analysis

It's quite likely that your company's current and future requirements for IT resources are different. The difference between where you are now and where you want to be is a gap. And a *gap analysis* can help identify all of the areas where gaps exist.

 Sometimes you will hear a gap analysis referred to as a *needs analysis* or a *needs gap analysis*.

Oftentimes, the output of a feasibility study will include data that can be used for a gap analysis. You can add information to that report or create your own system to identify and track progress toward closing the gaps. There's no one official gap analysis or way to do it—it's really a matter of being organized and tracking where you are and where you need to be. Figure 3.4 shows a simple template you could use for a gap analysis.

FIGURE 3.4   Gap analysis template

Category	Current State	Goal	Action Needed	Priority	Owner	Due Date
Business						
People						
Governance						
Platform						
Security						
Operations						

As you can see in Figure 3.4, we structured the categories based on the six areas of focus from the AWS CAF we discussed earlier in this chapter. Your business might or might not have gaps in all of these areas, and the template can be modified accordingly. In addition, there may be multiple gaps within one area. For example, let's say that under Platform, you have gaps in hardware needs and up-to-date applications. Those are gaps that require different solutions and should be treated separately.

One of the nice features about the template in Figure 3.4 is that it covers both business and technical gaps. One isn't necessarily more important than the other, but significant gaps in either area can cause a potential cloud solution to under-deliver versus expectations. Since you will be focusing on a cloud solution that is clearly rooted in technology, it can be easy to focus there and forget about the business or people side of things. It's just as critical to have the right staff in place with the proper training as it is to have the right number of virtual machines (VMs) in the cloud.

Gap analyses can also help with the following:

- Prioritizing the allocation of resources, such as where to assign technical staff or spend budget

- Identifying which technical features or functions have been left out of the migration plan

- Determining if there are compatibility issues between any components in the migration plan

- Identifying policies or regulations that are not being met with the current migration plan

The gap analysis itself doesn't provide a plan for remediation. It's just a road map surfacing the issues so they can be worked on. Some gaps may be showstoppers, while others are minor inconveniences. Having all of them laid out in one place can help the team and decision-makers understand what it will take to get from point A to point B and then decide if it's worth the investment in time and money.

Once the gap analysis document is created, it's a great utility to help measure progress against goals. It can tell you how close you are (or not) to achieving all of the goals set out in it, and if additional resources are needed to expedite the process. Much like with feasibility studies, CSPs will be happy to help with gap analyses with the goal of earning your business.

Using Reporting

Earlier in this chapter, we talked about the importance of running baseline reads to understand system performance. We also talked about running baselines over time. It's a good idea to put all of the baseline reads into once place and have some system for *reporting* the data. That is, share it with the people who need to know. It could be the network administration team, senior leaders, or a combination of stakeholders.

There are three key cloud performance metrics to baseline and report on.

- Compute
- Network
- Storage

Getting into the specific performance metrics to look at is beyond the scope of this book. Just know that performance in those three areas can make or break your network experience.

 Monitoring memory (RAM) usage is also important in real life. In the context of the cloud, memory is considered a compute resource. When you provision a virtual computer, you'll choose how many CPU cores and how much RAM is allocated to it. Because RAM is a compute resource, you won't see it explicitly listed as one of the reporting metrics in the CompTIA Cloud Essentials+ exam objectives.

If you have cloud services already, the CSP will provide usage reports that you can view and analyze. The usage reports will also be used to bill your company for services. We discuss that more in Chapter 5.

So, how does reporting fit into cloud assessments? If you don't have cloud services, then you can use whatever reports you have to help you determine the amount of cloud resources you need. For example, if your network has four servers and they're all pretty much at capacity, then you might want to invest in five or even six virtual servers. If you do have cloud services, then the reports can help you understand resource utilization. Based on that, you can recommend scaling up or down the number of resources you're paying for as appropriate.

Understanding Benchmarks

Earlier in the "Using Baselines" section, we talked about the importance of understanding system performance. We also mentioned that baselines without context can be hard to interpret. That's where *benchmarks* come into play. A baseline is a read of performance, whereas a benchmark is a standard or point of reference for comparison.

Let's go back to the example we used earlier of a server that has 30 percent CPU usage. If you know that the standard benchmark is to be at 70 percent or lower utilization, then the 30 percent reading looks really good. That's important context. Now, if users are complaining about the server being slow, you and the network administrators know that it's probably not the CPU's fault.

> You might hear the terms *baseline, benchmark,* and *reporting* (as in *performance reporting* or *resource reporting*) thrown around interchangeably. For example, some CSPs might show you tools they call benchmarking tools, but what they really do is baseline gathering and reporting, with no valid point of comparison. For colloquial purposes the mixed use of terms is fine, but for the Cloud Essentials+ exam you need to know the differences.

Within the cloud space, if you are assessing potential CSPs, there are few key areas to benchmark:

- Availability
- Response time
- Incident resolution time

Availability is important and should be specified in the service level agreement (SLA). The more nines you get, the more expensive it is—and you need to ensure that you're getting what you pay for. When performing a cloud assessment and evaluating a CSP, understand what their typical availability is for clients who pay for a certain level of service.

Response time is another key factor. Because cloud services are accessed over the Internet, there's always going to be a bit of latency. The question is how much latency is acceptable. You will probably have different expectations of acceptability depending on the use case. For example, a customer service or sales database needs to be very responsive. Pulling an email out of an archive created eight years ago and now in cold storage will take a little longer, and that should be okay.

Finally, there is incident resolution time. Clouds have a lot of great features and are generally reliable, but things happen. Hardware failures, security breaches, and other problems arise. How quickly the CSP typically responds to those incidents should be known before entering into any agreement.

Most CSPs will have benchmarking tools available for use. For example, AWS has EC2 Reports, and Azure has a suite of tools as well. If you don't happen to totally trust the CSP, third-party benchmarking tools are available too. For example, CloudHarmony (https://cloudharmony.com) provides objective performance analyses, iPerf (https://iperf.fr) can give you network bandwidth measurement, and Geekbench (https://geekbench.com) can measure cloud server performance.

Creating Documentation and Diagrams

Documentation always seems to get overlooked. The process of creating documentation can seem tedious, and some people wonder what value it adds. There are, of course, people who love creating documentation—those are the ones you want in charge of the process!

When performing a cloud assessment, and later a migration, documentation and diagrams are critical. We've already looked at documentation used for a gap analysis and creating reports and baselines for system performance. All of that should be kept in a central location, easily accessible to those who need it. In addition, consider documentation and diagrams for the following:

- Conversations with stakeholders and team members

- Location of all resources and applications pre- and post-migration

- Owners of capabilities and processes

- Internal and external points of contact

Many teams can benefit from using a collaboration tool to track and store documentation. For example, Microsoft Teams (`https://products.office.com/en-us/microsoft-teams/group-chat-software`) is a cloud-based platform integrated into Office 365 that allows for file storage, collaboration, chat, application integration, and video meetings. Slack (`https://slack.com`) is a popular alternative, and there are dozens more available such as Flock (`https://flock.com`), HeySpace (`https://hey.space`), and Winio (`https://winio.io`).

As a reminder, for the Cloud Essentials+ exam, you need to know how to use the appropriate cloud assessments, given a scenario. Be familiar with all of the following:

- Current and future requirements

- Baseline

- Feasibility study

- Gap analysis

  - Business

  - Technical

- Reporting

  - Compute

  - Network

  - Storage

- Benchmarks

- Documentation and diagrams

- Key stakeholders

- Point of contact

Understanding Cloud Services

The cloud has fundamentally changed the landscape of computer networking and how we use technology. That's a bold statement, but it's not an exaggeration. If you look back 10 or 20 years, companies that wanted a network had to buy hardware for the network, servers, and client machines as well as needed software packages. The internal or contracted support team had to install, test, and configure all of it. Any needed changes took time to test and implement. And of course, hardware and software became out of date, so companies would have to write off or depreciate their assets and buy new ones to stay with the times.

Now, all of this can be done virtually. A server still does what a server did back then, but the definition of the server itself may have completely changed. Instead of one collection of super-powerful hardware, there could be dozens of servers using the same hardware, and each can be turned on or off nearly instantly. Software is rarely purchased in perpetuity anymore but rather rented on a subscription basis. And while the support team is still important, a lot of technical expertise can be outsourced. In the majority of cases, the new model is also cheaper than the old one!

As cloud technology has matured, CSPs have also been under pressure to expand their business models. Many started to take services that are common in an on-premises network and make them available via the cloud. Others dreamed up new ways of doing business that could help their clients gain efficiencies and lower costs.

In this section, we are going to examine 11 different services that CSPs offer. Some of them exist thanks to the cloud, whereas others are simply made better thanks to cloud technology. Keep in mind that the cloud has been popular for business use for only about a decade now. CSPs have likely just scratched the surface on the types of offerings they can make, and more will be on the way. It's just the natural cycle of things when the landscape is being fundamentally changed.

Identity Access Management

You probably don't need us to lecture you on the importance of network security. The last thing you need is for your company to be in the news headlines for a security breach or for hackers stealing plans for a prototype before you can go to market.

Clearly, security was important before the cloud existed. Digital assets need to be protected, and the way it's done is to verify that the person trying to log in and access those resources is who they say they are. This is *identity access management*. A user is assigned a user account and told to create a password. When the user tries to log in, those credentials are presented to an authentication server that either grants or denies access. The same thing happens for individual resources once a user is logged in. If a user tries to access a file or other resource, their identity is compared to a security list to see if they have the appropriate level of permissions.

When you're using the cloud, though, all information—including login credentials such as usernames and passwords—is being transmitted across the Internet. Fortunately, it is generally encrypted, but having the Internet in play introduces an extra element of risk. So we'll spare the lecture for now and instead focus on three methods to simplify or strengthen identity access management in the cloud: multifactor authentication, single sign-on, and federation.

Multifactor Authentication

The simplest form of authentication is *single-factor authentication*. A single-factor system requires only one piece of information beyond the username to allow access. Most often, this is a password. Single-factor authentication is quite common, but it's probably the least secure of the authentication systems available. It's better than no authentication at all, though!

To increase security, your network or cloud services might require *multifactor authentication (MFA)*, which as the name implies requires multiple pieces of information for you to log in. Generally speaking, in addition to a username, MFA requires you to provide two or more pieces of information out of the following categories:

- Something you know
- Something you have
- Somewhere you are
- Something you are

Something you know is generally a password. If you forget your password, a website might ask you to provide answers to security questions that you selected when you registered. These are questions such as the name of your elementary school, father's middle name, street you grew up on, first car, favorite food or musical artist, and so forth.

One-time passwords can be generated by sites to give you a limited time window to log in. These are far more secure than a standard password because they are valid for only a short amount of time, usually 30 minutes or less. The password will be sent to you via push notification such as text, email, or phone call.

Something you have can be one of a few different things, such as a smart card or a security token. A smart card is a plastic card, similar in dimensions to a credit card, which contains a microchip that a card reader can scan, such as on a security system. Smart cards often double as employee badges, enabling employees to access employee-only areas of a building or to use elevators that go to restricted areas, or as credit cards.

Smart cards can also be used to allow or prevent computer access. For example, a PC may have a card reader on it through which the employee has to swipe the card or that reads the card's chip automatically when the card comes into its vicinity. Or, they're combined with a PIN or used as an add-on to a standard login system to give an additional layer of security verification. For someone to gain unauthorized access, they have to know a user's ID and password (or PIN) and also steal their smart card. That makes it much more difficult to be a thief!

A security token, like the one shown in Figure 3.5, displays an access code that changes about every 30 seconds. When received, it's synchronized with your user account, and the algorithm that controls the code change is known by the token as well as your authentication system. When you log in, you need your username and password, along with the code on the token.

FIGURE 3.5   RSA SecurID

Security tokens can be software-based as well. A token may be embedded in a security file unique to your computer, or your network may use a program that generates a security token much as the hardware token does. Figure 3.6 shows an example of PingID, which works on computers and mobile devices. This type of token saves you from having to carry around yet another gadget.

FIGURE 3.6   PingID

Somewhere you are, or the location you are logging in from, can also be a security factor. For example, perhaps users are allowed to access the company's private cloud only if they are on the internal corporate network. Or, maybe you are allowed to connect from your home office. In that case, the security system would know a range of IP addresses to allow in based on the block of addresses allocated to your internet service provider (ISP). Sometimes you will hear the terms geolocation or geofencing associated with this security mechanism.

Finally, the system could require something you are—that is, a characteristic that is totally unique to you—to enable authentication. These characteristics are usually assessed via biometric devices, which authenticate users by scanning for one or more physical traits. Some common types include fingerprint recognition, facial recognition, and retina scanning. It's pretty common today for users to log into their smartphones enabled with fingerprint or facial recognition, for example.

Single Sign-On

One of the big problems that larger networks must deal with is the need for users to access multiple systems or applications. This may require a user to remember multiple accounts and passwords. In the cloud environment, this can include some resources or apps that are on a local network and others that are cloud-based. The purpose of *single sign-on (SSO)* is to give users access to all of the systems, resources, and apps they need with one initial login. This is becoming a reality in many network environments, especially cloud-based ones.

SSO is both a blessing and a curse. It's a blessing in that once the user is authenticated, they can access all the resources on the network with less inconvenience. Another blessing is that passwords are synchronized between systems. When it's changed in one system, the change replicates to other linked systems. It's a curse in that it removes potential security doors that otherwise exist between the user and various resources.

While SSO is not the opposite of MFA, they are often mistakenly thought of that way. You will hear the terms one-, two-, and three-factor authentication, which refers to the number of items a user must supply to authenticate. After authentication is done, then SSO can take effect, granting users access to multiple types of resources while they are logged in.

A defining characteristic of SSO is that it only applies to resources contained within one organization's security domain. In other words, if Corporation X has Linux servers, Windows servers, apps, and files that are all under the Corp X security umbrella, then SSO can grant users access to all of those resources. What SSO can't do, however, is cross organizational boundaries. So if Corp X wants their users to access local resources as well as a cloud-based app such as Microsoft Office 365, SSO can't provide the login to both. In that case, federation is needed.

Federation

Let's continue with the example we just introduced: your company wants users to be able to access company-secured resources as well as the cloud-based Microsoft Office 365 with one login. Is that possible? The answer is yes, but it's not through SSO. The technology that enables this is called *federation*, also known as *federated identity management (FIM)*.

In simplest terms, federation is SSO across organizations or security domains. For it to work, the authentication systems from each organization need to trust each other—they're federated. Authorization messages are passed back and forth between the two systems using secured messages. One example of federation implementation is via Security Assertion Markup Language, or SAML. (It's pronounced like the word *sample* without the "p.") There are others as well, but SAML is very popular.

Let's take a look at how the federated login process works, continuing with our example:

1. User jdoe provides a username and password to log into the Corp X corporate network. Corp X's security servers authenticate jdoe.

2. User jdoe tries to open Microsoft Office 365 in the cloud.

3. Office 365 sends a SAML message to Corp X's security servers, asking if jdoe is authenticated.

4. Corp X's security servers send a SAML message back to Microsoft's security servers, saying that jdoe is legitimate.

5. User jdoe can use Office 365.

Again, it's like SSO, just across security domains. All the user knows is they type in their username or password once, and they can get to the resources they need. The same example holds true if the Corp X network is cloud-based, using AWS, for example. Finally, although we've been speaking of federation in one-to-one terms, know that an organization can be a member of multiple federations at the same time.

The primary benefit to using federation is convenience, but there is a financial upside as well. There is less administrative overhead required in setting up and maintaining security accounts, because the user's account needs to be in only one security domain. There are two primary disadvantages. First, there is a bit of administrative overhead and cost associated with setting up a federated system. Second, you do really need to trust the other federated partners and be sure their security policies match up to your own. For example, if your company requires government-level security clearances but another organization does not, they might not be a good federation partner.

Cloud-Native Applications

One of the big ways that the cloud has changed computing is in the application development space. The cloud has enabled more agile programming techniques, which results in faster development, easier troubleshooting, and lower cost to software companies. Two technologies that enable agile *cloud-native applications*—that is, apps that wouldn't exist outside the cloud—are microservices and containerization.

Microservices

For most of the history of application development, all executable parts of the application were contained within the same bundle of code. You could think of an application as one file, with anywhere from thousands to millions of lines of code. The key was, everything was in one bundle. Today we'd call that a *monolith*.

There was nothing inherently wrong with the monolithic development approach—it's just how programs were built. Yes, there were minor inconveniences. One was that to load the program, the entire program needed to be loaded into memory. This could be a serious drain on a computer's RAM, depending on how big the program was. And, if there was a bug in the program, it might have been a little harder for the development team to track it down. But again, there was nothing really wrong with the monolithic approach and it served us well for decades.

The advent of the cloud allowed for a new approach to software development, one where applications could be broken down into smaller components that work together to form an application. This is called *microservices*—literally meaning small services. You will also hear it referred to as *microservice architecture* because it is both a software development approach and an architecture. Either way you look at it, the point is that it's all about breaking apps into smaller components. Figure 3.7 shows a comparison of the monolithic approach to a microservices approach.

FIGURE 3.7   Monolithic vs. microservices app

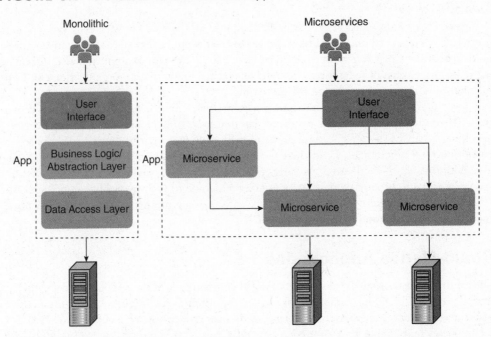

As an example of how this works, think of a shopping trip to Amazon.com. Amazon doesn't have just one big monolithic web app. The search feature could be its own microservice, as could the query that gives you additional product recommendations beyond your initial search. The "add to cart" feature could also be a microservice, as well as the part that charges a credit card, and finally the unseen portion of the app that transmits your order to the warehouse for order fulfillment. (To be fair, we don't know exactly how the Amazon site is set up, but it *could* be set up this way, so it's a good illustrative example.)

Microservices also are handy for letting multiple apps use the same service. For example, say that your company has a product database. The sales team needs to be able to query the database to check prices and make sure the product is in stock. The operations team, using a completely different app, also needs to check stock levels to ensure they reorder from the supplier when needed. The apps are different, but the mechanism to query the database for how much product is available could be the same microservice.

Using microservices ultimately results in faster app development and more flexible apps at a lower cost. It also makes apps easier to update and troubleshoot for the development teams. Finally, different parts of the app can be hosted or executed on different servers, adding to the flexibility of your total network.

Containerization

A container is simply a place to store items in an organized manner. *Containerization* is just a fancy term saying that items are being placed into a container. In terms of the cloud and software development, it means that all components needed to execute a microservice are stored in the same package or container. The container can easily be moved from server to server without impacting app functionality and can also be used by multiple apps if needed.

 Think of microservices as the way to build apps, and containerization as the way to store all of the microservice components in the same place.

Containers are often compared to VMs, which you learned about in Chapter 1, "Cloud Principles and Design." This is because both allow you to package items (in this case, app components; in a VM's case, OS components) and isolate them from other apps or OSs. And, there can be multiple containers or VMs on one physical set of hardware.

If a developer were creating a new app that needed features that were already containerized, his job would be much faster. Instead of re-creating those features, he could use the containers he needed and enable them to talk to each other through an API. He would just need to code the APIs and any new, unique aspects of the program rather than the entire thing. Much like microservices, containerization makes app development faster and cheaper.

Data Analytics

Many companies have realized, or are realizing now, that they are sitting on a ton of data regarding their customers or markets. They're just not sure how to make the best use of it. That's why the field of *data analytics* is hot right now. People with analytical skills are in high demand as companies attempt to find whatever edge they can with the troves of data they possess.

Most of the time, these companies are looking for analysts with experience in big data. We introduced the concept of big data in Chapter 2, "Cloud Networking and Storage." Big data doesn't necessarily mean a large data set—the data set could be large but doesn't have to be—but rather it refers to unstructured data. Unstructured data doesn't fit neatly into the rows and columns of a spreadsheet or database table, and it's hard to search or infer patterns from. Great examples are pictures and videos.

There are many tools in the marketplace designed to help companies manage and analyze big data. The cloud, with its flexibility and ample resources, has made this easier. Two technologies within data analytics that get a lot of love today, particularly in the realm of big data analytics, are artificial intelligence and machine learning.

Artificial Intelligence

For decades—maybe even centuries—science fiction has been filled with tales of machines or robots that look and act like humans. Depending on the story, this can be a good or bad thing. Most of the time, though, it seems that the human-like robot gets corrupted somehow and does evil deeds (or maybe it's just programmed that way), and nice, real humans need to come save our species. This book isn't a feel-good story about the indomitable human spirit, though—we're here to focus on the intelligent machines.

In essence, *artificial intelligence (AI)* is the concept of making machines perform smart, human-like decisions. Underpinning this is the fact that the machine needs to be programmed to do the task at hand. For example, you could have a robot that picks up and sorts marbles into bins by color. A properly programmed machine can do this tedious task faster and more accurately than a human can.

AI systems can be classified as applied or general. Most AIs fall into the applied category, meaning that they are designed to perform a certain task or set of tasks. A general AI, in theory, could complete any task set in front of it. This is a lot harder to accomplish, but it's the category into which machine learning falls. We'll talk more about machine learning in the next section.

We already used an example of AI performing a menial sorting task, but it's used in a variety of settings, including the following:

Virtual Personal Assistants   Many of us use Siri, Alexa, or Google Now to perform tasks for us. They can check the weather, play music, turn lights on and off, text or call people, set alarms, order products, and do a variety of other tasks.

Video Games   Anyone who has played a game with an in-game, computer-controlled character knows what AI is. Ask anyone who gamed a few decades ago and they will tell you how terrible, predictable, and honestly unintelligent the AI was. Today they've gotten much better at reacting to the human-controlled character's actions and the environment.

Digital Marketing   We have an entire "Digital Marketing" section later in this chapter, but AI plays an important role. Products or advertisements can be tailored to your Internet search history. Coupons may become available based on your purchase habits. These are both directed by AI.

The Financial Industry   Computers can be programmed to detect transactions that appear abnormal, perhaps because of the frequency or size of transactions that normally occur. This can help identify and protect against fraud.

The Transportation Industry   Smart cars are being tested today and might be within only a few years of becoming commonplace. In addition, tests have been conducted on smart semis, carrying freight from one end of the country to the other. AI enables these capabilities.

You can see that some of the actions that can be taken by AI are pretty complex. Driving is not easy, and financial fraud can be very hard to detect. Regardless of how complex the activity is, the key to AI is that it has to be programmed. The AI can only react to conditions it has been coded to react to, and only in the way it has been told to react. For example, if our marble sorting machine knows how to sort blue and red marbles only, it won't know what to do with a green one that it encounters.

Machine Learning

The terms artificial intelligence and *machine learning (ML)* often get confused with each other, but they're not the same thing. With AI, the machine needs to be programmed to respond to stimuli to complete a task. With *machine learning (ML)*, the idea is that data can be fed to a machine and it will learn from it and adapt. ML is a specialized form of AI.

ML "learns" through the use of a neural network, which is a computer system that takes input and classifies it based on preset categories. Then, using probabilities, it tries to make a decision or prediction based on new input it receives. A feedback loop to tell the system whether it was right or wrong helps it learn further and modify its approach.

For example, let's say you want to create an ML program that identifies fans of your favorite sports team. To help it learn, you feed it several images of fans in the right apparel or showing the correct logo. Then you would feed it new stimuli, and the program would guess if it's an image of that team's fan or not. You tell it whether it got it right or wrong. That process of feeding it new stimuli, it guessing, and you providing feedback gets repeated several times. Eventually, the system gets better at recognizing the correct elements in the photos and increases its accuracy.

The applications that AI and ML are used for are usually very different. AI needs to be programmed for all potential inputs and outcomes to work properly. ML can learn from new inputs whether it's correct or not. Here are some examples of where ML can be applied:

- Image recognition, including facial recognition
- Speech and audio recognition. For example, an ML program can hear a new song and determine whether the song is likely to make people happy or sad.
- Medical diagnoses. ML can take patterns of medical data and make a diagnosis of a disease.
- Financial modeling. An ML program can take inputs and predict what a stock or the market will do.

- General prediction models. We've used a few examples already (such as the last three), but ML is great at making predictions based on a set of rules when given new input.
- Data extraction. ML can take unstructured big data, such as pictures, videos, web pages, and emails, and look for patterns, extracting structured data.

The list here only scratches the surface of what ML can do. All of the major CSPs offer AI and ML packages, such as Google Machine Learning Engine, Azure Machine Learning Studio, and AWS Machine Learning. Other companies offer competing products as well; with an Internet search, you're sure to find one that meet your needs.

Digital Marketing

There are few guarantees in life besides taxes, death, and receiving junk mail. While it may be annoying to get emails that we didn't ask for, occasionally one of them catches our eye and we check it out—after verifying that the company is legit and it's not a phishing scam, of course. So even if you find them annoying, they *do* work! Emails from companies selling products or services is one example of *digital marketing*, that is, the marketing of products or services using digital technology. Contrast this with other types of marketing, such as commercials on the radio or television, billboards, or paper mail.

The CompTIA Cloud Essentials+ exam objectives specify two types of digital marketing: email campaigns and social media. Here's a quick description of each of them:

Email Campaigns   *Email campaigns* are when companies send automated emails out to potential customers. Most of the time, the email will contain a link for people to click, which will take them to a company web page or a specific product page.

Social Media   *Social media* refers to platforms such as YouTube, Facebook, Instagram, Twitter, Pinterest, and others where people post comments, pictures, and videos and digitally interact with other people. There are two ways advertising is usually done on social media. In the first, the social media marketing campaign will create a post in the same format as a "normal" post on the platform, in an effort to look like the message was posted by a friend. Like an email campaign, this post will have somewhere to tap or click to take you to a product page. Figure 3.8 shows a Facebook ad and a Twitter ad that look like posts. The second is used in formats that support video. Unskippable video ads can be inserted before (called pre-roll) or in the middle of (mid-roll) content the user is viewing.

Even though email and social media are different types of platforms, the benefits of each and the tools and methods used to activate them are quite similar, so we'll treat them together as digital marketing. Here are some of the benefits of using digital marketing:

- Better customer engagement, e.g., response rates
- Real-time results, monitoring, and optimization
- Enhanced analytics
- Campaign automation and integration
- Lower costs

FIGURE 3.8 Facebook (left) and Twitter (right) ads

Let's take a look at each of these in more detail:

Better Customer Engagement Social media companies have a frightening amount of data about their users. Some people are aware of this, so it's not uncommon to hear others say they don't do social media because of it. That's fine, but everyone uses a search engine, and Google (or whoever) stores and uses that information too. It's almost impossible to be truly anonymous on the Internet.

While it might be frightening from a user standpoint, all of that data is a gold mine for the digital marketer. The data that Google, Facebook, and others have can be used to create target audiences that meet a profile of customers your company wants to talk to. For example, say that your company is making organic baby food. You can have Google or Facebook create a target audience of women who have an interest in healthy eating and have children under the age of six. You can add more criteria as well, but the more you add, the smaller the target audience gets and the more expensive it becomes to reach people.

The Googles and Facebooks of the world will also let you use your first-party data to create target audiences. You can give them a list of email addresses, and they will match them up to people known in their database. They'll parse common characteristics and target people like the ones you've already provided.

All of this leads to better customer engagement, because you are targeting people who should be interested in your product. It's far more efficient than sending out glossy postcards to everyone in a postal code and hoping for a response.

All good digital marketing campaigns have a call to action (CTA), asking potential customers to tap or click somewhere to further interact with the company's materials or buy a product or service. When potential customers do tap or click, their profile information is tracked via cookies to help the marketers further optimize target audiences and messaging.

Real-Time Results, Monitoring, and Optimization   After you've kicked off a digital marketing campaign, you will want to analyze the performance to see how it did. Most platforms allow you to monitor results in real time, literally viewing how many clicks the ad gets by the minute.

Let's say you pick two different target audiences and show them your ad. You can see if one is performing better than the other and then increase or decrease your investment as appropriate. Or, you could take one audience group and split it into two and show each group a different message. Then, you can see which message performs better and optimize as appropriate. Some larger digital marketers will change messages and audiences daily, depending on how well their placements are performing.

Enhanced Analytics   Enhanced analytics goes hand in hand with results monitoring and optimization. Digital marketing platforms such as Google, Facebook, and others will have built-in analytics dashboards. You will be able to set your success measures—also known as KPIs—and measure progress against them. For example, you might want to look at click-through rate, video completion rate, or engagements (likes, comments, and shares).

Campaign Automation and Integration   Another beautiful feature of digital marketing is the ability to automate campaigns and integrate across platforms. Automation includes simple tasks such as turning ads on at a specific time or automatically sending emails to people who have clicked on your ad. Integration across platforms is handy to ensure that you're sending the same message to all potential customers.

Lower Costs   Digital marketing campaigns can be completed at a fraction of the cost of traditional marketing methods. For example, if you had to send a mailing out to people, you need to pay for the creation of the mail (either a letter or a postcard) as well as postage. And while you might be able to target an audience by sending it to people for whom you have addresses, the targeting capabilities are nothing like they are in the digital world.

Digital marketing existed before the cloud was popular, but cloud services have definitely made digital marketing faster, more accurate, and less expensive. We've mentioned a few digital marketing platforms, and certainly Google and Facebook are huge. Traditional cloud providers AWS and Azure have digital marketing services too, as do many others such as Salesforce, Nielsen, Oracle, and Teradata.

Autonomous Environments

Over the last decade or so, Google, Tesla, and Uber have been among the big companies making noise by testing self-driving cars. Some of the press has been good, but there have been bumps in the road as well. Embark, Peloton, and TuSimple have been experimenting with self-driving semi-trucks as well. In the computer field, Oracle has been working on automating routine database tasks such as backups, updates, security, and performance tuning. Many manufacturing facilities have nearly eliminated the need for human employees. All of these are examples of *autonomous environments*—a computerized environment where complex human actions are mimicked but without human intervention. You can debate whether autonomous environments are a good thing, but what's not debatable is that it's a growing trend.

Autonomous environments such as self-driving vehicles work by using a combination of programming, cameras, sensors, and machine learning. Think about driving a car, and all of the inputs that a person needs to be aware of. There's your speed, the speed of cars around you, the direction they are moving, pedestrians, stop lights, lane merges, weather, and probably 100 other things to pay attention to.

It might feel like there is some ambiguity about what defines AI versus an autonomous environment, and there is. Autonomous environments do use AI but are generally considered to be a more complex environment that likely combines several AI components into a bigger system.

All of this input generates a huge amount of data. A 2018 study by Accenture ("Autonomous Vehicles: The Race Is On") estimated that a self-driving car's cameras and sensors generate between 4 and 10 terabytes of data per day. The average laptop's fast, solid-state hard drive holds about 500 megabytes—it would take about 20 of these to hold 10 terabytes. That's a lot of data. Without the cloud, these ambitious projects wouldn't work.

It's Not Just the Data Storage

Endpoint devices within an autonomous environment (such as the car) need to be able to communicate with central planning and management devices. Current wireless cellular transmission standards are capable of supporting the bandwidth on a limited basis, but not on a massive scale. It's estimated that self-driving cars need to transmit about 3,000 times as much data as the average smartphone user. Wireless infrastructure will need massive upgrades before it can support widespread use of self-driving cars.

Using cloud services, your company may be able to save costs by automating certain processes. Of course, all of the usual suspects—big CSPs—will be happy to help you with your automation needs.

Internet of Things

The *Internet of Things (IoT)* is the network of devices that are able to communicate with each other and exchange data, and it's a very hot topic in computing today. It wouldn't be possible without the cloud. The term *things* is rather loosely defined. A thing can be a hardware device, software, data, or even a service. It can be something like a jet engine, or it can be multiple sensors on the fan, motor, and cooling systems of that engine. The key is that these things are able to collect data and transmit it to other things. In this section on the IoT, we'll start with places in which it's being used today and finish with potential concerns that your company may need to watch out for.

Consumer Uses

Thus far, most IoT-enabled devices have been produced for consumer use. The concept seems pretty useful—multiple devices in your home are IoT-enabled, and you control them through a centralized hub, regardless of where you are. Did you go to work and forget to turn the lights off? No problem. You can do it from your phone. Did someone just ring your doorbell? See who it is and talk to them in real time through your phone as well. Let's take a look at a few specific examples:

Home Entertainment Systems   Home entertainment is definitely the largest segment of IoT devices on the market today. Most new high-definition televisions are smart TVs with built-in wireless networking and the ability to connect to streaming services such as Netflix, Hulu, YouTube, or fuboTV. Other audio and video equipment will often have built-in networking and remote-control capabilities as well.

Not all smart TVs are really that smart, and large televisions are definitely not portable. For people who want to take their entertainment with them, there are streaming media devices. Examples include Roku, Amazon Fire, Apple TV, Chromecast, and NVIDIA SHIELD. Some are small boxes, like the slightly old-school Roku 3 shown in Figure 3.9, while others look like flash drives and have a remote control. Each has different strengths. For example, Amazon Prime customers will get a lot of free content from the Amazon Fire, and NVIDIA SHIELD has the best gaming package.

FIGURE 3.9   Roku 3

Security Systems   While home entertainment is currently the biggest market for smart home devices, smart security systems come next. Some systems require professional installation, whereas others are geared toward the do-it-yourself market. Many require a monitoring contract with a security company. Popular names include Vivint, Adobe Home Security, ADT Pulse, and SimpliSafe.

While specific components will vary, most systems have a combination of a doorbell camera and other IP cameras, motion sensors, gas and smoke detectors, door lock, garage door opener, lighting controls, a centralized management hub, and touchscreen panels. Of course, you are able to control them from your phone as well.

> If you don't want to get an entire security system, you can buy systems to control the lights in your house. You can also get smart wall outlets that replace your existing ones, which enable you to turn devices plugged into them on or off, as well as monitor energy usage.

Heating and Cooling   Programmable thermostats that allow you to set the temperature based on time and day have been around for more than 20 years. The next step in the evolution is a smart thermostat that's remotely accessible and can do some basic learning based on the weather and your preferences. Figure 3.10 shows a smart thermostat.

FIGURE 3.10   Nest smart thermostat

By Raysonho @ Open Grid Scheduler/Grid Engine. CC0, `https://commons.wikimedia.org/w/index.php?curid=49900570`.

Home Appliances   Do you want your refrigerator to tell you when you're out of milk? Or even better yet, do you want to have it automatically add milk to the grocery list on your smartphone? Perhaps your refrigerator can suggest a recipe based on the ingredients inside of it. Appliances like this exist today, even if they haven't enjoyed a major popularity spike. Many consumers don't see the value in the benefits provided, but perhaps that will change over time. Other examples include smart washing machines, clothes dryers, and ovens.

Small appliances can be part of the IoT as well, if properly equipped. You could control your smart coffee maker from bed, starting it when you get up in the morning. Even toasters or blenders could be made into smart devices. It will all depend on the consumer demand.

Modern Cars   Thirty years ago, cars were entirely controlled through mechanical means. The engine powered the crankshaft, which provided torque to rotate the wheels. When you turned the steering wheel, a gear system turned the wheels in the proper direction. There were even these nifty little handles you could turn that would lower and raise the windows.

Not today. While there are clearly still some mechanical systems in cars—most still have gas engines, for example—the cars made today are controlled through an elaborate network of computers. These computers determine how much gas to give the engine based on how hard you press the accelerator, how far to turn the wheels when you crank the steering wheel, and how fast to slow down when you hit the brakes. They can even do smarter things, such as transfer power to certain wheels in slippery conditions, sense how hard it's raining to adjust the wiper speed, and warn you if there is a car in your blind spot. Many drivers love their GPS systems, and these are integrated too. Other new enhancements to cars include collision avoidance systems, adaptive cruise control, automated parallel parking, interactive video displays, and more.

While much of this innovation is great, it can make cars more expensive to fix if components in this network break. It can also make them susceptible to hackers, who could get in remotely through the GPS, entertainment, or communications systems.

 Real World Scenario

Hacking Your Car

Most modern cars are basically computer networks, and with their communications, navigation, and entertainment systems, they connect to the outside world. And ever since computer networks have existed, someone has tried to hack them. Cars are no exception.

While the odds of having your car hacked are pretty low, the effects could be disastrous. Hackers could shut your car off on the interstate or render your brakes inoperable.

Auto manufacturers are of course aware of the threats, and in the last few years have taken steps to reduce the chances of a successful attack. Know that it's still a possibility, though. If you do an Internet search, you can find several articles related to car hacking. One such example is https://www.wired.com/2015/07/hackers-remotely-kill-jeep-highway.

In the previous section on autonomous environments, we talked about smart cars. These are only possible thanks to the IoT.

Fitness and Health Monitors   Fitness and health monitors are popular for people who want to keep track of their exercise, calorie consumption, and heart rate. Most are worn on the wrist like a watch, and some are advanced enough to be classified as smartwatches.

These devices too can belong to the IoT. They connect via Bluetooth, Wi-Fi, or cellular connections; collect data about us; and can transmit that data to another device. Popular companies include Fitbit, Garmin, Polar, Apple Watch, and Jawbone.

Commercial Uses

Any number of industries can benefit from interconnected devices. If you are out and about, take a few minutes to just look around at the variety of equipment and electronics in use today. It's something that we rarely take the time to observe, but when you look for opportunities to embed sensors or other data collection components into things, you can find quite a few. This section explores examples for a few industries.

Medical Devices   The medical industry is full of equipment. If you've been to a hospital or clinic, you know that the amount of machinery they have is pretty impressive. While there have been strides in interoperability, not all of the machines can talk to each other or react if something goes wrong.

Further, medical applications can be extended outside of the medical facility. Critical electronics such as pacemakers can be connected to a smart system, and patients can wear other devices that monitor their vital signs, such as heart rate and blood pressure. The readings can be transmitted back to an office and recorded and monitored. If something appears to be wrong, an application on the hospital computer can show an alert, notifying the medical professional of a problem. In this way, medical professionals can efficiently keep an eye on many people at once.

Manufacturing   Manufacturing plants have become heavily automated over the last few decades. Robots can do a lot of work, but historically, robots haven't been very smart. They do what they are programmed to do; if something goes wrong, they aren't able to adjust. For maintenance personnel, tracking down the problem can often be tedious and time-consuming. The IoT can greatly help here.

Sensors built into machines can monitor production rates. If a component in the machine starts to wear down or fails, the technician will know immediately what to fix. Ideally, the technician will even be able to fix it before it breaks, because the technician can tell that the part is wearing down and will fail soon. Other sensors can be attached to pallets of raw materials or produced goods, enabling instantaneous tracking of the quantity and location of inventory. Finally, perhaps a manufacturing plant has several different lines of products. A smart system could increase or decrease production on the appropriate lines based on real-time customer demand.

Transportation   We've already discussed autonomous cars and semi-trucks, which are obvious transportation plays. Another application could be in traffic signals. Have you ever waited at a red light for what seemed like forever, when there was no traffic coming from the cross direction? Some traffic signals do have sensors to detect the presence of cars, but not all do. If you take that one step further, sensors can monitor traffic to determine where there is congestion and then make recommendations to GPS systems to reroute vehicles onto a better path.

Finally, there are applications such as being able to set variable speed limits based on road conditions, electronic tolls, and safety and road assistance. Dozens of states use electronic toll collection systems. Users sign up and place a small transponder in or on their car. When they drive through the toll, a sensor records the vehicle's presence and bills the driver. Electronic toll systems are paired with IP cameras to detect those who attempt to cheat the system. Examples of road assistance apps include OnStar, HondaLink, Toyota Safety Connect, and Ford Sync.

Infrastructure   In 2007, an interstate bridge in Minnesota filled with rush-hour traffic collapsed, sending cars, trucks, and a school bus plunging into the river below. Thirteen people were killed, and 145 more were injured. This tragic event is a signal that infrastructure isn't permanent and that it needs to be repaired and upgraded periodically.

The IoT can help here too. Sensors can be built into concrete and metal structures, sending signals to a controller regarding the stress and strain they are under. Conditions can be monitored, and the appropriate repairs completed before another tragedy strikes. Sensors can be built into buildings in earthquake-prone areas to help assess damage and safety. In a similar way, IoT-enabled sensors can monitor railroad tracks, tunnels, and other transportation infrastructure to keep conditions safe and commerce moving.

Energy production and infrastructure can be monitored by IoT devices as well. Problems can be detected in power grids before they fail, and smart sensors can regulate power production and consumption for economic or environmental efficiency.

Finally, some cities are becoming smart cities using the IoT. Through the use of sensors and apps that residents can download, cities can track traffic flows, improve air and water quality, and monitor power usage. Residents can get some interesting benefits, such as knowing if the neighborhood park is busy or being able to search for an open parking space downtown.

Potential Issues

As you've learned, thanks to the cloud, the IoT has a tremendous amount of potential for revolutionizing how people interact with the world around them, as well as how devices interact with each other. All of this potential upside comes with its share of potential challenges and issues as well:

Standards and Governance   As with the development of most new technologies, there is not one specific standard or governing body for the IoT. There are about a dozen different technical standards being worked on. Most of them focus on different aspects of the IoT, but there is some overlap between standards as well as gaps where no standards exist. For example, organizations such as the United States Food and Drug Administration (FDA) are working on an identification system for medical devices, and the Institute of Electrical and Electronics Engineers (IEEE), the Internet Engineering Task Force (IETF), and the Open Connectivity Foundation (OCF) are all working on standards for communications and data transmissions.

In the smart home space, devices produced by different companies might or might not follow similar standards, meaning that interoperability can be challenging. Some people suggest that governments should get involved to enforce standards, while others think that's the worst idea possible.

Generally speaking, standards have a way of working themselves out over time. Just know that if your company invests in the IoT, there might be some interoperability challenges. How the IoT will ultimately turn out is anyone's guess, but one or two technologies will likely emerge as the winners.

Data Security and Privacy   Two of the reasons that governance can be such a hot topic are data security and user privacy. Stories about Random Company X suffering a data breach are all too common today. And let's face it: the purpose of many IoT-related devices is to collect information about people and their behaviors. That raises some huge security and privacy concerns.

 Real World Scenario

Security Vulnerabilities Create Risk

The vast majority of adults today carry at least one electronic device on them at all times, whether it be their smartphone, a smartwatch, or a fitness monitor. Because of how common they are and the potential benefits, a lot of kids have smartphones and smartwatches as well. One benefit is that parents can track their child's location using convenient apps such as Life360, GPS Location Tracker, Canary, and mSpy. One unintended consequence is that means other people might be able to as well.

In October 2017, a security flaw was exposed in certain smartwatches specifically made for children. The flaw allowed hackers to identify the wearer's location, listen in on conversations, and even communicate directly with the wearer. For most parents, the thought of a stranger having this kind of ability is horrifying.

No breach was ever reported with these devices, but the possibility is unsettling.

Although security and privacy may seem like the same thing, there are differences. Data security specifically refers to ensuring that confidentiality, availability, and integrity are maintained. In other words, it can't be accessed by anyone who's not supposed to access it, it's available when needed, and it's accurate and reliable. Privacy is related to the appropriate use of data. When you provide data to a company, the purposes for which it can be used should be specified. Also, this means that companies to whom you are giving data can't sell that data to another company unless you've given prior approval. If your company is going to use consumer-facing IoT products, be sure to have security and privacy concerns covered.

Data Storage and Usage   IoT-enabled devices generate data—a lot of data. Because of the massive quantities of data generated, most of it gets stored in some sort of cloud-based solution. Again, this poses potential security risks.

For companies, the question becomes what do they do with all of that data? Just because they have petabytes of data doesn't mean it will do them any good. But of course, data can be incredibly valuable. Companies that figure out how to mine the data and translate it effectively into actionable insights will be ahead of the curve as compared to their competitors.

Blockchain

A *blockchain* is defined as an open, distributed ledger that can securely record transactions between two parties in a verifiable and permanent way. You might or might not have heard about blockchain, but it's likely you've heard of the most famous example of blockchain use, which is Bitcoin.

Bitcoin is a digital cryptocurrency—it has no intrinsic value and is not regulated by any official bank or country—that can be used to complete Internet-based transactions between two parties. Blockchain was developed initially to support Bitcoin, but it can also support other types of secure transactions including financial services records, smart contracts, and even supply chain management. It's likely that over the next few years, additional uses for blockchain will become more common.

Blockchain Principles

Blockchain operates on three key principles: decentralization, transparency, and immutability.

Decentralization   No one organization or company owns blockchain, and the information is not stored in a central location. A copy of the full blockchain ledger is stored on all computers that participate in the blockchain. It's truly a democratized transaction system. The decentralized nature of the technology also makes it harder to tamper with data in the blockchain.

Transparency   Everyone in the blockchain has access to all the data in the blockchain. The data itself is encrypted and private, but the technology and ledger are completely open. This again makes data harder to tamper with, and everyone involved is accountable for their actions.

Immutability   Look at nearly any article about blockchain, and you will see the word *immutable*. It's just a fancy word that means unchangeable. Because of how transactions are conducted and verified (using cryptography and hashing), blockchain is immutable, which provides a high level of data integrity. If any data in the chain were to be altered, it would be painfully obvious to everyone in the chain that someone tried to alter it.

Each of these will make more sense as we look at how blockchain works.

How Blockchain Works

Data in a blockchain is stored in units called *blocks*. Blocks (transactions) are stored end to end like in a chain. Each block contains the following:

- Transaction information such as date, time, and amount
- Participants in the transaction
- A unique code, called a *hash*, to identify the transaction
- The hash of the previous block in the chain

All data in the block is encrypted. So, if user Jane Smith makes a blockchain transaction, the data inside doesn't say Jane Smith in plain text but is rather an encrypted user ID that will be unique to Jane Smith.

Let's look at how a transaction works. It's also shown in Figure 3.11, because in this case a picture is worth a thousand Bitcoin.

FIGURE 3.11   The blockchain transaction process

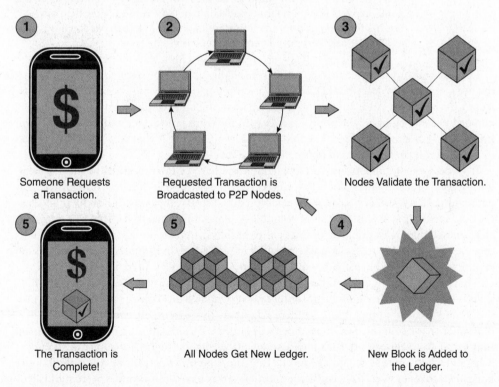

1. Someone Requests a Transaction.
2. Requested Transaction is Broadcasted to P2P Nodes.
3. Nodes Validate the Transaction.
4. New Block is Added to the Ledger.
5. All Nodes Get New Ledger.
5. The Transaction is Complete!

1. Someone requests a transaction, such as by making a purchase from a company that accepts Bitcoin payments.

2. The requested transaction gets sent to a peer-to-peer network of computers (called *nodes*) that participate in the blockchain network.

3. Using shared algorithms, the nodes validate and verify the transaction. This essentially means solving an encrypted mathematical problem, and this process can take a few days. Small transactions need to be verified by only one or two nodes, whereas large ones need to be verified by at least six nodes.

4. After verification, a new block containing the transaction information is added on to the end of the blockchain ledger. It's done in a way that makes the data immutable (permanent and unalterable).

5. Each party in the transaction is notified that the transaction is complete. Simultaneously, the new blockchain ledger, with the new block, is transmitted to all nodes on the peer-to-peer network.

Blockchain transactions carry no transaction costs—transactions are free! There may be infrastructure costs to support the hardware to participate in a blockchain network, though. Because of the lack of transaction costs, some experts speculate that blockchain could eventually replace businesses that rely upon transaction costs (such as Visa or MasterCard, or even Uber and Airbnb) to generate revenue.

Let's go back to the three principles of blockchain and see how they are relevant given the five steps we just described. Decentralization is apparent, because each node contains a copy of the ledger. And, anyone can participate in the blockchain. Transparency is handled because again, every node has access to the transaction data and the entire ledger. Immutability is a little trickier. The first part of immutability is that as a block gets added to the ledger, it contains a hash of the preceding block.

It's worth expanding on this "a block contains a hash of the preceding block" concept for a second. Let's say that block 105 is complete. Block 106 gets created, and part of the data within block 106 is a hash of the encrypted block 105. In a way, block 106 contains part of block 105—at least a hash of what block 105 is supposed to be. If even a single character changes within block 105, its entire hash is different. So if someone tries to alter the data within block 105 on a node, the data in block 106 on that node also becomes corrupt. Everyone in the blockchain would know that the data was altered.

That brings up the question, how do you know which data is correct? Remember that thanks to decentralization and transparency, every node has a copy of the ledger. This is the second pillar of immutability. If there's an issue, the system self-checks. The copy of block 105 that's contained on the majority of nodes is presumed to be the correct one, and that ledger gets sent back to the altered node, correcting its ledger. For someone to truly hack a blockchain, they would need to be in possession of 51 percent or more of all nodes. For perspective, even the largest Bitcoin mining farms have only about 3 percent of Bitcoin nodes. So, you can consider the data to be essentially immutable.

With the need for a large number of peer-to-peer nodes, you can see how cloud computing helps make blockchain more feasible and manageable. All major CSPs offer blockchain services.

Real World Scenario

Grab a Pick and a Shovel

In the Bitcoin ecosystem, solving the mathematical problem to validate a new block is rewarded with a payout of a small amount of Bitcoin. In the mid-to-late 2010s, some people felt they could make money by setting up their computer to be a Bitcoin node—this is called *Bitcoin mining*.

Originally, people used their home PCs. Then, some more hardcore miners found that the CPUs in most computers were too inefficient but that the graphics processing units (GPUs) in high-end video cards were better suited for mining. Once the news got out, the price of video cards skyrocketed, and it became nearly impossible to find them in stores.

Did Bitcoin miners strike it rich? Not really. Validating transactions takes a fair amount of computing power and time. After investing in mining hardware and paying for electricity to run the hardware, most miners didn't come out ahead. Today, even with specialized mining hardware, casual miners might make a few cents per day—in most cases not even enough to pay for the electricity it takes to mine in the first place.

If you're interested in learning more about becoming a Bitcoin node or a Bitcoin miner, visit https://bitcoin.org/en/full-node. For an interesting video of a large Chinese Bitcoin mine, take a look at https://www.youtube.com/watch?v=K8kua5B5K3I. In the meantime, it's probably not a good idea to quit your day job.

Subscription Services

Cloud service providers offer several different ways to pay for their resources. The two most popular models are pay-as-you-go and subscription-based. In the pay-as-you-go model, you pay only for resources that you use. For companies that use few resources or have wildly unpredictable needs, this can be the cheaper way to go.

Subscription-based pricing, or *subscription services*, usually offers a discount over pay-as-you-go models, but it also means your company is locked into a contract for the length of the subscription. Generally speaking, the longer the contract you agree to, the more of a discount you will receive. Your company either pays for subscription services up front or has a monthly fee. Reserved instances, which we talk about more in Chapter 5, are subscription-based services.

 Overestimating the amount of cloud resources needed and getting locked into a subscription can result in a company overpaying for cloud services.

Subscriptions are available for the standard cloud resources, such as compute, storage, network, and database. It's also becoming more and more common for software to operate on a subscription basis. Take Microsoft Office 365, for example. Several years ago, if a company wanted Microsoft Office, it would pay a one-time per-seat license fee, get some installation CDs, and install the software. Microsoft would try to hard sell the company on upgrading when the next version came out—usually about every three years—but the company could just ignore the request. Eventually Microsoft went to cutting off updates and technical support for older versions in an effort to get people to upgrade, but that still didn't convince everyone.

Now, instead of buying Office, you essentially rent it. You have no choice if you want to use it. And instead of a one-time fee, you pay a yearly subscription fee. Microsoft isn't the only company doing this, so we don't mean to sound like we're picking on it. Software companies will tout the benefits, such as always having the newest version, being able to cheaply test new options, and automatically getting updates over the Internet. Really, though, it's a fundamental change in their business model designed to increase revenue. It's neither good nor bad—your perspective will depend on your company's needs—it's just the way it is now and for the foreseeable future.

Collaboration

The nature of business today is that companies need to be quick and agile. This applies to everyone, from small, five-person tax preparation firms to multibillion-dollar global giants. A big enabler of agility, especially when team members are geographically separated (or work from home), is *collaboration* software. The cloud makes collaboration so easy that it's almost second nature to some.

Collaboration services will vary based on the package chosen, but in general, these are some of the things to expect:

- Shared file storage
- Video conferencing
- Online chat
- Task management
- Real-time document collaboration

Using collaboration software, it's completely normal to have five people from different parts of the world video conference together, reviewing and editing a presentation for senior management or a client. The collaboration software allows access regardless of device platform or operating system, because it's all cloud-hosted on the Internet.

Security on collaboration platforms is pretty good. Users will be required to create a user account and password and must be invited to the specific team's collaboration space. Some collaboration packages support SSO or Federation to make managing usernames and passwords a little easier.

There are dozens of collaboration software packages in the marketplace. They will have slightly different features as well as costs. Some are free for basic use but may have limited features or charge a small fee for storage. Examples include Microsoft Teams, Slack, Confluence, Podio, Quip, Samepage, and Bitrix24. Figure 3.12 shows a screenshot of the Microsoft Teams file storage area we have set up to collaborate on this book.

FIGURE 3.12   Microsoft Teams

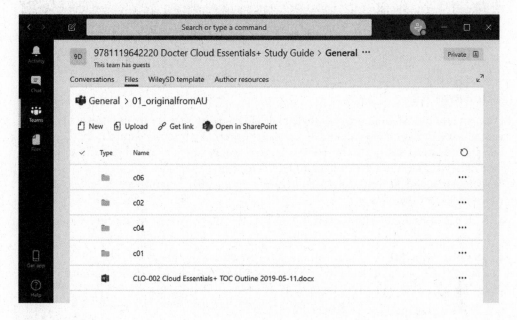

VDI

Virtual desktop infrastructure (VDI) has been in use since about 2006, so it predates the cloud. It's another example of a service that the cloud has made easier and cheaper to manage.

In a VDI setup, the administrator creates a user desktop inside a VM located on a server. When users log into the VDI, they are presented with their OS's graphical user interface (GUI) just as if they were logged into a local machine. Administrators can set up the virtual desktops in a few different ways. One is to let users customize their desktops just as they would on a personal device. The other is to make it so the desktops are effectively locked from modifications. It will always look the same every time someone logs in. The latter scenario can be useful if, for example, salespeople need to log into a kiosk within a store to complete a sale. Admins can also set up desktop pools, which are groups of similar desktops. For example, there could be one for the finance department with the software they need and a separate one for human resources with their software packages.

Technically speaking, a VDI is specifically run by a company within its internal data center—it's not cloud-based. CSPs may offer VDI under the name desktop as a service. It's the same concept as VDI—the only difference is where the VMs are hosted. As Citrix executive Kenneth Oestreich quipped, DaaS is "VDI that's someone else's problem."

The terms VDI and DaaS often get used interchangeably, even though they are different things. We'll continue to refer to the technology as VDI for ease and to match the CompTIA Cloud Essentials+ objectives. For purposes of the CompTIA Cloud Essentials+ exam, assume that VDI and DaaS are one and the same—*unless* you get a question on where one or the other is hosted.

VDI Benefits

From an end-user standpoint, the single biggest benefit of VDI is ease of access. The user can be anywhere in the world, and as long as they have an Internet connection, they can log into their desktop. Users also have the benefit of accessing their virtual desktop from any type of device, such as a desktop, laptop, tablet, or smartphone.

Companies benefit from using VDI because of centralized management, increased security, and lower costs.

- All desktops are managed centrally on a server. Any changes that administrators need to make, such as adding or updating software, can all be handled quickly and easily.

- Security is increased because all user files are stored on the server as opposed to on a laptop or PC. If a device were to get stolen, there is less risk of losing the data.

- In theory, VDI means that companies need to buy less hardware for their users, thereby reducing the total cost of ownership (TCO).

How VDI Works

To understand how VDI works, you need to dig up some of the technical concepts you learned in Chapter 1. VDI relies upon VMs that need a hypervisor. The virtual desktops are hosted on the VMs. VDI uses another piece of software called a *connection broker* that manages security of and access to the virtual desktops. Figure 3.13 illustrates a simple VDI system.

FIGURE 3.13   A simple VDI system

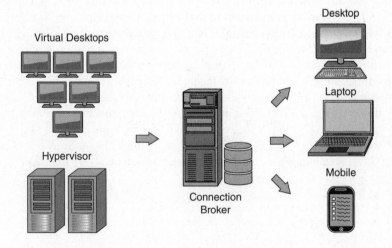

Self-Service

Finally, the last benefit of cloud services that you need to remember is *self-service*. We introduced self-service (or on-demand self-service) in Chapter 1 when we covered cloud characteristics. If you'll recall, it simply means that users can access additional resources or services automatically, 24 hours a day, 7 days a week, 365 days a year, without requiring intervention from the CSP.

Figure 3.14 shows the AWS S3 (storage) management screen. If another storage bucket is needed, all we have to do is click the Create Bucket button, set up the characteristics such as security and encryption, and create it. The whole process can be done in about 30 seconds, and supplier intervention isn't needed.

FIGURE 3.14   AWS S3 buckets management screen

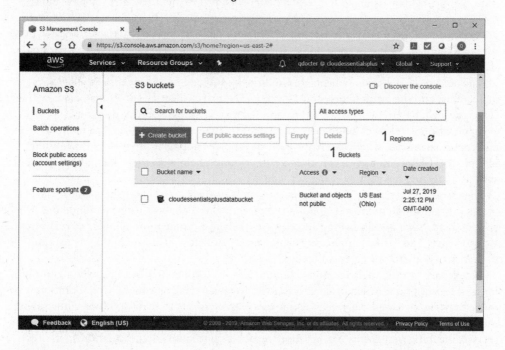

There are 11 cloud services that you need to be able to identify for the CompTIA Cloud Essentials+ exam, and some of them have multiple components. Be familiar with identity access management (including single sign, multifactor authentication, and federation), cloud-native applications (microservices and containerization), data analytics (machine learning, artificial intelligence, and big data), digital marketing (email campaigns and social media), autonomous environments, IoT, blockchain, subscription services, collaboration, VDI, and self-service.

Summary

In this chapter, we started to focus on the business principles of cloud environments. To start, we looked at using appropriate cloud assessments when given a scenario. When beginning a cloud assessment, you should be sure to understand current and future requirements. This means getting input from key stakeholders and establishing points of contact between your company and potential cloud providers.

After assessing current and future needs, run baselines to understand current network performance. Then, running a feasibility study can help you determine whether it's possible or what it would take to get to the desired future requirements. A gap analysis focuses on specific areas of the network or organization that need improvements to get to the desired state. Reporting can also help out with assessments, especially if you already have cloud services and are seeking to understand how much they're utilized. Benchmarks help you understand performance relative to other companies or established standards. Finally, make sure to document all important conversations and decisions and create diagrams for how cloud services will be constructed.

The next section was on benefits and solutions provided by cloud services. There are quite a few, and the exam focuses on 11 areas. The first is identity access management. The cloud can help by providing SSO, MFA, and federation across security domains.

Application developers will benefit from cloud-native applications such as microservices and containerization, which can help speed the app development process and save companies money. Many companies can also use the cloud to help with their data analytics needs, such as analyzing big data by using ML and AI.

Digital marketers can increase the effectiveness of their email campaigns and social media posts through improved cloud-based targeting and analysis tools. Autonomous environments such as self-driving vehicles are likely to become more popular over the next several years. The IoT has applications in a variety of fields such as manufacturing automation, security, and home entertainment systems.

Blockchain is a digital ledger made famous thanks to Bitcoin. Cloud providers offer billing as a subscription, which often saves money versus paying as you go. Collaboration is made easy via the cloud. VDI gives employees ease of access to their desktops while saving the company money, easing administration, and improving security. Finally, clouds are self-service, meaning that clients can get more resources without CSP intervention.

Exam Essentials

Know how to gather current and future cloud requirements.   The best method is to talk to key stakeholders, who are important people with a vested interest in how the cloud will work. Ask the right questions, and understand the time horizon for when changes should be implemented.

Understand what baselines are used for in cloud assessments.   A baseline is a test that captures performance of a system. For example, one could baseline normal network throughput or CPU utilization.

Know how a feasibility study is used in cloud assessments.   Feasibility studies are used to determine the practicality of a proposed move to cloud services. It gets at questions such as: do company needs require the use of the cloud, and does the company have the ability to migrate to the cloud?

Understand what a gap analysis does.   A gap analysis identifies where the network and organization are now and what needs to be true to get them to where they need to be. Gap analyses focus on business and technical readiness.

Know how to use reporting in a cloud assessment.   Reporting can help determine baselines for current network performance. If you already have cloud services, the CSP will provide reports on resource usage, such as compute, network, and storage resources used.

Understand how to use benchmarks for a cloud assessment.   A benchmark is a standard of performance or point of reference for comparison. For example, if you have a baseline read of your CPU utilization, you might not know whether it's good or bad. A benchmark can help you determine that by comparing your data to a known standard.

Know why it's important to create documentation and diagrams as part of a cloud assessment.   Cloud environments can get really complicated. Document conversations with key stakeholders and potential CSPs so you know what decisions were made and what the next steps are. Document and diagram layouts of where services will reside so a new business analyst or network administrator can look at them and understand how your cloud setup works.

Know who key stakeholders and POCs are.   A key stakeholder is someone with a vested interest in the cloud project. It could be an executive such as the CEO or CIO or even a cloud user. A POC is someone responsible for managing communication between a company and the CSP.

Know three areas of identity access management.   They are SSO, MFA, and federation.

Know what SSO is.   SSO is when users can access multiple systems or resources through a single initial login.

Know what MFA is.   Multifactor authentication occurs when a system requires multiple pieces of information to authenticate a user. For example, in addition to the user's password (which is one factor), the system might require a PIN, one-time password, security code, or answer to a security question.

Know what federation is.   Federation is much like SSO, but it applies across multiple corporations. It's when multiple companies' security systems trust each other to validate users; when users are validated by one, they can access resources in another federated security domain.

Understand the benefits of the cloud-native applications microservices and containerization. Microservices and containerization are designed to improve the speed of software development and also lower costs. Microservices breaks down a monolith program into smaller components, which are independently coded and managed. Containerization is a way to store all items needed for a program in one contained location.

Understand three areas of data analytics. The three areas you need to know are ML, AI, and big data.

Know what big data is. Big data refers to unstructured data sets, as opposed to structured data sets such as relational databases.

Know what AI is. Artificial intelligence is when machines are programmed to perform smart, human-like activities.

Understand what ML is and how it's different from AI. Machine learning is when data can be fed to a computer and it will learn from it and adapt. With AI, the computer or machine can only respond to input it's been programmed to respond to. With ML, the computer or machine can take novel input and respond to it. Based on feedback (was it right or wrong), it can learn and adapt for future input.

Know what digital marketing is and two common ways that it's executed. Digital marketing is the attempted selling of products or services using digital technologies. Two common methods are email campaigns and social media posts.

Understand what an autonomous environment is. An autonomous environment is a computerized environment where complex human actions are mimicked without human intervention. Examples include self-driving cars and robotic manufacturing facilities.

Know what the IoT is. The Internet of Things is a network of devices that are able to communicate with each other and exchange data. Common applications include home entertainment systems, security systems, heating and cooling systems, home appliances, modern cars, medical devices, and manufacturing, transportation, and infrastructure systems.

Know what blockchain is. A blockchain is an open, distributed ledger that can securely record transactions between two parties in a verifiable and permanent way. It's the technology behind Bitcoin, but it can also be used for other types of transactions.

Know what subscription services are. CSPs will often sell their services as subscription services, which means you pay for services for a period of time (such as six months or a year), often at a discount versus a pay-as-you-go model.

Understand how the cloud can help collaboration. There are dozens of cloud-based collaboration software packages, which allow users to share and edit files in real time, video conference, chat, and manage tasks.

Know what VDI is. With virtual desktop infrastructure, user desktops reside inside a VM located on a server. Users can log into their virtual desktops from any location with an Internet connection, on any type of device.

Know how clouds implement self-service.   The CSP will have an online management interface, where the client can acquire and use additional services without intervention from the CSP.

Written Lab

Fill in the blanks for the questions provided in the written lab. You can find the answers to the written labs in Appendix A.

1. James attempts to sign into the cloud, and it asks him for a username, a password, and a security code. This is an example of _____.

2. A _____ is someone with a vested interest in a project.

3. A _____ is a comparison of data versus a known standard.

4. The two types of gap analyses are _____ and _____.

5. Self-driving cars are an example of which cloud-based service?

6. Your company pays for cloud service for a year and gets a discount versus paying month-to-month. This is an example of _____.

7. A social media campaign is a type of _____.

8. Unstructured data sets are often referred to as _____.

9. When a computer is able to adapt based on input it's given, that is called _____.

10. Breaking down a large computer program into smaller parts and coding each part separately is an example of _____.

Review Questions

The answers to the chapter review questions can be found in Appendix B.

1. A network administrator wants to implement VDI in your future cloud solution. Which of the following is NOT an implication of implementing VDI?

    A. Centralized administration

    B. Remote user access

    C. Higher costs

    D. Increased security

2. Company A has a software development team with members located in Geneva and others in Chicago. Which cloud service will best help them manage a project that all of them are working on?

    A. Collaboration

    B. Self-service

    C. Autonomous environment

    D. Blockchain

3. Your company is trying to save money by using cloud services. Which of the following is most likely to help reduce the costs of software development?

    A. Federation

    B. Microservices

    C. ML

    D. AI

4. You have been asked to perform a cloud assessment for your company. Which of the following describes an appropriate order for conducting assessment tasks?

    A. Contact key stakeholders, run a baseline, perform a gap analysis, create documentation.

    B. Run a baseline, contact key stakeholders, perform a gap analysis, create documentation.

    C. Create documentation, run a baseline, perform a gap analysis, contact key stakeholders.

    D. Perform a gap analysis, run a baseline, contact key stakeholders, create documentation.

5. Your company recently signed up for a Microsoft Office 365 subscription. The network administrator wants to make it so that users only have to type in their login information once and don't need to log into the local network and Microsoft's cloud separately. What service does she need to implement?

    A. SSO

    B. Self-service

    C. Federation

    D. MFA

6. A network administrator who is part of the cloud assessment team mentions that the average server CPU utilization is at 40 percent. What do you use to determine if this is acceptable performance?

    A. Baseline

    B. Technical gap analysis

    C. Compute reporting

    D. Benchmark

7. In preparation for a cloud migration, your manager asks you to run a gap analysis. Which of the following is NOT a likely outcome of a gap analysis?

    A. Understanding if there are compatibility issues with software in the migration plan

    B. Identifying policies that are not being met by the migration plan

    C. Prioritizing allocation of resources within the migration plan

    D. Determining key stakeholder feedback about the migration plan

8. A small company needs to set up a security surveillance system to protect its building. Which cloud-based technology will the security system most likely take advantage of?

    A. VDI

    B. IoT

    C. SSO

    D. AI

9. The company CIO approaches you and asks you if the company should implement blockchain in the new cloud environment. Which of the following is the best explanation you can give on what blockchain is?

    A. It's an online cryptocurrency.

    B. It's an authentication system that securely validates users.

    C. It's a secure, open, distributed ledger.

    D. It lowers the TCO for application DevOps.

10. Your company recently merged with another, and the networks have been combined into a cloud solution. Users need to access multiple resources from different systems within the same security domain. What should your company implement to make access as easy as possible for users?

    A. SSO

    B. Federation

    C. MFA

    D. Self-service

11. Company A wants to assess the possibility of migrating to the cloud. What should they do to determine how much of their current server storage capacity is being used?

    A. Run a benchmark.

    B. Run a baseline.

    C. Determine current and future requirements.

    D. Run a gap analysis.

12. A member of your company's purchasing team is negotiating cloud services with a CSP. Over the course of the first year, which of the following would likely represent a cost savings over other types of payment models?

    A. Pay-as-you-go

    B. Self-service

    C. High availability

    D. Subscription services

13. To increase security of your company's cloud resources, the administrator decides to require users to enter a password and also a randomized security code to log into the cloud. What cloud service does the administrator need to enable?

    A. SSO

    B. VDI

    C. MFA

    D. Federation

14. You are performing a cloud assessment for your organization. It's time for you to determine which capabilities can be offloaded to the cloud and the level of support services needed. Which of the following assessments should you perform?

    A. Gap analysis

    B. Feasibility study

    C. Baseline

    D. Current and future requirements

15. When setting up a new cloud service, you want to ensure that you can get more storage space quickly without needing to call or email the CSP. What cloud service allows you to do this?

    A. Self-service

    B. SSO

    C. Subscription service

    D. Autonomous service

16. One of the company's developers is creating a software package that can identify human faces and mine footage from security cameras to determine whether someone is suspected of a crime. Which type of technology is best suited for this task?

    A. Big data mining

    B. Blockchain

    C. AI

    D. ML

17. The sales team needs to find better, faster, and cheaper ways to engage with potential customers. Which cloud service should they implement?

    A. Digital marketing

    B. Big data

    C. Blockchain

    D. Identity access management

18. You are performing a cloud assessment. What is the final step to take in the cloud assessment process?

    A. Engage key stakeholders

    B. Run a feasibility study

    C. Create documentation and diagrams

    D. Perform a gap analysis

19. A software developer at your company said he just used the cloud to place his program and all needed library files into one package. Which cloud service is he referring to?

    A. Microservices

    B. Blockchain

    C. Federation

    D. Containerization

20. Your company is debating which cloud-based data analytics solution to implement. Which of the following statements is NOT true when comparing AI to ML?

    A. AI can only react to conditions it's been programmed to react to.

    B. ML is a form of applied AI.

    C. ML uses neural networks.

    D. AI is when machines perform smart, human-like activities.

Chapter

4

Engaging Cloud Vendors

THE FOLLOWING COMPTIA CLOUD ESSENTIALS+ EXAM CLO-002 OBJECTIVES ARE COVERED IN THIS CHAPTER:

✓ **2.2 Summarize the financial aspects of engaging a cloud provider.**

- Capital expenditures
- Operating expenditures
- Variable vs. fixed cost
- Licensing models
  - BYOL
  - Subscription
- Contracts
- Billing
- Request for information
- Human capital
  - Training
  - Professional development

✓ **2.3 Identify the important business aspects of vendor relations in cloud adoptions.**

- Professional services
  - Time to market
  - Skill availability
  - Support
  - Managed services
- Statement of work (SOW)
- Service level agreement (SLA)

- Training
- Evaluations
  - Pilot
  - Proof of value
  - Proof of concept
  - Success criteria
- Open-source vs. proprietary

✓ **2.5 Compare and contrast cloud migration approaches.**

- Rip and replace
- Lift and shift
- Hybrid
- Phased

The first three chapters of this book had a pretty heavy technical slant. Regardless of whether you like learning about the tech side, it's important for you to understand how clouds work and what benefits they can provide to your company. Without that knowledge, you won't be able to order the right services and ensure you're getting what you really need without overpaying.

Now, we'll flip to more business-focused material in preparation for working with a cloud service provider. The CompTIA Cloud Essentials+ exam objectives separate the financial and business aspects of working with vendors, but they are inexorably related, so we'll treat them that way.

In this chapter, we will start off with defining business and financial terms you need to know related to expenditures and cost types, licensing models, human capital, and professional services. Then, we will go into detail on how to find and evaluate possible cloud vendors by soliciting bids, running evaluations, and working through contracts. Finally, we'll end the chapter with different approaches to performing a migration.

Understanding Business and Financial Concepts

For most companies, the entire point of moving IT infrastructure to the cloud is to save money. Generally speaking, using the cloud versus having on-premises infrastructure does do that. One way companies save money is by investing less in hardware and software that will become obsolete. Companies might also be able to save on taxes based on the types of expenditures they have. Choosing the right software licensing model can save money too, as can spending less on human capital and properly utilizing professional services. We'll look at each of these in the following sections.

Expenditures and Costs

While using cloud services might be cheaper than the alternatives, it's unfortunately still not free. When thinking of moving to the cloud, you need to be aware of different classifications of expenditures and costs. Understanding the differences and how each one can affect the bottom line will help you make the right decision.

Capital and Operating Expenditures

Money spent on buying, improving, or maintaining fixed assets is classified as a *capital expenditure*. The cool finance kids will shorten this to *CapEx*. Examples include buildings, business equipment, and computer hardware. Traditionally, most IT expenses have been CapEx, and the benefits of those expenditures are expected to last for several years. If you buy a new server or a building, you certainly hope that it's around for more than one fiscal year! Generally speaking, anything purchased with CapEx is added as an asset to the company's ledgers.

The other type of expenditure, called an *operating expenditure* (or OpEx), is used for the purpose of supporting the ongoing costs of conducting regular day-to-day business. Salaries, administrative expenses, office supplies, utilities, research and development, property taxes and insurance, licensing fees, and the cost of goods sold all fit into OpEx. The business benefits of OpEx are expected to be realized in the current year, and the goods or services purchased are not considered company assets for accounting or tax purposes.

> The costs associated with repairing equipment are generally considered OpEx. If the repairs extend the functional life of the equipment, though, those costs may be CapEx.

A company that needs to invest in IT can make the decision whether to use CapEx or OpEx. For example, imagine that a company needs to purchase several hundred terabytes of new storage space to support expansion. A CapEx solution might be to buy a new storage area network (SAN), whereas getting that storage space from a CSP would be an OpEx solution.

Those two solutions have profoundly different impacts from an IT management perspective. The SAN will require someone to purchase the hardware and then set it up, configure it, and manage it, and it might require acquiring more building space as well. Alternatively, setting it up in the cloud can be as simple as making a few clicks within the CSP's management software.

CapEx and OpEx also affect accounting and taxes differently. With CapEx, the cost of the equipment is depreciated over a certain time period, usually three to ten years. So let's say that the CapEx hardware upgrade costs $10 million and will be depreciated over five years. That means the company will pay all $10 million up front and can count the equipment as part of their assets. For tax purposes, though, they would get to deduct $2 million for each of the next five years.

> There are legal guidelines on what can be considered CapEx, how long the depreciation horizon can be, and how to handle CapEx for tax purposes. Companies need to follow generally accepted accounting principles (GAAP) to stay within the law. The accountants and tax professionals within a company should be familiar with these standards and can provide guidance on a proposed project or expenditure.

OpEx is always deducted in the current tax year. If $10 million is spent, all $10 million is counted as expenses for that tax year. There are no assets added to the balance sheet, though. The distinction between CapEx and OpEx can make a big difference for accounting and tax purposes! Table 4.1 summarizes the differences between CapEx and OpEx.

TABLE 4.1   Comparing capital and operating expenditures

	Capital Expenditures	Operating Expenditures
What it is	Spending on assets such as buildings or equipment	Spending on ordinary business activities
Examples	New servers Constructing a new server room A private jet for the IT staff	Cloud services Building utilities Employee salaries
Is it an asset?	Yes	No
When it's paid	Up front in a lump sum	Recurring monthly or annual payments
Tax treatment	Deducted over the asset's life span	Deducted in the current tax year

Many companies have chosen to go the OpEx route, treating their IT cloud services much like they would any other utility, such as electricity or water. Pay-as-you-go models facilitate this. If a company is just starting up or beginning a new project, this decision is probably pretty easy. For a company that already has an existing IT infrastructure, though, it might not be as clear. A company with a large data center that's three years old and is only partially depreciated might not realize immediate benefits from moving to the cloud. A cost-benefit analysis would need to be run, and the company may determine that it's not a good time to move to the cloud.

Companies often evaluate projects based on the return on investment (ROI), that is, the value realized by the project divided by the spending on the project. For example, if you spend $1 million on a project and it delivers $2 million in profit, then the ROI is 2:1. Many companies will write that as a $2 ROI, essentially saying, "For every dollar we spent, we made two dollars in profit." To make things more confusing, some companies will measure ROI based on topline sales, whereas others measure profit ROI. Clearly, an ROI below $1 is a problem because that means the project delivered less than it cost. Most companies will have higher thresholds they want to hit, such as $2.50 or $3.00, before they will agree to fund a project.

Variable and Fixed Costs

Continuing our foray into finance, it's time to turn our attention to variable and fixed costs. These are probably a little simpler than capital and operating expenditures. Simply put, a *variable cost* will change depending on how much is produced or used, whereas a *fixed cost* does not change regardless of how much is produced or used.

Let's use a noncloud example to illustrate the difference. Company X makes widgets. The company has a building, employees, and an assembly line. Fixed costs will include the lease paid for the building, because that won't change regardless of how many widgets the company makes and the cost for the assembly line. Variable costs will include the cost of raw materials, employee salaries (if the employees are paid by the hour or per widget), and utilities, most likely.

When working with a CSP, you might have the option of having fixed costs (if you go with a subscription) or variable costs (if you choose pay-as-you-go). Many companies like the certainty of fixed costs—after all, they're easy to predict. And, cloud providers may give you a discount if you sign up for a certain amount of resources for a specified amount of time. For example, you might be told you will pay $0.025 per gigabyte/month for up to 500TB of storage if you choose pay-as-you-go, whereas if you sign up for a year of 500TB of storage you'll only pay $0.022 per gigabyte/month. Yes, it looks like savings, but if you use only 100TB of storage, you will be wasting money on excess capacity.

Historically, most IT costs were fixed. With the cloud, many IT costs have switched to variable.

That example is very oversimplified, but buying a cloud subscription can be one way in which you'll overpay for cloud services. Not always, but it can happen. You'll need to run a cost analysis on a case-by-case basis to determine what's best for the situation.

Most CSPs will have online tools available to track and analyze costs. We'll look at more specific examples of analyzing cloud expenditures in Chapter 5, "Management and Technical Operations."

Licensing Models

Commercial software developers make their money by requiring clients to pay for a license. The license outlines the contractual rules by which the software, including operating systems (OSSs), can be used. For example, a license may specify that the software can be used on only one specific computer after it is installed. Or perhaps a license grants usage to five specific users, or allows for a maximum of five concurrent users, no matter who they are. There are a large number of *licensing models* out there, but in broad strokes, you might pay per user, per device, per server, or per network.

Some types of software don't require a license. If the software is classified as open source, public domain, or freeware, it can generally be used without cost to the user. Shareware may also be free of charge, but the developer often requests a donation to support their efforts.

Before acquiring software, always be sure to understand the licensing requirements. When the software is installed, the user must agree to the licensing terms or the software won't work—there is no negotiation. Figure 4.1 shows the introduction to the Microsoft Windows 10 license terms. Notice the bold text in the last paragraph shown, stating that you can either accept their terms or not use the software.

FIGURE 4.1   Microsoft Windows 10 license terms

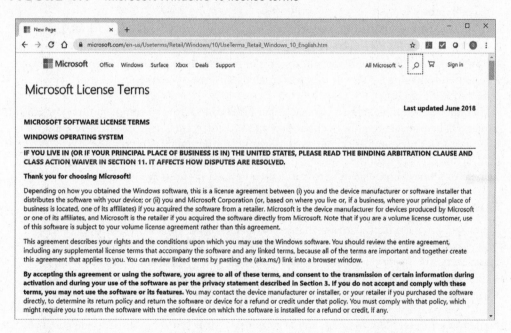

Companies that are not in compliance with licensing rules can be subject to large fines, and as with the law, ignorance is no excuse. It's good practice to ensure that all software licenses are cataloged and audited periodically.

The two types of licensing models you need to know for the CompTIA Cloud Essentials+ exam are BYOL and subscription. Unlike the expenditure and cost types we've discussed thus far, which are either-or (it's either a fixed cost or a variable cost), BYOL and subscription are not mutually exclusive.

Bring Your Own License

The *bring your own license (BYOL)* concept was introduced to give cloud clients flexibility to use existing licenses they've already paid for. BYOL terms let companies redeploy licenses from one device or user to another if needed, or even move them from an on-premises device to one in the cloud. There are three key benefits to using BYOL:

- **Greater flexibility:** Companies can move licenses as needed based on current business needs.

- **Reduced costs:** Up-front costs of migration or expansion can be significantly reduced, because the company has flexibility to move and reuse existing licenses as opposed to needing to buy concurrent licenses.

- **Enhanced license management:** Licenses can be tracked in the cloud, helping ensure compliance.

Let's take a look at an example of BYOL. Imagine that a company has 20 Microsoft Server licenses and is debating migrating to the cloud. With BYOL, if the company migrates to the Azure platform, Microsoft allows the company to bring those 20 licenses with them, as opposed to having to pay for new server licenses. This, of course, can save the client company a lot of money.

For another example, take a company that hires contractors to complete three-month projects. The projects require the use of specialized software whose licenses are good for one year. After the completion of the first project, the company can hire a separate set of contractors and reassign the licenses from the first group to the second group. Again, this helps save money versus needing to purchase a new set of licenses.

Subscriptions

Years ago, buying a license meant that you owned usage of that software for perpetuity. Today, many software developers have gone to a subscription model, which is more like a lease. Software subscriptions are typically one year in length, although that can vary.

The biggest downside to the subscription-based model is that in most cases, it has increased the cost of software ownership. For example, let's say that in the perpetuity model you paid $50 for a financial software package. As long as it still met your needs, you could use it forever. The company might offer new features or even discontinue updates of your version, but as long as it worked fine, you might not have had any incentive to upgrade. That $50 app could last you many years.

In the subscription model, you have no choice. You pay the $50 for one year. If by day 366 you haven't paid another $50, the software stops working. Software companies will tout the benefits of subscriptions, such as:

- Smaller up-front license costs.

- No upgrade costs for new features.

- Clients always have the most current version.

- Users have device flexibility as opposed to being tethered to one device.

- Tech support is included.
- The software may be installed in the cloud, which can lower on-premises IT staff needs.

The benefits aren't insignificant, but the overall costs might be higher. It's up to you to understand the pros and cons, run a cost-benefit analysis, and determine which licensing model is best for your organization. (However, you might not have a choice, as many software companies have moved to subscription-only sales.)

Human Capital

Implementing the cloud can have a big effect on a company's IT staff. On the positive side, the cloud can help free up IT capacity to work on important projects by eliminating the need for routine IT maintenance. Another aspect of moving to the cloud can be potentially controversial, because many companies are able to reduce the need for on-premises IT staff. Possibly affecting jobs or careers is not a decision to be taken lightly. Ultimately, a company needs to decide what the value of its *human capital* is—that is, the knowledge, skills, and experience possessed by the members of the IT staff.

The cloud reduces the company's capital cost of owning IT infrastructure. It also often reduces the operating cost of managing IT infrastructure.

For the staff at your organization, two important aspects to focus on are training and professional development. The two terms often get used interchangeably, but there are key differences between them. Let's take a look at each one.

Training   *Training* is a short-term process designed to have employees develop a skill or obtain knowledge in order to perform their job. Training can be provided for one person or for many people at the same time.

Cloud-related training will likely be required for both IT and non-IT employees. The IT staff will need to be trained on processes to manage cloud services or acquire new services. Non-IT employees may need training on how to access and effectively use cloud-based applications and storage.

Before migrating to the cloud, work with the appropriate departments to develop a training plan that identifies the training needs and develops and assembles the materials. During the migration, offer the training as it makes sense. You might also be able to enlist the help of the CSP in developing materials or providing training.

Professional Development   Professional development is a long-term educational process focused on employee growth. As opposed to training, which can be a group exercise, professional development is individualized and based on an employee's long-term career goals. Because of this, professional development requires a degree of self-reflection. Training is often a component in professional development, but only part of the broader plan.

Table 4.2 summarizes the key differences between training and professional development. Human resources professionals are often great partners for helping create training and professional development programs.

TABLE 4.2   Training versus professional development

	Training	Professional development
Who	Group	Individual
Timeline	Short-term	Long-term
Focus	Gaining job skills	Career growth
Learning objectives	Specific to job	Broad and open; based on career goals

Professional Services

Migrating to the cloud is not a simple task, especially for those who haven't done it before. Fortunately, there is a whole army of cloud providers and independent companies ready to offer assistance in assessing, planning, deploying, and optimizing cloud solutions. Acquiring the right *professional services* from a CSP or consultant can speed up migration time, enhance efficiency, and reduce cost while ensuring that the end solution meets a client's needs.

The Cloud Essentials+ exam objectives list four different professional services—time to market, skill availability, support, and managed services. We're going to group them into two general categories—time to market and managed services—and discuss them in more detail.

Time to Market

In business, speed is life. Companies that are late to market or slow to adapt often don't survive long in a competitive environment. That's why *time to market (TTM)*—the time it takes from having an idea to getting it into the market—is so critical.

Related to the cloud, there are two ways in which TTM plays a role:

- Performing a cloud migration quickly
- Enabling the launch of new products or services quickly

Getting the migration completed quickly and efficiently will likely enable launching new products faster. A cloud service provider or managed service provider can help with the first. Once a company is using the cloud, it can either launch new products or services faster or enable its clients to do so. For example, if you remember back to Chapter 3, "Assessing Cloud Needs," we introduced microservices. It's estimated that software development companies that use microservices can get to market 20 percent to 50 percent faster than those that don't.

Managed Services

Not every organization has the human capital needed to manage cloud services. As a consequence, an entire *managed services* industry has sprung up to meet the needs of these groups. Managed services, provided by managed services providers (MSPs), offer outsourced cloud management and technical support. This includes, but is not limited to, the following:

- Daily management and troubleshooting
- Performance testing
- Monitoring and reporting
- Backup and recovery

 Putting it in the language of the Cloud Essentials+ exam objectives, MSPs can offer *skill availability* and *support* for a cloud client.

Most of the big CSPs don't actually provide managed services. Amazon does through AWS, but as of the time of this writing, Microsoft and Google do not. Don't worry, though—all of them have readily available lists of dozens of authorized MSPs that are ready to help. Table 4.3 has links for each of the big three's authorized MSPs.

TABLE 4.3 Authorized managed service providers

Cloud provider	MSP link
Amazon AWS	https://aws.amazon.com/partners/msp/
Google Cloud	https://cloud.google.com/partners/msp-initiative/ (click the Find An MSP Partner button)
Microsoft Azure	https://azure.microsoft.com/en-us/partners/

MSPs offer varying levels of support. Some clients might only need a few hours per week, whereas others will want dedicated, full-time support resources. As with everything else, it's best to shop around to find the best combination of service and price when you're looking for an MSP.

As a reminder, for the CompTIA Cloud Essentials+ exam, you will be expected to understand the following:

- Capital expenditures

- Operating expenditures

- Variable vs. fixed cost

- Licensing models (BYOL and subscription)

- Human capital (training and professional development)

- Professional services (time to market, skill availability, support, and managed services)

Finding and Evaluating Cloud Vendors

For most companies, the IT budget represents a sizeable chunk of overall expenditures. It's no wonder that cloud services, with their promises of significant savings, have taken off in popularity. Finding the right cloud provider to support your business needs is essential to realizing the savings that you expect. But with several major cloud providers and dozens of smaller ones to choose from, how do you go about finding and evaluating the right fit?

The first step is to gather information about potential vendors. There's a fairly well-documented path to doing this, but it can be long and often very detailed. After gathering information and choosing one or more vendors to explore further, you can perform evaluations to see how well their services actually deliver. Finally, when you've made the final choice, you need to negotiate the contract and billing terms. We'll look at each of these steps in the following sections.

Gathering Information

Before you sign a contract and commit to spending large sums of money, it's always best to shop around for the best deal. The best deal isn't always the cheapest, because quality should factor into the value equation as well. With so many vendors in the marketplace, it can be challenging to find the right one—and no, they're not all the same.

First, understand if you want to pursue a solution that is open source or proprietary, because the differences can have a major impact on the service you receive and future cloud needs. Once you've determined that, you can begin the process of requesting information from potential vendors.

Open Source vs. Proprietary Technology

The open source versus proprietary debate is one of the most contentious in the history of computing. It's raged for decades and is certainly not unique to cloud computing. Perhaps the best-known arena for this debate is OSs. The open source side features

UNIX, Linux, and their derivatives, whereas proprietary OSs such as Microsoft Windows and macOS dominate the PC marketplace. In the mobile arena, Android is open source (although very tightly controlled by Google) and iOS is proprietary.

Even in the hardware arena, the debate carries on. Apple is notoriously controlling of its hardware platform and the devices its OSs can be installed on, whereas the PC and Android markets are far more open across vendors. There are pros and cons to each method, and as in any highly charged political debate, there are passionate and entrenched people on both sides.

Before we go further, let's take a second to define what the terms are. *Open source* means software whose source code is freely available and can be modified by other users. *Proprietary* software's source code is closely guarded, and users are not allowed to modify it. Open source is usually equated with free, but that's not always the case. A vendor might use open source code to create a software package and then charge users for that package. Of course, since it's open source, the user can likely modify it after purchasing it, depending on the licensing terms. Proprietary software almost always comes with a price tag.

 We've already mentioned some of the big players in the proprietary space—the big three are Amazon AWS, Microsoft Azure, and Google Cloud. Some of the most well-known open source providers are OpenStack, Apache CloudStack, and Eucalyptus.

In fact, the primary driver behind choosing one platform over the other is often cost. Open source might not be free, but it's generally far less expensive than its proprietary counterparts. Of course, that may come with trade-offs as well, such as reliability and available support.

Other than cost, what might sway you toward one solution versus the other? Here's a short list of benefits to using an open source cloud solution:

No Vendor Lock-in With open source platforms, you have more flexibility to move from one vendor or cloud package to another. Since proprietary software is owned by that software company, it's not easily transported to another vendor.

Greater Flexibility in Development If a feature doesn't exist, a programmer can create it. Even simple modifications such as changing styles can be accomplished by someone on the development team or a paid contractor.

Faster Updates Because you're not waiting on a big company to provide software updates or add features, any needed changes to support business needs can be done relatively quickly.

By no means is this an exhaustive list. Generally speaking, though, open source has two major advantages over proprietary cloud offerings—lower cost and greater flexibility. Proprietary clouds have advantages as well, including the following:

Support from a Big Company Some clients like to know that their technology solution has the backing of a major corporation such as Amazon, Microsoft, or Google. It's not likely that those companies are going to fail any time soon, so there's a certain level of security by going with one of them.

More Features   Proprietary cloud companies have large staffs of programmers cranking out features. The list of features may be way more than you'll ever need, but at least you know they are available if and when your business needs them.

Clear SLAs   Big CSPs can practically guarantee certain levels of performance through a service level agreement (SLA). We'll get into what an SLA is in the "Request for Information" section later in this chapter.

Again, this isn't a complete list of benefits, but it gives you an idea what proprietary clouds provide. If open source clouds focus on lower costs and flexibility, proprietary ones tout their features and stability. Neither is inherently better or worse—choose what makes the most sense for your company and business needs. Regardless of the type of cloud you choose, you can likely find an MSP that will help you with management if needed.

 Real World Scenario

Choosing the Right Cloud Solution

For large companies that have invested massive amounts of money into on-premises IT infrastructure, moving to public cloud services isn't an economically viable option. But even if moving their entire IT infrastructure to the cloud doesn't make sense, they can still make use of some cloud features by creating a private cloud.

Companies that create on-premises private clouds to augment their IT infrastructure mostly choose open source platforms such as OpenStack or Apache CloudStack versus a proprietary package. The biggest reason is lower cost. At the same time, these large companies have expansive IT staffs that can handle the cloud management and feature development required to customize the private cloud to their business needs.

Another option for companies is to not choose between open source and proprietary but rather to choose both for different needs. For example, a large company may decide to create an open source private cloud to provide benefits to its developers but use a public cloud for email and productivity software. Recall from Chapter 1, "Cloud Principles and Design," that this is considered a hybrid cloud solution.

Request for Information

The first official business process when looking for a cloud provider is a *request for information (RFI)*. The purpose of an RFI is to collect written information about a CSP's capabilities. RFIs are not unique to cloud services; they are standard documents for seeking information from any vendor on a major project.

When sending an RFI to potential vendors, it's important to be clear on the requests and specific about your objectives. There's no one "right" way to construct an RFI—if you've never done one before, an Internet search will give you a multitude of templates. No matter which template you use, follow these principles:

Be clear on the project objectives.   At this stage, project objectives can and should be high-level, but the potential CSP needs to know what you are trying to accomplish. If they're not designed to help you meet your goals, then everyone can quickly see that and move on.

Be clear on process, timelines, and next steps.   Ensure that you specify how you expect a response (e.g., email) and when you need a response. Give the potential vendors a reasonable amount of time to complete the RFI. Provide a single point of contact (SPOC) so the vendor can ask questions if needed. Finally, let the vendor know when they can expect a response or follow-up.

Ask for information in a standard format.   Provide a template that the vendor can fill out, perhaps in Excel or Word. This makes it easy for the vendor and also makes it easy for you to compare differences between potential providers.

Keep the request high-level.   Remember that at this stage, you are gathering general information about a vendor's capabilities. There will be time to get into specific details in later steps.

Make it as easy as possible for the vendor to complete.   You might be sending RFIs to a handful or even a dozen potential vendors, but in the end you are probably going to choose only one. Vendors don't get paid to fill out RFIs, but of course they need to spend resources to complete them. This isn't the time to ask for a treatise but to gather general information.

Consider the RFI as the first step in a multistep vetting process. After evaluating responses from the RFI, you can narrow down the list of potential vendors. Then, move on to the next step, which will be a request for quotation (RFQ) or request for proposal (RFP). Whereas you can cast a broad net with an RFI, an RFQ or RFP is usually sent to only a few finalists, generally no more than three to five.

Request for Quotation

If after the RFI you want to solicit a quote for a specific set of services, then you should issue a *request for quotation (RFQ)*. In an RFQ, you provide a breakdown of the services or products you need and a project timeframe and ask for a price quote. Some companies call this a request for tender (RFT), which is basically the same thing.

For example, let's say your company knows that it wants to buy IaaS and needs eight Windows Server 2019 VMs with four virtual CPUs (vCPUs) and 16GB RAM each. You also need 200TB of online storage and 500TB of archive storage. That's a specific ask, and the solution is standardized and readily available off the shelf.

When creating an RFQ, follow the same general principles as for the RFI. You can be a little more detailed in the request, but follow a standard format and be clear about the goals, process, timelines, expectations, and next steps. In most cases, the winner of the RFQ stage wins the business.

Request for Proposal

The more common follow-up to an RFI is a *request for proposal (RFP)*. RFPs differ from RFQs in that an RFP asks for solutions to a broad project or nonstandard problem rather than a quote for a specific solution. This is the formal request that gets into the nitty-gritty details of the proposed solution and tries to tease apart the benefits of choosing one vendor over another.

Before sending out RFPs, align internally on what the success criteria and scoring method will be. Outline what the top priorities are, and develop a methodology to fairly assess each proposal. If you don't, you may be dealing with a bunch of opinions and no definitive way to come to an answer. That will slow down the project and potentially cost money.

Here are some other features of an RFP:

- It's typical to ask for more depth on a vendor's background and capabilities as well as thinking from the vendor on how to solve the problem at hand.

- The requestor should be prepared to provide more information to the potential vendor, such as current structure, processes, and business needs. Because of this, a confidentiality or nondisclosure agreement may be required.

- Pricing and implementation timelines are included.

- This is probably the first time you will see a proposed statement of work and service level agreement. We'll cover each of them in the following two sections.

Based on this description, you can understand that an RFP takes a lot longer to complete than either an RFI or an RFQ does, because the vendor needs to put a lot more effort into it. Be sure to build in completion time, chances for both sides to ask follow-up questions, and internal review and alignment to your project timeline. An RFP process may require multiple rounds of negotiations. It's expected that the winner of the RFP process wins the business. Table 4.4 summarizes the characteristics of an RFI, RFQ, and RFP.

TABLE 4.4   Comparing an RFI, RFQ, and RFP

	RFI	RFQ	RFP
Purpose	Information gathering	Pricing request for a specific solution	In-depth project proposal
Example	Doing research on potential vendors	500 TB of storage space needed	Looking for cloud solutions to a broad business challenge
Number of vendors	Many	No more than three to five	No more than three to five
Next step	RFQ or RFP	Winner gets the contract	Finalize statement of work with the winner

Statement of Work

The *statement of work (SOW)* provided by a potential vendor is a critically important document because it outlines the specific work to be provided by the vendor. The SOW should be very detailed so as to avoid any ambiguity when the project starts. Depending on how you've set up your RFP process, the SOW will be either part of the RFP or provided after you accept an RFP. Getting the SOW hammered out is basically the final step in selecting the vendor.

The language in the SOW is considered legally binding once both parties agree to and sign it. This is one of the reasons why it must be crystal clear and leave no room for ambiguity on the services to be provided. That way, when one party or the other thinks that the contract isn't being fulfilled, it's easy to see who is correct.

There isn't one standard format for the SOW; it really depends on the vendor. Regardless of the format, it should include all of the following:

- Project objectives, including business, technical, security, administration, and others
- Description and scope of services, including key deliverables and timelines
- Key performance indicators (KPIs)
- Roles and responsibilities of both the vendor and the client
- Standards, compliance, and testing, if needed
- Terms and conditions, such as how long the SOW will be valid for
- Payment and/or billing terms
- Points of contact for both parties

It's not uncommon for the SOW to be 50 pages or longer. After all, it needs to provide specifics on what's expected so there are no surprises for either party.

Service Level Agreement

The SOW defines the scope of services that will be provided, and the *service level agreement (SLA)* defines metrics for measuring success. Both are critically important to have in the final contract. The SLA may be part of the SOW, or it might be a separate document. Either way, they're interdependent.

As an example, recall the concept of high availability (such as "four nines") we covered in Chapter 1. The SOW would define that the provider is responsible for high availability. The specific standard ("four nines") would be part of the SLA. Another common example is in software development, where SLAs specify how long a vendor has to implement change requests.

A good SLA will have the following elements:

- Required performance standards for services provided
- Reporting mechanisms for monitoring performance, including frequency of reporting
- Recompense or remediation plans if performance levels are not maintained
- Review and change processes to alter SLA terms
- Termination guidelines if performance consistently falls below expected standards

It's crucial to negotiate the terms of an SLA to ensure they meet your business needs before agreeing to them. Failure to do so can result in not getting the services your business needs and having no recourse to do anything about it.

Performing Evaluations

Talking to potential vendors and going through the RFI and RFP processes can uncover a lot of information. Ultimately, though, the real question is, can the vendor actually *do* what you need them to do? This is where *evaluations* come into play. In an evaluation, the potential vendor sets up a working environment, and users get a chance to test it. In this section, we'll explore three types of evaluations—proof of concept, proof of value, and pilot.

When to Run an Evaluation

The timing of when you might run an evaluation depends on your internal business processes and the scope of the project. There are basically three options.

- Run evaluations for each company that you have an RFP on. This usually takes the longest and is the most intensive. Some vendors might not be open to this unless you tentatively agree to move forward with them.

- Choose a lead vendor and then run evaluations, and sign the contract only if they are successful. This is the most plausible option.

- Don't run evaluations at all. This isn't recommended. You should require evidence that the proposed solution will work the way you expect it to.

Proof of Concept

A *proof of concept (PoC)* is a small project that demonstrates the feasibility of a solution or part of a solution. Again, the idea is to show that the vendor's technology can do what they say it will do and that it will meet your business needs. A PoC is generally short in duration, perhaps between one week and one month, and implemented in a nonproduction environment so as not to disrupt day-to-day operations.

   The production environment is the setting where hardware and applications are put into use for end users.

A good PoC will follow this process:

1. **Define success criteria.** The *success criteria* determine if a project succeeds or fails and should include business and technical success metrics.

2. **Create the PoC solution.** As noted already, it's best to do this in a test environment so as not to disrupt the business. Also, be sure to focus the solution on the specific task it's trying to achieve, and avoid scope creep.

3. **Evaluate the PoC versus the success criteria.** Have a small number of users (generally more knowledgeable or technical ones) use the solution, evaluate it, and provide feedback.

4. **Make a pass/fail decision.** Did the PoC work? If so, it might be time to move to a pilot or start scaling it for production. If not, it might be time for a different PoC test.

A successful PoC should not be immediately moved into a production environment. It likely needs to be tested further, optimized, and scaled before it's ready for a broad rollout.

We can't emphasize enough the importance of keeping the PoC focused on the right scope and aligning on the success criteria before starting the test. If a PoC doesn't meet success criteria, that is not a failed PoC—it's much better to fail in a test than to seriously damage the business! Having a poorly executed PoC or ambiguously defined success criteria is a much bigger problem, because it can lead to the approval of a project that shouldn't be deployed.

A PoC is usually fairly quick—about one to four weeks to complete. Because of the speed and relatively straightforward evaluation method, many companies are choosing PoCs instead of running a long and resource-intensive RFP process.

Proof of Value

Many people will use the terms *proof of concept* and *proof of value* interchangeably. While they can be similar in many ways, a *proof of value (PoV)* study includes understanding value realization from the proposed project. In other words, a PoC tells you if the technology works, whereas a PoV tells you whether it will save (or make) you the money that you think it will. It's all about the Benjamins. Otherwise, it's run just like a PoC.

Most of the time, a company will run either a PoC or a PoV. If the technology is new to the world or being adapted for your organization, then a PoC might make the most sense. If the technology is relatively standard and coming from a known vendor, you can be pretty certain that it works. In that case, you might want to run a PoV to make sure you're getting the savings you expect.

Pilot

A *pilot* project is a small-scale initial rollout of a solution into the production environment. The intent of a pilot is to test the solution among a smallish number of users to understand if it works on existing production hardware and apps.

Pilots are useful because you get additional feedback from a small group of users, and you can roll the project back or turn it off if there are problems, with little disruption to current business. During the pilot phase, additional technical support is often available to react to any problems. Often this is referred to as *hypercare*. If a pilot is successful, the project can be scaled to full production. Table 4.5 outlines some key differences between the PoC/PoV, the pilot, and the production environments.

TABLE 4.5   Comparing PoC/PoV, pilot, and production environments

	PoC/PoV	Pilot	Production
Goal	Prove that solution works or adds value, in a test environment	Prove that solution works in production with low risk	Enable the business to run
Number of users	Small (<10)	Less of 100 or 10 percent of future users	All users
User's role	Testing and feedback	Perform job tasks and provide feedback	Perform job tasks
Support system	Informal: development team	Formal hypercare: development team and/or help desk	Formal: help desk
Business impact of issues	Low	Medium	High

When Failure Is a Success

As contrary as it might seem, an evaluation doesn't need to be successfully completed for you to consider it a success. You might read that previous sentence and wonder if we've gone crazy, but we haven't.

The primary goal of a pilot is to learn if something works, in a noncritical environment. If the pilot or PoC/PoV fails but you learn from it and can either fix the problem to try again or walk away from the solution without costing the company significant money or time, that's success—even if the evaluation "failed."

Negotiating Contracts and Billing

The final step in the CSP selection process is to sign the contract. While doing so might seem simple enough after all of the technical and business evaluation that your company has done, there's more to signing a contract than meets the eye. It's not hyperbole to say that the contract is the most important part and that getting it wrong can cost an organization a significant amount of money or worse. Provisions in a contract could result in legal battles or the company not being able to retrieve its data.

So, after all of the work that's been done to evaluate and choose a CSP, make sure to spend ample time reviewing the contract as well. Unless you're trained in contract law, this is a great time to partner with lawyers or purchasing professionals to ensure that everything checks out.

We're not going to spend a lot of time talking about *how* to negotiate a contract. There are plenty of books on negotiation in the marketplace, and besides, that's not our area of expertise. Instead, we'll focus on elements you need to ensure are in place as well as the terms of those elements. After that, we'll look at some standards for billing.

Contracts

Every CSP will have a slightly different contract format, but each contract should have similar elements. We've said it before, but it's important to emphasize again that ambiguity in contracts is a bad thing. If something isn't crystal clear to you and the legal team, get that part rewritten. Also make sure that the terms are what you expect. For example, if you need a certain recovery time as part of an SLA, it needs to be clearly stated.

 The *contract* is a written document that is legally binding, specifying the rights and duties of the parties to the agreement.

All contracts should have sections for the following:

- Terms of service
- Privacy and security policy
- Acceptable use policy (AUP)
- Service level agreement
- Egress terms

We'll look at each of these in the following sections.

Terms of Service

The terms of service should contain all elements of the SOW, if you received one during the RFP process. If you didn't receive one, then those terms absolutely must be included now. This section will specify the responsibilities of the CSP, as well as client responsibilities. The following are areas that can be overlooked but should be understood:

- Where the data is physically located. Some countries have regulations on where data is or is not permitted to be stored.
- Intellectual property (IP) rights. Some CSPs may have contracts that make it sound like the client can use the service but does not retain IP rights to content created within it. If you create it, you should own it.

- Client control and visibility to subcontracting.

- Parameters for when and how the CSP can change services.

- Rights of the CSP to terminate services for either nonpayment or violation of an AUP.

- Liability limitations for both the client and the CSP. The CSP will likely try to severely limit its liability for either poor service or data loss.

- Jurisdiction and/or governing law. Legal terms differ from country to country or even within states, provinces, or regions. Understand where the legal jurisdiction is and if that comes with any potential consequences.

Privacy and Security Policy

Data is nearly every company's most precious resource today, and ensuring that it's secure and does not get compromised is a monumental task.

Privacy and security are two different things, but they're related. Security means that the data is not accessible to those who should not access it. This includes hackers of course, but also employees, contractors, and CSP employees or other vendor partners. Privacy means that data for individuals will remain hidden. If your company collects data that can be used to identify individual people, known as *personally identifiable information* (PII), you and the CSP have legal obligations to keep it private. The contract should state what those obligations are. Here are a few related areas to check:

- If the CSP is compliant with well-known privacy and security standards.

- Your ability to perform security audits of the CSP and its operations.

- How data is maintained for legal and/or regulatory purposes. This is especially important if your business has certain governmental regulation standards it needs to meet.

Acceptable Use Policy

There may be activities prohibited by the use of the CSP. For example, some CSPs may ban the creation or storage of material that is considered hate speech. Others might prohibit the use of their services to create spam messages. Prohibited activities will be specified in an AUP. Violation of these terms can result in termination of the contract and possible legal action.

Service Level Agreement

We introduced SLAs earlier when we talked about the SOW. As a reminder, the SLA is the document that specifies levels of performance expected. If you need three-nines uptime for a service, the SLA needs to specify that.

Some CSPs might try to get a bit tricky with SLA wording. For example, an SLA might say something like "target service levels," or "services are designed to be available." You don't want targets; you want guarantees. And if those standards are not met, the recompense needs to be specified. CSPs may offer additional services or a longer service period as recompense. If the service isn't working well, though, it's hard to see how getting more of that service is a good thing.

Egress Terms

Not all relationships are destined to last forever. This is true for people as well as the cloud. Perhaps the most important part of the contract is, how will the company get its data back if the contract ends? Again, data is an immensely valuable asset—having it all disappear because of a bad breakup with a CSP could be catastrophic. Here are some egress terms to negotiate:

- How to end the contract.

- If there are early termination fees.

- How data will be delivered to the client in the event of a contract termination. (Getting the data back is important. Getting it back in a usable format is essential.)

- A grace period to extend service while the client shops for a replacement.

- After the contract is terminated, the amount of time data is held for legal purposes.

Failure to negotiate how and when you will get your data back can result in vendor lock-in, which is a situation where it's basically impossible to get out of a contract. Clearly this is something to avoid!

 Real World Scenario

Real Life Contracting Mistakes

Nobody's perfect. If you have not negotiated cloud services before, it's entirely possible that something can slip through the cracks. To help eliminate any potential problems, be sure to have someone on your team review the terms as well—preferably a lawyer! Here are some of the most common mistakes that happen when negotiating cloud contracts:

- Not shopping around for better terms.

- Paying for all cloud services up front.

- Not checking for hidden charges.

- Signing a long-term contract with the wrong SLAs.

- Lack of penalties for noncompliance.

- Not negotiating different SLAs for different services or parts of the business.

- Buying services that the company doesn't yet need. (Needing it "soon" isn't a good excuse. Don't buy it until you need it.)

- Failing to negotiate future contract terms in advance. For example, if you plan on this being a long-term deal, negotiate renewal terms at the time of the initial contract to avoid sticker shock later.

Billing

Similar to contract terms, billing terms will vary by CSP. In general, there are two types of billing. The client can be invoiced, meaning a bill is sent electronically or via mail, or costs can be charged automatically (sometimes called self-serve). Think of this much like paying bills in your private life. Some bills might be just taken out of your checking account automatically every month, like rent or a mortgage, whereas for others you get a bill for and then need to pay it. Costs are either assessed on a monthly basis or when a certain usage threshold is reached.

For the CompTIA Cloud Essentials+ exam, you will be expected to understand the following:

- Contracts

- Billing

- Request for information (RFP and RFQ are not specifically listed in the exam objectives, but it's likely that they will appear in the exam itself)

- Statement of work (SOW)

- Service level agreement (SLA)

- Evaluations (pilot, proof of value, proof of concept, success criteria)

- Open-source vs. proprietary

Choosing a Migration Approach

After you've signed on with a cloud provider, the final step is to move the organization's data, services, applications, and workloads to the cloud. This process is called *migration*. A migration might involve moving everything to one cloud, transferring components to different clouds, or keeping some elements in an on-premises environment. Every migration will be a little different.

In this section, we are going to start by examining some general principles for a successful migration, including risks to watch out for. Then we'll talk about four different migration strategies: lift and shift, rip and replace, hybrid, and phased.

Migration Principles

If a company is looking forward to saving money by using the cloud, few things can be as disheartening as a failed migration. There are lots of things that can go wrong, even for small companies with relatively straightforward needs. Larger companies with complex systems and dependencies have even bigger risks.

Most problems can be taken care of by proper migration planning before a single bit of data is transferred. Going with an experienced CSP or MSP can also help out quite a bit. Nothing can guarantee a flawless migration, but here's a list of steps you can undertake to help ensure that the migration goes off without a hitch:

1. Catalog the data, applications, processes, or workloads that will be migrated. Classify them by size and complexity.

2. Prioritize the order in which items will be migrated.

3. Define how much of the migration will be handled by the CSP or MSP, and how much will be handled by internal staff. Processes and roles need to be clear to everyone.

4. Assign the right personnel to manage the migration.

5. Create the plan for the migration road map and schedule.

6. Establish KPIs for the migration plan and schedule.

7. Develop a security plan for pre- and post-migration.

8. Communicate the migration plan to key stakeholders.

9. Schedule check-ins (and perform them!) with the migration execution team.

10. Test the migration and fix issues as needed.

Before you start with the migration principles, it's assumed that you've already found a CSP that meets your needs; determined if you need a single cloud or multicloud environment; decided if the cloud will be public, private, or something else; and aligned on which items will be moved to the cloud. Also, not all of the steps listed here may be necessary for your situation. Obviously, tailor it as needed.

While following the right steps, be on the lookout for the following risks during and after the migration:

Complexity Creep   If your company has a lot of different systems or is moving to a multi-cloud or hybrid environment, things can get complex. Some installations can get too complex to properly manage. Make sure that the cloud structure is appropriate to meet business needs.

Application Issues   There are two things to watch out for regarding applications. The first is that some apps are better designed to run locally than they are in the cloud. For example, apps that suffer from latency, necessitate high security, or require transfers of large amounts of data could have issues being hosted in the cloud.

The second issue is of dependencies. Some applications are dependent upon another—that is, they require another app to operate properly. Finding this out after one (but not the other) has been migrated is too late.

Security Risks   Security should always be top of mind when it comes to a company's data and infrastructure. Work carefully with the CSP, MSP, or internal security experts to ensure that data security and privacy are fully accounted for. Run security testing immediately after the migration, and schedule periodic security audits after the migration is complete.

Now let's start looking at the specific methods that can be used to migrate data to the cloud.

Two terms that are not listed in the CompTIA Cloud Essentials+ exam objectives but are in the acronyms list are *virtual to virtual (V2V)* and *virtual to physical (V2P)*.

V2V refers to migrating apps or data from one virtual machine (VM) to another. For example, moving between instances within a cloud provider will be V2V.

V2P refers to migrating apps or data from a VM to a physical device, such as a hard drive, tape drive, or optical disc. With all of the talk about moving *to* the cloud, you might wonder why people use V2P. The most common use is for moving data to a physical medium for offline or archived data storage. V2P can also be used to transform a VM into a physical one.

Lift and Shift

In *lift and shift*, data and applications are moved to the cloud as is. They are literally picked up from one location, usually on-premises, and set down in another. You may also hear this called *rehosting*, because the app or data is now on a new host. The following are the benefits of a lift and shift:

- It's quick and easy.
- It requires few or no changes to existing apps.
- It can immediately save cost on hardware infrastructure.

You can also lift and shift from one cloud to another. Say for example that you have a cloud contract that is expiring soon, and you are moving to a new provider. Lifting and shifting is fast and generally has low complexity, so it's probably the right way to go.

The downside to a lift and shift is that applications moved to the cloud might not have been designed for cloud operation and therefore can't take full advantage of cloud features. Because of this, apps might not perform as well as they could, or the company might not realize the savings that it had hoped for.

Some companies will choose to lift and shift with an eye to upgrading the applications later. One such way is called *re-platforming*. In re-platforming, some minor changes are made to the app as it's moved to the cloud in order to help performance. For example, perhaps an app gets moved and placed behind a load balancer to spread out the work among multiple VMs. This is relatively low risk but can provide a performance boost.

A more complex transition is called *refactoring*. This means the app is migrated using lift and shift, and then it's re-programmed to take advantage of cloud features. This carries a little more risk than a basic lift and shift or a re-platforming, but it can pay big dividends in the long run. Refactoring is also called *rearchitecting*.

A common analogy in the cloud community is that a lift and shift is a lot like moving a houseplant from one area of the house to another. It could thrive better in its new environment, but not much changed. Refactoring would be more like moving the plant but also putting it into a bigger pot and giving it fertilizer.

Lift and shift is a good choice for disaster recovery and is required for commercial applications that can't be refactored. Refactoring is a good choice for resource-intensive or old monolithic apps.

Rip and Replace

Rip and replace means that the app will be completely redesigned from scratch, during migration, using only cloud-native components. This means that the app can take full advantage of cloud features, which will optimize the cost of using the cloud. Whereas a lift and shift is fast, easy, and usually cheap, a rip and replace has more complexity and risk, but also has higher cost savings.

A rip and replace is best used when you're migrating an old app or an app that is suffering from performance issues, such as slow speed or frequent crashes. As an aside, rip and replace probably isn't the best term to use for this type of migration. No self-respecting IT professional would rip out a necessary app or process before having a replacement. Technically speaking, it should be called *replace then rip*, because that's the order of operations. Perhaps that term just isn't as marketing-friendly.

Hybrid and Phased Migrations

If you're comfortable with lift and shift and rip and replace, then understanding hybrid and phased migrations should be pretty easy.

A *hybrid migration*, as the term implies, is a combination of the lift-and-shift and rip-and-replace approaches. It's generally defined in one of two ways. First, it can be a situation where you do some of each method. For example, let's say you have commercial software packages and a custom app that's old and needs to be upgraded. You will lift and shift the commercial software, and you can rip and replace the custom app. Second, it can refer to a situation where you migrate some of your infrastructure but not all of it. For example, perhaps you have a database that the team decides to keep on-premises. That won't get migrated, but user data and other apps will. That's a hybrid migration.

A *phased migration* takes place in stages. Really, nearly every cloud migration is phased in some way. It's uncommon to migrate everything at the same time. For example, user data is often migrated before applications are. Generally speaking, though, if the migration will be completed in a short time frame, say, a few weeks or a month, it probably won't be referred to as phased. If the migration will take a long time, such as if you were to migrate data now and apps next fiscal year, that would definitely be phased. Figure 4.2 shows an example of different potential phases of cloud migration.

FIGURE 4.2   Phased cloud migration

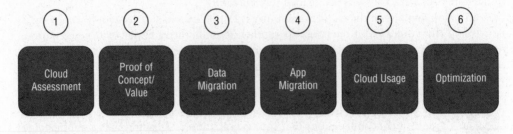

   The CompTIA Cloud Essentials+ exam will test you on the following migration approaches:

- Rip and replace

- Lift and shift

- Hybrid

- Phased

Summary

In this chapter, you learned about the financial aspects of engaging a cloud provider, business aspects of vendor relations, and cloud migration approaches.

The chapter started with descriptions of various business and financial terms you might hear when working with CSPs. These included capital and operating expenditures, variable and fixed costs, bring your own license (BYOL) and subscription licensing models, human capital, and professional services.

Next, we discussed finding and evaluating potential cloud vendors. The first thing to understand is if you need an open source or proprietary cloud platform. Then, you can send out a request for information (RFI), which usually leads to either a request for quotation (RFQ) or a request for proposal (RFP). The RFP also usually includes the statement of work (SOW) and performance metrics in the service level agreement (SLA). Suppliers can also be evaluated by running projects such as a proof of concept (PoC), proof of value (PoV), or pilot. Be sure to specify success criteria for all evaluations. Once your evaluation is complete, you can move on to negotiating and signing the contract and clarifying the billing process.

Finally, we looked at cloud migration approaches. The two discrete approaches are lift and shift and rip and replace. A combination of the two is a hybrid approach. Migrations aren't usually completed in one step; such migrations are said to be phased migrations.

Exam Essentials

Know the difference between capital expenditures and operating expenditures.   A capital expenditure is a one-time expense generally used to acquire a fixed asset. For tax purposes, capital expenditures are depreciated over time. Operating expenditures are used to support the ongoing costs of conducting day-to-day business, such as salaries, utilities, office supplies, and research and development. Operating expenditures are accounted for in the current tax year.

Understand the difference between a variable cost and a fixed cost.   Variable costs change from month to month or year to year. A fixed cost does not change.

Understand the BYOL licensing model.   The BYOL model gives users flexibility to use existing licenses they have already paid for. BYOL terms let the license be redeployed from one device or user to another. This gives greater flexibility, lower costs, and better license management.

Understand the subscription licensing model.   Under the subscription licensing model, users essentially pay to lease the rights to use the software for a specified period of time, generally one year. This is in contrast to a perpetual license, which grants use for the lifetime of the app.

Summarize the financial aspects of contracts and billing.   The contract is the legally binding document that outlines the roles and responsibilities of the cloud provider and the client. It should contain terms of service, privacy and security policies, acceptable use policy, a service level agreement, and egress terms.

Billing will happen either automatically or when a certain level of usage is attained.

Know how a request for information is used.   When seeking cloud vendors, an RFI is a document designed to collect written information about a CSP's abilities. It's the first formal request for information and is usually followed by an RFP or an RFQ

Understand what human capital is and the difference between training and professional development.   Human capital is the knowledge, skills, and experience possessed by the IT staff. Training is a short-term experience designed to teach skills specifically needed to perform a task. Professional development is a longer-term approach focused on employee growth.

Know the business aspects of the four professional services.   The four professional services you should be familiar with are TTM, skill availability, support, and managed services.

Know what an SOW is.   An SOW is a document provided by a CSP that outlines specific work to be performed by them.

Understand what an SLA is.   An SLA is usually associated with the SOW. It provides the metrics for measuring the success of the SOW.

Understand how a pilot is used.   A pilot is a small-scale initial rollout of a project into the production environment. The goal is to test the solution among a small number of users to see whether it works in the production environment.

Know the differences between a PoC and a PoV.   Both a PoC and a PoV are deployed in test environments with a small number of test users. A PoC is designed to prove that a technology works. A PoV should tell you whether the test will deliver the value (such as cost savings or extra sales) that you expect it to.

Understand the difference between open source and proprietary clouds.   Open source means that the software is usually free, or cheaper, and the code can be modified. Proprietary software has source code that cannot be modified except by the company that produced it. Open source clouds are generally less expensive, have less risk of vendor lock-in, provide greater flexibility in development, and are faster to update and upgrade. Proprietary clouds offer the backing and support of a big company, more features, and clear SLAs.

Know what a rip-and-replace migration is.   In rip and replace, the old software is completely rebuilt as it's moved to the cloud. It can take longer and initially be more expensive, but it allows older apps to take full advantage of cloud features.

Know what a lift-and-shift migration is.   In a lift-and-shift migration, apps and data are simply moved from one location, such as on-premises, to the cloud. They are comparatively fast and cheap. Older software that is not optimized for the cloud might not realize all of the efficiencies of the cloud migration, however.

Understand what hybrid and phased migrations are.   A hybrid migration is one that combines rip and replace or lift and shift, or one where some services stay on-premises where others move to the cloud. A phased migration is one that takes place in steps over time, such as moving data in the first year and applications in the second year.

Written Lab

Fill in the blanks for the questions provided in the written lab. You can find the answers to the written labs in Appendix A.

1. A(n) _____ expenditure will, for tax purposes, be depreciated over the lifespan of the asset.

2. A _____ license allows holders to move software from an on-premises device to the cloud.

3. When referring to employees, _____ is the long-term educational process focused on long-term career goals.

4. How fast an idea goes from the idea stage to being ready to sell is called what?

5. Hiring out cloud management and performance testing is an example of what?

6. What is the name of the document that specifies metrics used to determine whether the CSP is delivering what they are supposed to?

7. After approving an RFI, you want a company to provide a more detailed description of how they would solve your problem. What should you request?

8. What type of cloud evaluation is performed in a production environment?

9. In a cloud contract, which section specifies how a company can get its data back if the agreement ends?

10. Which type of migration allows all applications to fully benefit from the cloud?

Review Questions

The answers to the chapter review questions can be found in Appendix B.

1. For corporate tax purposes, which of the following types of expenditures would be depreciated over several years? (Choose two.)

   A. Employee salaries

   B. A building expansion

   C. Property tax

   D. Four servers

2. Sue, an IT employee, tells her manager that she wants to create a five-year plan to fulfill some career goals. What type of plan does Sue need?

   A. Training

   B. Managed services

   C. Support

   D. Professional development

3. Your company has decided to move to the cloud. However, a research and development database has high security needs and will be kept on-premises. What type of migration is best for this situation?

   A. Rip and replace

   B. Lift and shift

   C. Hybrid

   D. Phased

4. You have just approved an RFP from a cloud vendor. Which of the following could be logical next steps to move to cloud services? (Choose two.)

   A. RFI

   B. Pilot

   C. PoC

   D. RFQ

   E. Lift and shift

5. Your company is migrating to the cloud. Users need both commercial and proprietary software packages, and both types will be migrated. The migration needs to happen quickly. Which types of migration are most suited for this situation? (Choose two.)

   A. Rip and replace

   B. Lift and shift

   C. Hybrid

   D. Phased

6. The IT department is going to run a small cloud evaluation in the production environment to see if there are any app compatibility issues. Which type of evaluation will they be running?

   A. Pilot

   B. PoC

   C. PoV

   D. Managed service

7. Your organization is considering moving from an on-premises data center to the cloud. A finance manager asks about the benefits of using a pay-as-you-go model for services. Which of the following is a benefit of pay-as-you-go?

   A. It converts an operating expenditure into a fixed expenditure.

   B. It converts an operating expenditure into a capital expenditure.

   C. It converts a capital expenditure into an operating expenditure.

   D. It converts a capital expenditure into a fixed expenditure.

8. Your company is debating potential cloud solutions. Which of the following are benefits of going with a proprietary cloud platform? (Choose two.)

   A. Large company support

   B. Enhanced features

   C. Lower cost

   D. Flexible development

9. After migrating to the cloud, your company hires external technical expertise to perform cloud optimizations and troubleshooting. What is this an example of?

   A. Professional development

   B. Managed services

   C. Human capital

   D. SLA

10. Your company is moving all IT infrastructure to the cloud. The company has a five-year database license. Which of the following can save the company money on migrating the database to the cloud?

    A. BYOL

    B. Subscription

    C. Pilot

    D. PoV

11. A CSP has just completed an RFP, and you have accepted it. Which of the following is the most appropriate next step?

    A. Sign the contract

    B. Request an RFQ

    C. Agree to an SOW

    D. Agree to an SLA

12. You are acquiring new cloud-based software for your company. The developer will only sell you the software on a subscription basis. Which of the following is NOT an advantage of subscription-based pricing?

    A. No upgrade costs for new features.

    B. Smaller up-front license costs.

    C. Users should have device flexibility.

    D. The company is required to pay for the software only once.

13. A manager in your company wants to ensure that the cloud solution you are proposing will help with TTM. What does the manager mean by this?

    A. How much delay there is in accessing cloud resources

    B. How long it takes to send data from one cloud location to another

    C. How long it takes to get from the idea stage to selling a product

    D. How many evaluations are needed before the cloud can be launched

14. You are looking for a new CSP. Your company wants to ensure that any intellectual property rights are clearly owned by the company and that the CSP has no stake in them. Where will this be specified?

    A. Contract

    B. Billing statement

    C. SOW

    D. SLA

15. Your company is evaluating payment options for a new CSP. Which of the following could be an advantage of going with subscription-based pricing for the cloud as opposed to pay-as-you-go? (Choose two.)

    A. It allows you to cancel the contract at any time with no penalty.

    B. It allows you to count the costs as operating expenditures.

    C. It might be cheaper with discounts.

    D. It provides for easy planning with fixed costs versus variable costs.

16. You have received several RFIs from potential cloud vendors. Now, you want to know how much it will cost for a standard set of four VMs. What should you ask for next?

    A. RFQ

    B. RFP

    C. PoC

    D. PoV

17. You are seeking to pilot a new cloud-based service and have several CSPs to choose from. Which of the following should NOT be selection criteria for choosing which company to pilot with?

    A. Usability in the cloud environment

    B. Successful completion of the pilot

    C. Data security in the cloud environment

    D. Latency in the cloud environment

18. You are creating an RFI to seek out potential CSPs. Which of the following is NOT recommended to include in the RFI?

   A. Project objectives

   B. Timeline for response

   C. SOW

   D. Template for the CSP to respond with

19. Your company has decided to move its extensive on-premises IT infrastructure to the cloud. Because of the cost involved, management decides to move some services this fiscal year and move the rest of the services next fiscal year. Which type of migration will you be performing?

   A. Rip and replace

   B. Lift and shift

   C. Hybrid

   D. Phased

20. You have moved to the cloud and are now seeking out professional services. Which of the following is NOT an example of cloud professional services?

   A. Running a PoC and establishing proper success criteria

   B. Using developers who can program in a language your team can't program in

   C. Contracting part-time technicians to perform data backups

   D. Developing and selling a service more quickly than you did before using the cloud

Chapter

5

Management and Technical Operations

THE FOLLOWING COMPTIA CLOUD ESSENTIALS+ EXAM CLO-002 OBJECTIVES ARE COVERED IN THIS CHAPTER:

✓ **3.1 Explain aspects of operating within the cloud.**

- Data management
  - Replication
  - Locality
  - Backup
- Availability
  - Zone
  - Geo-redundancy
- Disposable resources
- Monitoring and visibility
  - Alerts
  - Logging
- Optimization
  - Auto-scaling
  - Right-sizing

✓ **3.2 Explain DevOps in cloud environments.**

- Provisioning
  - Infrastructure as code
  - Templates
- Continuous integration/continuous delivery

- Testing in QA environments
  - Sandboxing
  - Load testing
  - Regression testing
- Configuration management
  - Orchestration
  - Automation
  - Upgrades and patching

✓ **3.3 Financial planning of cloud resources.**

- Storage
- Network
- Compute
- Chargebacks
  - Resource tagging
- Maintenance
- Instances
  - Reserved
  - Spot
- Licensing type
- Licensing quantity

Management tools of resources in the cloud will be familiar if you have used relatively updated tools for on-premises virtualization technologies. This can be attributed to the shift to web-based management tools most software vendors have embraced over the last decade. Software vendors generally are no longer requiring "thick" clients to be installed on desktops to manage their software. One of the most common virtualization platforms is VMware. vSphere is its management system. It used to come only as a client-based install; however, starting with version 5.0, it now comes as a web-based client. The most recent version of vSphere, as of the writing of this book, is 6.7 and does not officially support the "thick" client anymore.

Thick vs. Fat vs. Thin Clients

You will often hear references to a thick or a fat client. Generally speaking, these terms are interchangeable in that they are referring to a software package that must be installed on a local system to work. We will use *thick* client in this book because it pairs better with the term *thin* client (no software installation required). In general, though, they can be used interchangeably.

Most of the major cloud service providers (CSPs) offer management tools that fall into one of three categories:

- Management console (web)
- Command-line interface (CLI)
- Software development kits (SDKs)

The interesting and important thing to keep in mind when using any of these management options is that most management operations ultimately make an *application programming interface (API)* call to perform the work. When you use the web management console to start an instance, it is the web application that makes an API call to the backend to do the work. When you use the CLI in a script to automate a build process, it is the CLI application that makes the same API calls. When you use an SDK in an application you write, it is the SDK that is making an API call. The interesting piece is that this generally holds true for most management tools, both on-premises and in the cloud. It is this shift to everything being an API call that has allowed the shift from thick clients to thin clients.

We would be remiss if we didn't mention two other management tools that do not fit in with the previous descriptions and are still considered thick clients. However, this management really only applies when you are accessing resources in the IaaS cloud model. Those management tools are Remote Desktop Protocol (RDP) and Secure Shell (SSH). If you spin up a Windows instance, you will still manage that instance through RDP. If you spin up a Linux instance, you will still manage that instance through SSH. Figure 5.1 is an SSH connection to an EC2 instance running in AWS.

FIGURE 5.1   SSH connection to AWS

```
Amazon Linux 2 AMI

https://aws.amazon.com/amazon-linux-2/
12 package(s) needed for security, out of 20 available
Run "sudo yum update" to apply all updates.
[ec2-user@ip-172-31-70-185 ~]$
```

Exam Note

You will need to know about RDP and SSH. They are both management tools, and they are both secure by default.

Explain Aspects of Operating within the Cloud

Operating within the cloud introduces new concepts and terminology because of the scale that CSPs can operate in. This scale was available only to larger enterprises, but now individuals and smaller organizations can benefit from a CSP's global infrastructure.

Data Management

Data is going to be your most valuable asset in the cloud. You are going to need to protect it and manage risk around its loss. Data comes in many different forms, from structured data like databases to unstructured data like files and objects. No matter its form, the loss of data can be catastrophic to a business from both a financial perspective and a customer retention perspective. There are three mechanisms when it comes to data management in the cloud:

- Replication: Data availability
- Locality: Location or proximity
- Backup: Disaster recovery

Replication

When you spin up either a server or a database instance, it is usually located on only one host or data center. This means that if the host or zone (covered later in the next section,

"Availability") becomes unavailable, then your server or database will also be unavailable. *Replication* offers greater data availability than this default behavior. Data is replicated (copied) to another storage location. This offers data redundancy; if one storage location goes offline, the other location can pick up without the end user or application ever noticing.

The location will be the next topic for discussion. However, there is an important distinction between CSP-driven replication and user-driven replication. A CSP will automatically replicate data within its own data center, and you will have no control or say in this replication. The CSP does this replication to achieve its guaranteed service level agreement. There is no direct cost to you; the cost of this replication is built into the cost of the storage offering. You can also choose to replicate your data and resources to achieve greater data availability and improve the next topic, locality.

Replication does not guard or protect against data deletion or data corruption. If something goes wrong with your data, the issue will just be replicated to the destination. Replication is a disaster recovery option for loss of infrastructure, not data deletion.

There are two types of replication: synchronous and asynchronous.

Synchronous

Synchronous replication is the type that a CSP perform on your data by default to achieve its SLA. Data is written to multiple locations in real time. When you save a file or write a record to a database, the data is written to several locations at the same time and in real time.

Synchronous replication is limited by distance between the locations. It is impossible to perform synchronous replication from one side of the globe to another, no matter the bandwidth available. Synchronous replication is subject to network latency. The general rule of thumb is that synchronous replication is not possible if the network latency between the two locations is greater than 30 ms (milliseconds). This usually means that synchronous replication is limited to that within a data center or with a data center that is in close proximity geographically to the source data center. This becomes a limitation of synchronous replication. When data cannot be transmitted with lower latency than 30 ms, we need to shift to the other type of replication, asynchronous.

Asynchronous

Asynchronous is the type of replication that solves the distance problem of synchronous replication. However, it presents a drawback that has to be accepted: data is *not* replicated in real time. There is a recovery point objective (RPO) that is associated with asynchronous replication. We have discussed RPO in Chapter 1, "Cloud Principles and Design." RPO and RTO will likely be on the exam. We have been discussing replication, but RPO and RTO also impact our next subject: disaster recovery.

Exercise 5.1 will give some perspective on latency and travel time of data across the Internet. Distance on the Internet can have significant impact on data speed and user experience. This exercise will demonstrate in real time the latency that exists between your location and various locations within the Azure network.

EXERCISE 5.1

Demonstration of Latency

1. Visit http://www.azurespeed.com.

2. Select various regions around the globe.

3. Review both the Closest Datacenters and Latency Test results.

   These results are from your current location to the selected Microsoft Azure regions you selected. Figure 5.2 displays the results from my current location, which is in Ohio, US.

FIGURE 5.2 Latency to Azure network locations

Latency Test

Geography	Region	Location	Average Latency (ms)
Asia Pacific	East Asia	Hong Kong	223 ms
Japan	Japan East	Tokyo, Saitama	180 ms
India	Central India	Pune	241 ms
Australia	Australia Central	Canberra	219 ms
United States	East US	Virginia	91 ms
United States	Central US	Iowa	80 ms
United States	West Central US	Wyoming	91 ms
Europe	North Europe	Ireland	142 ms
United States	East US 2	Virginia	90 ms

Locality

The speed of the Internet is still limited by the speed of light. Even the fastest routers using the latest fiber-optic cabling cannot transmit bits faster than it takes light to travel the distance. Therefore, *locality* of data will impact the end-user experience and how fast data or services will load. Locality refers to the location where your data is in the CSP's infrastructure. If you are building an e-commerce site that sells soccer apparel, your users could be located all over the globe. In contrast, if your e-commerce site sells baseball apparel, then the majority of your users will be located in North America. This difference between the end users and the data for the e-commerce site is what can drive the need for data replication and locality of data or services to the end user.

Backup

Backups are just as important in the cloud as they are on-premises. Backups go a step further than replication. Replication will help recover in the case of hardware failure, but replication cannot help you recover from data loss or data corruption. If someone either maliciously or by accident deletes data, replication will replicate the deletions. If data becomes corrupt by an error in application code, replication will replicate that corruption. Therefore, there is going to come a time when you will need to recover to a point in time.

Here the RPO, which was discussed previously, comes into play. You will have to determine what an acceptable RPO is for your needs. Thankfully, the cloud now offers technology that hasn't been available to on-premises data centers or has been cost prohibitive in the past.

 Real World Scenario

GFS Backup Rotation

One of the most popular backup rotations used is called Grandfather Father Son (GFS). The GFS name comes from three levels of retention. The most common rotation used is the following:

- Daily backups are kept for 90 days (son).
- Weekly backups are kept for six months (father).
- Monthly backups are kept for one year (grandfather).

Typically for archival purposes and regulatory requirements, the monthly backup that is taken at the end of the year is moved to permanent storage or off-site.

CSPs and virtualization technologies offer *snapshots* as a form of backups. A snapshot will capture all the data on a drive at a point in time and freeze it. This snapshot can be used in any of the following ways:

- Rolling back or returning a VM to the state of the snapshot.
- Creating a new VM from the snapshot, an effective copy of the original server.
- Copying the snapshot to object storage to be used for recovery at a later date. This is analogous to the typical backup performed on-premises.

There is typically no charge for snapshots. However, there is a limit to the number of snapshots a cloud account can have. If you make a new VM from a snapshot, there is a cost associated with the additional VM resource. Finally, there will be object storage cost for the data stored. You can implement data life cycle policies that will create a GFS backup rotation or whatever scheme is required for your needs.

Availability

One of the largest benefits of using the cloud is availability. CSPs offer a scale that would be difficult and costly for anyone to implement on their own. This scale can offer greater availability of the resources you place in the cloud. CSPs have multiple *data centers* that are in close proximity to each other. CSPs group these data centers into regions. The larger CSPs have regions all over the globe. These are the main topics we will be discussing:

- Zones
- Regions
- Geo-redundancy

Zones

Many CSPs use slightly different naming conventions when it comes to their infrastructure. The two terms that come up the most are *zones* and availability zones (AZs). In general, a zone is equivalent to a data center or a group of data centers that function as a single unit. Each data center will have its own security and redundant systems.

Let's talk about what we mean when we use the term *redundant systems*. This is an important topic to understand because it leads to one of the biggest reasons to move to the cloud. CSPs have to plan and build robust redundant steps for every part of the infrastructure. Redundancy provides fault tolerance, which we will discuss later. For now, keep in mind that fault tolerant means that the system is able to keep working even after multiple component systems have failed.

 Real World Scenario

Planning for Catastrophe

I used to work for a company that built data centers to not only host their own infrastructure but also sell floor space. When we sold floor space, we had to offer SLA that took into account the possibility of a catastrophic event. The planning that goes into minimizing risk is astounding. We had power lines from three different service providers into the building. We had dual diesel generators, each one capable of handling 125 percent of the average load. Additionally, we had contracts from multiple diesel providers to supply diesel to the facility in the event of extended power loss. We were guaranteed a minimum delivery no matter the current supply. This was just the delivery of power to the facility. Inside the facility, we had multiple UPS systems from different vendors, so that if one had a fault, the others could take up the load. We had multiple Tier 1 ISPs that provided their own redundant fiber-optic connections. We had multiple microwave connections to the Internet in the event that all hard lines to the facility were cut. There were multiple cooling units on separate power lines. The cooling units were even serviced in a staggered schedule to minimize the risk of multiple units failing under load.

All of this planning went into designing a data center for a relatively small facility when compared to the larger CSPs. I am trying to give you perspective on the level of detail that the larger CSPs go through with their larger customer base. Could you provide this level of risk mitigation? Could your current hosting provider?

If you have resources deployed in your cloud account, then the CSP dictates where those resources land on its infrastructure. The CSP needs to have this control to provide its SLA. Even if you purchase dedicated services, their location is determined by the CSP. This serves two purposes. First, CSP can provide the maximum service level by spreading load where there is capacity. Second, the CSP can provide a higher level of security. Resources are not identifiable at the data center level; even the data center technicians do not know which host is running your resources.

A zone is a logical unit that you can think of as a data center or collection of data centers whose implementation details you do not need to worry about. The CSP handles this infrastructure and offers a guarantee of the availability of those services through its SLA.

Regions

Multiple zones are grouped together to form a *region*. For the larger CSPs these regions are located all over the globe, and they usually have names that closely resemble their location. For example, here is a list of the public regions offered in North America from AWS and Azure as of the writing of this book:

AWS	Azure
US East (N. Virginia)	East US (Virginia)
US East (Ohio)	East US 2 (Virginia)
US West (N. California)	West US (California)
US West (Oregon)	West US 2 (Washington)
Canada (Central)	Canada Central (Toronto)
	Central US (Iowa)
	North Central US (Illinois)
	South Central US (Texas)
	West Central US (Wyoming)
	Canada East (Quebec City)

It is interesting to note that Azure offers more regions than AWS even though AWS was the first CSP to market with a cloud offering. AWS released its object storage offering Simple Storage System (S3) in spring of 2006.

Regions are used as an extension of zones to offer greater data availability and even locality for your data. It is important to note, though, that unless you are using regions located adjacent to each other, i.e., US East (N. Virginia) and US East (Ohio), you will only be able to utilize asynchronous replication. The latency between two regions that are geographically separated is too great to offer synchronous replication.

In general, highly available service offerings and options will be self-contained to a region. Everything within a region can be made highly available due to the nature of the well-connected zone.

Geo-Redundancy

Regions offer cross-zone availability. *Geo-redundancy* is the next level up and offers cross-region availability. Services are replicated between regions to offer greater availability. Unfortunately, physics and the speed of light rear their ugly heads and place limits on how quickly cloud services are in sync.

Geo-redundancy is implemented by a content delivery network (CDN). A CDN typically compromises edge locations, which are specialized servers maintained by the CSP. CDNs will keep a copy of the content located around the globe and offer greater locality. These edge locations will cache a copy of content and serve it locally from their locations. When the content gets updated or after a predetermined time period, the edge location will make a callback to the source and retrieve up-to-date content. Figure 5.3 is a map provided by AWS to represent its CDN.

FIGURE 5.3   AWS CDN: CloudFront

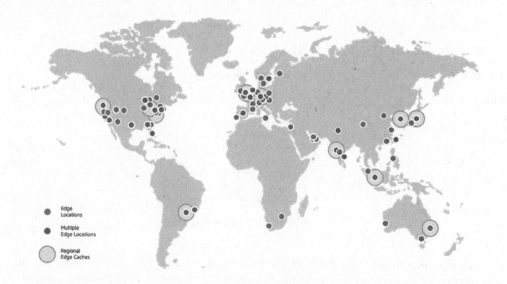

It is important to note that active data cannot be cached at the edge location. Think of a database entry; the entry must be unique and up to date. Otherwise, the data can be corrupted.

You have experienced this phenomenon whenever you have made an online order. Searching for items and looking at photos or reading text is typically quick and responsive (content is distributed across zones or regions). However, once you click Add Item To Cart, it takes a bit longer to update the cart. Even viewing the cart and making changes takes longer than browsing for items. The cart has to exist in a database, and only one database can be the master. So, any changes or additions must be written back to a single point. This is another reason why items in stock are not always accurate or items temporarily become out of stock. Stock quantities are typically distributed with the item data through regions and zones, but the actual quantity can exist in only one place.

CDNs and georedundant availability often use the term *eventually consistent*. This concept is important to understand in relation to the zone, regions, and geo-redundancy. Data within a zone can easily be kept consistent through synchronous replication. Data within a region or out to the geo-redundant points eventually will become consistent through asynchronous replication. For example, you are running an e-commerce site and using object storage for all the images. The primary database and source of the images lives on infrastructure in a Virginia zone. You are utilizing CDN and edges to replicate all of the images out to offer locality to your internal customers. You need to update an image of one of the products. So, you upload a new image to the object storage. The new image will synchronously replicate out everything that it needs in the Virginia zone. That makes the image updated in real time everywhere within the Virginia zone; i.e., it is immediately consistent. At the same time, asynchronous replication is copying the image out to the regions and edge locations that have an old copy. These remote locations will eventually get the updated image; size and distance will impact this time, thus the term eventually consistent.

Ultimately, geo-redundancy is a mechanism to offer greater availability as regions and zones do. It is just the next layer in the onion that is the cloud. It is a cool feature because you as a consumer can utilize this feature at a very cost-effective rate.

Exam Note

Zones, regions, and geo-redundancy are tools provided by CSPs to offer greater data availability. CDNs used to be out of the reach of most customers due to cost. CSPs are making these services more cost effective every day.

Disposable Resources

Going to the cloud offers agility and no up-front costs. No longer do you need to procure and rack and mount physical servers that will be stand-alone or part of a cluster providing virtual resources. Now everything can be virtual, just in the cloud. That is what we mean by *disposable resources*—virtual resources in the cloud that are not permanent. Compute, storage, and network resources usually can be created within minutes and can be destroyed in a similar time frame.

Servers being a disposable commodity has increased the use of the concept of *immutable infrastructure*. Immutable infrastructure is treating infrastructure resources as truly disposable. If a server needs to be updated or changed, don't update the production server. Update or make changes to a new server. Test it, and once it is validated, replace the production server with the updated server. There may come a time when, due to security reasons, a patch or a change needs to be made in production; it needs to be made on the live production server.

So, we don't want changes made on production servers. We want to spin up new servers and make changes to them instead. You are probably thinking, "I am going to spend all my time creating new servers and customizing them according to what I need. I need to install packages X, Y, Z, make changes to half a dozen configuration files, etc."

You would be correct, but that is what we don't want you to do. We want you to automate and procedurally set up the process for creating new servers. There are two methods for assisting with this task and a third way that is really just a combination of the first two.

- *Bootstrapping*
- *Golden image*
- Hybrid

Bootstrapping

Bootstrapping is taking an already tested and verified VM image and applying the post-deployment process after the initial start. Most modern OSs allow for software installations via scripts or the command line. All of the CSPs offer post-deployment execution options, i.e., commands. For example, you could deploy the CentOS 7 image to the cloud and use a post-deployment launch script of the following:

```
yum install epel-release -y
yum install nginx mariadb-server mariadb
```

This will effectively install Nginx and MariaDB on your instance automatically during its deployment. This will speed up deployment and makes the process procedural and repeatable. You could take it a step further and have the post-launch be an entire script that is stored in object storage. The servers you want to bootstrap could reference the script, and when you need to make changes, you can edit the script. Most of the CSPs offer an entire infrastructure as code deployments. We will be introducing that concept in our next section in this chapter.

If you haven't gathered it yet, the shortcoming of bootstrapping is the complexity of doing advanced deployments, e.g., editing configuration files or changing passwords. These are possible with bootstrapping but require more advanced scripting. Golden images are the next step in solving advanced deployment models.

Golden Image

A golden image is where you take an already tested and verified VM image and customize it to your needs and then deploy it. You can install any software needed for production. You make all configuration changes that are not machine specific, i.e., connecting to databases and setting up users and passwords. Once your VM is configured the way you want it, you create a new VM image from the server you just configured.

With your new VM image in hand, you can deploy new instances based on this new configured VM image. This solves the limitation of bootstrapping because you can make any change you want as long as it is not machine specific. You can't statically assign an IP address, for example.

Though this solves the limitation of bootstrapping, it adds a new limitation. You have to maintain this golden image. Every software update by you or a third party will require a new golden image. Maintaining these images will require a time commitment.

Hybrid: Utilizing Both

The hybrid is the cross between bootstrapping and a golden image. You perform any complex or advanced deployments through a golden image, but anything that is relatively easy to script you put in the post-deployment launch. Finding the right balance between the two and when to do more of one over the other will come with time and experience. The OS will play a role in how much of each you do. In Windows, for example, it is a little harder to do the bootstrapping, unless you are using the latest version and are familiar with PowerShell.

Monitoring and Visibility

We have now deployed some resources in the cloud, and we have started deploying in an automated way. This automation can lead to scenarios where we may not know when a server is deployed. The need to know what is deployed and in what state leads us to our next topic.

- *Alerts*
- *Logging*

 All the major CSPs offer alerts and logging. Their respective terms and definitions change over time, but the underlying principles stay the same. We will be referring to AWS CloudWatch in this section. CloudWatch performs both alerting and logging, but all the other cloud platforms offer a comparable platform.

Alerts

When it comes to the cloud, there are four main categories that we typically want to alert on: billing, compute, storage, and networking. We will be discussing the impact of billing or financials later in this chapter.

Alerts on billing, storage, compute, and networking are threshold based. In other words, when resource A reaches a threshold of X, an alert is generated. We use the term *generate* an alert for a very good reason. This is because of a common misconception about the difference between an alert and a notification. Not all alerts need to trigger a notification for the alert. In fact, we want to strive for an architecture in which alerts can be triggered and we are never notified.

Let's talk about a real example to clarify the difference. In a hypothetical web application deployment, we have two web app frontend servers with one database backend. We set an alert for CPU usage on the web app servers of 80 percent for 5 minutes. That means if CPU usage on one of the web app servers stays above 80 percent for more than 5 minutes, we want an alert to be triggered. The question we have to ask is what we want to do with the alert. Could we have the alert generate an email that is sent to us, asking us to investigate? Sure. However, a more elegant and advanced action would be to spin up an identical third web app frontend server and have the load spread between three servers instead of two. This action should lower the CPU load on the first two servers. This is an example of autoscaling, which we will discuss in the next section of this chapter.

Alerts can be used to trigger notifications as well. In fact, notifications sometimes are going to be the only possible result of an alert. A billing alert would be a good example of this. When I set up cloud tenants for both myself and my clients, one of the first alerts I set up is a billing alert. This alert is always along the lines of if my bill reaches $X for any given month, send an email. For a first-time setup or test tenants, my dollar value is typically very low, like $10. This will alert me or a client before an unexpected high bill is received.

The ultimate goal would be to set up a collection of alerts that indicate a suboptimal performance state. Then attach actions and/or workflows to these alerts to bring the systems back to an optimal performance state. If you think about it, that would mean no corrective action would ever need to be taken by you. This is a goal that can never be achieved with 100 percent accuracy. However, the more you can bring into this model, the less you will have to do. This will free up more of your time and allow you work more on advancement instead of putting out fires.

Logging

Logging is the recording of events or actions that have occurred against an asset. Logging is critical for any organization that utilizes technology. Working in IT, you have had to handle situations where someone has asked what happened after something goes sideways. Logs are going to be the primary source of information on past events. In Chapter 1, we discussed hypervisors and VMs that run on the hypervisor. This separation of host and VM leads to a separation of logs as well.

In the realm of the cloud, logging can occur at one of two levels, first the hypervisor and second the VM. You can think of the ordinary physical aspects of a computer as being visible to the hypervisor: CPU, RAM, storage, networking, power events, etc. These logs are not like Windows Event Viewer or the Linux SYSLOG system, which are at the VM level.

For AWS the logging system is called CloudWatch. CloudWatch natively logs events at the hypervisor level and with some setup can log events at the VM level. VM-level logging is usually dependent on an agent being installed in the VM. This agent is a software application or service that runs inside the VM and relays events out to CloudWatch. This agent requirement is not specific to AWS; it is required for all VM-level logging.

Optimization

The cloud offers an agility that is not realized when utilizing on-premises resources. You can scale up to the level of resources that your monitoring dictates (*autoscaling*). In theory, you can spin up and create as many resources as you want, the cloud is unlimited. AWS would love to charge you for these unlimited resources, but if you want to continue to use the cloud and remain fiscally responsible, then you need to scale down as well.

You will hear two terms when it comes to scaling: *horizontal scaling* and *vertical scaling*. Horizontal is scaling out to additional resources, i.e., adding servers to handle system load.

Vertical is scaling up by adding additional resources already deployed, i.e., adding more memory or CPU to current resources.

Before moving anything to the cloud, you need to take an assessment of your current resources you are wanting to move to the cloud. This assessment is the process of determining the correct need or the *right-sizing* of the cloud services. Right-sizing is a continuing process in order to save costs. Going to the cloud will not lower *total cost of ownership* (TCO) without right-sizing on an ongoing basis.

Autoscaling

One of the easiest and largest selling points of going to the cloud is getting the right resources at the right time, without having to set the resource levels manually. What you can do is set the parameters of an optimal or acceptable performance and have the cloud keep your application within those parameters.

For instance, you are designing an e-commerce website. You have all the necessary components already in place.

- Database in place with cross-availability zone setup, i.e., the master in one zone and the slave that is kept in synchronization with the master.
- Two web application frontend servers in multiple zones. One in each zone.
- Load balancer in place to spread the load between the two zones.

This setup should be fault tolerant at the zone level, so if any single zone went down, the e-commerce website would stay up and available. However, now we want to set some parameters if the site comes under heavy load due to a sale going on or a new hot product being released. Here are a few examples of parameters we could set:

- If CPU utilization on either web frontend reaches 80 percent for a sustained 5-minute window. Then, create a new web frontend in the zone that contains the web frontend that has high CPU.
- If memory usage is over 90 percent on the database server for a sustained 10-minute window. Then, increase memory on the master and slave DB servers in both zones by 25 percent.

The second action is relatively straightforward and if done properly would not require a restarting of services. The first action is dependent on the actions we learned in the disposable resources section earlier in the chapter, i.e., bootstrapping and/or golden images. If you want the CSP to be able to autoscale with additional server resources, you will need to do a lot of preparation and testing work. We will get more into the specifics of these steps in the next section of this chapter.

These parameters would allow the horizontal scaling of the web frontends and the vertical scaling of that database server. At this point, you may be asking which one is better—horizontal or vertical scaling? In general, horizontal is preferred, because it is usually more cost effective and definitely more fault tolerant. We will be discussing the pricing of horizontal versus vertical more in a later chapter. Horizontal is more fault tolerant because if a server fails and becomes unavailable, then our parameters will continue to add frontend servers until CPU load falls down to acceptable levels. Vertical scaling does not have these two benefits.

You should be asking yourself why we don't horizontally scale on the database server. The answer boils down to the need of writing data to a single source in order to keep data consistency; i.e., there is a single master DB that ensures data consistency. There can be multiple copies of the DB that can be read, but writing can occur at only one location. Therefore, the only option we have for scaling out the database server is vertically.

Multimaster database designs do exist. They allow the writing of data to multiple destinations, and the system keeps the data consistent. One example that you may have heard of is Active Directory (AD). AD has been around for a while, and the technology is mature. This is possible because the data being written is highly specialized and of a specific type. There are commercial database offerings that offer a more general database architecture with multimaster writing, but they are expensive and beyond the scope of this book.

We have discussed increasing resources to meet increased demand, but what happens when the demand drops? Luckily, autoscaling can scale down as well as up. Scaling down is a little more difficult than scaling up, and there are some restrictions. Let's take a look at a few example parameters building off our last example of the e-commerce site:

- If CPU utilization is below 25 percent across all web application frontends for a sustained 30 minutes, then remove one instance from one availability zone.

- If memory utilization on the database server falls below 30 percent utilization for a sustained 30 minutes, then decrease memory by 25 percent on both the master and slave DB servers.

These parameters are written as examples and are closely aligned with the previous parameters, but there are a few problems with them:

- The first example could easily put us in a nonredundant state; i.e., it could shut down servers in such a way that we don't have a server in each availability zone. To account for this, most CSPs offer service minimum and service maximum when creating scaling groups. Minimums set the minimum resources that a scaling group will scale down too, no matter what the parameters state. These minimums will guarantee a baseline that scaling will not go below. Maximums set the maximum resources that a scaling group will scale up to, no matter what the parameters state. These maximums can guard against runaway processes that come from bad code or design. These help ensure against an astronomical bill that can come from scaling out too much.

- The second example isn't even a valid parameter that could be executed. Software can expand to use new memory but cannot collapse back down if memory is removed. The application would have no way of knowing; the memory would just be gone. What happens to the data that was stored in the memory blocks that are not removed? This is similar if you have ever expanded a disk; you can increase the size but not decrease the size. This is a limitation of vertical scaling and another reason to use horizontal scaling where possible. The only method of shrinking back down from a vertical scale is a restart of the server itself to see the new memory size.

Scaling in the Real World

I have worked for a CSP running large-scale e-commerce websites during Black Friday and Cyber Monday. In every instance of services being negatively impacted, it has presented itself as a memory overrun on the database server. The client wanted to scale up the database server. The problem was that as soon as additional memory was added, all of the memory was consumed. If we added additional memory, it was consumed as well. Obviously, we could not continue this path because there is limited memory even in a large cluster or even offered by the large CSPs. Ultimately, the issue was poorly written code on the web application servers that were consuming the memory on the database server.

We are trying to bring to light that autoscaling is not the be-all and end-all for resource management. Autoscaling is a tool and a useful tool, but it must be monitored and not treated as a "set it and forget it."

Right-Sizing

As you and your organization start looking at making the move to the cloud, one of the first things you will have to evaluate is what to move or migrate. The easiest and most common trap that people fall into is, "We have X resources on-prem, so we need X resources in the cloud." Another common one is, "We have this critical application that requires 8 CPU cores and 16 GB of RAM; therefore, we must have the same resources in the cloud because that is the way it has always been done."

This evaluation, which you perform on all your on-prem resources that are candidates for moving to the cloud, is critical and cannot be overlooked. It is important to engage several sources for guidance, not just the vendors of the applications. Often, vendors can have two sets of system requirements: minimum and recommended. The recommended requirements are often the best in class for larger usage. The vendor wants the best experience for the users, so they want to be better safe than sorry. The minimum requirements are the minimum to receive support from the vendor, and they should be recognized. Each application and each company is different, but a nice starting point is somewhere between minimum and recommended. Keep in mind, if your selected resources cause poor performance, it is easy to scale up. However, it is harder to scale back down. In fact, most companies that come from on-prem will never scale down, because there is not a business case for it. On-prem resources are already purchased and are shared, so it is more efficient to leave the over-provisioned application. This is not the case in the cloud, though. You must break from this mind-set. They just do lift and shift, which will cause overrun on costs and increase TCO. This is the largest reason for cloud deployments to fail.

As stated earlier, right-sizing is an ongoing process. All the major CSPs offer cost analysis and cost calculators. We will discuss this later in the chapter when we review and report financial expenditures.

The first step in right-sizing either cloud resources or on-premises resources is to monitor and analyze the use of the resources. This is typically easier in the cloud than on-premises due to the availability of the tools in the cloud that are not readily available on-premises. You need to monitor both off-peak and on-peak times. With the autoscaling feature that is available in the cloud, you can get more granular when resources are scaled. This is another reason that horizontal scaling is the preferred method over vertical scaling. Here are a few tips for right-sizing:

- Focus on recent data; old data may not be actionable.

- Look at time periods that are large enough to not present any bias. Four weeks is a good starting point. It is large enough to capture any outliers on usage but not so large that the data won't be actionable.

- Separate your environments when right-sizing and looking at the numbers. Development, testing, and production will have different requirements and give different metrics.

Explain DevOps in Cloud Environments

What is *DevOps*? In short, it is the combination of software development (dev) and information technology operations (ops). This combination makes an even bigger impact when taken to the cloud. The reason is that all the major CSPs have had to embrace DevOps internally for their own processes. They have extended their own DevOps offerings to their customers. To take a page from the AWS DevOps page directly:

> DevOps is the combination of cultural philosophies, practices, and tools that increase an organization's ability to deliver applications and services at high velocity: evolving and improving products at a faster pace than organizations using traditional software development and infrastructure management processes. This speed enables organizations to better serve their customers and compete more effectively in the market.

Cultural philosophies, practices, and tools...of those three things, only one of them can be offered by CSPs: tools. However, it is crucial to understand the other two to effectively use the tools provided by the CSPs. There are two other important parts of this definition: "evolving and improving products at a faster pace..." and "...better serve their customers...." Think about these two points in conjunction and what their ramifications are if executed properly. Better serve customers with new features at a faster rate. Think about the cloud as a whole and how quickly it evolves. Do you think the CSPs are using DevOps for their own internal projects?

There is an acronym that is often used with DevOps that tries to encompass this definition in an easy-to-remember manner: *CALMS*. Culture Automation Lean Measurement

Sharing. This is not covered on the exam specifically, but we wanted to call it out. We will make references to this throughout the section. We will leave it up to the reader to draw parallels between CALMS and the quote from AWS given earlier.

Exam Note

You will not need to know CALMS or AWS's definition of DevOps for the exam. However, DevOps is a mind-set and a process. If you have never worked in an agile organization or one that uses DevOps, it is different from a traditional approach. We mention them as memory aids and an introduction to thinking in a DevOps way.

You will hear about a pipeline a lot when talking about DevOps. This pipeline is not specific to DevOps and is referred to for any application development and deployment. Depending on your source, this pipeline will have three to five different parts. We will standardize on a four-part pipeline that will be referred to in this order:

1. Development
2. Build
3. Test
4. Release

Steps 1 and 2 are the Dev part of DevOps. Steps 3 and 4 are the Ops part of DevOps. In the classic application development pipeline, these are separate teams and often siloed from each other. These silos are often by design because the two teams can have conflicting goals and priorities. Developers are incentivized to produce new features and fix old bugs; i.e., change is generally good. IT Operations, on the other hand, are incentivized to keep things running and stable; i.e., change is bad. DevOps for the most part is a solution to this conflict. Let's take a look at a classic application development pipeline example:

V1.2 Application release: 25 new features and 12 bug fixes

| Dev | -> | Build | -> | Test | -> | Release | - 6-month timeline

In this example, each step is siloed from the others. Here are some issues that arise from this pipeline:

- This pipeline takes three months to get any new features or bug fixes to the end users.
- Developers won't learn of any issues in their code until the build or test phase.
- Resources and time are wasted because often resources from one silo are waiting on resources from another silo to complete.

Let's look at a DevOps application development pipeline example:

V1.2.56.7809 Application release: 1 new feature or 1 bug fix

| Dev -> Build -> Test -> Release | - 12-hour timeline

In this example, the silos have been removed and everyone works together to get a release ready. Here are the benefits of using this model:

- Features and bug fixes are released to the end user at a faster pace.

- Developers find bugs or issues more quickly because building and testing happen right away.

- Priorities are more visible, and they can even be changed from day to day.

- Your team can be more flexible and adapt to changes in priorities or issues more quickly.

DevOps Tools

Each step of the pipeline requires tools to be used. We will list a few here, but this list is not exhaustive and changes as new/better tools become available.

Source tools: GitHub, Apache Subversion

Build tools: Jenkins, Microsoft Visual Studio

Testing tools: Selenium, Pester, Vagrant

Release tools: Chef, Puppet

One term that you will hear a lot because it is critical to the DevOps process is Source Control Management (SCM). SCM falls under the Source Tools.

Provisioning

We are going to need resources to work along this pipeline. We are going to need to create these in the cloud, or *provision*. To build on what we have learned in a previous section, we should build *immutable* or disposable resources. We will not change these resources directly; if we need new features, we will deploy new resources and test. Not only do we want to use disposable resources, but we want these resources to autoscale as needed. We want horizontal scaling both in and out, depending on the demand placed on our resources. *Infrastructure as code* will be our next topic to accomplish these goals

Infrastructure as Code

Infrastructure will be used at every step of the pipeline, including development workstations, build servers, test platforms, and release platforms. Infrastructure can mean a lot of different things, but in general infrastructure can be broken into three categories that we will expand on in the next section: compute, storage, and networking. In the classical model, how would we set up this infrastructure? We would have a process or a checklist that we would follow. Some of the steps would include things like: install OS, apply patches, add additional storage or diskspace, set IP address and DNS settings, install needed software, set network security, etc. This setup is what is called *imperative* or *expressive*. Yes, it is defined and probably even defined well, but a human still must perform the actions. Human error will occur, and steps will be missed or duplicated. Compute or storage resources will fail, and then the process must be repeated to get back to a working state. If there is a different OS or a different patch level or there are different storage options, then we will need to define a new imperative process, and we will have to test it as well.

There is a better way. If we could use a declarative model instead of imperative, then we solve a lot of these shortcomings. By declarative, we mean we will declare what our infrastructure should be and let the CSP work out the details. We define a good state. For example, we can specify that we need four Linux servers with 100 GB disk drives. These four Linux servers will have software packages X, Y, and Z installed. Network security will allow traffic from the Internet destined for port 80. This is a lot simpler on our part, because it can also be self-healing. Turn off one of the four servers, and the system could automatically deploy another server to bring the infrastructure back to a good state. This is the concept of *infrastructure as code* (IaC).

One thing to clarify is the word *code*. Oftentimes people, when they hear the word code, think of some programming language like C, Java, or Python. Now these languages can be used to define infrastructure (Python is more common than the other languages), but usually their definition of infrastructure is imperative. We want to be declarative in our definition, so we will use configuration file(s). These files are in the form of a structured data set in text format. One of the most widely used formats is the JSON format. We will show an actual example of IaC using JSON in the next section. For now, just know that JSON files are structured around tab characters, curly braces ({}), colons, and commas.

Since the infrastructure is now defined as code, we can use the application development pipeline. SCMs will be used extensively in a DevOps model. In fact, an SCM is a critical piece and even a requirement in the section covering continuous integration/continuous delivery.

This IaC automates the setup and configuring of all compute, storage, and networking. It allows you to copy and rebuild the same infrastructure over and over. You can use this to build your test environments. The test environments will look and act just like production, because the same code is defined in both environments. There is no difference between the two if done properly.

You often can't start with IaC right out of the gate because there are too many unknowns on what the infrastructure should look like. Additionally, the JSON files can get pretty complex pretty quickly. New users to the cloud may not have a lot of experience with JSON or even know where to start. There can be a learning curve, and that is where templates enter the picture to assist with this hurdle.

Templates

Most CSPs offer prebuilt templates that can provide easier deployment and entry into provisioning and IaC. There are also third-party websites that offer downable IaC template files. The following is a template for creating an AWS Elastic Cloud Computing (EC2) instance. This would be part of a larger template, but you can see how this is declarative and not imperative. We are not defining the steps to build the infrastructure. We are defining what the infrastructure looks like.

```json
  "Ec2Instance" : {
    "Type" : "AWS::EC2::Instance",
    "Properties" : {
      "ImageId" : { "Fn::FindInMap" : [ "AWSRegionArch2AMI", { "Ref" :
"AWS::Region" },
                        { "Fn::FindInMap" : [ "AWSInstanceType2Arch", { "Ref" :
"InstanceType" }, "Arch" ] } ] },
      "KeyName" : { "Ref" : "KeyName" },
      "InstanceType" : { "Ref" : "InstanceType" },
      "SecurityGroups" : [{ "Ref" : "Ec2SecurityGroup" }],
      "BlockDeviceMappings" : [
       {
        "DeviceName" : "/dev/sda1",
        "Ebs" : { "VolumeSize" : "50" }
       },{
        "DeviceName" : "/dev/sdm",
        "Ebs" : { "VolumeSize" : "100" }
       }
      ]
    }
  }
```

This code is in JSON format. It defines several things, but the most important are the following: Type, ImageID, and BlockDeviceMappings. We will discuss these individually.

- **Type:** This simply defines what this block of JSON code defines. For example, AWS::EC2::Instance is simply read as Amazon Web Services : Elastic Cloud Computing : Instance.

- **ImageID:** This defines the computer image to use in this template. The image will define the OS and the patch level. The bit of code uses Fn: and Ref: for this logic that would reference other parts of the template that are not listed.

- **BlockDeviceMappings:** These are the disk drives that will be presented to the OS. There are two entries here, and each entry defines three things: first, the device name that will be presented to the OS, i.e., /dev/sda1, and second, the type of volume, Ebs, which is elastic block storage. Third is the volume size or the size of the drive presented to the OS.

This is just an example and is not a complete template. You can deploy these templates as is or modify them to suit your needs.

You can find templates that offer complete stack deployments. They can literally be one-click complete system deployments. Here are a few examples:

- Microsoft Windows Server Active Directory

- WordPress multisite

- Magento e-commerce site with Redis cache

Continuous Integration/Continuous Delivery

Continuous integration and continuous delivery, also known as CICD or CI/CD, is a hot topic and referenced a lot by the CSPs and online sources. CICD has become synonymous with DevOps. In short, this where application updates and changes are constantly being released. We are building on our previous topics to deliver this concept of CICD. To be efficient with this continuous change, we need disposable resources, IaC, and autoscaling. We need our infrastructure to be predictable, reliable, scalable, and changeable. We will break down continuous integration from continuous delivery.

Continuous integration (CI) is the continuous execution of the first three steps in our application development life cycle: dev, build, and test. By continuous we mean the process can be executed at any time and by anyone, and the infrastructure needs to support it. A centralized SCM is the first and the most important aspect of CI. Your developers and your Ops team need to have a centralized point where anyone can view and check out both source code for the application and the IaC. Git, a distributed version control system, is probably the most widely used because it is free and open source. CSPs offer their own SCMs, but usually they are just implementations of Git. A centralized Git server either on-premises or in the cloud is a single point of authority, also known as a *repository.*

Continuous delivery (CD) is the last step in our application deployment pipeline: release. We need to have a continuous process to be able to release our application to either production or a test environment. Our developers and Ops need to be able to use and experience their work without waiting for someone or a process.

It is important to draw a distinction between continuous delivery and continuous deployment; they are often confused. Continuous deployment is the automatic deployment to production once all the other steps have taken place; i.e., the code is pushed to production in real time. Continuous delivery is the ability to deploy to production at any given time, but with a control in place for final approval. Continuous delivery is what is used in the real world, because no large project should ever be pushed to production automatically without managerial approval for release.

NOTE

Code is released into an environment. Most people are familiar with the production environment, but organizations have more than just a production environment. There can be as many environments as an organization needs. In reality, though, cost and time are the limiting factors of too many environments. Whatever the number, each environment will generally fall into one of three categories:

- **Production:** This is the prod environment and the one your end users use. This should be the most stable.

- **User acceptance (UA):** This is the environment where select users can use and provide feedback on a version of the application. This should be stable; otherwise, the users will not want to use it.

- **Dev/test:** This is the environment for your developers and Ops personnel to test and make whatever changes are needed.

To implement CICD we need *automation*. Automation is what is going to complete the build and test phases of our pipeline. We don't want to expend human resources on any process that can be automated. We will be discussing automation later in this chapter. Automation is not enough, though; we need something that can push things along and to the next steps. That is where *orchestration* comes into the picture, which we will talk about later in this chapter. This will speed up the time to delivery. This can free up time for your developers and Ops personnel.

We have freed up developer time, and ideally the developers are writing and committing code at a faster pace. We have orchestration in place that automates the build and testing of the software. As long as everything passes, we can move on to the next phase, which is delivering the software to users. Our aim is to shorten up this process and times as well, thus the continuous delivery.

Testing in QA Environments

We have discussed application development (CI/CD) pipelines and the part it plays in DevOps. The third stage of DevOps is testing. We are going to take a deeper dive into testing needed in our DevOps model. If we are going to test, we need an environment or infrastructure to test in. As mentioned previously, environments typically fall into one of three categories: production, UA, and dev/test. Quality assurance (QA) can span all three, but usually falls into UA or dev/test. The type of QA testing is different for each environment.

Sandboxing

Sandbox testing by definition is testing that happens in a sandbox or a separate environment that is isolated from other environments. That means either dev/test or UA will work for this type of testing. The benefit or the use case for sandbox testing is when you have changes in infrastructure. For example, your application is in production running on the Windows Server 2016 OS. You want to test the current production application code on Windows Server 2019. We would create a new IaC or template that will deploy a scaled-down copy of the production infrastructure with the only change being the host OS is Windows Server 2019. This is where all of our previous work starts to shine. Our Ops personnel can check out the IaC from our SCM and update the OS to Windows Server 2019. CICD kicks into gear and validates that the IaC is of the correct format and passes other checks. Once all the checks pass, we can push out the deployment of our new dev/test infrastructure.

Once our isolated Windows Server 2019 infrastructure is deployed, our developers can deploy a copy of the production application to the new sandbox environment. This is part of the CICD as well; we have empowered the developers to push production code to a dev/test environment that will not impact the production environment. This new environment is our sandbox; it's part of the production code of the application in the dev/test infrastructure.

Load Testing

Load testing typically happens in a UA environment. Load testing is testing that tries to mimic or reproduce real-world use scenarios of the application. This is one of the hardest types of testing to execute in the real world. The problems: What is the proper load to test? How do you simulate the load without real users? What other load testing besides user load do we need to test, i.e., DB load? How do we simulate load test but then get real-world user experience? You will not be able to do a true one-to-one real-world load test. There are too many unknowns, and there is no true way of testing real-world user experience.

There are software packages that are specialized for this testing. Some are commercial, and CSPs do offer packages that can perform load testing. Selenium is an open source tool for load testing. It is supported by all the major CSPs.

Regression Testing

Regression testing happens in both the UA and dev/test environments. Regression testing is testing that validates that new features and bug fixes don't cause a negative impact on production code; i.e., new code does not regress the production code. There are two important things to keep in mind when it comes regression testing: system-wide testing and previous issue testing.

Regression testing needs to run against the entire system and on as close to a production environment as possible. We are trying to capture bugs or issues that were unintended. A developer could be working on a new feature for scheduling appointments that allows the software to check a person's availability. They do a unit test and validate that the new feature works for scheduling new appointments. Does this feature impact appointments that are already scheduled? Does the new feature lock already scheduled appointments and prevent their modification? In this case, the software has regressed. It would be difficult to test this scenario without using a copy of a production calendar with a user's real-world appointments.

Throughout the testing process, bugs and issues are going to be discovered. These bugs need to be tracked through their life cycles from discovery to resolution or mediation. There are software issue tracking packages that will assist with this tracking. One of the most widely used is called Jira from Atlassian. Jira will assist with the other important aspects of regression testing, such as previous issue testing. Since we have documented and tracked all previous bugs, we need to retest them to validate that they have not recurred or manifested differently.

Regression testing, while critical to the application development pipeline, is often the most time-consuming and resource-intensive. Ideally it requires a complete copy of a production environment and testing against every known previous bug. This daunting task would be impossible without automation in our DevOps world. In reality, complete issue testing cannot be performed on every single update, especially as the number of previous bugs grows.

Configuration Management

We have our code for both our application and our infrastructure. Both have configurations, and we need a system to manage these configurations. Fortunately, the tools we have already been using, SCM and issue tracking, will be part of this system. In the case of the SCM and infrastructure, the SCM is literally the maintainer of our infrastructure configuration. The SCM is also the maintainer of our source code for the application. The configuration of the application source code will be managed in both the SCM and the issue tracking package. These tools are not going to be enough, but they are the foundation of our next topics: orchestration, automation, upgrades, and patching.

Orchestration

Orchestration is the glue or the coordination between automation tasks. Orchestration will free up resources both digital and human so they can perform other tasks. Orchestration strives to make automation efficient and manageable. Managed automation is great and necessary for DevOps, but unmanaged automation will lead to issues of who, what, and when. Orchestration can not only answer those questions but can also create workflows that connect separate pieces of automation.

Orchestration is ultimately a pipeline itself. If we have complete orchestration, it will span our application development pipeline. Orchestration is going to use the tools SCM, IaC, CICD, issue tracking, and testing that we have been discussing in this chapter. Here are some of benefits that we gain from orchestration and using these tools:

- **Centralized management:** We can utilize the SCM and issue tracking tools as a centralized point of our automation processes.

- **Auditing:** In a previous section, we discussed monitoring and logging. With our orchestration running from a central point, we can audit all the events. This is critical because orchestration will break or go awry at some point.

Orchestration can be broken into three parts. They may be called different things by different CSPs, but generally every part of orchestration falls into one of these three:

- **Runbook:** Collection of distinct steps that either a person or an automation process follows

- **Workflow:** Collection of runbooks and the logic needed to execute a task that is being automated

- **Pipeline:** Collection of workflows that define the overall automation being performed

Let's look at an example pulling from the previously discussed items. We know that we will need to perform regression testing, and we also know that we should be running this against production data. This is our pipeline, and we want to orchestrate the automation needed.

- The first workflow is going to first check whether we have a test environment ready to accept the database from production.

  - If the test environment is up and ready, then we will move on to our second workflow of copying that database.

- If the test environment is not up and ready, then we will execute our Build Test Environment (BTE) runbook.

    - The BTE runbook will first clean up or destroy any remnants of a failed test environment deployment.

    - The BTE runbook checks out the latest IaC for the test environment from our SCM.

    - The BTE runbook then executes IaC and deploys the environment.

    - The BTE runbook finally validates that the test environment is up and healthy and returns control back to orchestration, which will execute the next workflow.

- The second workflow is going to copy databases from production to a staging server (first runbook). The staging server will execute a masking process on the databases to protect confidential information not needed for testing (second runbook). Finally, we will copy the new databases into our test environment as "production" like databases to perform our regression testing (third runbook). We won't go into detail on all the runbooks but will give an example of the first one.

    - The first runbook will perform the following tasks:

        - Temporarily stop log processing on a read copy of our production database. This will prevent the database from changing while we copy it. The changes will queue for processing.

        - Copy database files in a recoverable format to a staging server.

        - Reenable log processing on the read copy of our database.

        - Monitor the delta between read copy and production to validate that the two are syncing.

Automation

Automation is the technique, method, or system of operating or controlling a process by highly automatic means, reducing human intervention to a minimum. The key point of this definition is "reducing human intervention to a minimum." Humans are a costly resource; if we can eliminate or reduce their involvement in a repeatable process, then we can free them up to work on other processes.

There is a lot of buzz around the concept of automation, but not all of it is positive. There is a sense that companies are just trying to replace humans with robots. This carries a negative connotation that we want to get rid of employees. That is not the goal of automation in the DevOps model. We don't want replace humans with automation. We want processes that have set repeatable steps performed by humans to be performed by an automated process. The employee no longer has to perform a rote set of steps every day. The employee now has that time to work on other tasks. This makes the overall process more efficient.

Let's give an example of a process that can and should be automated within any decent size company and user account life cycle. The user account life cycle falls into one of three categories: creation, modification, or termination.

User account creation is the process of onboarding or creating new user accounts as employees are hired. One sign of a successful business is the number of new employee hires. Here's an example of the manual user creation process:

1. An email is sent from the head of HR to Tom, who works in IT, requesting a new user account creation. The email should include basic information about the user, i.e., name, title, manager, department, etc.

2. Tom logs into the identity management system and opens the user account creation tool.

3. Tom enters the basic minimum information required for account creation, such as the name and password.

4. Tom then must look up the manager and department to determine which groups the new user needs to be a member of in order for the new employee to perform their job. This step alone is very error prone.

5. Tom then creates a new share on a file server for the new user.

6. Tom logs the new user onto a test workstation to validate the password, permissions, and share access.

This entire process is rote and mundane. It is also prone to error because a small step can be missed due to human error. It can also be time intensive. At a minimum it will take 10–15 minutes per account. If Tom must create 20 accounts in one day, then that is 5 hours of work without any breaks. If we could automate this process, then all Tom really needs to do is a validation process. All 20 accounts can be validated in the amount of time it takes to create a single user account.

What would automation look like? First, we need to collect information. This information is included in the email from HR, but the format can be different from email to email. We need a better or more automated way of collecting the information we need. Second, we need some logic that we can take action on. For example, if the new user is a member of the sales department, then they become a member of the NA-Sales, GotoMarket, and Prospects groups. Additionally, the new user file share will be created on the file server dedicated to the sales team.

The collection of the information is critical because the source of the information must be accurate and authoritative. HR will be the source, but how do we capture the information needed? Companies of almost any size are going to have an HR database system. It may come in different forms, such as a payroll system, for example. This will be the source of our information because the information has legal processes in place to ensure accuracy. We are going to set up some sort of monitoring of the HR database. This monitoring will include triggers. A trigger will simply wait and watch for an event; when that event occurs, it starts the automation.

Once the automation is started, the logic that we have defined has to be evaluated. The automation process will look at the department value that is in the HR database. The automated process will look up the logic based on the value and determine the next steps it needs to perform. Here's an example of our automated process:

1. A new employee named Sally is hired. HR collects all the information needed to process the new hire and inputs the data into the HR database.

2. A monitor recognizes the new user added and triggers the automation process.

3. Automation evaluates all the values of the HR database entry for Sally. It determines group membership and file share location.

4. Automation logs into the identity management system and creates the account and sets a password. Additionally, it modifies the group membership of the needed groups by adding Sally.

5. Automation creates the file share on the required server.

6. Automation performs a synthetic login to validate account availability and password.

Upgrades and Patching

We have all the pieces and parts we need to deploy our application. Next come changes to our application. We will need to add new features and fix discovered bugs. We want to use all the tools and topics we have learned in this chapter to upgrade or patch our applications.

Exam Note

The exam may include questions about applying a patch into a production environment. This is will be worded in an attempt to trick you into selecting that you want to apply a tested patch straight into production. Historically, this is what a lot of companies do, but this goes against the principles we have learned this chapter, namely, disposable resources, IaC, availability, CICD, and orchestration. The correct answer is going to be to deploy into a copy of production and then shift this production load onto the copy. This kind of deployment is referred to as a blue/green deployment.

Blue/green deployments have been the standard to strive for when deploying upgrades and patches to production. Unfortunately, they were typically cost prohibitive with on-premises environments due to the needed resources. Let's lay out some parameters before we start building our blue/green environment.

We have an application that is deployed in a production environment. Users are actively using the application. Users have been requesting a new feature for the application. Developers have written the new code for the feature. This new code has gone through all the unit, load, QA, and regression testing. Everything has gone through the pipeline up to delivery. Thanks to our CICD process, we are ready and capable of deploying the upgrade with the new feature.

There are two things we need to perform to get our upgrade into production. The first is a critical aspect of configuration management and business as a whole. *Change management* is the process of committing a change that will have an impact on production workload. Change management is a large topic that deserves a deep dive into the details. However, for the exam, keep in mind it is the final step, and approval for making a change will impact production in some way. The second is to configure a blue/green deployment. Let's walk through that process now:

- Our current production environment that is running the current code will have several parts to it: application servers, database servers, network security, load balancers, etc. We are going to designate this environment as blue.

- We will take our IaC or templates and deploy an exact working copy of our blue environment. There will be one difference with this copy; it will not have a load balancer. Additionally, we are going to deploy the copy of the blue environment to be behind blue's load balancer. This copy of blue will be designated as green.

- We will keep the load balancer configured to only direct traffic to the blue environment.

- We will then deploy our upgrade to the green environment.

- We have identical infrastructure deployments; one is running current live production code, and the other is running our new tested and updated code. Currently all traffic is being directed to the blue environment by the load balancer. The end user is not impacted by any of these changes so far.

- We will configure the load balancer to start directing a percentage of the traffic to the green environment. The percentage will be dependent on your business needs. Typically, it starts around 10 percent, but the biggest takeaway is that the starting percentage is below 50 percent. Remember, we are directing real production end users to the new code at this point.

- We are going to utilize our monitoring and logging to ideally identify any issues. However, we are also going to be looking for feedback from the end users.

- Dependent on feedback and monitoring, we start increasing the traffic sent to Green. While increasing the percentage, we continue to monitor and provide feedback.

- We continue the increase of traffic being directed to green until all the traffic is going through green.

- Our new application upgrade has been deployed into production and is running on green.

- To save costs, we shut down the blue environment and mark it for deletion. It is no longer a production environment. We are back at our steady state. When we want to deploy a new application, we will treat this as blue and repeat the process.

If we have executed properly, we will have upgraded our application and provided a new user-requested feature, there was no downtime, and the end users were never aware of the change except the new feature. The real benefit of the blue/green deployment is if something goes wrong. Since we initially are directing only a small percentage of traffic to green, the risk of data loss or corruption is limited to 10 percent of the end user data.

API Integration

An API is a method for a user or a process to interface with a service. For example, the storage service provided by a CSP will have a supported API. This means you could write code that could make changes to the storage that deployed in one of your environments. Before you start worrying about having to write code to use this feature, you need to know you already have been using your CSP's API. For CSPs, everything is an API call. If you log into their web portal, the web portal itself is making an API call to the identity provider. If you create a new VM to test a new setting, you initiated an API call to create the VM.

Everything to CSPs is already an API call. Therefore, we just need to explore how we can interact with their API and integrate into our processes. The three methods of API calls by the major CSPs are: web, CLI, and SDK.

Everything we have been doing so far has been through a web portal, so this method of integration is familiar. Even the IaC we did earlier was a web call; we uploaded a JSON file to define the infrastructure. The CSP's web portal performed an API call to parse and process the JSON file. Then the CSP's orchestration started dozens or potentially hundreds of work-flows that started hundreds of runbooks to deploy our infrastructure. We hope this is starting to sound familiar. CSPs use the same tools that we have been discussing the whole chapter.

A web portal to API is the most obvious and readily apparent API integration to a CSP's services. However, a web portal does not lend itself very well to orchestration. The next step in accessing the API so we can really start orchestrating is the CLI. CLI stands for command-line interface. As its name suggests, this is the API integration you can utilize by typing out individual commands to perform actions. All the major CSPs have download-able and installable CLI packages available for all the major OS platforms. You install this package on your Mac or Windows machine. You set some configuration settings, i.e., cre-dentials and region. Then from the command prompt or from a shell, you can execute com-mands like the following:

```
New-vm -instanceid ubuntu18.04.02 -NetworkID eastprodlab01 -storagesize 100GB
-name ProdLabServer01
```

This would deploy a server with the name ProdLabServer01 with a 100 GB drive on the network eastprodlab01 with the OS Ubuntu 18.04. This allows us to start scripting. We can start incorporating scripts into our larger orchestration pipeline. Our scripts can also become part of the development tools we have already discussed, i.e., SCM.

The next step in our journey and advancement after the CLI is SDK. *SDK* stands for Software Development Kit. All the major CSPs have downloadable and installable SDK packages for all the major OSs. SDKs on the surface look and feel like scripting through the CLI. However, that is where the similarity ends. First of all, SDKs are language specific, i.e., Python, .NET, PowerShell, etc. You need to download and install for the programming language that you are familiar with. Second, you are going to write code in the language you decide. This code will interact with the CSP's API directly. Your code does not have to go through an abstraction layer to be used by the API. These API calls will be even faster than the CLI scripts because of the lack of abstraction layer.

When utilizing the SDK, our interaction with the CSP is code. We can use everything we have learned so far in the chapter and get all the benefits we have been talking about.

Financial Planning of Cloud Resources

We decided that we want to start utilizing the cloud and provisioning resources in the cloud. We are shifting our costs from on-premises resources to cloud resources. We need to understand whether such a move makes sense from a financial perspective. We need to consider some of the following questions:

- CSPs offer several different types of storage. What are the use cases for the different storage types?

- Do we need to use commercial software that needs to be licensed?

- We have a department that wants to move everything to the cloud. How can we track expenses and pass along the charges to the department?

We will be addressing all these questions in this section. We are going to try to leave this discussion very general and not tied to any specific CSP. However, there will be times that we will refer to a specific CSP. There will be at least four questions on the exam that are related to this section. All the questions will be either math based or about licensing and chargebacks. You will not need to know specific pricing. You will need to know which service offerings are cheaper in relation to the others; i.e., SSD storage is more expensive than HDD storage.

Let's dive into the three main categories of services you can purchase from CSPs:

- Storage

- Network

- Compute

Storage

Storage is generally offered as three different services: object, block, and file storage. Pricing for each service will be different because the underlying technologies are so different from each other.

Object Storage Was the First Public Cloud Service Offering

AWS launched the first publicly available cloud offering in March 2006, called S3. S3 stands for Simple Storage Service. AWS had been using S3 for a few years. It served all the pictures and static content of the Amazon Store. Amazon Store is the largest customer of AWS.

Object Storage

Object storage is used for files that are not structured. Object storage does store individual files like a normal file system, but there is no hierarchy as there is in a file system. Object storage is not designed for frequent file changes like block storage or file storage. Object storage is accessed almost exclusively as HTTP or web calls. Web calls can be broken into two categories: retrieval requests and creation/modification requests.

Pricing for object storage will fall into one of three categories: storage pricing, object access/transfer within the CSP's infrastructure, and object access/transfer out of the CSP's infrastructure.

- Storage pricing is the cost the CSP will charge for storing the data in their infrastructure. For example, if you store 5 TB (terabytes) of training videos in Amazon's S3 standard, it will cost $117.76 every month, using current pricing as of writing this book.

- Object access/transfer within the CSP infrastructure contains the actions of: list, create, copy, and get processes using the CSP's tools. Listing all the objects that you have uploaded to object storage using either a web portal or API calls is an example. Making a copy of an object is another example. Basically, any interaction you have with an object using CSP tools falls in this category. These prices are the lowest of all three categories.

- Object access/transfer out of CSPs infrastructure is any access to the objects that goes over the public Internet or is accessed by infrastructure outside the CSP's infrastructure. Transferring the same 5 TB of training videos out of S3 will cost $460.80 per transfer. This is priced per gigabyte of transfer, and the cost per gigabyte goes down as you transfer more.

Durability vs. Availability

Data availability refers to the ability to access specific data at a point in time of the request. Data durability refers to the ability of data to survive a failure of the underlying infrastructure. All the CSPs offer really high data durability. In other words, your data will not become corrupted or lost if you keep your data in our object storage. However, the CSPs guarantee that you can access that data at any given time depending on availability and how much you want to pay. To put it another way, just because you cannot access specific data at this time does not mean the data is lost.

Block Storage

Block storage is the storage of files as blocks or sectors on a disk drive. When most people think of or use storage, this what they are using. Your disk drive in your computer right now is a block storage device. The thumb drive that you copy your PowerPoint presentation onto is a block storage device. The computer system does not store the file as a whole file; it breaks the file up into blocks and writes them to the disk as blocks. All physical disk drives are block storage devices. Therefore, any OS you want to run requires and expects a block storage device to operate.

Block storage is what all of your VMs or servers will use. It is where your databases will store their files. Block storage is for the storage of files in hierarchical structure for retrieval by a computer system. You can purchase disk drives for a computer in several different flavors, so you can purchase block storage for a VM in several different flavors. The difference between the different tiers boils down to speed; i.e., SSD is faster than HDD.

SSD vs. HDD

There is a common misconception that SSD is always better and preferred to an HDD. However, this is not always the case, and the key difference boils down to the physical differences between the two types of drives. An HDD is a hard disk drive. It is a spinning platter that write and reads data sequentially. An SSD is a solid-state drive that can read or write any order to any memory cell. Therefore, an SSD is better and more efficient at random read and writes. An HDD is better and more efficient at sequential read and writes. Where the misconception comes from is that the normal day-to-day use of a computer is random by nature; therefore, SSD performs better for average daily use. However, there are applications such as video processing or data processing that by their nature are not random and are sequential. These applications can benefit from the older technology of HDDs.

In general, SSD is more expensive than HDD. However, CSPs have started offering different tiers of each, and depending on what tier, that rule may not always apply. Additionally, the price difference between a standard SSD and HDD is so minimal that SSD is the default block storage offering on VMs. The speed increase justifies that minimal cost difference. The standard HDD offering is an option, but you have to specifically select it.

The block storage offering to keep an eye on and that might come up on the test is the guaranteed Input Output Per Second (IOPS). If you have a database application that needs a sustained throughput on random reads and writes, you can provision a block storage device with a minimum IOPS provided, and the CSP will guarantee the throughput. You will pay a premium for this feature; it is the most expensive tier.

RAID-0 with Multiple Block Storage Devices

There is a relatively new trend making its way through the best practices articles. Since the CSPs offer such a high availability for standard SSD block devices, why not utilize the software RAID that is present in all modern OSs to achieve a high throughput? For example, if I attach four 25 GB standard block storage devices to a Windows machine, I can use the built RAID functionality of the OS to create a RAID-0 striped set. In theory, we are now getting the throughput of four simultaneous SSDs. The risk is that if one of the block storage devices becomes unavailable, then all the data is unavailable until the missing device is brought back online. We have yet to see this used in a production environment, but it is an intriguing possibility.

File Storage

File storage as a service is a relatively new offering because the applications are specific to the needs. However, this concept has been used in the IT arena for so long that the CSPs have recently started offering them. File storage solves the problem of how multiple endpoints can write to the same destination at the same time. Object storage allows multiple reads from multiple endpoints at the same time. Block storage offers multiple writes from a single endpoint. Neither of these offers multiple writes from multiple endpoints. This is actually a difficult problem to solve in the IT field. The best solution we have found so far is the Network File System (NFS). NFS is an older protocol that is still used. It has wider acceptance in the Linux OS than Windows.

All of the current file storage solution offerings are NFS mount points that can be used in the VMs. Their pricing is similar to that of object storage. The pricing tiers break down by availability. How often you need to access the data in file storage will determine the price.

Network

We have already touched a little on network costs when we discussed object storage and the costs associated with data transfers out. In general, the major CSPs don't charge for creating a network as long as the network stays within their infrastructure. You can create VMs in a CSP's infrastructure and have IP addresses assigned and even move data back and forth between VMs without accruing any costs outside of the storage costs. Additionally, CSPs don't typically charge for data transfer into their infrastructure. They do charge for data transfer out of their infrastructure. They are all for taking all your data; they charge for you to get it back.

The pricing structure for outbound data transfers is tiered, and the price decreases as the amount of data transfer goes up. They charge per gigabyte of transfer per month. Some CSPs have different rates depending on the region you are wanting to transfer out of; for example, data transfers are more expensive out of Asia than out of North America. Table 5.1 shows the pricing structure for AWS data transfer outbound from North America.

TABLE 5.1 Pricing Structure for AWS Data Transfer Outbound from North America

Tier	Price
First 10 TB per month	$0.15/GB
Next 40 TB per month	$0.11/GB
Next 100 TB per month	$0.09/GB
Over 150 TB per month	$0.08/GB

There are two other network features that can incur costs depending on your CSP:

- First is a publicly available IP address, in other words, an IP address not in the RFC 1918 space. Most CSPs offer the first public IP address used for a VM free of charge. However, if you need an additional public IP for a VM, then there is a charge.

- Second is the use of a load balancer. If you recall in our blue/green deployment built in the previous section, we used a load balancer to direct traffic between the two. There is typically either an hourly fee or a data transfer fee associated with data sent through a load balancer.

Public vs. Private IP Address Spaces

If you have ever worked with a network engineer, you have probably heard the term RFC 1918. Network engineers use this term when discussing public and private IP address spaces. RFC 1918 is a real document that was released by the Internet Engineering Task Force (IETF) in 1996. You can read it at https://tools.ietf.org/html/rfc1918. This document defines the difference between public and private and the communication that can occur between the two. It also defined three private IP address ranges that are available for anyone. Table 5.2 lists the three reserved RFC 1918 private IP blocks.

TABLE 5.2   Reserved RFC 1918 Private IP Blocks

Network Address	Broadcast Address	Prefix	Block
10.0.0.0	10.255.255.255	10.0.0.0/8	24-bit
172.16.0.0	17.31.255.255	172.16.0.0/12	20-bit
192.168.0.0	192.168.255.255	192.168.0.0/16	16-bit

Compute

Unless you are storing a large amount of raw data in the cloud, most of your cloud expenditure will be on compute resources. Charges for compute are dependent on CPU and memory availability to systems being provisioned. A VM with four CPUs and 8 GB of RAM will cost more than a VM with two CPUs and 4 GB of RAM. All the major CSPs have broken their compute offerings into different classes that optimize a feature of the compute node being requested. Table 5.3 lists the most common classes of compute used by CSPs.

TABLE 5.3 Common Classes of Compute Used by CSPs

Class	Purpose
General	General day-to-day operations
CPU optimized	CPU-intensive workloads, e.g., video processing
Memory optimized	Memory-intensive workloads, e.g., large databases
GPU accelerated	GPU-enabled applications, e.g., AI
Storage optimized	Storage-intensive workloads, e.g., data warehousing

The general class is the cheapest of all the classes as long as you don't need the resources of another class. In other words, adding more memory to a general class VM in order to run a large database will be more expensive than running a memory-optimized class VM. The general class works great for proofs of concept and running some basic testing. However, production environments will often use the specialized classes to save costs.

So far, we have been talking about a VM being created in the cloud and the cost associated with it. From the topics we covered in Chapter 1, this should sound like IaaS. We are creating infrastructure for our own use. We will have access to the underlying systems and can make changes. We covered other cloud models in Chapter 1, specifically PaaS. PaaS still needs compute resources, but you will not have system-level access. So, they are referred to as serverless compute resources. Serverless compute resources are also called *managed services* or *microservices*. An example of a managed service would be a hosted database service, e.g., MySQL. You can interact with the MySQL instance using MySQL tools and any application can access the database. However, you don't have system-level access; you can't update the MySQL software, for example. When you create the managed MySQL instance, you will have the option to select a compute class with required CPU and memory resources. The cost of the managed service will depend on the class and options you select.

Chargebacks

One of the great advantages of going to the cloud is the self-service aspect. If you have a credit card and an email address, you can sign up for either AWS, Azure, or Google Cloud and start provision resources immediately. This self-service ability can apply to people in addition to the original account creator.

The company Congruence Corp decided to start using the cloud. A new cloud account was created, and a company credit card was used to handle monthly charges. Because Congruence

Corp is a large corporation, it authorized department heads to create cloud resources at their own discretion. The marketing department wanted to be on the cutting edge of technology and decided to lift and shift its current marketing on-premises resources to the cloud. The marketing department didn't utilize any of the concepts we have been discussing, like auto-scaling and right-sizing. This kind of go-to cloud strategy happens more often than not, and it is one of the primary examples of a go-to cloud strategy that fails. The reason for the fail-ure is going to be the large bill on the corporate card for all the cloud resources.

Chargebacks is the process of charging departments or creators of cloud resources for the resources they have provisioned. These chargebacks are a tool for holding consumers of the cloud resources responsible for their actions. We are trying to address and prevent the scenario just outlined for the marketing department at Congruence Corp. Once the market-ing department starts seeing the actual costs of their decisions and go-to cloud strategy, they will realize the TCO is higher than their on-premises resources. This is not a failing of the cloud model; it is a failing of the cloud strategy.

Resource Tagging

Congruence Corp has more departments than just marketing. These other departments may be forming their own cloud strategies. How can we go about knowing which cloud resources belong to which department? *Resource tagging* is the process of tagging cloud resources with identifiers that allow them to be categorized and grouped into logical units. These identifiers are determined by the consumer of the cloud resources. Here are a few key takeaways from implementing such tagging in the real world:

- Always create a tag for every resource with the identifier "Name: <Value>." CSPs will assign names to every resource created. However, these CSP-provided names are going to be globally unique identifiers (GUIDs) that are human-unfriendly to use in the real world. These GUID names assigned by the CSP have to be unique to their entire envi-ronment. A tag of Name: MarketingServer01 will be unique to the cloud account, not to the CSP.

- Create additional tags that will follow logical separation that you already have present in your business hierarchy. An organizational chart can be a good starting point. The most common will be "Department: <Value>."

- Don't neglect unstructured files, i.e., object storage. Remember, object storage is designed for unstructured file storage. These files can group to terabytes, and some CSPs offer petabyte-scale object storage.

Maintenance

Whenever you make a technology purchase, whether it be hardware or software, there is typically a yearly maintenance fee. This maintenance fee ranges from 10 to 25 percent of the base up-front price of the technology. As long as you continue to pay the annual maintenance fee, you will receive both technical support and access to upgraded and newly released features.

Do not confuse a maintenance agreement with a subscription-based purchase. The difference is the license type: owned or leased. If you make a large up-front payment for a piece of technology, either hardware or software, you will typically receive a perpetual license to use that version until update or replacement. With a subscription model, there is typically no large up-front payment to license the technology purchase. The license will not be perpetual and will expire as soon as the subscription is cancelled. We will discuss licensing more later in this section.

To minimize risk, you will typically purchase maintenance on your hardware and software purchases. Maintenance on software provides support and upgrade paths. Maintenance on hardware provides support and warranty for the hardware. If something goes wrong, you will have access to experts on the hardware and replacement of defective parts. Maintenance does not typically cover hardware upgrades. If there is a version of the hardware with increased performance, you will need to make an additional purchase with its own maintenance. If your current hardware cannot perform under your increased load as the business grows, then you will need to make an additional purchase. Either one of these scenarios is called a hardware refresh. The cost of this hardware refresh and subsequent maintenance costs that are not covered by the current maintenance is the number driver we have seen for businesses wanting to go to the cloud. They are looking at a large up-front payment to procure new hardware with continuing maintenance costs. In their minds, if they spread that large up-front payment across a monthly bill from a CSP, then they are saving money because they don't need to purchase maintenance for support.

Instances

Instances are usually mistaken for provisioned VMs, i.e., full servers. In the classic IaaS model, instances equal VMs, but that is not the only model we are going to utilize. For a more complete definition, think of instances as compute resources, as we have discussed previously.

By default, instances that are created in the cloud use the pay-as-you-go pricing model. That means you pay for the time the instance is powered on and any storage required for the instance. Some CSPs offer billing by the minute, but some bill in a minimum hour cycle; i.e., you are billed for an hour even if the instance was used for only 5 minutes. Pay as you go is also referred to as *on-demand pricing*. On-demand pricing is the most expensive pricing model if the instances are utilized 24/7. It is intended for short run or proof-of-concept instances.

Reserved

Reserved instances are instances with a capacity of CPU and RAM that you are willing to pay even if the instances or capacity are not used or even powered on. This becomes a guaranteed minimum payment; obviously, the CSPs like such instances. It provides a guaranteed revenue stream, and it becomes easier for them to resource plan their own infrastructure. Reserved instances smooth out the resource utilization spikes that will occur on a daily basis.

Reserved instances are purchased in either a one-year or three-year commitment. It will be easier to understand why you as a customer would want to use reserved instances if you use some real-world numbers, as I've done in Table 5.4. We will use current AWS pricing models as of the writing of this book. All the rates will be hourly for the on-demand and the effective hourly rate for one-year and three-year commitments. The last column will give the annual cost of on-demand versus a three-year commitment if the instance is run 24/7, 365 days a year.

TABLE 5.4 AWS Hourly Rates

CPU	RAM	On Demand	One-Year	Three-Year	Annual Cost
2	4	$0.0416	$0.026	$0.018	$364.67 vs. $157.79
4	16	$0.1664	$0.104	$0.072	$1,458.66 vs. $631.15
8	32	$0.3328	$0.209	$0.144	$2,917.32 vs. $1,262.30

As you can see from the numbers, if you need an instance with eight CPU cores and 32 GB of RAM and if the instance will be on all the time because it is business critical, e.g., a database server, you can save $1,655.02 per year if you purchase a reserved instance with a three-year commitment.

Fifty Percent Rule for Reserved Instances

If you know that an instance will be powered on and thus billable for at least 50 percent of a calendar year, then you will save money on a reserved instance. The instance being off for half a year and paying for it to be off is cheaper than paying the on-demand price for half a year.

Finally, I'll clear up some common misconceptions about reserved instances. Reserved instances are not tied to a specific VM that is turned on. You are purchasing a reserved capacity of a type. In our example VMs in Table 5.4, if we purchase a three-year commitment for two CPU cores and 4 GB RAM, then we can use that capacity for any VM we want to utilize at that point. We could use the reserved capacity for a web server in the first quarter. Then we could terminate our web server instance and create a new automation server for the freed-up reserved capacity. You cannot combine or use partial instance types. You are purchasing an instance type, i.e., two CPUs and 4 GB RAM, and you must consume it as that.

Spot

Spot instances were created to solve two problems. First, customers have unused reserve instances lying in wait. This is an unused resource. Could the customer recoup some of the cost of the reserved instance, since it is unused? Second, a customer has the need for instances for a small window of operation, i.e., minutes or hours. The instance would not be mission critical or for production use, but there is a need for compute resources. Could the customer get access to unused resources at a steeper discount than on-demand pricing?

Spot instances bridge this gap of unused supply that is available to a specific demand that is temporary in nature. We will approach it from both sides independently.

- **Supply:** Congruence Corp has purchased four reserved instances, each with a capacity of 32 CPU cores and 64 GB RAM. Three of the four are actively being used for Congruence Corp's production systems. The fourth one is currently off but can be turned on if demand on the other three becomes too great, i.e., autoscaling. Congruence Corp would like to recoup any amount of money they have already paid for the reserved instance. Their effective hourly rate for a three-year commitment is $0.634. The hourly rate for the same instance as an on-demand instance is $1.73. Congruence Corp decided to offer the reserved instance at a spot instance hourly rate of $0.45 per hour. Congruence Corp determines the hourly rate based on how quickly it wants the reserved instance to be picked up.

- **Demand:** Flying Widgets Inc. needs to do some video streaming processing for a new podcast it is releasing. The podcast is just a proof of concept and is not critical. Flying Widgets Inc. determines it needs 32 CPU cores and 64 GB RAM to process the video stream. Processing could take up to 48 hours to complete. On-demand pricing put the costs at $83.04 just for the instance. Since this is not a critical application and there is acceptance of the instance becoming unavailable, Flying Widgets makes a bid for a spot instance with 32 CPU cores and 64 GB RAM. Flying Widgets is willing to pay $0.50 per hour for the instance; again, Flying Widgets makes their bid based on their need and the speed of availability.

- Since Flying Widgets Inc.'s bid is above Congruence Corp's reserved price, a spot instance is created for Flying Widgets Inc., using the Congruence Corps reserve instance. As long as Congruence Corp doesn't pull back the instance (which they can at any point), then Flying Widgets Inc. can use the spot instance for a price of $24 versus the $83.04 of on-demand. Congruence Corp gets to recoup some of its already allocated expenditure.

Exam Note

Spot instances are specific to CSPs where there is a shared tenancy, and we haven't seen a lot of their use in the real world. However, they are covered on the exam. The important things to keep in mind: spot instances are won or created on a bidding process. Spot instances are a means of utilizing unused reserve instances. Spot instances can offer significant resources at a significant cost savings. There is a risk that a spot instance may go away without warning and whatever task(s) you have running need to recover from such an event.

Licensing Types

All software comes with a license that specifies the conditions of its use. There are hundreds of different licenses, more than we could cover. However, they can be broken into two broad categories:

- *Free for use*
- *Pay for use*

Free for Use

There are software license types to provide a right to use the software for a specific use. Some licenses limit free use to academic purposes. Some licenses are free only if used in conjunction with a separate pay-for-use license. The most common free-for-use software license is the GNU Public License (*GPL*). GPL is the license type used for the Linux kernel, which is the core software of any Linux distribution. One can argue that it is the popularity of the Linux OS that led to the popularity of the GPL. On the other hand, one can argue that the Linux OS wouldn't be as popular as it is without the permissive GPL license.

GPL has become synonymous with open source, but the two are not the same. *Open source* means that the source code for the software is freely available to download, view, and modify. It is not a license type, and it does not provide a right to use the source code for any purposes. Open source just means the source code is open to everyone. GPL is a license type; it grants the right to use the software with restrictions. GPL has several parts. First, the source code must be open. Second, it grants the right to modify and create derivative works from the source code. Third, it requires that all derivative works must also follow the GPL license.

This requirement that all derivative works that come from a GPL license must also use GPL is a thorny issue with developers who want to produce pay-for-use software that started with a GPL license. This created a need for a free-for-use license type that could be used as a basis for derivative works that could be pay-for-use license. The Berkeley Software Distribution (BSD) license type is currently the most common. BSD is a permissive right license type. It allows the distribution and use of the software and any derivative software as long as the BSD license is included in the subsequent license type. There are still more free-for-use BSD license types than pay-for-use, but a BSD license is the basis for many pay-for-use licenses.

Pay for Use

Pay for use, sometimes referred to as commercial software, is software that you must pay a fee to use. Microsoft Windows, Adobe, Oracle, Citrix, and Microsoft Office 365 are examples of common pay-for-use software. Most of these software packages do offer heavily discounted or sometimes free usage under specific conditions, but none of them can be used commercially without paying a license fee.

Pay-for-use licenses come in two different pay models: perpetual and subscription.

- The Windows OS is an example of a perpetual license. You pay a flat up-front cost and have the right to use the software forever. Windows XP is no longer supported, but if you have an old computer somewhere, it could still be running Windows XP and you have the right to continue using it.

- Office 365 is an example of a subscription model. You pay Microsoft $20 per user per month, and you will get access to the Office 365 E3 license. The Office 365 E3 license provides access to the Office suite, i.e., Word, PowerPoint, Excel, etc. E3 also provides access to Exchange Online and SharePoint Online. You can use email and create a website in the Office 365 Cloud using the E3 license. There is no up-front cost associated with an E3 license; it is a flat rate of $20 per user per month. However, if you stop paying the $20, then Microsoft will lock your data stored in the cloud. The Office applications will enter a reduced functionality state and prevent you from saving any new work.

BYOL

With the advent of the cloud, a new pay-for-use license had to be created, which resulted in Bring Your Own License (BYOL). You have already invested in a perpetual license for a commercial software product. You need to use it in only one place, currently on-premises. However, you know your CSP has the ability and resources to run the commercial software. Do you have to buy a second perpetual license even if you want to shut down the license that you are running on-premises? The answer is, it depends on the software vendor. Some do not allow the transfer of licenses. Some do only under specific conditions or with specific restrictions. Some do allow it. We will give two examples from different software vendors: Cisco and Microsoft.

Cisco, a standard in the networking world, has invested in the cloud and virtualization technologies. Its firewall offering is called Cisco Adaptive Security Application (ASA). Cisco offers a virtual ASA that you can download and incorporate in your own on-premises virtualization stack. You will have to license it and obtain a license key file from Cisco for the ASA to allow traffic. The license key file is perpetual but tied to an OS version. AWS marketplace offers deployable machine images. Cisco has provided and supports these AWS virtual ASAs. Table 5.5 shows the estimated costs for running ASAs in AWS.

TABLE 5.5   Estimated Costs for Running ASAs in AWS

Service Offering	Estimated Hourly Cost
Cisco ASA: BYOL	$0.10
Cisco ASA: Standard	$0.79

As you can see, there is a significant increase in cost if you want to use a subscription license that is maintained through AWS.

Microsoft Windows OSs must be licensed for commercial use. Microsoft licensing is extremely complex and could fill an entire book. We will just cover the basics.

Microsoft does not currently offer a formal BYOL, even into its own cloud offering, Azure. Microsoft does not offer or recognize transfer of licensing from on-premises servers to servers hosted in the cloud. You must license your Windows OSs in the cloud separately from your on-premises licenses, with one exception. If you or your company is under a current Microsoft Software Assurance contract, then you can apply to use license mobility. License mobility has several restrictions and requirements. It will require licensing experts on your part to properly manage.

All the major CSPs thankfully have partner status with Microsoft and can offer Microsoft licenses under Microsoft's service provider license agreement. This places the burden of Microsoft license compliance on the CSP. The CSPs have included Microsoft licensing costs in the instance pricing they offer, so it is not something you need to manage. While most of the Microsoft OSs are offered by the CSPs, not all Microsoft products are available from all CSPs. Microsoft Exchange Server is an example of a product that is not licensed by the CSP. So, if you want to run an Exchange server in the cloud, you will have to acquire and apply your own license.

License Quantity

We have covered the different types of licenses that could be required to run services in the cloud. How many of what type of licenses do you need? The short answer is you need whatever quantity you are using. However, the details are in what "using" means. If an instance is powered on and running, then you need to have a license for any pay-for-use software. Even if the instance is not actively participating in traffic flow, you need a license if the instance is on. This becomes more apparent when you look at the hourly rate for instances in both AWS and Azure. The hourly rate is for powered-on instances. If the instance is turned off, then there is no charge. Remember that the Windows OS license is included in the hourly rate. You could have hundreds of Windows instances deployed, but as long as they are turned off, then they are not being used. Therefore, there is no licensing requirement.

In our previous example with the Cisco ASA, the cost associated with the BYOL was not a license cost. It was compute resource cost for the instance that ran the ASA image. The Cisco example where we used an AWS subscription for the Cisco ASA Standard image incurred an hourly charge because it was powered on.

Licensing is a complex topic and is oftentimes vendor-specific. For the exam, you will need to know that you need a license for every running instance that you have deployed. The key part is running and powered on. It does not matter if the instance is not handling production traffic or workload.

Summary

We covered a lot in this chapter, from aspects of operating in the cloud and introducing DevOps to explaining the financial impact of operating in the cloud. We introduced data management and how to keep your data available and consistent.

We introduced the infrastructure of CSPs and the breakdown of zones, regions, and geo-redundant locations. Cloud has enabled the concept of immutable infrastructure or disposable resources; this is where cloud resources are treated as commodities, not permanent fixtures. We showed the importance of alerts and logging to keep an eye on your cloud resources. They allow you to know what is going on and set up self-healing resources. This self-healing is enabled through autoscaling. Before any organization decides to make the leap to the cloud, they need to take a closer look at their on-premises resources to perform a right-size analysis.

We introduced DevOps in general and how you can use tools provided by CSPs and how to provision resources in the cloud and utilize code to define your infrastructure. There was in important concept of imperative versus declarative when defining infrastructure and resources. We discussed CI and CD and how they are central to every DevOps implementation, in the cloud or on-premises. There are various forms of testing that any DevOps team will need to perform as part of the CICD pipeline. Automation and orchestration are the cornerstone and the glue that make the CICD pipeline work. We talked about how to perform an upgrade on an application, using all of the tools we discussed this chapter. CSPs have built their infrastructure and consumption model around APIs and their integrations; i.e., everything in the cloud is an API call.

We discussed the financial side of going to the cloud and how the CSPs offer different tiers of their products. Service offerings will usually fall into one of three categories: compute, network, or storage. We discussed the importance of resource tagging to accurately track expenditures of services in the cloud. There are currently three instance types offered by CSPs: on-demand (default), reserved, and spot. We discussed the use case and when you would want to use one or the other. Finally, we talked about license quantities and license types.

Exam Essentials

Know about data availability and the part replication plays. Data availability is the concept of making and keeping data available to users and applications. Replication is the process of storing data in multiple locations to provide other means of data availability if one location is no longer available. There are two different kinds of replication: synchronous and asynchronous. Synchronous replication keeps data synced in real time. Asynchronous replication replicates data on time determined by RTO and RPO.

Know what locality means and understand the benefit the cloud offers.   Data locality is the impact distance has on data access to the end user. Data does not flow through the Internet instantaneously, and it will take time to deliver content. The distance between the end user and the data is directly related to the time it takes. CSPs have a global presence and can store data in multiple locations around the globe, thus decreasing the distance and time for delivering content.

Know the part backups play in restoring data or services.   Backing up is the process of copying data to a medium that can be restored in the event that the data is lost or compromised. Backup processes in the cloud are similar to other backup processes performed in on-premises virtualized infrastructures. Snapshots are executed and copied to object storage on a schedule that is aligned with the required RTO and RPO.

Know the difference between zones and regions.   A zone is are either a data center or a collection of data centers within a CSP's infrastructure. The CSP's infrastructure within a zone is within close proximity of each other and offer high bandwidth and low latency to facilitate synchronous replication. Regions are logical collections of zones within a CSP's infrastructure. Regions are named after their locations around the globe, e.g., US East, Canada, US Central, and US West.

Know what geo-redundancy is and the part a CDN plays.   Geo-redundancy is the process of replicating data and services between regions. Geo-redundancy has two main goals: keeping data and services running if a region becomes unavailable and offering a closer locality to end users. CDN is a distributed (i.e., in multiple regions) delivery network of data to facilitate the locality.

Know what disposable resources are and the shift in deployment processes.   Having disposable resources is the concept of treating infrastructure that supports data access as immutable, or unchangeable. If you have new versions of applications or OSs, then do not deploy them on the current infrastructure. Deploy new infrastructure with the updates and changes. There are two techniques for deploying infrastructure more quickly: bootstrapping and golden image. Bootstrapping is having the deployment of infrastructure include customization and installation through a scripting process. Golden image means having the customization and installation be part of the image that is deployed and already present at the moment of deployment.

Know the importance of monitoring and visibility.   Monitoring and visibility provide insight and notify when events occur in the cloud. Alerts monitor and produce actions based on the properties of the deployed infrastructure, i.e., storage, compute, and networking. Logging is the recording of events or actions that occur either in the cloud or on the resources in the cloud. Logging the cloud is already present and needs to be configured. Logging on resources will require additional setup.

Know the process and benefit of autoscaling.   Autoscaling is one of the coolest features with the largest benefit of moving resources to the cloud. You can set parameters that will scale both in and out based on resource health and usage. The cloud can be self-healing when events occur that would normally have a negative user impact.

Know the importance of right-sizing in the cloud. The biggest reason for cloud initiatives to fail is cost overrun. This is due to organizations performing lift-and-shift strategies—they move everything to the cloud. The cost model between cloud and on-premises is in direct conflict and not compatible. Right-sizing is the process of performing an analysis of on-premises resources and providing the correctly sized resources in the cloud.

Know the DevOps process and mind-set. DevOps is a change in historical deployment processes. The CALMS acronym is a good thing to remember to help understand: Culture, Automation, Lean, Measurement, and Sharing. DevOps tries to turn down the silos that exist in most organizations. The process needs to be iterative and have a feedback loop.

Know the benefits of infrastructure as code (IaC). IaC makes your infrastructure be defined as code. This allows the use of the tools used in the development process for infrastructure. IaC allows for imperative defining of resources instead of declarative. You define what the resources should be, not what the resources are. There are templates available online that have complex infrastructure deployments and can be tailored to your needs.

Know what CICD is and how it relates to DevOps. CICD is an implementation of the DevOps process. It uses the tools from software deployment to execute the four steps of application deployment: Dev, Build, Test, and Release.

Know various testing processes. Sandboxing is the process of testing changes in an environment that is close to production but cannot impact the production environment. Load testing is the process of testing new code under circumstances that are close to real-world use, i.e., under load. Regression testing is the process of testing changes through a detailed and documented process that won't reintroduce previously discovered issues.

Know the process and tools used for configuration management. Automation is a method of controlling a process in such a way as to limit or even remove any human intervention. This removes the human error aspect and also makes the process repeatable. Orchestration is the coordination between multiple automation techniques. Orchestration brings all the pieces and parts of the DevOps process together with logging, monitoring, and auditing of the entire process.

Know the importance of API in the cloud. Every action, whether performed as part of orchestration or viewing logs in a management console, is an API call. This means there is no difference between web tools, CLI tools, or SDKs; they all perform the same way.

Know the differences and examples of costs using storage, network, and compute. Storage costs depend on the type: object, block, or file. Object storage costs are based on transfer and access, including replication. Block storage costs are based on the type and speed of the storage. File storage costs are based on transfer and access. All three have costs associated with the amount of storage used. Network costs are based on the amount of data transferred in and out of the CSPs infrastructure. Compute costs are based on the resources, i.e., CPU and RAM provisioned.

Know what chargebacks and tagging are. Chargebacks are the process of assigning costs of cloud resources to either individuals or departments that are responsible for the resources. Tagging is used to correctly assign properties to resources to identify who is responsible for a resource.

Know the three types of instances and their differences.   By default, any instance is an on-demand instance type. This is a pay-as-you-go model, and you pay for only the amount of time the instance is on. Reserved instance type is the pre-pay model. You pay for the resources up front even if you are not actively using instances. Spot instances are instances that are renting reserved instances not currently being used. On-demand is the most expensive option.

Know the different licensing types and the impact they have on cloud licensing.   Free-for-use licenses that have become synonymous with open source are software that can be used freely without having to pay any licensing fees. Pay-for-use licenses, which have become synonymous with commercial software, are software that you must pay a fee to use. Use of either in the cloud is available, but the pay-for-use license is impacted. Use of commercial software in the cloud is dependent on the software vendor and must be treated individually.

Written Lab

Fill in the blanks for the questions provided in the written lab. You can find the answers to the written lab questions in Appendix A.

1. _____ replication keeps data in sync between two or more locations in accordance with RPO and RTO.

2. CSP infrastructure is broken into logical units called _____, which offer high bandwidth and low latency connectivity.

3. _____ is the process of scripting or writing code that will configure and customize any cloud resource at the point of deployment.

4. Setting up parameters and resources that will grow or shrink with demand is called _____.

5. Software defined networking is an example of _____.

6. _____ testing is where new application code is tested against past bugs.

7. Creating a system that is able to perform the same steps in a repeatable and consistent manner is _____.

8. _____ is the underlying technology in all management tools for CSPs.

9. _____ are the cheapest instance type one can utilize in the cloud.

10. _____ is the technique of being able to use your already purchased license on a cloud resource.

Review Questions

1. The CIO wants to cut the cost of the instances that are running in the cloud. The instances that have the highest cost are all production instances and are required to be on 24/7. Which instance type should you look into utilizing?

   A. On-demand

   B. Spot

   C. Reserved

   D. Quick

2. You have been tasked with creating a WordPress site using open source software and making the primary site highly available within a region. Which option of software and locality would fulfill the requirements?

   A. Nginx and MariaDB installed on Ubuntu 18.04 running in both US-East-1 and US-East-2 zones

   B. Nginx and MariaDB installed on Windows Server 2012 R2 running in both US-East-3 and US-East-2 zones

   C. IIS and MariaDB installed on Windows Server 2016 running in both US-East-1 and US-East-4 zones

   D. Nginx and MariaDB installed on CentOS 7 running in both US-East-1 and Canada-1 zones

3. You are designing the infrastructure for an e-commerce website that plans on selling sporting apparel for football (soccer) clubs around the globe. Which technology should you look at that offers the lowest latency and best performance for your shoppers?

   A. Immutable infrastructure

   B. Synchronous replication

   C. Content delivery network

   D. Autoscaling

4. You need to update all the Windows Servers from Server 2012 R2 to Server 2016. You decide the best course of action is to do an in-place upgrade and install Server 2016 over the top of Server 2012 R2. Is this a recommended course of action? Why or why not?

   A. Yes, because you are saving money by not creating more servers.

   B. Yes, because the software is already installed on the servers and you know Server 2016 is compatible.

   C. No, because you are not treating the servers as disposable resources.

   D. No, because you have not performed any load testing of the software on Server 2016.

5. You have decided to test your application on Server 2016 and want to deploy new instances. Which technologies will you use to speed up the deployment and make sure all the servers are deployed in procedural and repeatable fashion? (Choose two.)

   A. Bootstrapping

   B. API

   C. Golden image

   D. Tagging

6. Which of the following cloud resources will have a cost associated with any transfer of data out of the CSP's infrastructure? (Choose all that apply.)

   A. Object storage

   B. Network

   C. Compute

   D. Block storage

7. Which storage offerings will have a cost associated with the amount of data stored, even if the resource using the storage is powered off? (Choose all that apply.)

   A. Object storage

   B. Block storage

   C. File storage

   D. Replicated storage

8. Your legal department wants to start using cloud resources. However, since all of their work will be associated with legal cases, they need an accurate usage and billing breakdown to bill the clients. What are you being asked to implement?

   A. Right-sizing

   B. Maintenance

   C. Chargebacks

   D. Monitoring

9. The development team has added a new search feature that has never been tested before. Which testing process is more important than the others?

   A. Load testing

   B. Regression testing

   C. Sandbox testing

   D. Penetration testing

10. Your manager wants to do a lift-and-shift migration from on-premises servers to cloud servers. He has determined that the cloud will save money. Which process is the manager forgetting to complete?

    A. Templating

    B. Autoscaling

    C. Orchestrating

    D. Right-sizing

11. The CFO wants to be notified whenever the monthly estimated costs reach $2,000. You will set up _____ to notify once the threshold is met.

    A. Logging

    B. Alerts

    C. API

    D. Autoscaling

12. What has become synonymous with DevOps and is referred to as a pipeline and used in the real world by organizations?

    A. Continuous integration continuous diversity

    B. Continuous integration continuous development

    C. Continuous integration continuous delivery

    D. Continuous integration continuous discovery

13. Which of the following cloud deployment models offers the best scalability and cost effectiveness?

    A. Public

    B. Private

    C. Community

    D. Hybrid

14. A blue/green deployment is a deployment used primarily when doing_____ on production infrastructure.

    A. Regression testing

    B. Upgrades and patching

    C. Sandbox testing

    D. Development

15. Which of the following is not a common characteristic of public clouds?

    A. Self-service

    B. Pay-as-you-go

    C. Higher cost

    D. Availability

16. Your company uses a financial transactions database that updates frequently. If a natural disaster occurred, any data backup older than one hour would not be useful to the company. To ensure that backups are always more current, what needs to be specified in the disaster recovery plan?

    A. RPO

    B. RTO

    C. TSO

    D. SLA

17. API integration can be used to manage cloud resources by which of the following methods? (Choose all that apply.)

    A. Web

    B. CLI

    C. SDK

    D. SSH

18. What storage type is used for the OS boot partition of an instance running in the cloud?

    A. HDD

    B. File

    C. Block

    D. Object

19. What is the process of combining a series of automation steps into a repeatable process that can be audited?

    A. Automation

    B. Orchestration

    C. Autoscaling

    D. Patching

20. Which of the following are examples of free-for-use license types? (Choose all that apply.)

    A. Linux

    B. Apache

    C. Windows

    D. Cisco ASA

Chapter

6

Governance and Risk

✓ **4.1 Recognize risk management concepts related to cloud services**

- Risk assessment

  - Asset Inventory

  - Classification

  - Ownership

- Risk Response

  - Mitigation

  - Acceptance

  - Avoidance

  - Transfer

- Documentation

  - Findings

  - Risk register

- Vendor lock-in

- Data portability

✓ **4.2 Explain policies and procedures**

- Standard operating procedures

- Change management

- Resource management

- Security policies

  - Incident response

- Access and control policies

- Department specific policies

- Communication policies

Compliance is a word that can make people groan in annoyance or that they ignore with apathy. Most seasoned IT professionals view compliance requirements as busywork or just documentation. They feel it takes time away from real work. However, for large organizations and for any organization in certain fields (banking, healthcare, insurance, manufacturing, government, etc.), compliance is critical to operations.

Being in compliance requires actions by individuals and/or organizations that are aligned with laws or regulations imposed by regulatory agencies. These actions can come in many different forms: documentation, policies, procedures, forms submissions, and board reviews, to name a few. We will be discussing several of these and giving examples in this chapter.

Any cloud plan will require some compliance knowledge. Compliance helps protect organizations and individuals from civil and criminal liabilities. This isn't something that can be ignored or done later. Compliance audits are time sensitive and must be performed annually.

 Real World Scenario

Payment Card Industry Data Security Standard (PCI DSS)

PCI DSS is an example of a compliance requirement that is dictated not by law but by contractual obligation. It governs the security of credit card information and is enforced by agreements between businesses that accept credit cards and banks that process the transaction. PCI DSS is a requirement of all the major credit card vendors and administered by the Payment Card Industry Security Standards Council. So, any organization that wants to issue a credit card, process a transaction using a credit card, or accept credit cards as a form of payment must follow the 12 PCI DSS requirements:

- Install and maintain firewall configuration to protect cardholder data.

- Do not use vendor-supplied defaults for system passwords and other security parameters.

- Protect stored cardholder data.

- Encrypt transmission of cardholder data across open, public networks.

- Protect all systems against malware and regularly update anti-virus software or programs.

- Develop and maintain security systems and applications.

- Restrict access to cardholder data by business justification (i.e., "need to know").

- Identify and authenticate access to system components.

- Restrict physical access to cardholder data.

- Track and monitor all access to network resources and cardholder data.

- Regularly test security systems and processes.

- Maintain a policy that addresses information security for all personnel.

You will not need to know the 12 requirements for the certification exam. They are listed to show an example of a compliance requirement for processing credit card information. You will need to know that PCI DSS stands for Payment Card Industry Data Security Standard and that it is required.

You can read more about PCI DSS and get more details at https://www.pcisecuritystandards.org.

Recognize Risk Management Concepts Related to Cloud Services

The major underlying theme of this chapter will be *risk*. CompTIA offers another certification that is security focused: CASP+ (CompTIA Advanced Security Practitioner). Sybex has a Study Guide for the CASP+ certification where *risk* is defined as the probability or likelihood of the occurrence or realization of a *threat*.

The key words are *probability* and *threat*. Probability is the chance or likelihood that something might occur. We will use the definition of threat from the same book:

> A *threat* is any agent, condition, or circumstance that could potentially cause harm, loss, damage, or compromise to an IT *asset* or data asset. The likelihood of the threat is the probability of occurrence or the odds that the event will actually occur.

Agent, condition, or circumstance: these are either individual(s) or events. Harm, loss, damage, or compromise: these refer to any kind of loss of value. The last key term from this definition is *asset*.

Asset

An *asset* is an item of value to an institution such as data, hardware, software, or physical property. An asset is an item or collection of items that has a quantitative or qualitative value to a company. Quantitative and qualitative will be covered in the section "Risk Assessment."

To put it another way, risk is the probability that some sort of harm or damage will occur to an asset. An asset is anything that is of value to a company or organization. In the most general sense, an asset does not have to just be an IT item. Employees are also an example of an asset. Additionally, harm or damage can be generalized to be a less than ideal state of the asset, e.g., service being inadvertently turned off. In this section, we are going to discuss strategies and methodologies to manage risk.

Instead of talking about risk by definition or abstractly, let's give a few examples of both IT-related risk (Table 6.1) and non-IT-related risk (Table 6.2).

TABLE 6.1   IT-Related Risk

Risk	High probability of employees unintentionally interacting with malware in today's connected workforce. Employees digitally interact with others via email, sharing of files, or web pages.
Threat	Immediate harm would be loss of company data and files. Secondary would be loss of employee time—both the employee who became infected and the IT employee's time to recover the company's data and the employee's infected device.
Asset	Company data and employees

TABLE 6.2   Non-IT-Related Risk

Risk	High probability of car being stolen if parked in a busy parking lot with keys lying on the front seat
Threat	Immediate loss of vehicle and potential damage
Asset	Vehicle

You most likely have dealt with these risks before and haven't thought much about them. You already have a risk response in mind for either of these examples: install anti-malware and lock your car. Realize that you deal with risk every day and you already have built-in responses. We want to expand on that and apply similar techniques to new risks that come with going to the cloud. We will be discussing risk response later in this chapter.

Risk Assessment

Now that we have an idea of what risk is, let's talk about how to assess the risk. When we measure risk, we are talking about risk that can affect assets. So, we need to explore and understand assets more. Assets are any items that have value to a company. This value is measured through either a *quantitative* risk assessment or a *qualitative* risk assessment.

Quantitative risk assessment deals with dollar amounts. It attempts to assign a monetary value to the elements of risk or the assets themselves. Qualitative risk assessment deals with the quality of risk or assets. It will rank the threats based on experience, intuition, or a specific scenario.

Quantitative is the most intuitive because it has a dollar amount attached to it. For example, a laptop costs $1,200 new. If it is lost or stolen, it easy to do the risk assessment on the hardware. However, that $1,200 is not the complete picture of the asset's value. What about the data that is on the laptop? Let's say that laptop was used by the director of marketing for a company. On that laptop there were all the slides and marketing material for the go-to-market strategy for the coming year. Those materials took employees time to produce. Maybe that work was tracked, and we could place some quantitative assessment on the work. We could probably put a monetary value on replacement or redoing the work. So, the quantitative risk assessment for this laptop has now increased in value.

We are not done with our risk assessment of our laptop. What if the laptop was stolen by a competitor of the company? What if the competitor learns the new go-to-market strategy and they get a jump on the strategy? The competitor could execute a similar strategy or a strategy that effectively renders your company's strategy mute. What is the cost to the company now? This is where qualitative risk assessment comes into play. The only way to assess this risk is based on the experience and intuition of experienced people. Since the assessment is based on a person's perception, we need to have a way of measurement, which is the difficult part. The best way and really the only way of measuring qualitative risk is comparison or ranking. Measuring the risk of a competitor learning your strategy is difficult, but we could compare it or rank it against other components of quantitative analysis.

At the core of this risk analysis is the asset. Before we explore assets in depth, we need to define two topics that are critical to the assessment process: value and threat. We will be discussing these two topics throughout this chapter, and they are critical to understanding risk. Value is typically thought of as monetary or quantitative, but it is not limited to monetary value. An asset can have a higher value than other similar assets if it is critical to the functioning of a business. As an example, think of an ice cream truck. All the ice cream obviously is an asset and has a monetary value. However, the ice cream truck itself would be considered more critical than the ice cream because all the ice cream would melt and be ruined without a functioning ice cream truck. Additionally, the ice cream itself cannot be thought of just in terms of the monetary value of its purchase. Ice cream in this case also has revenue value.

We have defined threat previously, but we need to add a new term that is often confused with threat, *vulnerability*. Vulnerability is a threat, but not all threats are vulnerabilities. A vulnerability is attached to a specific asset. Vulnerabilities are threats to assets that have not been mitigated. We will be discussing mitigation and other risk responses later in this chapter. We need to know which assets we have.

Asset Inventory

Before we can secure or protect any asset, we need to know what we are going to secure or protect. This is where an *asset inventory* becomes essential. Many organizations lack an accurate and timely inventory of their assets. By timely we mean accurate inventory when timing is important. Think of a scenario where a fire broke out at a warehouse. Would the organization have an accurate head count and the names of the individuals in the building? This information is needed quickly and needs to be accurate.

Broadly, assets can be broken into two categories: tangible or intangible assets. Tangible assets are assets that can be appraised with a monetary value. Intangible assets cannot be directly appraised with a monetary value. These have a close parallel to qualitative assessment and quantitative assessment. For the sake of brevity, we are going to keep our discussion of assets to hardware, software, and data.

 Real World Scenario

Hardware vs. Software and Physical vs. Virtual

Typically, people think of hardware as being something physical, i.e., something you can touch. The cloud and virtualization have blurred this definition. Simply, is a virtual server that you spin up in the cloud or in your own data center considered hardware? Well, it isn't physical and not as straightforward to define. The answer is a little muddied, but the short of it is this: Software has the properties of not being physical and performs a specific function. Software is created by a software developer. A VM emulates hardware even though it is not physical. It is not an application that is created by a software developer. The hypervisor that runs the VM is software, but the VM is considered hardware. It may sound counterintuitive to say that hardware has a dependency on software. However, hardware that you typically consider a physical hardware device still depends on software to run, e.g., a firewall or router.

The majority of cloud resources that you create will be considered hardware even though they are not physical, i.e., VMs, networks, databases, etc. CSPs are making a push for managed services, i.e., database as a service, Docker as a service, etc. This blurs the line even more, and some instances are considered software. Additionally, SaaS applications like Office 365 or Google Suite are considered software packages.

Hardware

Hardware on the surface should be easy to track. A hardware device can be seen or touched or can be scanned once it registers with the network or our cloud management console. Organizations will use databases or automated applications to perform inventories and track hardware through its life cycle. If you look at your company-provided machine or phone, there is probably an asset or property tag, as shown in Figure 6.1. This tag will have a unique number for the organization on it that identifies it within a database.

FIGURE 6.1   Example of a property tag

In Chapter 3, we discussed reporting on virtual hardware. CSPs offer three categories of virtual services: compute, storage, and network. These virtual items cannot be seen, touched, or property tagged. We need to come up with some other mechanism to inventory these items. Fortunately, almost all CSPs provide some means of inventory. The larger CSPs will offer move advanced inventory mechanisms.

Software

Software by its nature is more difficult to inventory than hardware; it is not physical. Inventorying software is just as important, if not more important. An inaccurate software inventory can have significant financial impact and security risk. It is important that software inventory be accurate and up to date. Otherwise, unlicensed software can and will be used in an organization.

Unlicensed software can have significant financial impact on an organization. Risk can come from multiple sources, but the most common are unpatched software and software audits.

Modern software for patches and updates has to be online to download the patches. The software vendor will check for a valid license either before allowing the download or before the installation of the patch is allowed. An unpatched software package is inherently vulnerable to exploitation and attack. This vulnerability is a threat. We discussed vulnerabilities and threats previously. Remember our definition of risk; unpatched software increases the probability of harm or damage to an asset.

Periodically major software vendors perform software audits. These audits typically start as voluntary but can become compulsory if ignored. In short, if a software vendor decides to perform a software audit, there will be a smaller risk if you perform it rather than ignore it. The software audit will come in one of two flavors or a combination of the two. First is self-reporting. The software vendor will ask how many installations of software X you have. Second is some sort of licensing manager check. The software vendor will run a check against either an internal or external-based licensing manager; i.e., you purchased 100 installations of software X, but the licensing manager is reporting 150 installations.

This gap in proper licensing is a risk that has monetary impact. The software vendor will require a true-up, a realignment of purchased software to actual. However, the software vendor may also require payment for software that was used in the past. Organizations need to have an accurate software inventory and have controls in place to either audit or prevent unapproved software installations.

 Real World Scenario

Software Editions Impact Licensing

I worked for an organization that needed to purchase several hundred licenses of Microsoft Visio and Project. It was determined through use-case scenarios that Visio Standard edition was enough to the meet the use-case requirements. However, Project Professional edition would be required to meet the use case. The order was put through, but when it came back, the license editions got flipped. The license count was for Project Standard and Visio Professional. No one noticed, and the IT department installed the software based on user requirements, i.e., Visio Standard and Project Professional.

This went on for several years, and the error was never recognized or corrected. Microsoft did a software audit several years after the original purchase. The organization reported correctly the hundreds of Visio Standard and Project Professional installations. Microsoft found the organization to be out of license compliance and issued a new bill for the use of Project Professional installations when only Project Standard was licensed. Unfortunately for the organization, because of the age of the original purchase, we could not prove that it was an error on Microsoft's part or on the organization's original order.

We were able to negotiate with Microsoft and get some relief from paying the full price of the difference, but there was still a monetary impact.

Data

Data, when discussing assets and risk, is the broadest and most diverse topic. We need to make a distinction between data and information here, because they are often confused. *Data* is in raw format. *Information* is collated and categorized data. For example, the number of units sold of a particular product in the last quarter would be considered data. However, the comparison of units sold last quarter to those sold in the same quarter of the previous year would be considered information.

We are going to discuss the inventorying and risk of both data and information. There will be overlap between the two, but we will call out the difference when necessary.

In general, information has a higher value placed on it than data due to its meaning. Information is processed data and has greater value.

Another difference between data and information is use. Business processes is an example of information that is not derived directly from data. Business processes are based on data.

Classification

We have our assets inventoried with their values. We need to add the other part of the risk definition, which is threat. We will discuss the difference between threat and vulnerability later in this chapter. It is easier to understand risks and formulate the appropriate risk response if they can be grouped with similar risks. Once grouped, the risks can be ranked according to the likelihood of the realization of threat or the asset's value. This ranking of risks becomes its own classification.

Risk *classification* systems come in one of two flavors: grades (A, B, C, D, F) or a scale from 1 to 5. The systems are interchangeable and function the same way. The goal of the classification is to help determine the appropriate risk response or appropriate level of security to provide to an asset. One should never spend more on resources to protect an asset than the value of the asset itself.

There are two parts of the classification: asset value and the probability of a threat occurring. These two parts will help produce the risk classification for the asset and threat. The higher the asset value and the higher the probability of a threat occurring, the higher the risk classification, e.g., level 5. Lower asset value and lower probability of a threat occurring will mean a lower risk classification, i.e., level 1. The balancing act and the middle ground is where you have an asset of high value but low probability of threat, or an asset of low value with a high probability of threat. Your organization will need to come up with policies on how to handle the middle classifications, but being able to compare one risk to another risk will assist greatly.

Table 6.3 shows a few examples to help clarify how an organization might set up their classification system.

TABLE 6.3   Example Classifications of Risk

Asset	Threat	Classification Level
Data center	Loss of network connectivity	5
Company vehicles	Theft from parking garage	4
Office supplies	Used for non-business-related projects	2
Laptops and mobile devices	Loss or theft by or from remote employees	3
Office space	Loss of power	1

Obviously, different organizations would give different classifications. Some might classify loss of a laptop at a higher level than the loss of a company vehicle because of the likelihood of recovery or not. A company vehicle is less likely to be stolen and more likely to be recovered than a laptop. A manufacturing company that produces its product at an office space would rate loss of power higher than an accounting firm might. The accounting firm could relocate required staff or have them work from home. The production would stop for the manufacturing firm and could not resume until power was restored.

Each organization has to determine its own classification system and criteria. The ranking or grading, though, becomes important when determining appropriate risk response. This risk response will be determined by the risk and asset owners, our next topic.

Ownership

Ownership is a critical concept and role when it comes to risk management. There are two roles that need to be identified when discussing ownership: risk owner and asset owner. In smaller organizations, the same person can play both roles, but in larger organizations, they are often different people. Let's take a deeper dive into each role.

Risk Owner

The person who takes on the role of *risk owner* needs to be in a management position. The risk owner is going to be the individual who will decide and assume the risk response for the risk they are owning. We will be discussing risk response in our next section. The importance of the risk owner being part of management cannot be overstated. Remember, risk is a function of management; it is not a function of IT or technical services. Risk must be managed as a whole from the organization top down, not the bottom up.

The risk owner is often a department head or a director and is someone other employees report to. The risk owner will have a larger picture view of the organization and have management-level knowledge to make informed decisions when choosing an appropriate risk response. They report to upper management and in layman's terms the "buck stops with them" when it comes to risk response and outcomes.

An example of a risk owner for a larger organization would be VP of cloud services. As you can surmise from the title, they would be responsible for everything having to do with the cloud, including all IaaS, PaaS, and SaaS offerings. For a large organization, this individual would not be able to have the technical expertise or the background to be the asset owner for all the cloud offerings. However, the risk owner would have the managerial experience and expertise to rely on asset owners to make informed risk response decisions.

Asset Owner

An *asset owner* may be known by several different names, depending on the asset: product owner, data owner, or information owner. A product owner is someone who has extensive knowledge or background in the product or data they own. An asset owner is responsible for the execution and operation of the software or systems that control and manage assets.

An example could be someone who owns a cloud SaaS product like Office 365 for an organization. The product owner should have training, skills, and experience to provide guidance to the risk owner. The product owner provides advice and counsel to the risk owner in order for them to make an informed decision about risk response.

In smaller organizations, the risk owner and asset owner are often the same individual, and a single person can be the risk and asset owner of multiple assets. A CTO or CIO of a small organization may own all the technology and risk assets.

Risk Response

Once assets have been inventoried and classified and ownership has been determined, the owners can use the risk assessment to determine their risk response. We need to bring up an important concept when it comes to risk response. We should never exert more effort or pay more or expend more resources than the value of the asset itself. This is where an asset's value becomes important. For example, we should not spend the money and resources for 24-hour armed security guards and biometric scanners to secure a server that is worth only $5,000. The level of securing must be dependent on the value of the asset. This is where the quantitative and qualitative analyses we performed earlier become important. This also goes back to our classification of risks.

In general, there are four responses to risk: mitigation, acceptance, avoidance, and transfer. We will be discussing them each individually.

Mitigation

Risk *mitigation* is the most common response to risk. In short, mitigation is the act of reducing risk through the expenditure of resources of the organization. An organization is going to invest in either technology or staffing to lower the probability of the realization of the threat against its assets.

Firewall, anti-malware, proxies, and identity management are all examples of risk mitigation responses. They all require an investment from an organization, and their purpose is to lower the probability of threats against assets. This is by no means an exhaustive list, but you get the idea.

Mitigation strategies are usually technological in nature in that they entail hardware or devices to implement. Simple locks on doors help prevent the theft of assets from your home or place of business. Do you lock your car when you park? What is the reason for locking your car? If you park your car farther away from the store where no other cars are parked because you don't want your car to get dinged by other cars, that is an example of risk mitigation. The expenditure of resources is the longer walk and increased time.

CSPs offer several mitigation responses, and most of these strategies are included or enabled by default. None of the CSPs allow network traffic from the Internet to resources by default. You must enable or allow traffic from outside your network or the CSP's network inside. This is in the best interest of the CSP as well. Threats against your resources are partial threats against their resources. CSPs have taken additional risk mitigation responses that you may not be aware of. They have specialized hypervisors that isolate resources and help prevent "runaway" use of their resources. The shared responsibility model that we discussed in Chapter 1 is the framework for risk response from both the CSP and you.

Acceptance

Risk *acceptance* is similar to mitigation in that the organization is going to handle the risk themselves. The critical difference is that the organization will not expend any resources on the risk. The organization is accepting the probability of the threats against the identified assets as is. Acceptance is the "do nothing" response to risk. Management has decided to self-insure.

The reasons why the organization chooses acceptance over the other risk response falls into one of two categories: either value of the asset or probability of the threat.

- If the value of the asset is low enough that damage or loss is not significant, then cost of replacement is not significant.

- If the probably of a threat is very low, then it can be effectively ignored.

A couple of examples will help clarify risk acceptance. A bank with pens in the lobby that anyone can use and take is an example of risk acceptance. The pens' value is so low that the bank accepts the probability of occasional theft. Almost every occurrence of an asset being treated as a commodity or disposable is risk acceptance. An organization deciding to take no protective action on employees' Internet usage is an example of risk acceptance. Internet filtering technologies can be expensive, and for smaller organizations, it may not be cost-effective to filter and/or monitor Internet usage. The organization is relying on reactive measures as responses to any risk that become realized from inappropriate Internet usage.

Avoidance

Risk *avoidance* would be the preferred risk response for every risk manager. The risk is nullified, and no damage or loss of an organization's asset will occur. However, in the real world, risk avoidance is the rarest and hardest to attain. Risk avoidance is where the probability of a threat is eliminated or reduced to zero. The threat is removed or the chance of the occurrence no longer exists.

Moving a data center from an area that is prone to natural disasters is one example of risk avoidance. If you look at the major CSPs and the regions discussed in Chapter 5, none of the regions is in a high natural disaster area. Amazon and Microsoft did not build their eastern data centers in the areas of high hurricane occurrence.

AWS Data Centers

AWS has an interactive web page that introduces the workings of its data centers.

https://aws.amazon.com/compliance/data-center/data-centers/

It covers a lot of the topics discussed in this chapter.

The difference between risk mitigation and avoidance can be difficult, because resources are typically expended to avoid a risk entirely. The expenditure of the resources would typically indicate mitigation versus avoidance. The difference is that most mitigation responses only lower the probability and don't eliminate it.

Transfer

Transfer is the last risk response we will discuss. When an organization transfers all the risk from itself to a third party, that is risk transfer. Insurance is the largest example of risk transference. Think of homeowner's insurance; you pay a third party a monthly fee. In return, the insurance company will make a large payout to you if your home is damaged. Your average homeowner cannot self-insure (risk acceptance), because they already have a mortgage out on their home; i.e., they couldn't replace their home if it was destroyed.

Organizations utilize risk transfer all the time through purchase of third-party insurance: fire, flood, property, liability, etc. Insurance is not the only example of risk transfer. Organizations will often realize that they need third-party technical expertise to achieve their technical goals. They will often reach out to consultants and rely on their expertise. Organizations will hire these consultants on a temporary basis to complete a specific set of steps that are specified in a statement of work.

Lastly, using CSP services is an example of risk transference. You are paying the CSP for services, and in turn they are accepting the risk of maintaining the infrastructure that you are "virtually" using. The shared responsibility model details which risks the organization is transferring to the CSP and which they still need to mitigate or accept.

Documentation

Documentation is a word that can strike fear and pain into IT professionals. It isn't entirely their fault. Most IT professionals are tasked with building or creating something that hasn't been done before. So, they spend a lot of time trying different things, with a lot of trial and error. When they finally come across the solution and are able to implement it, the question becomes what to document. Do they really need to document the 99 things they tried that failed or only the one that was successful? The answer is somewhere in between, but you can see how documentation in general is not something that is enjoyed.

The first thing that needs to be documented is anything that is required by law or regulation. We discussed this previously in this chapter. Looking at the 12 requirements of PCI DSS, all of them will require some level of *documentation* to prove compliance. Any publicly traded company will have SEC documentation requirements that must be met.

Next, the items that need to be documented are anything that is required by an organization's policies and procedures. Any documentation that is required by law or regulation is most likely covered by policies and procedures. However, there will be documentation requirements spelled out in policies and procedures that go beyond laws and regulations. Policies and procedures written in response to risk realization events are a good example. We will be talking about risk realization events in the next section. For now, understand that when a risk event occurs or when damage occurs against an organization's asset, we need to perform a findings documentation.

Findings

Findings are the documentation of a risk event. When a risk event occurs, an investigation is typically warranted. This investigation may be brief or may take months, depending on the circumstances. Investigations may involve third parties and even law enforcement. Investigators are tasked with determining whether proper procedures were followed or whether there is a gap in procedures to handle the event(s) that occurred. Since findings are the product of an investigation, we will break down the four general investigation types in Table 6.4.

TABLE 6.4   General Investigation Types

Type	Details
Criminal	Investigations are typically conducted by law enforcement. The goal is to produce evidence that can be used by law enforcement or counsel. Proper chain of evidence (chain of custody) procedures most be followed. Criminal cases must meet the *beyond a reasonable doubt* standard.
Civil	Investigations typically do not involve law enforcement and are conducted internally by an organization. They may involve legal counsel, but the human resources (HR) department will be involved. Civil investigations have a lower standard than criminal, called *weaker preponderance of evidence*. Proper chain of evidence procedures should still be followed but are not a strict requirement.
Regulatory	Investigations are performed by either government officials or regulatory body personnel. Investigations are different from audits. Audits can occur at any time and are performed to meet compliance requirements. Investigations occur after a risk event occurs. Investigations will often perform the same steps as an audit but will also dig deeper into the procedures that relate to the risk event.
Operational	Operational investigations are the most common and the investigations you are most likely to run into as IT professionals. The goal is to resolve operational issues that occur from email phishing attempts, malware outbreaks, deleted files, etc. There are no evidentiary requirements unless spelled out in policy. A lot of your day-to-day tasks could fall under this type of investigation.

Whatever type of investigation you are performing, the ultimate goal is to provide the findings of the investigation to management. Management takes these documented findings and will help direct policies and procedures or change the risk response in the future. If the findings uncover a new risk or if a previously known risk is changed, then the information needs to be entered into the *risk register*.

Risk Register

A risk register is the documentation of every risk that has been identified by an organization. It lists all risks for management to evaluate and determine the best risk response. ISO 73:2009 defines *risk register* as a record of information about identified risks.

The register allows management to look at all the risks that have been identified as a whole. This allows for a more holistic approach and response to risk. For example, firewalls are a standard risk mitigation response to the risk of having servers connected to the Internet. If management was siloed into individual departments, then each department may determine the need and purchase their own firewall. This response not only is a waste of resources but can lead to fragmented configurations across the organization. The auditing and management of several disjointed firewalls becomes harder and more time-consuming. With every identified risk in one location, more informed risk responses can be implemented.

Risk registers come in many different forms, and the form is determined by management preference and number of risks identified. If you search online for risk register examples or look at most risk management textbooks, the example given is a scatter plot. Each axis will have either probability or impact. However, these are hardly ever used in real life. If an organization is attempting to list all identified risks, then the scatter plot would be too large or the dots would become meaningless.

Risk registers in the real world are often filled in using Excel. They resemble more of a log entry than a scatter plot. Each identified risk has its own row or multiple rows. The columns help categorize and group identified risks. With enough details, management can sort and filter on the information. The organization determines the individual columns, and they often change. However, almost all risk registers contain the information shown in Table 6.5. A lot of the terms should be familiar.

TABLE 6.5 Example of risk register entry

Column	Description
ID	Identifier that is unique to the risk
Description	Description of the risk at a high level, e.g., newspaper headline
Threat	Details the threat or the vulnerability of the asset(s)
Impact	Nature of the risk and harm or damage to assets
Assets	List of assets that are affected by the risk
Likelihood	Probability of the risk occurring
Grade/Level	Either numerical or alphabetical representation that allows comparison to other risks

TABLE 6.5   Example of Risk Register Entry *(continued)*

Column	Description
Owner	Names of the risk and asset owners
Response	Details of the chosen risk response
Date Created	Date of the original risk identification and addition to the risk register
Change Log	Any changes made to the identified risk and what those changes were
Date Modified	When changes were made to the risk register, the date the changes occurred for the risk

Management may want to have more columns, but the 12 listed are in almost all registers in one form or another. Ideally you recognize the terms, and you can see we have been building on these ideas throughout the chapter.

False Sense of Security with Risk Registers

Risk registers have a downside once they become large, as they tend to in organizations. Management can become complacent and believe that all risks are in the register. This leads to tunnel vision where management only sees the risks that have been identified. Obviously, this becomes very dangerous. There will always be new risks, especially when working in the cloud.

Vendor Lock-in

Vendor lock-in is a risk that existed for organizations well before the cloud. The cloud has resurfaced this risk, and organizations need to choose the appropriate response that aligns with their strategies. Vendor lock-in is the difficulty of switching from one vendor to another because of proprietary hardware or software provided by the vendors. One can argue that we should just use open standards (hardware and software that any vendor can produce). However, the reality of the situation is that the leading vendors are leading because of their IP. This IP is what makes them leaders in the industry. Vendors cannot protect their IP unless they use proprietary hardware and software.

Corporate America Embracing Open Source

It is not an absolute that organizations will ruthlessly protect their IP. In fact, in recent years there has been a trend, especially in the technology space, for organizations to embrace open source.

Microsoft, one of the largest technology firms, has started integrating Linux into its flag-ship OS. You can download and install Windows Subsystem Linux (WSL) on Windows 10 today. Microsoft has developed and released free-to-use implementations of the OpenSSH suite on modern Windows desktop and server editions. Microsoft recently purchased GitHub, which is a publicly available cloud-based implementation of Git.

When it comes to CSPs, let's be honest, vendor lock-in is a very real risk. There is little incentive for CSPs not to promote vendor lock-in. The cloud is a subscription-based pric-ing model. CSPs want continual revenue from their cloud offerings. If it was easy to switch between CSPs, then why wouldn't end users hop from vendor to vendor as prices change? If I am spending $200 a month with AWS for two VMs and I find out that Microsoft Azure's cost for the same VMs is only $175 a month, then I would have to evaluate the costs and impact of moving the VMs to Azure. After 12 months, I would have saved $300, which is more than a single month's bill.

The *risk response* to cloud vendor lock-in is either acceptance or mitigation. Acceptance is often the choice because it mirrors the history of the organization's own infrastructure. Before moving to the cloud, an organization's infrastructure is already vendor locked. Organizations standardized their infrastructure so their staff could support it. Cisco or Juniper ran the network. All the servers in the data center were made by Dell or HP. All the storage ran on EMC or NetApp arrays. Organizations didn't have the resources or the technical expertise to avoid vendor lock-in.

The cloud does offer an easier path to a different response, mitigation. Vendor lock-in can be mitigated by diversification. Instead of running all infrastructure in either AWS or Azure, run some applications in both. Looking at the different cloud models we have discussed such as IaaS, PaaS, and SaaS, ideally you can see where we have abstracted dif-ferent components. For example, I don't need to care or worry about what is running my Windows Server 2016 computer. I don't need to care whether it is running in AWS or Azure. I just need some way of accessing it or for my clients to access it.

Organizations will still need technical expertise with diversification. However, the simi-larities between the CSPs is converging. At a high level, the terms are the same between them, i.e., *zones* and *regions*. The specifics are different, but you can usually draw paral-lels. AWS calls its object storage offering Simple Storage Solution (S3). Azure calls its object storage offering Blob storage. They have different names and the underlying technologies are different, but the use cases and presentation to the end user are nearly identical.

Data Portability

Data portability is another risk when going to the cloud. It is similar to vendor lock-in in that it is difficult to port data from one vendor to another. However, the difference is in the difficulty of porting data from one information system to another. This goes back to our discussion about data versus information. Data that is raw and unchanged in general is not useful in itself to business operations. Information, on the other hand, is processed data and what individuals typically use. Information is data that is processed in some manner that is typically software.

For the most part, CSPs cannot hold your data hostage as long as you are in good standing with the CSP (no outstanding bills, no legal holds, etc.). Your data is your data, but that does not mean the CSPs are under any obligation to make the transfer of data easier beyond the bare minimum.

Exam Note

Risk was the major theme in this section. The main takeaways from this section for the exam are how to identify risk and what are possible responses to identified risks.

Data Privacy

You will need to be familiar with the concept of *data privacy* for the exam. You will not need to know the individual CSP's particular data privacy policies, but the broad concepts they cover. Additionally, you will need to know about *General Data Protection Regulation (GDPR)*. GDPR was passed by the European Union (EU) parliament in April 2016. It applies not only to any businesses that are located in the EU but also to any businesses that want to offer services to residents of the EU. Any business that wants to process or hold the personal data of individuals residing in the EU must comply with GDPR. Businesses must take steps to protect PII. Because of the global scale of the major CSPs and the size of the EU market share, GDPR is becoming the default even for non-EU residents. It is simpler and easier for CSPs to have only one set of rules for all users than separate rules for different regions.

Getting your data out from the CSP will be determined by the type of data you want to extract. If it is raw data contained within a database, then you can just export the data as raw SQL. All major CSPs do charge egress bandwidth, i.e., data moving out of their network. Extracting an entire VM is more technical than just dumping a SQL database. There are tools and services that will assist with the extraction of the VM. However, extracting the VM is not enough; you need to have a place for the extracted VM to land. Where you want the VM to ultimately live will dictate the file format you need the VM to be in. You may have to extract the VM a couple of times to get it in the correct format.

 Real World Scenario

Virtual Machines Are Just Files

One of the underrated or misunderstood advantages of virtualization is that VMs are just files that get "played" by a hypervisor. You can think of them as almost like a

PowerPoint presentation, a very large PowerPoint presentation. The PowerPoint file can change and grow, but as long as you have the entire file and a "viewer" (compatible hypervisor), then the PowerPoint presentation can be run anywhere. The devil is in the details on the compatible hypervisor, but you get the point.

Thankfully, there is an open source standard for VM file formats, Open Virtualization Format (OVF). All CSPs support this standard for importing. Few CSPs allow you to export into OVF format. Therefore, the trick is to get a VM into OVF format. There is a process called Physical 2 Virtual (P2V) that makes this process doable. There is freely available software that you install on a machine, and it goes through the process of converting the machine into an OVF file. Even though the process is called P2V, the software does not make a distinction between physical or virtual. In other words, you can install the P2V software on a VM and have it work the process and output an OVF. You can then take the OVF file to import into any CSP that supports the OVA file format, which most do.

Explain Policies or Procedures

The terms *policies* and *procedures* are often confused, not because they describe the same thing but because they are almost always used together in the same sentence. We are as guilty of this as anyone. Looking back through this chapter; almost every occurrence of the word *policies* is followed by *procedures*. So, what is the difference between the two?

Policies are thoughts, ideas, or principles that give a direction for actions to be performed by individuals or organizations as a whole. Sexual harassment, anti-bullying, wellness, anti-smoking, etc., are all examples of policies that organizations will typically have. Policies also define what qualifies as certain actions, i.e., sexual harassment, bullying, etc. This definition is often the standard to determine what course of action is to be taken. This course of action is a procedure.

Procedures are steps that should be taken once an event takes place or steps that need to be taken to follow a policy. If an individual believes they have been sexually harassed after reviewing the sexual harassment policy, then they are to follow the sexual harassment claim procedure. This procedure will have well-defined steps to be taken, including who they should report the sexual harassment to and which forms and/or evidence to present.

We are going to be discussing policies for the most part, because we want to leave you with broad examples. In general, policies are typically dictated by laws, regulations, or industry standards. An organization may tweak the wording of a policy to fit their specific needs, but network security policies are pretty similar from one organization to another. Procedures are often specific to an organization, because they detail specific steps/actions to take.

Public Policies and Procedures

If your head is spinning with the difference between policies and procedures, there is a great resource that you can tap into to understand them better. Your local public-school district (and certain private schools) will have publicly available policies and procedures. They are public because schools are required to follow open meeting laws in states. Additionally, policies and procedures cannot be added to or modified without school board approval. This means there are public meetings and readings of policies and procedures to make changes. Check your local school district's website; in all likelihood, there is a section for policies and procedures where you can browse, download, and even search through their policies and procedures.

Standard Operating Procedures

Standard operating procedure (SOP, pronounced *ess-oh-pee*, not *sops*) are the documented and defined steps that an individual or an organization takes once an event occurs. These are critical when we get into security events and incident responses, which we discuss in a few sections of this chapter. SOPs are not just made for when a risk event occurs or if something unfortunate happens. SOPs are also appropriate for day-to-day, mundane matters.

SOPs help explain when something out of the ordinary occurs. Generically speaking, Event A just occurred. What led up to the event occurring? An engineer made changes to System B. What changes did the engineer perform, and did they follow SOP?

Let's walk through two examples.

- Cindy recently got married and changed her name to Cindy Jones. Cindy initiated a name update with the HR department. The HR department updated the payroll and employee records. HR then created an IT ticket for the name change in all the IT systems. Tracy in user account management received the ticket and updated her name in Active Directory (AD). Tracy then forwarded the ticket to the messaging and collaboration team to update the email address. Alex made the appropriate name change in Microsoft Exchange and closed the ticket. When Cindy opens a ticket that she is unable to receive emails with her new email address from outside the organization, Holly on the messaging and collaboration team can review Alex's step and easily determine that he did not follow SOP and forgot the last step. Holly needs to make the name change in their external SPAM filter so outside emails can be delivered.

- Kim is reviewing the monthly charges from her CSP when she notices a discrepancy between the bill and what her IT department reporting says should be provisioned. Kim opens a ticket with IT to check the bill and what is present in the CSP management tools. Bill takes the ticket and opens the CSP management console and quickly determines that there are two VMs in the management console that are not reporting to the IT cloud reporting tools. SOPs for provisioning VMs in the cloud require using a pre-approved template. The template has the agents pre-installed that will report into the IT cloud reporting tools. The template also has approved OS images and security patches. Bill reviews the cloud audit logs and determines that Kevin created the two VMs that are not reporting. Bill asks Kevin if he used the template when creating the two VMs in the cloud. Kevin responds that he did not because the new software he was trying to test was not supported on the template's OS version.

The first scenario is a real-world example that happens all the time in any large organization when an employee's name changes. SOPs assist and shorten the amount of time needed for issue resolution. The second scenario actually highlighted two SOPs. First, Kim was following an SOP when she was reviewing the CSP monthly bill. That SOP led to the evidence of a breakdown in another SOP (Kevin). This breakdown in SOP is an indication of a gap in the SOP, not a fault on Kevin's part. Kevin is trying to test new software and needs a requirement out of the SOP. Either the SOP needs to be updated or a different SOP needs to be created to account for testing new software outside of the SOP with the approved template.

SOPs are critical for large organizations, especially where a change can have far-reaching implications. Changes are going to occur in the world of IT, and following SOPs can make management of those changes easier.

Change Management

Most IT professionals will groan or mutter under their breath when change management comes up. They see it as a waste of valuable time and just another process that slows down getting work done. If viewed strictly from the perspective of an IT professional who is trying to maximize the work done and issue resolution, then it can be understood. However, a properly functioning change management system for an organization is critical to business success.

Change management is the process of approving and managing approved changes to an organization's assets. These changes must have two properties: an accepted risk and an increased value to the organization. Any change is going to have an inherit risk to the organization because it is a change, but the accepted risk needs to be counterbalanced by an increased value to the organization.

Never making changes in IT has several drawbacks: no security patches, no new features, no enhancements. Services become frozen and never change. Not only is this a huge security risk (because attackers are definitely changing), but it is a poor end-user experience. End users will not get access to tools that are designed to improve their efficiency. Therefore, change management is not going away, and ideally you will see that it is an essential part of going to the cloud.

Change management in the era of the cloud actually causes frustration and headaches for change managers. The reason is that CSPs are going to make changes to their service offerings, and these changes can and will impact organizations. This is not to say that CSPs are negligent and do not communicate changes to their customers. On the contrary, CSPs have their own rigorous change management process, and they do communicate changes. However, the impact of a change is not fully understood by the clients. The other piece that causes heartburn for change managers is an inability to either block or roll back a change in the cloud. For example, let's say there is a business procedure spelled out that an individual is to check a certain web page and document the failed login events for the last 24 hours. Let's ignore that unautomated and human requirement for this procedure for the time being. The CSP has developed a new and improved web interface to bring the most used reports to the central dashboard. The new interface could very well move the location of the last failed login events in 24 hours to a new area of the website. The individual tasked with the procedure would have to adapt and change their process to fulfill the requirement.

Microsoft has recently made changes to its Office 365 admin center. Figure 6.2 shows the current version as of the writing of this book.

FIGURE 6.2   Office 365 admin portal

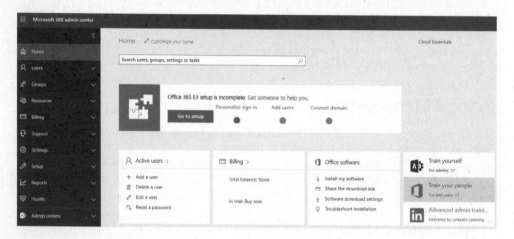

Figure 6.3 shows the new and improved change management interface.

FIGURE 6.3   Office 365 admin portal preview

As you can see, the navigation pane on the left has changed. The dashboard on the right has also changed. For the most part, all of the previous information is still present, but the location is changing. Organizations that are wanting to make the move to the cloud are going to have to embrace change. The cloud is inherently about change. That is the double-edged sword; you get the benefit of another organization's innovation, but you are also beholden to their changes. Going to the cloud means you are going to experience change, change, change.

Change Management History

Many of the concepts of change management are derived from the Information Technology Infrastructure Library (ITIL). ITIL identifies best practices for an organization to increase availability. ITIL was created in the 1980s by the UK government as a framework for technology adoption. The most recent version is 4 and was released in February 2019. There are still five core volumes as in ITIL version 3. One volume has been present in all versions, Service Transition. Service Transition details and spells out the change management process. Organizations do not need to adopt ITIL to use change management, but the concepts and the framework come from ITIL.

Resource Management

Resource management in the cloud is going to touch on many subjects that we have already discussed: asset inventory, provisioning, continuous integration and continuous delivery (CICD), configuration management. At the heart of any resource management are the resources. In the cloud the resources we are going to manage are going to be storage, compute, and network. These three terms should be very familiar to you by this point. By management we are referring to the ability to create and/or destroy and make changes to resources we want to manage.

The major CSPs have a concept of *resource groups*. Resource groups are a collection of resources that are "similar" in either their resources or their management of the resources. For example, an organization may create an "Internal-Testing" resource group. This resource group would be used for any internal IT projects that engineers or developers need to test ideas on. This should sound familiar; think back to when we were discussing CICD. This resource group can have security policies and access control policies applied to it as a whole (security and access control policies are coming up later in this chapter). Everything in a resource group is going to be an asset, and this is where an accurate asset inventory becomes critical.

CSPs have recently made a push for resource management for noncloud resources. This typically starts with mobile device management (MDM); think of email on your phone or access to internal corporate web applications. Microsoft's cloud offering is currently more robust than those of at other CSPs. This is due mainly to its cloud offering of Intune. Intune can manage both of the major mobile device platforms: Apple and Android. Additionally, Intune can be used to manage nonmobile device platforms such as Windows, macOS, and Linux.

Security Policies

A *security policy* is the top or even one of the first policies an organization decides to adopt. We will reference another Sybex book, *CISSP (ISC)² Certified Information Systems Security Professional Official Study Guide, Seventh Edition*:

> A security policy is a document that defines the scope of security needed by the organization and discusses the assets that require protection and the extent to which security solutions should go to provide the necessary protection.

Let's dive into this definition a little more; a lot of the terms should already be familiar to you. The "assets that require protection": this is where the assets inventory becomes essential. We need to know the assets that we need to protect. "Extent to which security solutions": this is where the risk register becomes essential. "Provide the necessary protection": this is where the policy becomes important. We have already discussed having an appropriate level of response to an identified risk, but this is where we define it.

Security policies will also define the roles and assign responsibilities to individuals, i.e., asset owners and risk owners. Security policies will define audit requirements and compliance steps for both laws and regulations. Some security policies will define acceptable risk levels, though the risk levels are typically defined by risk management. Risk and security for large organizations are separate departments but work closely together. This is because most security events or functions are risk related, but not all risk is security related. For example, risk involving employee interactions, i.e., sexual harassment, is not security related.

There are three basic categories of security policies, which are detailed in Table 6.6.

TABLE 6.6   Security Policy Categories

Category	Description
Regulatory	Security policy that is required by either law or regulation. Details the regulation or law that is to be followed and the procedure(s) that must be followed to be compliant.
Advisory	Security policy that defines behaviors and activities that are acceptable in the organization. Will also lay out the procedures and consequences for an individual who violates the security policy. A network usage policy or mobile usage policy are examples of advisory security policies.
Informative	Security policy that provides reasoning and/or information about goals and mission statements for the organization. Will provide the proper procedures for working with third parties.

Incident Response

All three categories of security policies have *procedure* in the description, and if you recall, a procedure spells out a set of actions for the policy. An incident response is going to be a procedure. *Incident response* is the set of actions or steps taken once a risk event has occurred. Most organizations have three steps in an incident response procedure.

Step 1: Detection and Identification

Identification here means to identify that a security event has occurred; it does not mean we have identified all involved parties. Detection is different than identification. Detection means just to recognize an anomaly or events that occurred outside of normal operating parameters. Identification is the recognition of events that are in violation of a security policy.

The key to detection and identification is logs and/or access control policies. Additionally, you need to know what normal behavior and events are. You must know how your systems operate. The tools used for detection and identification should be familiar. Anti-malware, firewall logs, OS event logs, and physical security systems, to name a few.

The last step in detection and identification is notification. You need to notify the appropriate parties once a security event has been identified. This notification starts the next step in the incident response.

Step 2: Response and Reporting

Once the appropriate parties have been notified, someone or something needs to form a response to the security event. The response should be spelled out in the security policies by a procedure. Additionally, parties that are responding to the event need to document any actions taken. Responding parties need to assume that all their actions will be reviewed. This would be part of the security policies. For example, an organization has a security system with monitored door access. Part of this monitoring is the alerting of any doors that remain open for longer than 60 seconds. The response to a door remaining open for longer than 60 seconds would be to dispatch a security guard to investigate. There are several outcomes once the security guard is at the door. Maybe it is 8 a.m. and lots of people are entering the building and the door was never shut. Maybe someone is having a long conversation at the door and is just holding it open. Maybe someone forgot their badge and propped the door open with a bag to run back out to get their badge. Whatever action is determined by the security guard to take must be logged.

The initial response to a security event should be isolation and/or containment. You want to minimize the continuation and prevent further harm to an organization's assets. However, the isolation should not destroy evidence of the security event itself. For example, if you believe a server has been compromised, then turning off the server will clear the memory of the server. There could be useful evidence in memory. However, if you can either take the server offline or move it to a different network or isolate it from everything else, that provides time for investigation without potentially destroying evidence.

Gathering evidence is the next step in response and reporting. Evidence gathering when the equipment is owned by the organization is easier than when equipment is owned by a third party. If an organization owns a piece of equipment, then the user of said equipment doesn't generally have a right to an expectation of privacy. This is one of the main reasons why organizations issue laptops, desktops, cell phones, etc. Since they are owned by the organization, they can seize these devices and perform any actions they need without a user's say in the matter. Evidence gathering on third-party equipment can get into the legal realm of warrants and subpoenas, which we will not cover in the book. The takeaway is that the gathering of evidence needs to preserve the evidence but also contain it; therefore, the seizure of equipment may be necessary.

Analysis and reporting are the last step in response and reporting. We have the evidence gathered. We need to analyze the evidence and get rid of unneeded information or noise. We need to just focus on the pieces that are related to the security event. Summarize the appropriate evidence and relate it to the actionable security policy. Once summarized, provide a report to management. It is appropriate to theorize and make conjecture about causes and motives, but you should spell out which conclusions are based solely on fact and which are speculations, even if educated.

Step 3: Recovery and Remediation

The last step in the incident response can be the most difficult and time-consuming. You need to return your organization's affected system to a normal operating state, which depending on the security event may not be possible or could take months. Think of a data breach, where all of your customer PII has been leaked. How do you return to a normal operating state? What does a normal operating state look like? Those decisions could take time and may not even be known. A security policy should state what a normal state is, but a security policy cannot handle every event.

Lastly there needs to be a lessons learned step. This is where you and/or management takes a look at the incident response and the underlying security policies and find where there are any gaps. Gaps will be either in the security policy itself or in the technologies that support the security policy. It is important to note that this is not a "who can we blame" step. Some individuals will think this step is management looking for a fall guy. In some organizations that may be true. However, any member of management who makes the lessons learned step a blame game is not a good manager. Experienced and good managers know this.

Access and Control Policies

Access and control policies are a subset of security policies. They will be some of the most important and the bulk of security policies. At the heart of access and control policies is a three-letter acronym, CIA. We will be discussing CIA more in-depth in the next chapter, but for now it stands for confidentiality, integrity, and availability. Access and control policies are all about ensuring CIA.

Access and control policies spell out how an organization's assets can access and change other assets owned by the organization. You can think of who has access to what files on a file server, who has access to the server room, and who has access to change employee data. Access and control policies are between two or more assets.

There are three primary types of control when it comes to access and control policies, which are explained in Table 6.7.

TABLE 6.7   Access and Control Policies

Control Type	Description
Preventive access controls	Controls that actively attempt to block or prevent any security events from occurring. Think of doors, locks, data classification, penetration testing, etc.
Detective access controls	Controls that detect when a security event occurs. Some security events cannot be prevented, or an unknown security event occurs. Think of motion detectors, security cameras, logs, honeypots, audit trails.
Corrective access controls	Controls that return assets to a normal operating state after a security event occurs. Think of anti-malware, backup and restore, or active intrusion detection.

The next piece of access and control policies is an access control list (ACL). An ACL should define which assets are involved and what rights one asset has over the other. Some OSs or control systems can have ACLs with hundreds of rights to assets. However, all rights can generally be broken into one of three categories: Read, Write, and Execute, as explained in Table 6.8.

TABLE 6.8   ACL Categories

Right	Description
Read	The ability of an asset to read or even access another asset. Sometimes referred to as read-only if this is the only right granted to an asset. This right does not grant the right to change or modify an asset. One thing to keep in mind that a lot of individuals forget is if I can read or have access to an asset, I can usually make a copy of the asset.
Write	The ability of an asset to be changed or modified in any way. Most people consider write access as having full access, but that is not the case. The reason is that if an asset has write access, then the underlying asset can usually be deleted. This is one area where more advanced ACLs have split deletion away from the ability to change the asset. However, if I can write to an asset, then I can write "nothing" to it, which effectively deletes the data.
Execute	The ability of an asset to execute or take action on another asset. This is the last right needed for full access to an asset. Some assets can perform an action that will affect other assets. This is an important distinction because if an asset has write rights to other assets, then the parent asset can make changes to assets it might not normally have rights to, if the parent can execute the middle asset. This is another area where advanced ACLs have broken the execute right into further rights.

Even though read, write, and execute ACLs appear to only apply to files or printers or databases, that is not the case; we said that read, write, and execute are the three generic types of rights granted by ACLs and apply to assets protected by ACLs. These rights can be interpreted in the case of physical security as well. Read access could be the ability to open a door and access a protected room. If an individual has only read access, then they may be required to be escorted by another individual, i.e., cannot be alone. Write access could be the ability to enter a protected room without being escorted. Additionally, write access could be the right to leave without having to be let out. Execute access could be the ability to leave with an item that was protected by the room. These are just examples, but ideally you can see how ACLs work for more than just technical items.

Authentication vs. Authorization

For the exam you will need to understand the difference between authentication and authorization. They are often confused, and many people think they are one and the same.

Authentication is proof or validation of who or what an asset is. A password or a fingerprint is an authentication method. It is something used to confirm who an individual is.

Authorization is the rights an asset has. An asset should be authenticated first to prove they are who they say they are. Then authorization determines which actions an asset can take.

Department-Specific Policies

Department policies are policies that may or may not fall under the umbrella of security policies. Department policies will definitely refer to security policies, but security policies should be applied at the organization level.

Department policies can be security in nature, but they should apply only more restrictive policies rather than less restrictive policies. The organization's security policies need to be the baseline, and any department-specific policies should only enhance the organizations.

Departments can have policies that are not security related but are risk related. Human resources and legal departments are the two largest examples of departments that would need such policies. Their department policies are going to be centered around confidentiality, because of the type of information they have access to. Employee files, pay scales, depositions, testimonies, and evidence are some examples. These policies will lay out the conditions and procedures for sharing this information both inside and outside the organization.

IT departments will also have *department-specific policies*. These policies stem from their ability to grant or remove access to and control of assets. Since most things live digitally in an IT infrastructure somewhere, IT is usually the department that can grant or take ownership of an asset. Taking ownership is one of the most important rights that can be granted to an individual. Usually only IT personnel have this right. If control of an asset is lost because of negligence or nefarious means, then someone needs to be able to assume control of the asset. Once control of the asset is regained, then access can be granted to the appropriate parties.

Let's talk through a few examples to help clarify some of the policies an IT department might have. When an employee's employment needs to be terminated, what happens to the assets the employee had access to? In some cases, this employee may be the only individual with access to certain assets, i.e., files or emails. An IT department will have the rights to take control of this employee's technical assets, but maybe IT shouldn't have access to the employee's assets. Who does IT grant access to? The employee's manager? What if it is a manager who gets terminated? These are questions that should be answered in a policy and procedure for IT professionals to follow.

Another example is a request for access to assets an individual doesn't normally have. IT professionals get requests all the time along the lines of: "John is out for vacation for a couple weeks. He was working on an important proposal but forgot to email it to me. Can you give me access to his files or send a copy over to me?" What is the appropriate IT response to such a request? Does someone need to approve it? Does John need to be notified? All these questions should be answered or given a path of last resort in policies.

Communication Policies

Communication policies are the last kinds of policies we are going to discuss and one of the most important. When discussing communication policies, we are not referring to notifications as part of an incident response. We are referring to communications that happen after a security event occurs. Some communication policies may be required by law or regulation. The federal laws that mandate disclosure or reporting of events only involve financial records. These are not security-related in nature. The two laws that are most referred to when talking about mandatory reporting or communications are the Sarbanes-Oxley Act and the Dodd-Frank Wall Street Reform and Consumer Protection Act. Neither will need to be known for the exam. We wanted to point out that currently the only federally mandated communications involve financial records.

Every state in the United States including the District of Columbia has enacted some sort of data breach notification laws. We obviously are not able to cover the individual laws in all 50 states. However, we wanted to point out that state laws mandate notifications when it comes to personal information in data breaches.

Most organizations have adopted communication policies when it comes to security events. These policies may be internal only unless mandated by state law. One of the most critical aspects of communication policies is the right to privacy. Individuals have the right to certain aspects of privacy, and an organization cannot breach this without breaking other policies. The privacy rights that individuals typically enjoy fall into one of two categories: life events outside of work or disciplinary actions.

- In general, life events that take place outside of the workspace and don't impact an organization or its other employees are considered private. An individual cannot be required to disclose them to an employer.

- Disciplinary actions taken against an individual in general cannot be communicated to anyone other than the affected parties. This is to ensure that the perception of guilt does not impact the disciplined individual. This is the restriction that puts most organizations in a bind when it comes to communication policies. Other individuals believe they have the right to know about events that impact an organization, but in general right to privacy trumps right to know when it comes to the individual versus the organization.

We have gotten the gotchas and required stuff out of the way. What should be in a communication policy? After a security event does occur, the communication policy should specify who should be notified and what should be communicated. The what will depend on the who. You should not communicate the technical details and findings of a server being taken offline to the sales staff. However, technical details may benefit members of the IT department.

Communication policies must take larger risk events into consideration as well. For example, what if a fire broke out in a warehouse and the fire made the local news? How should an organization communicate the safety of staff members to their families? What if workplace violence occurs? What sort of communication should be relayed to the family but also to the press? It is important for an organization to have clear policies in place to handle such events to cut down on misinformation.

It is important for organizations to have defined communication policies when utilizing the cloud. These policies need to describe who, what, when, and where should be communicated after a security event. Additionally, there should be a catchall communication policy to address unknown or unforeseen events when they occur.

Summary

We covered a lot in this chapter, not all of it technical in nature, but it is important and needed for the exam. We started the chapter with compliance and the importance it plays in any organization. We discussed what it requires to be compliant and gave the example of PCI DSS, which lists the requirements for processing credit cards.

Risk was introduced and was the primary focus of this chapter. We defined risk at both an IT level and a non-IT level. We discussed how to assess risk both quantitatively and qualitatively, which you need to understand for the exam. At the core of any risk assessment is an asset. An asset is any object or material that has value to an organization. The next key aspect of risk is threat. Threat is any set of circumstances that may cause damage or harm to an asset. We discussed the need for an accurate and up-to-date asset inventory. We then moved on to asset classification and how classification will help determine the level of protection of an asset against a threat.

Ownership was the next topic, and we defined the difference between a risk owner and an asset owner. Every identified risk needs to have a response. There are four standard risk responses: mitigation, acceptance, avoidance, and transfer.

We discussed the importance and need for documentation to be compliant with laws and regulations. Findings is the documentation that is produced whenever a risk event occurs. Findings flow from an investigation and four types of investigations can occur. A risk register is the document that details all the identified risks to an organization. It is a tool that is used by management to help formulate the appropriate risk response to each identified risk.

We briefly introduced vendor lock-in and data portability when working in the cloud. The cloud plays a significant role in both topics, and you need to be aware of its potential impact. We also introduced a few tools and concepts that will help mitigate the impact of both vendor lock-in and data portability. Data privacy was discussed and the need to know what GDPR is and the requirements.

We introduced policies and procedures and the difference between the two. Change management plays a pivotal role in the management of risk and cannot be ignored. Change management will make the life of an IT professional easier. We also brought up the difference in change management when utilizing the cloud; i.e., change will happen, and it will be out of your control. Resource management was our next topic, and we touched on some of the tools CSPs offer.

Policies were our next big topic, and we went through security, access and control, department-specific, and communication policies. With security policies we dived into incident response and the steps needed to be taken. Last, we introduced the concept of ACLs and how they control the access of one asset to another asset.

Exam Essentials

Know what compliance is.   Compliance consists of the actions an organization takes to be compliant with laws and regulations that govern the industry the organization operates in or a state/country an organization operates in.

Know what risk is and its three parts.   Risk is the probability of the occurrence of a threat. Threat is any condition or circumstance that can cause harm, damage, or loss of an asset. An asset is an item or material that has value to an organization.

Know the difference between quantitative and qualitative analysis.   Quantitative analysis is the analysis of the value of an asset that is based on monetary value, also known as a tangible asset. Qualitative analysis is the analysis of the value of an asset based on its perceived qualities. This analysis is often done by experts who have experience with the assets and are able to compare assets to other assets to provide a perceived value.

Know the importance of an asset inventory.   Risk is all about protecting assets. An organization needs to have an accurate and timely asset inventory to protect against threats. Asset inventory examples are hardware, software, and data.

Know what risk classification means and its importance to the level of protection.   All identified risks should be classified and ranked against other risks. This ranking or grading will help determine the appropriate risk response and also work as a check mechanism with other risks.

Know what ownership is and the difference between the risk owner and the asset owner. The risk owner will be a member of management who decides the risk response to an identified risk. The asset owner will be more technical and have the expertise to manage an asset. They can be the same person but don't have to be.

Know the four risk responses.   Mitigation is reducing risk through action(s) of expenditure of resources. Acceptance means that the organization chooses to not reduce risk. Avoidance is the removal of risk. Transfer means that a third party accepts the risk.

Know the importance of documentation and be able to give examples.   Documentation is a requirement to be in compliance with laws and regulations. Findings and a risk register are two examples of often-required documentation.

Know the impact of vendor lock-in and data portability in the era of the cloud.   Utilizing resources in the cloud has an inherent risk of vendor lock-in. CSPs will not make it easy for you to switch or move between different CSPs. CSPs cannot hold data hostage, but they don't have to make it easy for you to port your data to another vendor either.

Know the difference between policies and procedures.   Policies give direction, guidance, and provide goals for an organization. Procedures provide specific steps to achieve or work toward a goal.

Know the importance of standard operating procedures.   SOPs can shorten the time involved in basic troubleshooting to come to issue resolution quickly.

Know the importance of change and resource management.   Change management is the process of managing change for an organization when consuming cloud resources. Changes must increase the value or benefit to an organization in some fashion when there is a corresponding level of risk. Resource management is managing cloud resources: compute, storage, and networking. Cloud offers additional resource management that was not possible with on-prem resources, e.g., Intune.

Know the various policies discussed: security, access and control, department-specific, and communication policies.   Each one of these policies plays a different role in risk management. Security is at the top and should be organization-wide. Each subsequent policy adds on another layer that helps manage risk.

Know the steps for an incident response.   The steps are detection and identification, response and reporting, and recovery and remediation. Understand how the workflow goes from one step to another step.

Know the three basic rights of an ACL.   Read, write, and execute are the rights that more advanced ACLs are built on. Understand how these can be generically applied to nontechnical assets as well.

Written Lab

Fill in the blanks for the questions provided in the written lab. You can find the answers to the written labs in Appendix A.

1.   _____ is the probability or likelihood of the occurrence or realization of a threat.

2.   _____ is any agent, condition, or circumstance that could potentially cause harm, loss, damage, or compromise to an IT asset or data asset. The likelihood of the threat is the probability of occurrence or the odds that the event will actually occur.

3. _____ is an item of value to an institution such as data, hardware, software, or physical property. An asset is an item or collection of items that has a quantitative or qualitative value to a company.

4. _____ and _____ risk assessments are used to assign value to an asset.

5. _____ is the determined appropriate action once a risk has been determined.

6. _____ are thoughts, ideas, or principles that give a direction for actions to be performed by individuals or organizations as a whole.

7. _____ are a set of steps that should be taken once an event takes place or steps that need to be taken to follow a policy.

8. _____ is a document that defines the scope of security needed by the organization and discusses the assets that require protection and the extent to which security solutions should go to provide the necessary protection.

9. _____ policies are policies that dictate the mechanisms and level of interaction between two or more assets owned by an organization.

10. _____ is the process of controlling planned events that are aimed at increasing value for an organization while also minimizing risk.

Review Questions

1. You are working the service desk for your organization and get a request from a manager to immediately disable a user account, because they are being terminated. You ask him to wait while you validate the user's manager and contact HR to verify termination. However, the manager is insistent that you disable it now or he will report you to your manager. What process would you be violating if you disabled the user account right away?

   A. Security policy

   B. Change management

   C. Standard operating procedure

   D. Access and control policy

2. You have put in a request to install a security update on your organization's firewalls. The security update is needed to address a potential security vulnerability with the firewall authentication system. Your manager agrees with the value the security update offers but asks if there are any known issues with the patch and if there is a rollback plan if the fire-walls stop functioning. What process is your manager requesting?

   A. Change management

   B. Resource management

   C. Risk avoidance

   D. Asset inventory

3. The new iPhone was just released, and your management has decided that the company will purchase iPhones for all engineers who are on an on-call rotation. This is to help ensure availability and provide a standard for all on-call engineers. Since the iPhones are being purchased by the organization, your management wants to have a level of control over the iPhones, i.e., the ability to wipe data, enable security settings like PIN, and enable Find My iPhone. What should you look into to meet this request?

   A. Vendor lock-in

   B. Asset inventory

   C. Resource management

   D. Security policies

4. An accounts payable staff member received an email from the organization's CEO request-ing they immediately cut a check for $40,000 and mail it to a P.O. box in another state. What process should you initiate?

   A. Risk mitigation

   B. Incident response

   C. Communication policy

   D. Findings

5. Your manager has requested a list of staff and contractors who report to you that need to enter the building after normal business hours. He also requested justification for each member. This is an example of:

   A. Access and control policy

   B. Department-specific policy

   C. Standard operating procedure

   D. Risk assessment

6. You are creating a summary report of potential new hires to share with directors in your office. You include the following information for each applicant: name, experience, contact information, and salary requirements. After the report is completed, you send it to the directors. The director of HR requests that you remove the salary requirements from the report because the directors should not view salary requirements until after the first round of interviews to keep the hiring process as fair as possible. This request is an example of:

   A. Risk transfer

   B. Standard operating procedure

   C. Communication policy

   D. Department-specific policy

7. You are asked to compose an email to send to clients who were unable to access your organization's sales portal over the weekend because of a power outage that affected the whole area. Your email should be brief but explain the unforeseen circumstances that caused the portal being down and what additional steps the organization is taking to prevent such an outage in the future. The email is an example of:

   A. Risk transfer

   B. Communication policy

   C. Findings

   D. Incident response

8. What are two factors that will impact the decision to adopt the cloud and move all your organization's on-premises resources to the cloud?

   A. Change management

   B. Resource management

   C. Vendor lock-in

   D. Data portability

9. The CEO wants a detailed report of events that occurred over the weekend that caused all the cash registers at a store to go offline and prevent sales from completing. The CEO is asking for elements of:

   A. Incident response

   B. Risk assessment

   C. Change management

   D. Findings

10. ＿＿＿ contains all assets and the determined response to the identified risks.

   A. Ownership register

   B. Standard operating procedure

   C. Security policy

   D. Risk register

11. The municipality has approved the construction of a new water treatment plant that will be directly adjacent to your current data center. This will increase the likelihood of flooding in the area. You make a recommendation to move all of your infrastructure to the cloud. This risk response type is:

   A. Acceptance

   B. Avoidance

   C. Mitigation

   D. Transfer

12. The only parking garage near your office building is across the street at a busy intersection, and all your employees must cross the intersection. There is a parking garage that is farther away on the same side of the street, but your employees either can't or don't want to use it because of the distance. The organization decides to purchase and offer a shuttle service from the distant parking garage free of charge to the employees. This risk response type is:

   A. Transfer

   B. Acceptance

   C. Mitigation

   D. Avoidance

13. Over the past three months, two windows have been broken in your store's front. Each window has cost several thousands of dollars to replace. You contacted a security company that will install video surveillance cameras and also will patrol the area at random intervals throughout the night for $200 a month. They will also pay to replace any broken window and prosecute any individuals caught damaging property. You weigh the options and determine that it will save you money for at least the first two years. This risk response type is:

   A. Transfer

   B. Avoidance

   C. Acceptance

   D. Mitigation

14. Sales personnel who do not come into an office on a regular basis represent 2 percent of your organization's workforce. Through historical records it is determined that terminated sales personnel return their company equipment 50 percent of the time if they are terminated while out of the office. One of your sales personnel has been found to be in violation of company policy and must be terminated immediately. This risk response type is:

   A. Avoidance

   B. Acceptance

C. Mitigation

D. Transfer

15. Your company's firewall vendor will end support for the version of software that you are using in January of this year. They have an update that will be supported for three more years. However, if the upgrade fails, you will have to continue to use unsupported software unless the firewall vendor is able to fix the upgrade process. All other firewall vendor options are cost prohibitive. The firewall vendor has had only two firewall upgrades fail out of thousands and was able to get the firewalls to work eventually. You decide to move forward with the upgrade. This risk response type is:

A. Mitigation

B. Avoidance

C. Acceptance

D. Transfer

16. How many classifications of risk do most organizations have?

A. 3

B. 5

C. 10

D. 8

17. Who is responsible not only for an organization's asset but also for the risk response to any identified threat to said asset? (Choose two.)

A. Risk owner

B. Asset owner

C. Change manager

D. CEO

18. A risk is the probability or likelihood of the occurrence or realization of what?

A. Vulnerability

B. Threat

C. Security breach

D. Phishing attempt

19. A threat is any agent, condition, or circumstance that could potentially cause harm, loss, damage, or compromise to an IT asset or data asset. A threat causes a decrease in what in an asset?

A. Harm

B. Value

C. Risk

D. Importance

20. _____ is an item of value to an institution such as data, hardware, software, or physical property. An asset is an item or collection of items that has a quantitative or qualitative value to a company.

    A. Policy

    B. Asset

    C. Threat

    D. Value

Chapter

7

Compliance and Security in the Cloud

✓ **4.3 Identify the importance and impacts of compliance in the cloud**

- Data sovereignty
- Regulatory concerns
- Industry-based requirements
- International standards
- Certifications

✓ **4.4 Explain security concerns, measures, or concepts of cloud operations**

- Threat
- Vulnerability
- Security assessments
  - Penetration testing
  - Vulnerability scanning
  - Application scanning
- Data security
  - Categories
    - Public
    - Private
    - Sensitive
  - Confidentiality
    - Encryption
    - Sanitization
  - Integrity
    - Validation

- Availability
  - Backup
  - Recovery
- Breach
- Application and infrastructure security
  - Audit
  - Access
  - Authorization
  - Hardening

We have brought up *compliance* in the previous chapter, and anyone who has worked in a regulated industry will tell you that it can require a lot of resources (time and capital) to be compliant. Fortunately, CSPs have already expended resources in making their infrastructure compliant. We are going to be covering lots of different aspects of compliance in the chapter, and we have broken down the various compliance requirements by the following areas:

- Data sovereignty
- Regulatory concerns
- Industry-based requirements
- International standards
- Certifications

It is important to note that compliance is not solely up to the CSP or the user of the CSP resources. Similar to the shared responsibility model, which we covered in Chapter 1, compliance is shared as well. CSPs can offer compliance certifications for their resources, but you as a consumer of those resources will have to show compliance as well if required.

Identify the Importance and Impacts of Compliance in the Cloud

Meeting or exceeding compliance requirements demonstrates a commitment to customers as well as regulators. End users can be confident that CSPs have developed tools and resources that allow end users to be compliant.

Amazon's Simple Storage Service (S3) was the first generally available cloud service provided. S3 was released on March 14, 2006, and since then, there have been numerous new stories about "hacks" or security breaches involving S3. However, all of them have been because of a misconfiguration or breakdown in security on the part of the end user and not of AWS.

If you or your organization has chosen to utilize the cloud, then you have also chosen to store data in the cloud. Not all the data may be sensitive in nature, but almost all data will have value to someone. You and your organization need to make a commitment to protecting and safeguarding data from unauthorized third parties. A large part of this chapter will be showing tools and concepts that CSPs offer to help you meet that commitment.

We will be giving examples of tools that you can utilize offered by CSPs later in this chapter, but in general, compliance with regulations fall into one of the following three areas:

- Activity logging and auditing
- Encryption and key management
- Identity access and control

Data Sovereignty

Data sovereignty is the concept that data is subject to laws and regulations of a particular nation. There is an important distinction to make here on data sovereignty that is often misunderstood. Often people assume that the data sovereignty laws of the nation where the data is stored are the laws that must be applied. However, that is not the case; the data sovereignty laws of the nation where data is located are to be applied.

Let's go back to a previous example of the e-commerce website we run. We have not started using the cloud yet and still run all our infrastructure out of our data center located in the United States. We routinely sell to customers located in the European Union. When we collect their credit card information for payment processing, there are two regulations that will apply, GDPR and PCI DSS. We have discussed both in the past, but it is important to understand that even though the data is stored in the United States, it is the EU data sovereignty laws that apply. Now that does not mean we are not subject to U.S. laws and regulations. Our organization is still located in the United States and incorporated in the United States; therefore, we are subject to laws and, more important, litigation in the United States.

 Design Scenario

U.S. and International Data Sovereignty

United States v. Microsoft Corp. is a good lesson in international data sovereignty. The basics of the case are the following. In 2013, the Department of Justice issued a warrant under the Stored Communications Act of 1986 to Microsoft for account information and emails related to a drug trafficking case. The account information was stored on servers located in the United States, but the emails were stored on servers located in Ireland. Microsoft turned over information on the account but challenged the warrant in court over the email data since it was stored in Ireland. Microsoft claimed the email data was governed by Ireland/EU data sovereignty laws, not by the Stored Communications Act. Lower courts found in favor of the DOJ, but upon appeal the Second Circuit Court found in favor of Microsoft in 2016. The Supreme Court agreed to hear the case in 2017. Arguments were heard in February 2018. While still under deliberation by the Supreme Court, Congress passed the Clarifying Lawful Overseas Use of Data Act, or CLOUD Act.

The CLOUD Act, passed and signed into law in 2018, states that U.S. companies must provide data stored on any server owned and operated by the U.S. company, no matter the location, when requested by a warrant. However, it provides mechanisms for the companies to reject or challenge the warrant if they believe the request violates the privacy rights of the foreign country where the data was stored. Additionally, the CLOUD Act authorizes the Executive Branch to enter into bilateral agreements with foreign countries for sharing data stored about each country's citizens.

After the passage of the CLOUD Act, the DOJ issued a new warrant under the CLOUD Act instead of the Stored Communications Act. Microsoft complied with the warrant, and the case before the Supreme Court was rendered moot and dropped.

Links to resources on the web:

Supreme Court Case: *United States v. Microsoft Corp.*

```
https://www.supremecourt.gov/docket/docketfiles/html/public/17-2.html
```
CLOUD Act

```
https://www.congress.gov/bill/115th-congress/senate-bill/2383/text
```
The exam will not cover these cases, but there may be mention of the CLOUD Act. It is important to remember that it is the current law that covers U.S. companies and release of data stored outside of the borders of the United States.

It is important to realize the advantage and real value that global CSPs offer over either local CSPs or your own data centers. Global CSPs offer data locations around the globe, so if you must meet a data sovereignty requirement concerning location, then they will offer locations that could meet these requirements.

 Design Scenario

Other International Data Sovereignty

China and Russia are two examples of countries that have restrictive data sovereignty laws. China has a requirement that any personal information or important data must be stored on a server located within China. Additionally, China has licensing requirements for any company doing business with Chinese citizens. You may have heard about the Great Firewall of China, which places technological restrictions on all Internet traffic in and out of China. Microsoft provides documentation on data sovereignty and China regulations that would apply to any business:

```
https://docs.microsoft.com/en-us/azure/china/overview-sovereignty-and-
regulations
```

Russia recently has taken a different route than China. Russia has started blocking Google and Amazon cloud services entirely instead of implementing regulations. Russia has taken issue with the messaging/communication platform of Telegram. Telegram offers end-to-end encryption messaging, which prevents anyone from being able to view messages, even Telegram. In an effort to block access to Telegram (which runs on Google Cloud and AWS) to Russian citizens, most, if not all, services of both are blocked. Russia has recently hinted at a desire to build its own Internet separate from the current Internet based/controlled in the United States.

Regulatory Concerns

Regulatory concerns actually fall into one of three buckets, and we will be discussing all three. These three are not mutually exclusive, and there will be a lot of overlap.

- Local, state, and federal
- Industry-based requirements
- International standards

Local, state, and federal regulations is the catchall section for any organization doing business in the United States. In general, the other categories can fit into this category. However, industry-based requirements and international standards are more specific and targeted to particular organizations or customers.

There is a hierarchy to regulations as there is with laws in general in the United States. In the United States there is the *doctrine of preemption*, which in short states that state law preempts any local laws and federal law preempts any state laws. This is an important concept to understand because it provides the framework and guidance if you are ever presented with regulations that appear to be in conflict.

Net Neutrality

On June 11, 2018, the Federal Communications Commission (FCC) overturned previous regulations that enacted net neutrality. Net neutrality in essence barred Internet service providers (ISPs) from blocking, slowing down, or speeding up delivery of online content at their discretion. The FCC transferred jurisdiction of ISP network management to the Federal Trade Commission (FTC). Additionally, the FCC preempted any states from enacting their own net neutrality rules. Several states have brought lawsuits against the FCC, but no decisions have been handed down as of the writing of this book.

Outside of the doctrine of preemption, regulations follow the reverse order, i.e., local then state then federal. This is derived from specificity; state laws are more specific than federal laws. This specificity is intentional and based on local control.

Getting into specific local or state regulations is beyond the scope of this book. Therefore, we will focus on federal regulations and requirements in this section of the book. There are federal regulations that won't be mentioned in this section because they fall under either industry-specific or global regulations, which will be covered later in this chapter. There are too many regulations to cover all of them in this book. However, we will cover a few that are more well-known and tend to appear on the exam. We recommend that you visit each of the global CSPs' compliance pages to view the regulations they are compliant with; you can find a list of them in Table 7.1.

TABLE 7.1 CSP Compliance Links

CSP	Compliance Page
AWS	https://aws.amazon.com/compliance/programs/
Azure	https://azure.microsoft.com/en-us/overview/trusted-cloud/compliance/
Google	https://cloud.google.com/security/compliance/

Federal Risk and Authorization Management Program (FedRAMP)

FedRAMP was established to provide a standardized approach for assessing, monitoring, and authorizing cloud computing services under the Federal Information Security Management Act (FISMA, which we discuss next). CSPs desiring to sell services to a federal agency must demonstrate FedRAMP compliance either by earning a Provisional Authority to Operate (P-ATO) from the Joint Authorization Board (JAB) or receiving an Authority to Operate (ATO) from a federal agency. FedRAMP authorizations are granted at three impact levels based on NIST guidelines—low, medium, and high. These rank the impact that the loss of confidentiality, integrity, or availability could have on an organization—low (limited effect), medium (serious adverse effect), and high (severe or catastrophic effect).

Federal Information Security Management Act (FISMA)

FISMA is a federal law that requires U.S. federal agencies and their partners to procure information systems and services only from organizations that adhere to FISMA requirements. The FISMA requirements are controls identified by NIST 800-53 rev 4 and NIST 800-37. We have mentioned NIST previously in this book, so you should be familiar with who they are. Mentioning all NIST documents that detail or relate to federal regulations is beyond the scope of this book. However, if you are interested in reading further, Table 7.2 contains NIST document numbers and web addresses. If you choose to pursue further certifications specifically in the security field, you will need to become familiar with these.

TABLE 7.2 CSP Federal Links

NIST	Description	Web Address
800-53	Security Controls	https://nvd.nist.gov/800-53
800-37	Risk Management	https://csrc.nist.gov/publications/detail/sp/800-37/rev-2/final
CSF	Cyber Security Framework	https://www.nist.gov/cyberframework

Federal Information Processing Standard (FIPS)

FIPS is a federal standard that details the security requirements for cryptographic modules that protect sensitive information. Cryptographic modules are hardware devices (usually, but can be software) that are used to encrypt sensitive information. The current FIPS standard is 140-3, which was released on March 22, 2019. This standard is maintained by NIST, and it publishes a list of vendors and their cryptographic modules that are validated as FIPS 140-3 compliant. FIPS 140-3 is so new that no CSP is FIPS 140-3 compliant as of the writing of this book. Currently each CSP has information and a list of services that can be FIPS 140-2 compliant. You can get additional information about each of the standards from the websites shown in Table 7.3.

TABLE 7.3 CSP FIPS Links

FIPS Standard	Website
140-3	https://csrc.nist.gov/publications/detail/fips/140/3/final
140-2	https://csrc.nist.gov/publications/detail/fips/140/2/final

> **Exam Note**
>
> You will not need to know specific details about FedRAMP, FISMA, or FIPS. You will need to be familiar with these terms, as we have seen them used in exam questions.

Industry-Based Requirements

We have already covered one industry-based regulation in the previous chapter, PCI DSS. It is a regulation that covers credit card processing for any business. This is one regulation that spans multiple topics, because it is also global. It would be impossible to cover every industry-based requirement here. Therefore, we will cover a wide range, a few that will be mentioned on the exam, and a few that you may have come across previously.

- FERPA
- FINRA
- GLBA
- HIPAA
- MPAA
- SOX

Family Educational Rights and Privacy Act (FERPA)

FERPA is often called the HIPAA of educational systems. It is a federal law that protects the privacy of student education records. There are in essence two parts of FERPA: first, that educational information will not be shared with any unauthorized individuals, and second, it guarantees access to educational information to authorized individuals. FERPA does not require or recognize audits or certifications. So, any education institution that wants to use cloud services must assess its ability to comply with FERPA. CSPs can really only address the first part of FERPA, and it is important to understand their commitment if you or your organization deals with educational information. One thing to note, though, about CSPs' FERPA commitment is that the CSP itself needs to be designated as a "school official" to be compliant with FERPA. This can be a point of contention for some academic institutions.

Table 7.4 shows links to each CSP's FERPA documentation.

TABLE 7.4   CSP FERPA Links

CSP	Link
AWS	https://d1.awsstatic.com/whitepapers/compliance/AWS_FERPA_Whitepaper.pdf
Azure	http://download.microsoft.com/download/2/8/3/2839FB21-353E-472E-BE57-883EC9C6185F/FERPA_Compliance_Backgrounder.pdf
Google	https://cloud.google.com/security/compliance/ferpa/

Financial Industry Regulatory Authority (FINRA)

FINRA is a financial institution regulation that stipulates and outlines the books and record-keeping requirements. Financial institutions must retain financial transactions and related communications in a nonerasable and nonmodifiable state. The specific rule is known as 4511, and it can be one of the most challenging to implement in the cloud.

> **FINRA 4511 and SEA Rule 17a-4**
>
> FINRA is the regulation that we are referring to, but the text of the rule calls on SEA Rule 17a-4. SEA Rule 17a-4 is Section 17(a)(1) of the Securities Exchange Act of 1934. We wanted to call this out if you do any web searches. In fact, AWS documentation is listed as SEC 17-a1, whereas Microsoft documentation is listed as FINRA 4511.

The difficulty is the requirement that records be stored in a tamper-proof medium with no ability to alter or delete them until after a specific retention period. In every digital device there is a root or admin user who has the ability to do anything to the device. How do you set up a mechanism in a device that can prevent an action that is allowed by default?

As of the writing of this book, only AWS and Azure have FINRA-compliant storage offerings. Neither one of them is intuitive or easy to implement, but they are there. Links to AWS's and Azure's FINRA compliant documentation are found in Table 7.5.

TABLE 7.5   CSP FINRA Links

CSP	Link
AWS	https://aws.amazon.com/getting-started/projects/set-up-compliant-archive/
Azure	http://download.microsoft.com/download/6/B/2/6B20520B-E264-4B58-9EE2-DD6C87D9E254/FINRA-Compliance.pdf

Gramm-Leach-Bliley Act (GLBA)

GLBA is a U.S. law that reformed the financial services industry and specifically addressed concerns about protecting consumer privacy. Financial institutions covered by the Gramm-Leach-Bliley Act must tell their customers about their information-sharing practices and explain to customers their right to "opt out" if they don't want their information shared with certain third parties. The FTC is charged with this regulation, and you can read about it on the FTC's website:

https://www.ftc.gov/tips-advice/business-center/guidance/how-comply-privacy-consumer-financial-information-rule-gramm

At the time of this writing, only AWS and Azure offered GLBA compliance. Links to their documentation on GLBA are found in Table 7.6.

TABLE 7.6 CSP GLBA Links

CSP	Link
AWS	https://d1.awsstatic.com/whitepapers/compliance/AWS_User_Guide_for_Financial_Services_in_the_United_States.pdf
Azure	http://download.microsoft.com/download/2/A/C/2AC21A04-CE23-4963-BE1A-515DB4A17C6E/GLBA-Compliance.pdf

Health Insurance Portability and Accountability Act (HIPAA)

HIPAA is a U.S. law that establishes requirements for the use, disclosure, and safeguarding of individually identifiable health information. It applies to covered entities: doctors' offices, hospitals, health insurers, and other healthcare companies with access to patients' protected health information (PHI), as well as to business associates, such as cloud service and IT providers, that process PHI on their behalf. As with the FERPA regulation, the CSP will have to be designated as an "authorized party" in transactions. This is an important detail that any organization must understand.

Links to CSP documentation concerning HIPAA are found in Table 7.7.

TABLE 7.7 CSP HIPAA Links

CSP	Documentation
AWS	https://aws.amazon.com/compliance/hipaa-compliance/
Azure	http://download.microsoft.com/download/4/6/B/46BB3C98-AE2B-42C1-A2CD-F7C0040FB6B8/HIPAA_Compliance_Backgrounder.pdf
Google	https://cloud.google.com/security/compliance/hipaa-compliance/

Motion Picture Association of America (MPAA)

MPAA is the association that provides best practices guidance and control frameworks to help major studio partners and vendors design infrastructure and solutions to ensure the security of digital film assets. Everyone is familiar with or at least has heard of MPAA if they have ever seen a movie. MPAA serves other functions besides securing digital film assets, but in the cloud, security is the main focus. MPAA does not offer a certification; it just provides the framework and guidelines.

At the time of this writing, only AWS and Azure offered MPAA compliance documentation. Links to their documentation are found in Table 7.8.

TABLE 7.8   CSP MPAA Links

CSP	Documentation
AWS	https://aws.amazon.com/compliance/mpaa/
Azure	http://download.microsoft.com/download/7/A/1/7A19B051-3399-4222-BEF1-E6E3E0A17961/MPAA_Backgrounder.pdf

Sarbanes-Oxley Act (SOX)

SOX is a U.S. law that requires publicly traded companies to have proper internal control structures in place to validate that their financial statements accurately reflect their financial results. SOX does not just apply to financial institutions; it applies to any publicly traded company. Additionally, there is no SOX compliance certification. SOX is mainly about reporting, so there are SOC reporting requirements. It is these SOC reporting requirements that CSPs can assist with.

At the time of this writing, only AWS and Azure offer SOX or SOC compliance documentation. Links to their documentation can be found in Table 7.9.

TABLE 7.9   CSP SOX Links

CSP	Documentation
AWS	https://aws.amazon.com/compliance/soc-faqs/
Azure	http://download.microsoft.com/download/5/D/2/5D278460-AF57-470F-B166-5BD9258BCE3E/SOX-Compliance.pdf

---

Exam Note

The examples list is not an exhaustive list and by no means are you expected to know all these regulations. These regulations are specific to industries, and unless you work in one of the affected industries, you do not need to know details about them. We mention them as examples of the many regulations that CSPs must work with and to introduce the names of regulations that have appeared on exam questions. The exam will not ask specifics about any of the regulations, but it is important to recognize them by name and know they are regulations.

International Standards

International standards would be an even bigger list than industry standards if you went country by country. Therefore, we won't provide a list of them, but we will provide links to global CSP compliance home pages that you can browse. International standards are going to be specific to you. We can offer assistance and tools that will help you adhere to whatever standards you must comply with. Additionally, we can give a few examples of common standards.

CIS Benchmarks

The Center for Internet Security (CIS) on a regular basis publishes benchmarks for technology products. These benchmarks are a great tool and assist in the process of becoming compliant. They cover a wide range of topics including: OSs, server software, cloud providers, mobile devices, network devices, and desktop software.

You must register with CIS to access the benchmarks, which are all available for free download in PDF. These benchmarks, while not specific regulations, are a great starting point for meeting security regulations. You can register for free here:

```
https://www.cisecurity.org/cis-benchmarks/
```

CIS offers benchmarks for all three of the major global CSPs: AWS, Azure, and Google. Figure 7.1 shows the cloud benchmarks.

FIGURE 7.1   CIS benchmarks for CSPs

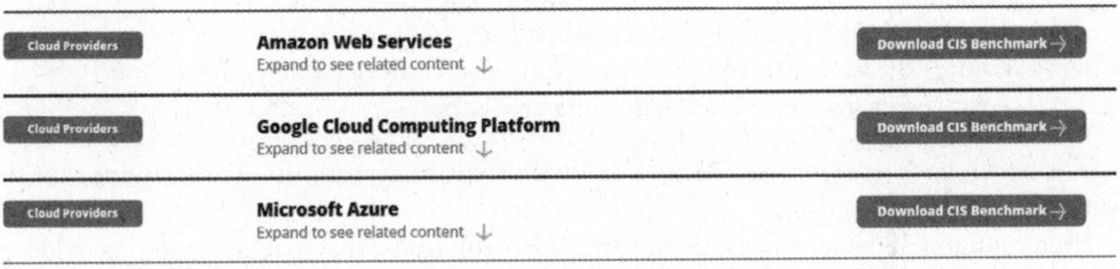

Here is an excerpt from the CIS benchmark for AWS:

> This document provides prescriptive guidance for configuring security options for a subset of Amazon Web Services with an emphasis on foundational, testable, and architecture agnostic settings. Specific Amazon Web Services in scope for this document include:

- AWS Identity and Access Management (IAM)
- AWS Config
- AWS CloudTrail
- AWS CloudWatch
- AWS Simple Notification Service (SNS)
- AWS Simple Store Service (S3)
- AWS VPC (Default)

As you can see, it covers several services offered by AWS; a few we have mentioned before and some we will talk about later in this chapter.

The benchmarks have levels, scores, descriptions, audits, and remediations. The ISO 27001 standard, which we discuss in the next section, has a requirement of multifactor authentication (MFA) on all administrator accounts. Once you have registered with CIS for access to the benchmarks, you can download PDFs for Azure, AWS, and Google. All three PDFs give detailed steps to perform in the respective platforms that will require MFA for all administrative account access. Here is an excerpt from the AWS CIS benchmark concerning MFA:

> 1.2 Ensure multi-factor authentication (MFA) is enabled for all IAM users that have a console password (Scored)
>
> **Profile Applicability:** Level 1
>
> **Description:**
> Multi-Factor Authentication (MFA) adds an extra layer of protection on top of a user name and password. With MFA enabled, when a user signs in to an AWS website, they will be prompted for their user name and password as well as for an authentication code from their AWS MFA device. It is recommended that MFA be enabled for all accounts that have a console password.
>
> **Rationale:**
> Enabling MFA provides increased security for console access as it requires the authenticating principal to possess a device that emits a time-sensitive key and have knowledge of a credential.

The benchmark goes into technical detail with steps to perform to ensure (audit) that the benchmark was achieved.

Even though CIS benchmarks are not specific regulations, they will assist and provide guidance on steps needed to become compliant.

Exam Note

You will not need to know specific CIS benchmarks for the exam. However, we have seen several questions make reference to CIS benchmarks. You will need to know that they cover securing technology resources, and they cover a wide range including CSPs, servers, desktops, network devices, and mobile devices.

International Organization of Standardization (IOS)

ISO is an international body that creates and maintains standards. These standards don't just deal with the cloud or technology, but there are several that do and CSPs have compliance documentation on them. You will recognize and see a lot of overlap between these standards and regulatory requirements at both the federal and industry-specific levels.

- ISO 9001 – Global Quality Standard
- ISO 27001 – Security Management Controls
- ISO 27017 – Cloud Specific Controls
- ISO 27018 – Personal Data Protection

ISO 9001 – Quality Standard

ISO 9001 establishes the criteria for a quality management system. The standard has several components, including a clear focus on meeting customer requirements, a strong corporate governance and leadership commitment to quality objectives, a process-driven approach to meeting objectives, and a focus on continuous improvement.

An organization that is ISO 9001 compliant has demonstrated a commitment to quality in the services they provide. At the time of writing this book, only AWS and Azure provided links to a CSP's ISO 9001 documentation, as shown in Table 7.10.

TABLE 7.10   CSP IOS 9001 Links

CSP	Documentation
AWS	https://aws.amazon.com/compliance/iso-9001-faqs/
Azure	http://download.microsoft.com/download/E/6/3/E63F54DC-766E-477C-98D8-ADDB6A94F5C5/ISO-9001-Compliance.pdf

ISO 27001 – Information Security Management Standards

ISO 27001 is the basis of several other regulations that we have already discussed; basically any security-related regulation has its roots in this standard. It is intended to bring information security under explicit management control. As a formal specification, it mandates requirements that define how to implement, monitor, maintain, and continually improve an information security management system. It also prescribes a set of best practices that includes documentation requirements, divisions of responsibility, availability, access control, security, auditing, and corrective and preventive measures.

Links to CSPs' documentation on ISO 27001 are listed in Table 7.11.

TABLE 7.11   CSP IOS 27001 Links

CSP	Documentation
AWS	https://aws.amazon.com/compliance/iso-27001-faqs/
Azure	http://download.microsoft.com/download/1/2/9/12926039-8F90-4BAF-AC8F-7124D48F400B/ISOIEC_27001_Compliance_Backgrounder.pdf
Google	https://cloud.google.com/security/compliance/iso-27001/

ISO 27017 – Controlling Cloud-Based Information Security

ISO 27017 is specific to CSPs and details information security. It is designed to be used as a reference for selecting cloud services information security controls when implementing a cloud computing information security management system. This standard is the basis for the shared security model that we have discussed throughout the book. Here are a couple of other examples of topics covered in this standard:

- Removal and return of cloud service customer assets upon contract termination
- Alignment of security management for virtual and physical networks
- Protection and separation of a customer's virtual environment from that of other customers
- Virtual machine hardening requirements to meet business needs

Table 7.12 includes links to the CSPs' documentation on ISO 27017.

TABLE 7.12   CSP ISO 27017 Links

CSP	Documentation
AWS	https://aws.amazon.com/compliance/iso-27017-faqs/
Azure	http://download.microsoft.com/download/7/7/9/7799D02B-A97A-48E0-A057-C19DD543BB24/ISO-IEC-27017_backgrounder.pdf
Google	https://cloud.google.com/security/compliance/iso-27017/

ISO 27018 – Protecting Personal Data in the Cloud

ISO 27018 governs personal identifiable information (PII) in the cloud. It is based on EU data protection laws and gives guidance to CSPs acting as processors of PII on assessing risks and implementing controls for protecting PII. There are four main requirements for the 27018 standard.

- Customers of CSPs know where their data is stored.
- Customer data won't be used for marketing or advertising without explicit consent.
- Customers of CSPs know what's happening with their PII.
- CSPs will comply only with legally binding requests for disclosure of customer data.

Links to CSPs' documentation on ISO 27018 are shown in Table 7.13.

TABLE 7.13   CSP ISO 27018 Links

CSP	Documentation
AWS	https://aws.amazon.com/compliance/iso-27018-faqs/
Azure	http://download.microsoft.com/download/F/D/A/FDA4697E-D72D-4513-8626-A5F294DC7A0F/ISOIEC_27018_Compliance_Backgrounder.pdf
Google	https://cloud.google.com/security/compliance/iso-27018/

> **Exam Note**
>
> You will not need to know the specifics of each ISO standard. We have seen exam questions that make mention of an ISO number, but they usually refer to a specific number. It should be enough to know that ISO details international standards that CSPs can be certified on.

Certifications

We have already touched on certifications in this chapter. A certification is testament to the compliance of standards, practices, or regulations by an independent third party. Certifications typically have a lifetime and must be renewed. Some certifications must be renewed annually and some every three years. Getting certifications can be an arduous and expensive process (as you may well know). Organizations usually must pay not only for the infrastructure and processes needed to become certified, but also for the third party to certify them.

The list of certifications available would be too large for the contents of this book. As of the writing of this book, Microsoft listed 72 certifications that it has attained for its Azure cloud services. Many of the standards and regulations that we have discussed previously have certification processes. There is a certification process for a hardware device to become FIPS 140-3 compliant from NIST, for example.

Table 7.14 provides links to each individual CSP's certification list, where you can read more about requirements and how often third-party review must be completed to be compliant.

TABLE 7.14   CSP Certification Links

CSP	Certification
AWS	https://aws.amazon.com/compliance/programs/
Azure	https://www.microsoft.com/en-us/TrustCenter/Compliance/complianceofferings
Google	https://cloud.google.com/security/compliance/

Explain Security Concerns, Measures, or Concepts of Cloud Operations

We discussed *risk* at length in the previous chapter.

Threat

In the previous chapter when we discussed risk, we defined risk as any agent, condition, or circumstance that could potentially cause harm, loss, damage, or compromise to an IT asset or data asset. The likelihood of the threat is the probability of occurrence or the odds that the event will actually occur.

We are going to dive into this definition a little more and give a few examples that might not seem as obvious at first. One term that is not explicitly listed in the definition but is implied under loss is denied access. If access to an asset is denied in any way, even if only temporarily, then that is a threat that needs a response.

You have probably heard of a distributed denial of service (DDoS) attack. With today's advanced networking and content delivery networks (CDNs), most normal DDoS attacks can be mitigated by CSPs. Only the largest DDoS would have a chance of taking down a properly architected network in a CSP's network for an extended period of time.

FIGURE 7.2 DDoS Example

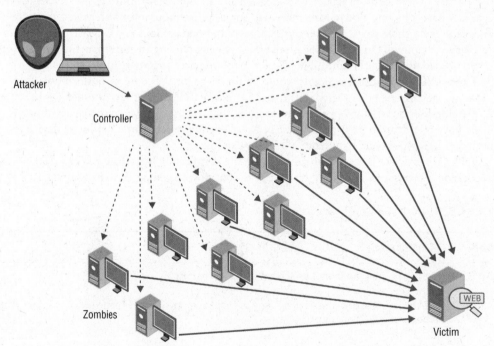

However, normal DDoS attacks can definitely interrupt and cause a loss of connectivity, at least temporarily, to make services unavailable. This can manifest itself in long load times or buffering of content. There is an old saying for video content makers, "Buffering is suffering." Have you ever closed a web page or a video online if the content buffered for too long? The point is, there are threats to assets that will not cause a total loss of the asset but can make the asset unavailable to your customers. This can lead to another threat, which is harm to your organization's reputation, which is an asset as well.

DDoS Maps

If you do a web search for *DDoS attack maps*, you will find several online that can display in near real time. One that I like is the Kaspersky Labs one located here:

```
https://cybermap.kaspersky.com/
```

Agent, condition, or circumstance are the first three key terms in the definition of threat. By agent we mean any entity that acts with a sense of agency or acts on its own. This can mean a person that is acting in either their own self-interest or another's. Agent could mean a literal agent, such as a software agent installed on a server or desktop. Agent is simply anything that performs specific actions to achieve some goal, whether that goal is beneficial, malicious, or benign in intent. By condition we mean the state or properties of an asset. Think of power state or access control—anything that describes the current state of an asset. By circumstance we mean actions performed by nonassets or agents that are out of your control. Think of weather, software bugs, catastrophic events, etc. These are things typically outside of your control that you will need to identify and manage.

Harm, loss, damage, or compromise are the next key terms in the definition of threat. Harm is either injury or damage to an organization's assets. This is the larger term for damage and is usually applied to nontechnical assets; think of employees. A natural disaster like a hurricane could cause harm to your employees, for example. By loss we mean either partial or complete loss and also permanent or temporary. The first terms are measurements of degree of loss, while the other two measurements of time. We gave DDoS as an example of temporary loss of an asset. However, a fire that takes place in a storage closet that contains past years of financial records would also be a loss. Damage means to impair the soundness or the value of an asset. The asset may not be lost, but its soundness may not be whole. What if a threat deleted all the credit card transactions from a point-of-sale system? There would still be inventory change and some record of the sales, but the system is no longer whole or accurate. Damage can also decrease the value of an asset; this can be either quantifiable or qualitative in nature depending on the asset, e.g., cracked screen, failed hard drive, etc. Compromise can mean lots of things, but in general it refers to either the ability to trust an asset or the asset being used to initiate threats against other assets. Most hackers who are looking to compromise systems are looking for monetary gain. Once a system is compromised and the hacker has control, they will use that system and attack other systems from it. This allows them to not use their own systems and allows them to cover their tracks more easily.

Vulnerability

We discussed *vulnerability* in the previous chapter when we discussed risk and threat. All vulnerabilities are threats, but not all threats are vulnerabilities. The key difference is that vulnerabilities are assigned to a specific asset. Additionally, a vulnerability is a threat that has not been mitigated. Most of the large technology companies have implemented bug bounty programs. This is where the companies will pay real money for information on new vulnerabilities. The bounty programs have restrictions on them to ensure that the technology companies have time to respond or patch a vulnerability before the release of the details. These vendors are both software and hardware manufacturers. You can read more about Google's bounty program, Project Zero, here:

https://googleprojectzero.blogspot.com/

Other vendors have different standards and restrictions, but you can get an idea of statistics and how successful these programs are by reading their FAQs.

For vulnerabilities that are publicly known, you need to look at the Common Vulnerabilities and Exposures (CVE) database. Except for zero-day vulnerabilities, which are fairly rare, CVEs are the most common attack vector for nefarious individuals. CVE is a dictionary of publicly disclosed cybersecurity vulnerabilities and exposures. The CVE database is freely available and searchable. You can access the CVE database here:

https://cve.mitre.org/cve/

Two of the largest vulnerabilities that have happened in recent years are Meltdown and Spectre. Meltdown and Spectre are two separate issues that have had a significant impact on organizations that utilize virtualization technologies. They affect virtually all processors on the market, meaning that they cause a hardware issue. Any processor on the market that is used for virtualization is impacted by both of these vulnerabilities. The basics of the vulnerabilities lie in the fact that virtualization technologies use shared resources; in other words, the host's memory is used by all resources running on the host. Resources running on a host could use these exploits to read memory addresses that they were not authorized to access.

Mitigation strategies for Meltdown and Spectre are limited because they exploit a fundamental feature of the hardware and features needed for virtualization. The major OSs and hypervisors have been patched and they do mitigate some of the risk, but they don't eliminate it entirely. Complete mitigation will require new processor hardware. Table 7.15 delineates where you can read about the Meltdown and Spectre specifics.

TABLE 7.15 Meltdown and Spectre Links

Name	CVE Number	Link
Meltdown	2017-5754	https://cve.mitre.org/cgi-bin/cvename.cgi?name=CVE-2017-5754
Spectre V1	2017-5753	https://cve.mitre.org/cgi-bin/cvename.cgi?name=CVE-2017-5753
Spectre V2	2017-5715	https://cve.mitre.org/cgi-bin/cvename.cgi?name=CVE-2017-5715

Security Assessments

Now that we know about assets, risk, and threats, we need to discuss securing those assets. We have touched briefly on the subject of security in previous chapters; here we dive in a little more and give examples and expand on previous definitions.

Security assessment is a systematic examination of an organization's security policies and underlying security controls to see if they're adequate to perform their assigned function.

We have explored security policies in depth in a previous chapter. In this section, we are going to discuss the process and tools to perform the systematic examination. An important concept that should be overarching when we discuss processes and tools is a security audit. A security audit is an independent review of an IT system, whether it be software or hardware. Independent is the key term here: IT personnel who manage and maintain an IT system should not be the personnel who perform the audit. Confirmation bias is very real and will occur even under the best intentions and conditions. The difficulty is finding an independent party who has enough domain knowledge of the IT system to perform an adequate audit.

Penetration Testing

Penetration testing (pentest) is an exploratory or directed examination of a network or system to achieve one or more of the following goals: information gathering or vulnerability exploitation. A pentest uses the same methodologies and techniques that attackers use, except they are performed with an organization's knowledge and permission.

Important Note on Informing an Organization

When performing a penetration test, it is important to have permission from the organization, not just from an ethical perspective but also from a legal perspective. The Computer Fraud and Abuse Act of 1986 makes it a crime to perform potentially compromising actions without permission. You can read more about the Computer Fraud and Abuse Act here: https://www.justice.gov/sites/default/files/criminal-ccips/ legacy/2015/01/14/ccmanual.pdf

On the other hand, performing penetration testing when all of the organization's IT and security staff know about it beforehand will not result in an accurate test. Penetration testing needs to be accurate and simulate real-world scenarios as much as possible. In short, someone at the organization needs to give permission, but the entire organization should not know about the testing. The information should be compartmentalized. Microsoft uses red vs. blue teams for penetration testing. If you would like more information about how Microsoft runs these two competing teams, there is a video here:

https://azure.microsoft.com/en-us/resources/videos/red-vs-blue-internal-security-penetration-testing-of-microsoft-azure/

Penetration testing comes in one of two forms: internal and external. Typically, organizations only look at external penetration testing, but it is important to also do internal penetration testing. If one system becomes compromised and is unknown to you, then the attacker will do their attack from the internal compromised system. Internal testing is also important in the case of a disgruntled employee.

The most basic form of pentest is a network port scan. *Nmap* (https://nmap.org) has become the industry standard. It is free and can be installed on almost any platform; most hardware vendors even have a lightweight version installed by default. Nmap can perform lots of different tests, but the most basic will scan a network for any IP addresses that respond. In addition, it will scan ports 1–1024 and see which will answer a request from any IP address. Figure 7.3 is a sample output from a run of nmap. The output in the figure took less than 2 seconds to run—nmap is very quick.

This type of network scan is really just information gathering and not exploiting or gaining unauthorized access. Once we have gathered information, we need to see what kind of access, if any, we can gain. Typically this access is going to be through exploitation of a vulnerability; we will discuss vulnerability scanning next. However, once access is granted, there are additional steps in pentesting: maintaining access and covering your tracks.

Maintaining access can come in several different forms including trojans, hidden accounts, hidden keys, reverse proxies, and SSH tunnels. All of these are designed to allow access to the asset even if the vulnerability that was exploited is patched; i.e., once exploited, the asset remains usable.

Covering your tracks is often missed when nefarious individuals attack, but if done properly, it can make investigations impossible. The first step in covering your tracks is making as few noticeable changes to the asset as possible. This will decrease the likelihood of detection in the first place and minimize evidence during an investigation. The second step is log sanitization. All modern OSs and network devices have basic logging enabled by default and virtually all of them log administrative events, i.e., logins, logouts, and admin changes. A good penetration test will remove any logged events using the exploits or maintaining access actions. A surgical approach is best; i.e., remove only the events that indicate you were there. However, removal of all logs can severely impact and hinder investigations. Removal of all logs obviously breaks our first step in covering tracks, but logs are the primary source of evidence. If there are no logs to review or investigate, then evidence will be limited.

FIGURE 7.3   Nmap example

```
Starting Nmap 6.47 ( http://nmap.org ) at 2019-08-20 16:26 EDT
Nmap scan report for 172.18.105.1
Host is up (0.0047s latency).
Not shown: 1022 filtered ports
PORT     STATE SERVICE
22/tcp  open  ssh
443/tcp open  https

Nmap scan report for 172.18.105.2
Host is up (0.0048s latency).
Not shown: 1022 filtered ports
PORT     STATE SERVICE
80/tcp  open  http
443/tcp open  https

Nmap scan report for 172.18.105.5
Host is up (0.0047s latency).
Not shown: 1015 closed ports
PORT     STATE SERVICE
22/tcp  open  ssh
53/tcp  open  domain
80/tcp  open  http
111/tcp open  rpcbind
139/tcp open  netbios-ssn
389/tcp open  ldap
443/tcp open  https
445/tcp open  microsoft-ds
901/tcp open  samba-swat

Nmap scan report for 172.18.105.11
Host is up (0.0036s latency).
Not shown: 1015 closed ports
PORT     STATE SERVICE
53/tcp  open  domain
88/tcp  open  kerberos-sec
135/tcp open  msrpc
139/tcp open  netbios-ssn
389/tcp open  ldap
445/tcp open  microsoft-ds
464/tcp open  kpasswd5
593/tcp open  http-rpc-epmap
636/tcp open  ldapssl
```

Vulnerability Scanning

Vulnerability scanning will be part of a pentest because it is what is going to grant unauthorized access. Vulnerability scanning will probe assets looking for known weaknesses that can be exploited to gain any kind of access. The goal of vulnerability scans is to identify potential exploits. This exploitation happens in two phases: gain access and elevation of privileges. It is important to understand the difference because vulnerabilities will fall into one of these phases but not both.

Gain access is an exploitation to gain any kind of access to an asset, i.e., to get in the front door. These exploits are the low-hanging fruit and usually the last to be patched. Let's use an analogy of wanting to steal a car. Assuming the car is locked, the first step is getting inside the car. You can't drive away a car from the outside.

Elevation of privileges is an exploitation that grants access to actions that are limited on an asset. These exploits are more well-known and patched quickly. The reason is that the access to an asset may not be enough access to harm or damage the asset. Typically root or administrative access is required to make changes. Using the stealing a car analogy again, once in the car, you need to get around the security measures that a key disables inside. You need a way of starting the car. You need a way of getting around the locked steering wheel, etc.

Steps in performing a vulnerability scan will depend on the environment and access to the tools you may need. At a basic level, without any tools, an experienced hacker can use just telnet and make requests to open ports from the nmap scan. Most services have a response to basic requests. This response can include useful information like the names of the software running on that port and even a version number.

As you can see from Figure 7.4, I have a software name and version. I can start searching the CVE database for any exploits that affect the software and versions.

FIGURE 7.4 CVE example

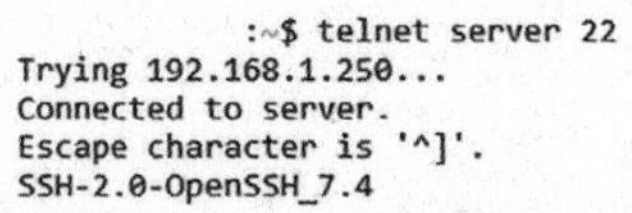

```
:~$ telnet server 22
Trying 192.168.1.250...
Connected to server.
Escape character is '^]'.
SSH-2.0-OpenSSH_7.4
```

There are tools that will automate the previous manual steps, but these tools require hardware to run. *Nessus* is the industry standard for vulnerability scanning. Nessus started out as an open source project, and you can still use a free version of it. However, there is a commercial version that is maintained by Tenable. Nessus is modular in nature, and most of the nice modules that can do the recent exploitation require paid-for modules. Don't discount the free tier, though; I have gathered and successfully exploited assets with it. It just cannot perform a full or complete vulnerability scan, but its information is still valuable. You can download and get additional information about Nessus here:

https://www.tenable.com/products/nessus

Another invaluable tool is Metasploit. Metasploit is also free, and anyone can run it if they have hardware. Metasploit actually attempts to execute the exploits that are identified. Metasploit is the tool used to gain access and to elevate privileges. It is not an easy software to use. It requires a lot of time to learn and successfully execute an exploitation. Metasploit is heralded as a penetration testing framework, which it is, but that is because exploitation is part of pentesting. You can download and get additional information about Metasploit here:

https://www.metasploit.com

⊕ **Real World Scenario**

Kali Linux Swiss Army Knife of Security

If you are not familiar with Kali Linux and are interested in information security, then get familiar. Kali Linux is a specialized distro of Linux that has all of the tools we have mentioned so far and hundreds of others already installed and ready to run.

One of the best executed and properly done exploits I have ever seen was done with a Raspberry Pi that had Kali Linux installed on it. An individual gained access to a building and found a computer that looked like it hadn't been used in a week or more. They plugged the Raspberry Pi into the network jack used by the computer and supplied power. The Raspberry Pi was set to phone home to AWS, i.e., an SSH tunnel to a VM running in AWS. Now the individual had remote access into a private network. Not only that but from that Raspberry Pi they were able to scan and exploit other systems inside the network.

Thankfully, this was part of a sanctioned penetration test, so no actual assets were harmed or damaged, but the tester was able to successfully exploit other systems. The exploited systems were thought to be protected because they were not publicly accessible. However, the Raspberry Pi was inside the network already.

Application Scanning

Application scanning differs from vulnerability scanning because you are scanning for unknown vulnerabilities. Application scanning is for the most part a manual and peer review process. An application's source code needs to be reviewed by peers and tested for best coding practices. We touched on this subject briefly in Chapter 5 when we were covering DevOps and the CICD pipeline.

Outside of peer reviews, the scanning of applications is done by testing the application. There are three types of testing that are generally performed: data, interface, and misuse.

Data testing is sending data to an application and reviewing how the application responds. The sending of data can be benign in nature, like synthetic transactions (transactions that look and act like normal transactions but are fake). Testing data can also be nefarious, as in SQL injection or cross-site scripting attacks. These are tried-and-true exploits that all applications need to be able to handle gracefully without crashing or elevating privileges.

Interface testing is testing the interface for unintended consequences. Any UI or UX developer will tell you that users rarely use an application the way developers intended. What inputs will an application accept: touch, keyboard, mouse, voice, and so on? Interface testing usually requires a focus group or user acceptance testing; i.e., you need to get it in front of users. Users will use an application's interface in ways you have never dreamed of.

Misuse testing can be a lot of fun but also most time-consuming. This is where you intentionally do something wrong in an application to see how the application handles it. Here are a few examples:

- Inputting text in a field that expects a number
- Providing more than 10 digits when entering a phone number
- Entering the same values for username and password, i.e., username = password
- Closing an application in the middle of use before a process is complete

There are many more examples, but you get the idea. It is using the application in intentionally stupid ways to make sure the application can handle unintended actions.

Open Web Application Security Project (OWASP)

OWASP is a nonprofit organization that produces tools for application scanning and testing. These tools can simulate and track a lot of the testing we just mentioned. As the name suggests, it is only designed for testing web applications, but it is pretty extensive in the information that can be gleaned from it. With the recent push for most web applications to be web-ized, OWASP tools are gaining in popularity and could become the standard.

Data Security

Data is ultimately the thing of value to most nefarious individuals. Compute and networking can be compromised and exploited, but the exploitation is typically used as a vector to access data. If you follow the technology news, recently the high-profile stories have been about data breaches and the effect they are having on individuals.

Whenever data becomes compromised, it usually contains personal information. This personal information either is freely released on places like the dark web or is sold to third parties. Whoever gets ahold of the personal information can use this information to perform several forms of *identity theft*. In this context we are using the term identity theft to include the broader category of identity impersonation.

The most common and well-known form of identity theft is when an individual uses another individual's information for monetary gain, i.e., to open bank accounts or credit cards, etc. However, there is a broader context of identity impersonation, e.g., when an individual gains access to enough personal information to perform a password reset on an email account. With access to an email account, nefarious individuals can act on your behalf because they are acting as you. They can use the email address to either gain access to other accounts or just send communications that are disparaging to someone's character.

Categories

Not all data can be treating equally, even personal information. Before we dive into how organizations use data categories, let's step through an example that is about personal information. You are already familiar with this topic, but you may not have thought about it in the context of categories. When we talk about PII, you typically just think of bank account information, Social Security number, credit card number, health history, etc. However, that is only private PII or information that you don't want unauthorized individuals to know.

Your name is an example of PII that you don't typically mind other individuals knowing. If no one knows your phone number or your mailing address or your email address, then no one would be able to communicate with you. You may not want certain individuals or organizations communicating with you, but in general you control that contact by requesting that they don't communicate with you. What about your favorite food or pet's name or your first car or favorite teacher? These are pieces of information that may not be damaging if other individuals know, but do you want the general public to know everything about your life? The point we are making is not all of your personal information should be treated equally; there are different categories, and each should be treated differently.

Public

All organizations must have public information or data; otherwise, they would never be able to conduct business with other individuals or organizations. *Public* information is information that you yourself treat as public: name, address, phone number, email, etc. These are required to facilitate communication between parties.

The easiest way to think of public information is that it is information that can be freely shared with little or no harm to an individual or organization if known. For an organization, examples include press releases, approved marketing materials, ads, etc. This is information that is actually required to be known to function as a business.

Private

The next level of data categorization is *private*. Private information presents potential harm to an organization if made public but is not sensitive (next level) in nature. Information or data in this category typically has the following properties: unauthorized access, disclosure, and/or destruction can have an impact on an organization or its clients.

Information that is categorized as private should be shared only with the proper contractual agreements in place, e.g., nondisclosure agreements (NDAs). Organizations will need to enter into agreements with other organizations or individuals to perform their business functions. NDAs help ensure that information that should be private remains private. Some examples of information that is generally considered private are general email correspondence and internal company communications.

Emails as Private Information

Emails being classified as private comes as a surprise to most individuals when they first learn about data categorization. Most people think of email as public information because of its ease of use and ease of sharing outside an organization. Additionally, almost everyone nowadays has a personal email that they use to communicate with anyone freely. However, it is important to treat business and even your own emails as private as the default and then assume that some emails are to be treated as public. It is this default behavior of private and then some as public that is critical because the inverse is far more problematic.

Sensitive

Information that presents the greatest harm to an organization or individual if released is represented by the *sensitive* category. Sensitive information is information the access or even the management of which could be governed by regulatory laws and requirements. We talked about regulations and standards earlier in this chapter. The data security standards discussed apply here, such as required encryption, restricted access, etc. Information with the sensitive categorization has the following properties: unauthorized access, disclosure, and/or destruction could have a serious adverse impact on an organization or its clients.

Organizational or individual examples include detailed IT and/or network designs, legal/HR investigation reports, and risk assessment reports.

Exam Note

The exam will have questions that will ask you to identify which category should be used for some information or data. You will need to determine what the risk is for the three levels: public, private, sensitive. Think of it as hierarchical. Public means anyone can view the information; there is little risk in everyone knowing. Next is private, which means only internal personnel should be able to view it, but everyone internal can. Finally is sensitive, which means only management or privileged personnel should have knowledge of the information.

 Real World Scenario

Government Categorization

Originally most organizations based their data categorizations on the U.S. government model. Prior to 1982 the U.S. government had a five-level data categorization.

- Top Secret

- Confidential Restricted

- Confidential

- Internal

- Public

Executive Order 12356 changed and streamlined the classifications to the ones shown in Table 7.16.

TABLE 7.16 Data Categorization

Level	Definition
Top Secret	Applied to information the unauthorized disclosure of which reasonably could be expected to cause exceptionally grave damage to national security
Secret	Applied to information the unauthorized disclosure of which reasonably could be expected to cause serious damage to national security
Confidential	Applied to information the unauthorized disclosure of which reasonably could be expected to cause damage to national security

Organizations must decide for themselves which is the best model and how many categories they need. I have never seen an organization with a mature and well-documented categorization scheme have less than three (similar to the three covered in this chapter). I have seen a few organizations that have had as many as six.

Confidentiality

Confidentiality or privacy is simply the assets that are protected from unauthorized assets. The unauthorized assets are both owned and not owned by the organization that owns the asset that is being kept confidential. This is the first principle of the CIA triad, which we mentioned earlier in the previous chapter. We will be discussing all three parts of the triad in this chapter.

Security mechanisms that offer confidentiality are designed to protect an asset from other entities. They are designed to prevent access outright, or if access is achieved, the asset is rendered useless or of no value. The level of protection is dependent on the sensitivity and value of the asset as well. We discussed sensitivity previously in this chapter, and the levels will determine the security mechanisms. Additionally, remember that more resources should not be expended than the value of the asset that is being protected.

When securing data that needs to be private, there are two mechanisms: encryption and sanitization.

Encryption

Encryption is the process of hiding or obfuscating data in such a manner that only authorized individuals can read the data. Encryption mechanisms date back to antiquity. If you have ever studied encryption algorithms, one of the first you learn about is called the Caesar cipher, named after Julius Caesar. The Caesar cipher is a simple shift character encryption. One letter is equal to another letter in the alphabet. For example, a shift of 5 means "A" becomes "F," "B" becomes "G," etc. A message of "This must be kept secret" would be encrypted as "Ymnx rzxy gj pjuy xjhwjy." Ideally only the individual who knew that a shift of 5 was used would be able to read the encrypted message. In reality, all shift ciphers can be broken in a matter of seconds by a computer or in a few minutes by a human.

The first massively produced encryption machine that used advanced encryption mechanisms was the Enigma machine used by the Germans during World War II. The Enigma machine's encryption was eventually broken by the English using a rudimentary computer at Bletchley Park.

Encryption mechanisms depend on two things: an encryption algorithm and a key. The encryption process takes a message or a data block that we designate as plain text. Plain text and the key are fed into the algorithm. The algorithm outputs a cipher text. To get the original plain text back, you feed the cipher text and key back into the algorithm, and the plain text is produced. This type of encryption is called *symmetric key encryption* (Figure 7.5) and accounts for the vast majority of encryption mechanisms.

FIGURE 7.5   Symmetric key encryption

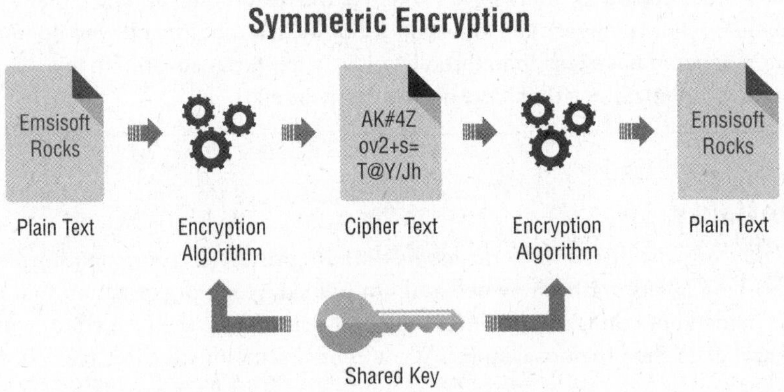

There are a couple of problems with this setup. First, you must assume that the algorithm is not confidential; you must assume everyone knows the encryption algorithm used. Second, the key itself is the only unknown in the process. If anyone gets ahold of the key, then they can decrypt any cipher text. So, I now need to keep the key private or confidential. However, if I want to send an encrypted message to you, then you will need the key. How can I get the key to you and keep it confidential? Asymmetric encryption is the process that solves the shortcomings of symmetric encryption, but it introduces its own set of problems.

In asymmetric encryption, there is still plain text or a data block, there is still an algorithm, and there is still outputted cipher text. What is different is the keys. There are now two keys: one public and one private, and both the sender and receiver have their own public and private keys. An example is shown in Figure 7.6. If Alice wants to encrypt data with asymmetric encryption and send it to Bob, then Alice either requests or accesses Bob's publicly available key. Alice takes the data and Bob's public key to the algorithm and sends Bob the cipher text. Bob takes the cipher text and feeds it and his private key into the algorithm and out comes the plain text. The public and private keys are paired. Only the private key can decrypt a message that is encrypted with the corresponding public key. Bob just needs to keep his private key confidential, and people can communicate via encrypted messages using his public key.

FIGURE 7.6   Secure communication

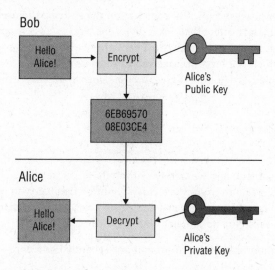

The main issue with asymmetric encryption is that it is considerably more complicated than symmetric. The resources it takes is orders of magnitude greater than symmetric. Additionally, four keys have to be maintained just for two parties to communicate, which is a lot more keys than the one needed for symmetric. The solution is to use both. First use asymmetric encryption to validate the identities of the parties wanting to communicate; this is part of integrity in the next section. Once identities are validated, the sending party (i.e., Alice) will generate a symmetric key and encrypt the symmetric key with Bob's public key. Bob can now decrypt the symmetric key with his private key. The symmetric key has been kept private, and we also know only Bob has it. Alice and Bob can now communicate using symmetric encryption securely.

So far we have been discussing secure communication or secure transferring of information and data; this is called *encryption in flight.* This is the type of encryption people are most familiar with and see most often. If you have ever ordered anything online and looked for the secure padlock on the address bar, then you have used HTTPS, which is a secure form of web communication. HTTPS literally uses the same process we discussed earlier. Encryption in flight secures the transmission of data but does not secure data itself. Think of a USB drive with important documents on it. The medium provides no way of securing transmittal of the data; in other words, I can just hand the USB stick to someone or I can leave it on a bus. We need to encrypt the data on the USB stick itself; this is called *encryption at rest.*

Encryption at rest is the act of encrypting the data as it is stored in whatever manner we choose: thumb drive, hard drive, CD, file share, cloud storage, etc. Encryption at rest will still use the symmetric encryption we discussed previously. It is the software package that we use to encrypt the data that will maintain the symmetric keys for us. This is good and bad because we are not having to maintain or transfer a key ourselves, but what happens if software is unavailable or crashes or becomes corrupted? Without the proper symmetric key, you will be locked out of the data that you are trying to secure. Encryption software will provide a mechanism to back up the symmetric keys, but they need to be secured.

Encryption-at-rest software typically comes from the systems themselves that you are trying to protect. Microsoft offers BitLocker as its encryption-at-rest option. BitLocker can be used to encrypt an entire hard drive. There are several other options, though. Apple has its own. EMC, which is a large storage vendor, has its own. There is even an open source alternative named TrueCrypt. They all come with different feature sets and levels of encryption.

Exam Note

Encryption is a large subject, and we barely skimmed the surface. However, we have seen terms used in questions on the exam that you may not be familiar with. We wanted to cover a laundry list of terms you might see and a short description. You do not need to know the technical details; just be familiar with the terms.

3DES Upgraded symmetric key algorithm that has recently been deprecated due to key collision.

AES Current standard for symmetric key algorithm. Used by the U.S. government, it's one of the few FIPS-compliant algorithms.

DES Symmetric key algorithm that is no longer used because of the short key length.

Diffie-Hellman Asymmetric key algorithm that is older but is still used.

Key Length The length of an asymmetric or symmetric key measure in bits. It ranges from 56 bits all the way to 4,096 bits in length. The longer the key, the stronger the encryption but the more resources required. A rule of thumb for key length as of writing this book is a minimum of 128 bits, but 256 bits is better. 128 bits is starting to show its age, and compute power is reaching the point of being able to decrypt any 128 bits in a "reasonable" amount of time.

RSA Asymmetric key algorithm, which is the pseudostandard used by most organizations.

Sanitization

Sanitization is rendering data unusable either digitally or physically. You have probably heard the term *redacted* when it comes to legal documents (documents that have parts blacked out). Redaction is a form of data sanitization, meaning removing sections of information if the document needs to be shared.

Data can also be obfuscated; credit card numbers are a good example. A requirement of PCI DSS is that credit card numbers cannot be stored in a readable format after the transaction is processed. Some companies encrypt the credit card information for later use for ease of re-orders. Some companies will obfuscate or scramble the numbers so that they cannot be retrieved. They will require you to enter a credit card number for every transaction.

Data can also be destroyed in such a manner that it is unrecoverable, and this is generally expected if data needs to be sanitized. Data can be destroyed either digitally or physically. The medium of the storage device or reuse of the medium determines the best method of destruction. For example, if data is stored on CDs or DVDs, there is no method of erasing the discs; therefore, the discs need to be destroyed. Conversely, data stored on a computer's hard drive could be destroyed or digitally wiped.

 Design Scenario

Data Deletion Does Not Equal Sanitization

Deleting files/data from a medium does not mean the data is sanitized. File systems that store files do not delete the data from the drives when you delete (even if you empty the recycle bin). File systems merely remove the references to the data, thus freeing up the space to be overwritten later, but the data is still present. File restoration software can scan drives and look for data that is not referenced and can re-reference the data. To digitally delete data, not only must the data be deleted, but space on the drives where the data was stored must be written over.

The Department of Defense (DoD) has a standard for sanitizing nonremovable rigid disks, i.e., hard drives. It includes the following requirements:

- Every bit on the drive must be flipped, i.e., 0 to 1.

- Then the entire drive must be written with a random sequence of bits.

- Or, the drive must be physically destroyed, which includes disintegrate, incinerate, pulverize, shred, or melt.

Integrity

Integrity is the second principle of the CIA triad and is closely related to confidentiality. If an asset is kept confidential, we also need to make sure that it has not been modified or altered. We need to be able to trust that it is accurate and in the state we expect it to be.

Modifications to an asset should not occur without proper authorization (confidentiality). Integrity includes the controls that prevent unauthorized modification on an asset. In the case of data, that would include ACLs and identity management controls.

Integrity also must include the ability to validate that an asset has not been modified or that the identity of a third party can be trusted. There are several other forms of validation, including authentication, that we will discuss later in this chapter.

Validation

We will be discussing two types of *validation* as examples. The first we have already introduced and was a large part of confidentiality when we discussed asymmetric key algorithm. The second will be a new concept but was a precursor to the encryption algorithms we have discussed, i.e., hashes.

Asymmetric key encryption can be used to validate the identity of a third party and therefore is part of integrity as well as confidentiality. Let's go back to our previous example of Alice and Bob.

Thinking back to Figure 7.6, Alice receives an encrypted message from Bob that says "Hello Alice!" but Alice wants to validate that Bob was actually who sent the message. Remember, Bob used Alice's public key, which is accessible by anyone. Therefore, anyone could have sent the message. Here are the steps that Alice can perform to validate that Bob was the sender:

1. Alice requests Bob's public key.

2. Alice requests that a third party validate that Bob's public key is valid and was issued to Bob.

3. The third party has digitally signed Bob's public key with its own public key.

4. Alice sees that the third party is a trusted third party and accepts Bob's public key as being valid.

5. Alice sends a message to Bob that is signed with Bob's public key. Message details include "Send this back to me with this text using my public key."

6. Bob receives the message, and only his private key can decrypt the message signed with his public key. He now needs to send the message back to Alice.

7. Bob goes through the same steps as Alice did in steps 1 through 4.

8. Bob sends the same message that Alice sent him back to her using her validated public key.

9. Alice receives the message and only her private key can decrypt the message signed with her public key.

10. Alice compares sent message to received message. If they match, then Alice has validated that Bob is who he claims to be and only he could have sent the message.

Alice is reasonably confident in Bob's identity, since only he could have decrypted the message sent to him and send it back to her exactly as she sent it.

Hashing is similar to encryption in that the output is not humanly readable and is not similar to the input of the hashing function. The main difference is hashing is a one-way mathematical process; there is no way to go from a hash to the original data that was the input. What is unique to hashes is that no two data inputs will ever produce the same hash as output. It is important to understand this. No matter the data inputted into a hashing function, the following two statements must be true:

- The same data input into a hashing function will always produce the same hash output.

- Different data input into a hashing function will never produce the same hash output.

Hashing is sometimes thought of as fingerprinting. You are producing a fingerprint of a data file or some other data asset. These fingerprints are always unique. Hashes also have the property of being the same length. A 256-bit hash will always be 256-bit output even if the input is much smaller or much larger. Output length is always the same; it is dependent on hash length.

In Figure 7.7, we hashed the text "What is the hashing?" and "What is the hashing!" The only difference between the two is the change of "?" to "!" but as you can see, the outputs are nowhere near each other even though the difference between the inputs is so similar. The outputs of both inputs are the same length.

FIGURE 7.7 Hash example of changing "?" to "!"

```
:~$ echo "What is the hashing?" | sha256sum
e01269bf5979fb671303d94e87fe56f37bb835cab2dda752c4a857f82f682279
:~$ echo "What is the hashing!" | sha256sum
cc2ec09b6290ada2ee9e18fab0e4bc66fdeb2dc4e84430a85cf9a15963e1da0b
```

In Figure 7.8, we hashed the text "What is the hashing!" several times, and the output is always the same. The output lengths are the same as well.

FIGURE 7.8 Hash example of "What is the hashing!"

```
:~$ echo "What is the hashing!" | sha256sum
cc2ec09b6290ada2ee9e18fab0e4bc66fdeb2dc4e84430a85cf9a15963e1da0b
:~$ echo "What is the hashing!" | sha256sum
cc2ec09b6290ada2ee9e18fab0e4bc66fdeb2dc4e84430a85cf9a15963e1da0b
:~$ echo "What is the hashing!" | sha256sum
cc2ec09b6290ada2ee9e18fab0e4bc66fdeb2dc4e84430a85cf9a15963e1da0b
:~$ echo "What is the hashing!" | sha256sum
cc2ec09b6290ada2ee9e18fab0e4bc66fdeb2dc4e84430a85cf9a15963e1da0b
:~$ echo "What is the hashing!" | sha256sum
cc2ec09b6290ada2ee9e18fab0e4bc66fdeb2dc4e84430a85cf9a15963e1da0b
```

Because of these properties, we can start building a fingerprint database of data that we want to be able to validate that the data has not be altered in any fashion. Keeping the hashes of data assets stored securely in a location that is separate from that of the data assets, we can always check current hashes against previously recorded hashes. If they do not match, then we know the data has been altered since the date of the original hash being stored.

Availability

The third principle of the CIA triad is *availability*. Availability means authorized assets can access assets in a timely and uninterrupted manner. Availability does not mean always available. Highly available, as discussed in Chapter 5, is the concept of trying to achieve being always available. Availability is different than confidentiality and integrity in that it doesn't typically involve controls as they do. There are some controls that can help with keeping an asset available, e.g., firewalls.

Backup and recovery are important for availability, and they will bring back two concepts that we discussed in Chapter 1, RTO and RPO.

Backup

*Backup*s are a mechanism of making copies of data or assets in such a manner that they can be retrieved, should the parent asset become unavailable or damaged and cannot be repaired. Since backups are making copies of data, it is virtually impossible to copy all the data every time anything changes; therefore, backups are taken at points in time. An RPO is important here, and as discussed previously, we need to know at what point we need to be able to recover from, e.g., 2 hours, 12 hours, 1 day, 3 days, 1 week, and so on.

 Real World Scenario

Protect Backups

It cannot be overstated that backups must be protected. There are several reasons, but the two that have a significate impact are the following.

First, backups are copies of your data. Anyone who has a copy of your backups has a copy of your data. I have worked with so many organizations that have taken great pains to secure their data with encryption and complicated ACLs to ensure confidentiality of their data. Then the organization throws backups on a network-attached storage (NAS) unit that anyone can access because all the systems need to back up to it. When I bring up the problem with anyone being able to access backups, their response is typically "But they are backup files. No one would be able read those files." Yes, they can!

Second, backups may and will most likely be the only recovery option if you ever fall victim to ransomware. Ransomware is where nefarious individuals will encrypt all files a user has access to with a symmetric key algorithm. If the user who fell victim to the ransomware had a lot of or even admin access to file shares, then all those file shares are now encrypted as well. I have worked with an organization in which ransomware encrypted almost all the file shares in the organization. Unfortunately, one of those file shares also contained the nightly backups of the file share. Again, it was a case where everyone has to have access to that file share for backups to run. Not only were all the files encrypted, but the backups that would have allowed restoration of the encrypted files were also encrypted. There was no recovery option, so the organization ended up paying the ransomware ransom just to regain access to the files.

Recovery

Recovery is the other side of backups. It entails the copying of data from a backup either to the original data location or to a separate recovery location. This has already been defined. The recovery location will play a large part in being able to achieve the desired RTO. Do we need new hardware? Can it be restored to the same location without impacting the availability?

The goal of recovery is to restore the availability of an asset. What that looks like and the process depends on the asset and the backup method utilized. There is an added risk when performing a recovery. Since you are replacing data with old data, you may inadvertently destroy evidence of a breach.

Breach

We discussed responses to breaches in the previous chapter. Now we are going to discuss the impacts of a breach when it comes to the CIA triad.

A *breach* in confidentiality is a breakdown and a loss of privacy of data. Depending on either your industry or regulatory requirements, a breach may have to be publicly disclosed. The ISO 27018 standard requires that a customer be informed if their personal information is lost or leaked outside of an organization's control. Currently there are no federal laws requiring disclosure of data breaches. However, most states have some sort of disclosure requirement. The disclosure may not have to be public, but the affected individual needs to be notified.

Breaches in integrity are a breakdown in the confidence in the accuracy of data. Data that cannot be trusted anymore has no value. Breaches in integrity that involve communications can lead to a mistrust between parties or even nefarious individuals executing a man-in-the-middle attack. Additionally, if the integrity of an asset has been compromised, it needs to be assumed that the confidentiality of the asset is also compromised.

Man-in-the-Middle (MITM) Attack

MITM is an attack where a third party inserts itself in a communication stream between two parties (A and B). A and B think they are communicating with each other, but in reality the third party is intercepting all communications and forwarding them on. This allows the third party to view all communications and even alter them if needed.

Breaches in availability are a breakdown of availability controls or the business continuity plan (BCP)/disaster recovery (DR) plan. The BCP and DR plan are an organization's road map if critical assets are no longer available. They can have significant impact on an organization's business functions.

Any breach that impacts one or more of the CIA principles can also have an impact on the organization's reputation. Having a tarnished reputation can impact not only current customer engagements but prospective customers as well. Any organization needs to take breaches seriously and understand the CIA triad.

Exam Note

The CIA triad will play a prominent role on the exam. You need to be familiar with the terms and the difference between the three. Additionally, you need to understand how encryption and sanitization offer confidentiality, how validation offers integrity, and how backups and recovery offer availability.

Application and Infrastructure Security

We are going to get a little more specific on topics we have discussed in the previous chapter and give some examples and tools that you can use that CSPs offer. We are wanting to secure applications and infrastructure at this point. This goes beyond the general concepts of security we have been discussing and is more specific than just data.

Audit

Auditing is a large topic that can include regulatory requirements and compliance. However, we are going to be referring specifically to audits as related to application and infrastructure security. An *audit* quite simply is a record of actions that occurred on an organization's assets.

In Windows operating systems, the Event Viewer is the default auditing tool. In Linux it is the /var/log directory for a default logging location. Infrastructure devices usually do not have storage for any kind of logging outside of basic troubleshooting. Therefore, most organizations set up SYSLOG servers to ingest events from network devices. Then there are specialized third-party applications that are geared specifically for application and infrastructure logging, like Splunk or QRadar.

The CSPs split the auditing process into separate pieces, and this can lead to confusion about which service offering to use. We will use AWS for our example. AWS's two auditing services are called CloudTrail and CloudWatch. Their definitions from the AWS website are as follows.

AWS CloudTrail

AWS CloudTrail is a service that enables governance, compliance, operational auditing, and risk auditing of your AWS account. With CloudTrail, you can log, continuously monitor, and retain account activity related to actions across your AWS infrastructure. CloudTrail provides event history of your AWS account activity, including actions taken through the AWS Management Console, AWS SDKs, command-line tools, and other AWS services. This event history simplifies security analysis, resource change tracking, and troubleshooting.

AWS CloudWatch

AWS CloudWatch is a monitoring and management service that provides data and action-able insights to monitor your applications, understand and respond to system-wide performance changes, optimize resource utilization, and get a unified view of operational health. CloudWatch collects monitoring and operational data in the form of logs, metrics, and events, and can set high-resolution alarms and automate actions.

AWS CloudWatch has benefits over the traditional auditing tools you may be used to, especially if you are using AWS images. AWS has created an agent-based monitoring system that is baked into all AWS images. If you have ever used agent-based management tools like SCCM or LANDesk, then you are familiar with the headaches of managing agents. However, you are also familiar with the advantages of agent-based management versus nonagent. CloudWatch gives you the best of both worlds. If it is set up properly, you can get Windows events from specific VMs running in AWS into your CloudWatch dash-board without ever having to touch the VM.

AWS CloudWatch is a more traditional auditing tool that users are used to. However, you can't discount AWS CloudTrail, as it plays a pivotal role in our next discussion of access and authorization.

Access

Access is the rights or permissions an asset has been granted or been denied by an asset owner. We want to clarify the difference between a right and a permission. They are often confused and used interchangeably, but there is a difference. A permission is authorization to perform some action on an individual asset that has been granted by the asset owner. Does a user have the permission to edit or delete a file? Does a service or application have the permission to delete old accounts?

A right is authorization or permission to perform an action of an entire system, like a computer or network device. Does a user have the right to act as a service on a computer? Does a user have the right to shut down or restart a router? The difference is subtle but important; rights are control over the entire system, whereas permissions are control over individual parts.

Another concept that is important to understand is that a deny permission will always trump an allow permission. It has become an unofficial universal rule because all vendors follow it. Access control comes in either granting or denying a right or permission. In the event of a competing or conflicting access assignment, if there is ever a deny permission, then that will supersede any allow permission, even if granted after the deny permission. I have yet to come across a system that didn't follow this rule. From the security perspec-tive, this rule can be pretty nice, especially if you need to deny access to an asset quickly. However, from a management perspective, it can cause some hardship when applying gran-ular with advanced access controls. You must always be permissive in your granting.

Grant vs. Allow and the Confusion of Deny

There is some confusion about the difference between *grant* and *allow*. Rights and permissions to an asset can be granted or denied. The rights and permissions that have been granted to an asset can be either allowed or denied.

I can be granted access (right) to a firewall. Once I have access, I will be granted or denied permissions to the firewall. I can be granted the allow permission to read the configuration, but denied the permission to change the configuration.

The confusion stems from deny being used in both cases as the negative, while two different words (grant and allow) are used for the positive.

Strictly speaking, grant does not equal allow (or mean the same thing), but they are oftentimes mixed up.

Every CSP has a central access management console. It is actually a requirement for one of the ISO standards. AWS calls it Identity Access and Management (IAM). Through IAM you grant access to resources to identities. We have intentionally left that description vague because of the power and number of customizable options in IAM. IAM allows almost all access management between assets, and those assets don't even have to be in AWS. IAM is beyond the scope of this book, but it has the most advanced feature set of all the CSPs.

Authorization

Authorization determines what an asset is and not what it is allowed to do (access). Authorization consists of the properties of an asset that are used to bestow or grant access to other assets. The easiest example of this is admin access. If a user has been authorized as an admin, then they have complete system access and can perform almost any action on the asset they are an admin for.

Authorization should be administered and maintained to groups, not to individual assets/users. If you want to grant administrative access to an individual, create a group called FullAdmins. Put the assets/users into that group and then grant the administrator access to the group. This has authorized the group and its members to be administrators.

Utilize tools like CloudTrail to audit and monitor actions by users/assets. Something is going to go wrong; it is not a question of if but when. When something does go wrong, you should be able to show what happened and when it happened.

Hardening

Hardening is the process of looking at threats against assets and the past events to determine a plan of action that will improve the security posture of an organization. Hardening can be as broad a subject as updating an entire OS to the latest release to get up-to-date security and features, or as focused as disabling outdated communication protocols because they are not using secure encryption algorithms.

In general, if you are running the latest software on the latest operating systems, then there is not a lot of hardening you can perform that won't have an impact on supported software configuration. For example, enabling and setting a high restriction on Security-Enhanced Linux (SELinux) will make a Linux installation really hardened, but almost no software will run on such a configuration.

Hardening is always a balance between security and user acceptance. Making a system so secure that nothing can ever be compromised sounds great for the security aspect. However, I can guarantee no user will willingly use the system. We have worked on systems that needed to integrate with CSPs but did not have Internet access. How can a server interface and integrate with a CSP if it doesn't have Internet access?

> **Exam Note**
>
> Audit, access, authorization, and hardening will be covered on the exam. Look at the examples we provided and understand the part these four things play in the security of applications and infrastructure.

Summary

A lot has gone into this chapter. You will not need to know every aspect of this chapter. We introduced you to a wide range of concepts and examples to prepare you for subjects you at least need to be familiar with, but also touch on many other things to meet the needs of a wide range of readers.

We dived deeper on to data sovereignty and the impact that working on a global scale has. You can't just think of the United States anymore; there are other players that need to be considered.

U.S. regulatory requirements were introduced. These are specific for doing business in the United States and also doing business with any federal agency. Topics included risk management, information security, and information processing requirements.

We then moved on to regulations that were industry-based. We covered a broad range from privacy (HIPAA and FERPA) to reporting (GLBA and SOX). We also included record retention (FINRA) and compliance with industry expectations (MPAA).

International standards were the next topic; we discussed general requirements and frameworks. There is no international body that can impose regulatory requirements, but there are international bodies that provide guidance. CIS benchmarks are recognized as universal benchmarks that help ensure information security. ISO has standards that are the basis of regulation requirements for other requirements.

The first section wrapped up with certifications and links to CSPs' documentation on their certifications that meet regulatory requirements. Not all standards/regulations offer or require certification.

The second section started by revisiting what a threat is. We discussed distributed DDoS attacks and provided some resources. Vulnerability was the next topic, and we introduced the very important CVE database, which is a free database of known vulnerabilities of both hardware and software.

Security assessments, which are a systematic approach to testing security controls an organization has in place, were next. Then we moved on to several assessments, including penetration testing, vulnerability scanning, and application scanning. We introduced several tools that are critical to any security assessment, including Metasploit, OWASP, nmap, Nessus, and Kali Linux.

Securing data was a large part of this chapter. We covered the concepts of data categorization. Most organizations use a minimum of three categories for data, but some use up to five or six.

The CIA triad is one of the most important concepts in the security field. If you plan on advancing further in the security realm, you will need to completely understand these three. Data encryption and sanitization were covered in regard to confidentiality. With integrity we need to validate the data, and integrity goes hand in hand with confidentiality. The last principle of the CIA triad is availability, meaning the need of backups and proper recovery processes that can be validated. We touched on breaches, which we also discussed in the previous chapter.

Moving on from data to applications and infrastructure security, we discussed audit, access, authorization, and hardening. Auditing is logging or tracking actions that occur against an asset or by an asset. It is a critical component after a breach has occurred. Access consists of the controls that are placed on protecting a specific asset. Authorization consists of the controls placed on a system as a whole. Rights and permissions play a part in both.

We finished the chapter with hardening, which is the process of updating or applying changes to assets to protect against vulnerabilities.

Exam Essentials

Know what compliance is.   Compliance consists of actions an organization takes to be compliant with laws and regulations. These laws and regulations come from the industries the organization is doing business with or the state/country that the organization does business in.

Know what data sovereignty is.   Data sovereignty is important to understand the impact when doing business with organizations. Data is stored one or more places in the cloud. The data location can have an impact on the sovereignty of the data. Data sovereignty deals with privacy and rights of access of third parties.

Know the difference and hierarchy of regulations from local, state, and federal levels.   It is important to know how conflicting regulations are to be followed. We gave examples of federal regulations from a range of federal agencies. These are to serve as an idea of the requirements that exist required at the federal level.

Know the terms and have a general understanding of industry-specific regulations. There will be questions on the exam that mention terms that are industry-specific. You do not need to know the details of the regulations, but you need to recognize the terms as regulations. Additionally, you need to have a sense of the type of regulations that will be required, whether it is security or reporting.

Know that international standards are the basis of other regulations. CIS benchmarks are used as tests and the benchmarks for regulations at both the international and national levels. Be familiar with the terms and that they cover most forms of technology used today. Know that ISO is the organization that sets many of the regulations discussed previously. There are standards for privacy, security, and cloud.

Know that certifications are an important standard of regulatory compliance. Certifications are proof that an organization has been able to demonstrate to a third party that they can fulfill the requirements for a regulation. They need to be renewed on a regular basis and require investment of resources by an organization.

Know what a threat is and be able to identify one. Threats can come in many different forms, but DDoS is one of the most common. Know that threats have many different parts and include not just loss or damage of assets. Impaired functionality or reduced access are also threats.

Know the difference between threat and vulnerability. Vulnerabilities are known threats that need to be addressed. Know about bug bounty programs from technology vendors.

Know that penetration testing, vulnerability scanning, and application scanning are the primary tools for security assessments. Penetration testing is the process of actively attempting to break in or test security controls. Vulnerability scanning is scanning for specific vulnerabilities. Application scanning is using tools and human testing on applications.

Be familiar with the various tools that are used in security assessment. Nmap is for network discovery. Metasploit and Nessus are for vulnerability scanning. OWASP is for application scanning.

Know the basic three categories for data security and their meaning, with examples. Public is data or information that can be shared with anyone inside or outside an organization.

Private is data or information that should not be shared outside an organization and should be kept internal.

Sensitive is data or information that is critical to be kept confidential, even inside an organization, and to which access is restricted to personnel who have to a need to know.

Know the principles of the CIA triad. Confidentiality: Privacy or keeping data secret.

Integrity: Validation of the data.

Availability: Assets being able to access other assets in a timely manner.

Know the tools used for confidentiality.   Data encryption: Encrypting data in a manner that allows sending of data to another party that they can unencrypt and read.

Data sanitization: Scrubbing or obfuscating data, which prevents anyone from reading or accessing the data later.

Know the tools used for integrity.   Validation: The process of validating the integrity of data; making sure the data has not been modified since its creation or the last approved change.

Know the tools used for availability.   Backup: This is the process of copying data to a secure location that is separate from the original location. RPO is critical for backup.

Recovery: This the process of copying data from a backup location to either the original location or a separate restore location. RTO is critical for recovery.

Know that the response to a breach is one of the principles of CIA.   A response may be a required reporting either to a regulatory body or public disclosure. Data may need to be destroyed if it is no longer trustworthy. Communication with a third party may not be trusted anymore. An organization may need to execute its BCP/DR plan.

Know auditing and its place in application and infrastructure security.   Auditing or logging is critical for application and infrastructure security. It can be both reactive and proactive to events. There are tools provided by CSPs that offer logging, not only at the tenant level but also at the resource level.

Know the difference between access and authorization.   Access means rights and permissions to assets that are part of a larger system. Authorization means rights and permissions to a system as a whole, like a tenant console or computer system.

Know rights and permissions and that deny trumps all other permissions.   Permissions are authorizations to perform actions on an asset that have been granted by an asset owner. Rights are either an authorization or a permission to perform actions on an asset as a whole. Any permissions or rights that apply a deny will trump any allow rights or permissions even if explicitly applied later.

Written Lab

Fill in the blanks for the questions provided in the written lab. You can find the answers to the written labs in Appendix A.

1. _____ is the data category used for a press release from an organization that is being sent to the newspapers.

2. _____ is the data category used for salaries earned by everyone in the organization.

3. _____ is the data category used for an email sent from HR stating when and where employees can get their flu shots.

4. _____ ensures the privacy or prevents the unauthorized access to assets.

5. _____ ensures the validity of an asset.

6. _____ ensure the timely access of an asset.

7. _____ are a set of steps that should be taken once an event takes place or steps that need to be taken to follow a policy.

8. _____ is the process of testing the resolved security issues in a patch that was applied to an organization's software.

9. _____ is the concept that data is subject to the laws and regulations of a particular nation.

10. MPAA is an organization that enforces _____ regulations.

Review Questions

1. You are working for a multinational public corporation. There are offices in India, China, and Germany. You are helping to deploy a chat application to be used by all three offices. The accounting department wants to be able to use the chat software. You will also be required to save all chat communications. Which regulations do you need to worry about? (Choose all that apply.)

   A. Federal

   B. Data sovereignty

   C. Industry-based

   D. Security assessments

2. You just received an email from your CEO announcing a change in health benefits offered to employees. What data category is this an example of?

   A. Private

   B. Classified

   C. Public

   D. Sensitive

3. Your manager has asked you to compose an email that will be sent to potential new clients detailing the availability and SLA of services you offer. You will need to gather from internal metrics to provide examples. What data category would the email be an example of?

   A. Private

   B. Classified

   C. Public

   D. Sensitive

4. You are in your manager's office and notice there is a pros and cons list about giving new bonuses to the staff. What data category is the list an example of?

   A. Private

   B. Classified

   C. Public

   D. Sensitive

5. PCI DSS requires encryption both at rest and in transit for any communication where a credit card number is transmitted to keep it private. What data security principle is this an example of?

   A. Categorization

   B. Confidentiality

   C. Integrity

   D. Availability

6. The network diagrams have finally been digitized, and the paper diagrams that have been hanging on the wall can be destroyed. Which data category and data security principles are being used?

   A. Sensitive, integrity

   B. Sensitive, confidentiality

   C. Private, integrity

   D. Private, availability

7. You just received an email reporting suspicious activity from the CEO's account. The email provides a link to review the suspicious activity and immediately lock the account. You want to review the suspicious activity before manually locking the CEO's account, so you click the first link. Which data security principle did you just violate?

   A. Categorization

   B. Confidentiality

   C. Integrity

   D. Availability

8. A new software patch is available for the organization's firewall. Before proceeding with the software update, you make a copy of the firewall's configuration. Which data security principle are you performing?

   A. Categorization

   B. Confidentiality

   C. Integrity

   D. Availability

9. You have been working on a new script that will make copies of the firewall configuration before a software update. You ask a colleague to review it before running it. The colleague recommends that the script not be run because it would store the firewall's admin passwords in clear text. This is an example of what kind of assessment?

   A. Penetration testing

   B. Vulnerability scanning

   C. Application scanning

   D. FISMA

10. Security assessments that test against known threats and bugs in software that can cause data corruption are called what? (Choose two.)

    A. Vulnerability scanning

    B. Data scanning

    C. Audit

    D. Application scanning

11. A security mechanism that should be maintained by groups and not individually and describes the properties of an asset, not the rights of the asset, is:

    A. Categorization

    B. Vulnerability scanning

    C. Authorization

    D. Availability

12. A client for which your organization offers off-site backups has reported they have been a victim of ransomware. All of their files on the shared network file share have been encrypted. They cannot access any files without paying a ransom. What suggestions could you recommend?

    A. Recovery

    B. Pay the ransom

    C. Vulnerability scanning

    D. Threat analysis

13. What is the difference between a threat and a vulnerability?

    A. Threats have been mitigated; vulnerabilities have not.

    B. Vulnerabilities have to be accepted; threats do not.

    C. Vulnerabilities have not been mitigated; threats can be mitigated, but other responses are possible as well.

    D. All threats are vulnerabilities.

14. Your manager gave you a new key that allows you to enter the server room anytime you need to. This is a type of:

    A. Authorization

    B. Access

    C. Sensitive

    D. Audit

15. Your organization's network file share was crypto-locked (encrypted), and a ransom was demanded for access to the files. You were able to recover the files from a backup. However, management has requested that you review and lock down access to the file share. They want only authorized individuals to be able to make changes to the entire file share. What is management asking you to perform?

    A. Vulnerability scanning

    B. Penetration testing

    C. Hardening

    D. Audit

16. How many classifications of risk do most organizations have?

   A. 3

   B. 5

   C. 10

   D. 8

17. You use security tools that perform a network discovery and are able to list all servers on the network and the services they provide. What are you performing?

   A. Vulnerability scan

   B. Application scan

   C. Audit

   D. Penetration test

18. _____ are proof by a third party of compliance with either federal, international, or industry regulations.

   A. Backups

   B. Certifications

   C. Requirements

   D. Benchmarks

19. A spreadsheet that has the admin passwords for the networking equipment at an ISP would be categorized as what?

   A. Private

   B. Sensitive

   C. Public

   D. Classified

20. An email between two CEOs about a merger between the two organizations with profit sharing numbers is an example of which data category?

   A. Private

   B. Public

   C. Classified

   D. Sensitive

Appendix A

Answers to Written Labs

Chapter 1: Cloud Principles and Design

1. Recovery Point Objective (RPO)
2. Software as a Service (SaaS)
3. Shared responsibility model
4. Broad network access
5. Self-service
6. Private
7. Elastic
8. High availability
9. Pay-as-you-go
10. Recovery Point Objective (RPO), Recovery Time Objective (RTO)

Chapter 2: Cloud Networking and Storage

1. Remote Desktop Protocol (RDP)
2. Virtual Private Network (VPN), direct connect
3. Resolving host names to IP addresses
4. Firewall
5. Hypertext Transfer Protocol Secure (HTTPS)
6. Object
7. Cold, hot
8. Deduplication
9. Content delivery networks (CDNs)
10. File

Chapter 3: Assessing Cloud Needs

1. Multifactor authentication (MFA)
2. Key stakeholder
3. Benchmark
4. Business and technical

5. Autonomous environments
6. Subscription services
7. Digital marketing
8. Big data
9. Machine learning (ML)
10. Microservices (or microservice architecture)

Chapter 4: Engaging Cloud Vendors

1. Capital
2. Bring your own license (BYOL)
3. Professional development
4. Time to market (TTM)
5. Managed services
6. Service level agreement (SLA)
7. Request for proposal (RFP)
8. Pilot
9. Egress terms
10. Rip and replace

Chapter 5: Management and Technical Operations

1. Asynchronous
2. Zones
3. Bootstrapping
4. Autoscaling
5. Infrastructure as code (IaC)
6. Regression
7. Automation
8. Application Programming Interface (API)
9. Spot
10. Bring your own license (BYOL)

Chapter 6: Governance and Risk

1. Risk
2. Threat
3. Asset
4. Quantitative, qualitative
5. Risk response
6. Policies
7. Procedures
8. Security policy
9. Access and control
10. Change management

Chapter 7: Compliance and Security in the Cloud

1. Public
2. Sensitive
3. Private
4. Confidentiality
5. Integrity
6. Availability
7. Procedures
8. Vulnerability scanning
9. Data sovereignty
10. Industry-based

Appendix B

Answers to Review Questions

Chapter 1: Cloud Principles and Design

1. **B.** The software as a service (SaaS) model provides software applications, including apps such as Google Docs and Microsoft Office 365. Anything as a service (XaaS) is too broad and can mean a combination of multiple services. Platform as a service (PaaS) provides development platforms for software developers. Infrastructure as a service (IaaS) offers hardware for compute, storage, and networking functionality.

2. **D.** Multicloud means using multiple cloud vendors for different service models, such as SaaS and IaaS together. This provides additional flexibility. The downsides are that it can be more complex to manage and cost more. The security will probably be a little worse than using a single cloud provider, due to having multiple systems to manage. A combined public and private cloud is a hybrid cloud.

3. **C.** Broad network access means that clients of different types, such as laptops and mobile devices, running different operating systems (OSs), such as Windows, macOS, and Android, can all access network resources. Self-service is the cloud characteristic that allows clients to get additional resources without supplier intervention.

4. **D.** Fault tolerance and redundancy are synonymous terms in cloud computing. Redundant systems can provide backups for other systems, so if one fails, the other can take over. Redundancy can help ensure high availability of resources. High availability means that the system is always or almost always available and is often specified in the SLA by the number of nines of uptime that are guaranteed. Disaster recovery is for after a system fails. Shared responsibility is the cloud security model.

5. **A, D.** Infrastructure as a service (IaaS) offers a client company capacity such as processing power (compute resources), storage, and network services. Applications are offered as part of software as a service (SaaS), and a database is typically offered as database as a service (DBaaS).

6. **A.** Availability is expressed in terms of nines. More nines means more availability. Four nines means 99.99 percent uptime. Some CSPs offer smaller increments with a five at the end. For example, four nines five means 99.995 percent availability, which is higher than four nines. Four nines five means no more than 4.32 seconds of downtime per day.

7. **A.** Elastic means that cloud resources can grow or shrink as a client's needs change. Self-service is when the client can get more resources without supplier intervention. Broad network access refers to the cloud being accessible regardless of client device. Availability means that resources are always (or almost always) accessible.

8. **C.** Backups are a form of disaster recovery. Redundant systems are typically online and do not need to be activated or restored. High availability means that resources are almost always accessible. A recovery time objective (RTO) defines how long services can be down before they are restored, in the event of a disaster.

9. **A.** The shared responsibility model defines security duties within the cloud. The CSP is responsible for the security of the cloud, and the client is responsible for security in the cloud.

10. D. PaaS provides software development tools for development teams. It allows geographically dispersed teams to easily operate as one. IaaS provides hardware capacity. SaaS offers web-based apps such as Google Docs. DBaaS is for databases.

11. B, C. Disaster recovery plans should include a recovery point objective (RPO) and a recovery time objective (RTO). The RPO specifies how old data can be when it's restored to be useful to the company. The RTO specifies how long services can be down after a disaster, before being restored. There are no recovery process or recovery cost objectives.

12. B. In the shared security model, the CSP is responsible for the security of the cloud, and clients own security in the cloud. Customer data, access management, and firewall configurations are examples of items in the cloud and are therefore the client's responsibility.

13. A. Public clouds, such as Microsoft Azure and Amazon Web Services (AWS), offer the best in scalability, reliability, and cost effectiveness. Private clouds do not offer as much cost effectiveness. Community clouds and hybrid clouds are between public and private in terms of scalability and cost effectiveness.

14. B. The RTO is the maximum amount of time a system can be offline in the event of a disaster. Maximum data age is the RPO. There are no common disaster recovery terms associated with cost or chain of command.

15. C. Cloud services should lower the cost of network operations and software use for companies. Cloud characteristics include elastic, self-service, scalability, broad network access, pay-as-you-go, and availability.

16. A. The RPO defines the maximum age of files that must be recovered from backups in order to restore normal operations. In this case, the RPO needs to be less than an hour. The RTO specifies how long services can be down in the event of a disaster. There is no TSO in disaster recovery plans. The service level agreement (SLA) usually contains a section for the disaster recovery plan.

17. D. The most cost-effective cloud solution is a public cloud, but the best security comes with a private cloud. Since both elements are needed in this case, the best solution is most likely a combination of the two, or a hybrid cloud. A community cloud is one that is owned by multiple organizations with shared interests.

18. C. In a pay-as-you-go model, clients pay only for resources that are used. Scalability and elastic can refer to the ability to get more resources, but the key component of this question is paying only for used resources. Availability means that resources are always (or almost always) accessible to clients.

19. B. Redundancy means having a backup of existing systems or processes—if one fails another can take over. Common redundancy types include hardware, network, geographic, process, software (apps), and data. OSs are easily replaceable, so redundant ones are not usually needed.

20. D. A community cloud is one that is essentially public but is shared between multiple organizations. In a sense, it's like a public cloud but has better security. Public clouds are accessible to everyone. A private cloud is for only one organization. Hybrid clouds are both public and private.

Chapter 2: Cloud Networking and Storage

1. A. Object storage is the best solution for large archives that do not need to be modified often. File storage is for smaller storage solutions and individual computers. Block storage is good for databases. Hot storage is more expensive than cold storage and is not recommended for archives that do not need frequent access.

2. B. Domain Name System (DNS) resolves host names to IP addresses; it's what will help end users locate your web server. Software-defined networking (SDN) abstracts network hardware in the cloud. Software-defined storage (SDS) allows for the virtualization of cloud storage solutions. A content delivery network (CDN) is load-balancing for websites.

3. D. The Hypertext Transfer Protocol Secure (HTTPS) is used in conjunction with a web browser to access cloud resources. Remote Desktop Protocol is used to remotely access a Windows-based computer, and SSH is used to remotely access a Linux-based one. Hypertext Transfer Protocol (HTTP) is not secure.

4. B. The Secure Shell (SSH) protocol is used to remotely access a Linux-based server. Remote Desktop Protocol (RDP) is used to access Windows-based servers. Direct connect is for a company to directly connect its network to the CSP's network. HTTPS is used in conjunction with a web browser to access cloud resources.

5. C. Hot storage is designed to be readily accessible at all times. It is more expensive than cold storage, but access time is much faster. Block and object are storage types. Block will be a little faster for structured data, and object storage is better for unstructured data. One won't necessarily be more expensive per gigabyte than the other.

6. D. A load balancer is designed to spread work among multiple computers in order to maintain or improve performance. It's also scalable and can handle spikes in network traffic. DNS resolves host names to IP addresses. A firewall is the network or computer's security device. SDN abstracts the cloud networking hardware.

7. A. A virtual private network (VPN) is a secure point-to-point tunnel over a public network such as the Internet. RDP is used to access Windows-based servers. The SSH protocol is used to remotely access a Linux-based server. HTTPS is used in conjunction with a web browser to securely access cloud resources.

8. B. The sales team needs a CDN to ensure quick access to the same materials globally. SDS allows for the virtualization of cloud storage solutions. DNS resolves host names to IP addresses. SDN abstracts network hardware in the cloud.

9. A, C. Cold storage and tapes are likely to be the least expensive, because neither are designed to be online for quick and immediate access. Hot storage will be the most expensive. Warm storage will be somewhere in between hot and cold.

10. A, B. Compression and deduplication are technologies that save space by reducing redundancy within files or between files. They can both reduce the needed storage space and help lower costs. Capacity on demand means that you can get additional storage space as needed. Object and block storage do not inherently help you save space and reduce costs.

11. C. SDN makes networks more agile and flexible by separating the forwarding of network packets (the infrastructure layer) from the logical decision-making process (the control layer). SDS separates the physical storage of data from the logical data storage controller. DNS resolves host names to IP addresses. A CDN is like load balancing for web content.

12. C. Block storage is the best option for databases. Object storage is great for unstructured data or large archives that don't need to be accessed frequently. File storage is good for PCs. Cold storage would not be appropriate, because it has longer latency times to access and update data.

13. D. Capacity on demand allows clients to get extra storage space instantaneously, or at least very quickly. SDS separates the physical storage of data from the logical data storage controller. SDN makes networks more agile and flexible by separating the forwarding of network packets (the infrastructure layer) from the logical decision-making process (the control layer). A CDN is like load balancing for web content.

14. A. Software-defined storage separates the physical storage of data from the logical control over drive configuration, independent of the underlying hardware. This means storage volumes can be created from multiple physical devices. DNS resolves host names to IP addresses. SDN makes networks more agile and flexible by separating the forwarding of network packets (the infrastructure layer) from the logical decision-making process (the control layer). A CDN is like load balancing for web content.

15. D. A CDN is like load balancing for web content. It uses edge servers to replicate data that's on the web server, serving the data to users closer to the edge server than to the web server. SDS separates the physical storage of data from the logical control over drive configuration, independent of the underlying hardware. This means storage volumes can be created from multiple physical devices. DNS resolves host names to IP addresses. SDN makes networks more agile and flexible by separating the forwarding of network packets (the infrastructure layer) from the logical decision-making process (the control layer).

16. A. Direct connect is used to provide a physical connection between your company's on-site network and the CSP's network. It's the best connectivity option for a large number of users. A VPN can also work for a large number of users, but it will use the Internet as its connection medium, so it will be a little slower than direct connect. HTTPS is for single users to access cloud resources using their web browsers. RDP is for a user to remotely access a Windows-based server.

17. D, E. A VPN can be used to set up a point-to-point connection between a corporate network and a CSP. Direct connect means directly connecting the client's internal network to the CSP's network. Both allow multiple users to use the connection simultaneously. RDP, SSH, and HTTPS are for single-user connections only.

18. D. A firewall is a hardware or software solution that serves as a network's security guard. It's also what lets you create a demilitarized zone (DMZ), which is a semi-public, semi-private network. SDN abstracts the networking hardware and separates routing from routing logic. A load balancer spreads work among servers. DNS resolves host names to IP addresses.

19. B. Most SANs use block storage to store data. Block storage is also commonly used for databases and by VMMs. Load balancing spreads work around to multiple servers. File storage is used for small-scale storage, such as on PCs. Object storage is for unstructured data.

20. C, D. The SSH protocol is used to remotely access a Linux-based server, and RDP is used to access Windows-based servers. HTTPS is used in conjunction with a web browser to securely access cloud resources. A VPN is used to create a secure point-to-point connection over an unsecure network, such as the Internet.

Chapter 3: Assessing Cloud Needs

1. C. Virtual desktop infrastructure (VDI) is when user desktops are created inside a virtual machine (VM) located on a server. VDI can centralize administration, increase security, and allow users to access their desktops remotely. VDI most often reduces the total cost of ownership and does not result in higher costs.

2. A. For the team to work together better, they should use collaboration software. Using it, they can video conference and share files with ease. Self-service refers to getting more cloud resources without CSP intervention. An autonomous environment is one in which human intervention is not needed, such as a self-driving car. Blockchain is a secure ledger system.

3. B. Microservices describes the breaking down of a larger program into smaller pieces— literally small services. It can reduce the cost of software development and ownership. Federation is a security mechanism. Machine learning (ML) and artificial intelligence (AI) are two services that can help with data analytics.

4.   A. The first thing to do when conducting a cloud assessment is to determine current and future requirements, and you do so by contacting key stakeholders and asking the right questions. After that, you can run a baseline to see where current performance is. That will let you perform a gap analysis to understand where the business and technical situations fall short. Finally, at the end you will create documentation and diagrams.

5.   C. Federation allows users to perform a single sign-on across different companies' security domains, whereas single sign-on refers to users logging into multiple systems within the same security domain. In this case, since it's the company's local network and Microsoft's cloud, it will be federation. Self-service refers to getting more cloud resources without CSP intervention. Multifactor authentication (MFA) means that users need to provide more information besides a username and password to log in, such as a temporary security code.

6.   D. A benchmark is a standard or point of reference for comparison. It should be used to determine whether performance is acceptable. A baseline can give you a performance read but doesn't provide context. A technical gap analysis will help you determine whether the company has the technology needed to implement cloud services or what is needed to do so. Compute reporting will give you CPU and RAM utilization from the CSP.

7.   D. Key stakeholders should input into a cloud assessment, but their feedback is particularly valuable when gathering current and future requirements. A gap analysis can be technical, business-related, or both. A gap analysis can help find compatibility issues, policies that are not being met, and priority calls that need to be made.

8.   B. Security systems are an example of a technology that relies upon the Internet of Things (IoT). VDI creates virtual user desktops. SSO is a security mechanism for computer logins. AI is when computers perform complex, human-like tasks.

9.   C. Blockchain is an open, distributed ledger that can securely record transactions between two parties in a verifiable and permanent way. The most famous example of blockchain usage is for the cryptocurrency Bitcoin, but Bitcoin and blockchain are not the same thing. Blockchain is not an authentication system, nor does it lower the TCO for application DevOps.

10. A. The purpose of SSO is to give users access to all of the systems, resources, and apps they need with one initial login. Federation is like SSO but applies across security domains. MFA means that users need to provide multiple pieces of information to log in—it makes access harder, not easier. Self-service refers to getting more cloud services without CSP intervention.

11. B. A baseline tells the company how its systems are currently performing. A benchmark compares performance numbers to an established standard or point of reference. Determining current and future requirements tells you what is needed but does not tell you about current performance. A gap analysis helps determine what gaps exist between current performance and desired performance standards.

12. D. Subscription-based pricing, or subscription services, usually offers a discount over pay-as-you-go models, but it also means your company is locked into a contract for the length of the subscription. Self-service refers to being able to get more cloud resources without CSP intervention. High availability is a feature of clouds (and more guaranteed availability will cost more), but it is not a cloud payment model.

13. C. Requiring users to enter multiple pieces of information to be authenticated is called MFA. SSO requires a username and password and allows access to multiple resources within a security domain. VDI is for creating virtual user desktops on a server. Federation is like SSO, but for across organizations.

14. B. A feasibility study can help determine whether it's possible for a company to move to the cloud. This includes determining which capabilities can be offloaded to the cloud as well as the level of support services needed. A gap analysis tells a company what the gap is between their current levels of business or technical readiness and where they need to be. A baseline is a measure of current performance. Determining current and future requirements is done before figuring out what can be offloaded or what support is needed.

15. A. Self-service means clients can get more cloud resources automatically without CSP intervention. SSO is a security mechanism. Subscription service is when a company pays for a level of services for a specified period of time. Autonomous environments are when computers or machines perform complex human-like actions without human intervention.

16. D. With ML, data can be fed to a computer, and it will learn from it and adapt. ML is a specialized form of AI and is perfect for facial recognition programs. Big data refers to unstructured data; mining it could help find data or data patterns. Blockchain is a secure ledger system. AI can make human-like decisions, but it can't learn, which is needed for facial recognition.

17. A. Digital marketing is when companies market products or services using digital technology. Examples include email campaigns and social media posts. Big data refers to unstructured data. Blockchain is a secure transaction ledger. IAM refers to capabilities used to authenticate users.

18. C. The final thing to do in a cloud assessment is to ensure that documentation and diagrams have been created. Conversations with the key stakeholders and CSP should be documented. Service coverage and locations should be diagrammed as needed. Engaging key stakeholders should happen very early in the process, as should feasibility studies and gap analyses.

19. D. Containerization is a fancy term meaning that all items are placed into a container. Developers can do this with a program they have created along with all components needed to execute that program. Microservices is a way to build apps by breaking them into smaller components. Blockchain is a secure digital ledger. Federation is a security mechanism.

20. B. ML is a form of general AI, not applied AI. Applied AIs are designed to perform a specific, smart, human-like activity. And, AIs can only react to conditions they have been programmed to react to. ML learns through the use of neural networks.

Chapter 4: Engaging Cloud Vendors

1. B, D. Physical, tangible assets such as a building (or building expansion) and servers are examples of capital expenditures. Capital expenditures are depreciated over the lifetime of the asset. Employee salaries and property taxes are operating expenditures, which are deducted in the year they are paid for.

2. D. Professional development refers to a long-term educational process focused on employee growth. Training plans are shorter-term and focus on acquiring a specific skillset to perform a job. Managed services and support are professional services that you might buy to help support the cloud.

3. C. A hybrid migration can be one of two things: either a combination of rip and replace or lift and shift or one where some assets remain on-premises. Rip and replace means that software gets re-created to take advantage of the cloud as it's migrated. Lift and shift means that assets are taken as is from the current site and moved to the cloud. Phased migration means that the migration happens in stages over time.

4. B, C. After the request for proposal (RFP) has been approved, there could be a few logical next steps. One might be to verify the statement of work (SOW) and SLA and then sign the contract and migrate. Another could be to run an evaluation such as a pilot or proof of concept (PoC). A request for information (RFI) comes before the RFP, and a RFQ is in lieu of an RFP. Lift and shift is a type of migration and would not be started until the contract has been signed.

5. B, C. The lift and shift, where data and applications are picked up as is and moved to another location, is the quickest and cheapest migration option. It's also appropriate for commercial apps that can't be reprogrammed. In a rip and replace, software needs to be redeveloped to take advantage of cloud services. Rip and replace migrations are not fast. A hybrid is a combination of the two, or a migration where some items stay in the original location. Phased migrations happen over time.

6. A. A pilot is a small-scale initial rollout of a solution into the production environment. The intent of a pilot is to test the solution among a small number of users to understand if it works on existing production hardware and apps. A PoC and PoV are run in test environments. Managed services are professional services used to support cloud installations.

7. C. On-premises data centers are capital expenditures, which come with high up-front costs. Cloud-based services are operating expenditures, which generally do not cost as much up front. Capital and operating expenditures can both be fixed.

8. A, B. Two choices when looking for a cloud are open source technology and proprietary technology. Proprietary clouds will give large company support, usually have more features, and have clear SLAs. Open source clouds are less expensive, provide greater development flexibility, have faster updates, and don't have concerns with vendor lock-in.

9. B. Hiring external professional services such as tech support is an example of managed services. Often these are contracted through a MSP. Professional development is long-term career development of internal employees, who are human capital. A SLA specifies metrics for determining whether the CSP is delivering what is expected.

10. A. BYOL allows for the transfer of existing licenses from one app, user, or location to another. If the database license can be used as BYOL, then the company does not need a new license, which saves money. A subscription license might or might not be transferrable. A pilot and PoV are evaluation types.

11. C. After accepting an RFP, the next step is to continue defining what the service provider will deliver. This is done through an SOW. The SOW might be part of the RFP, but it might not be. Once the SOW is agreed to, then the SLA can be finalized. A request for quotation (RFQ) is an alternative to an RFP, if you are looking for the price on a standard solution. You won't sign the contract until the SOW and SLA are agreed to.

12. D. A subscription is for a certain time period, such as one year. Consequently, the user will need to pay to continue to use the software after the license expires. Subscriptions should offer no upgrade costs for new features (which also means users should always have the newest version at no extra cost), smaller up-front license costs, and device flexibility.

13. C. Time to market refers to the ability to get a product or service from the idea stage to selling it as quickly as possible. It does not refer to delay or data transfer rates to or from the cloud or the number of cloud evaluations needed.

14. A. The contract will specify terms of service, which include items such as intellectual property (IP) rights. The billing statement shows how much is owed. An SOW specifies the work to be done by the CSP, and the SLA calls out metrics to determine whether the CSP is delivering on the SOW.

15. C, D. Subscription-based models might come with discounts and usually offer fixed costs. However, they lock a company into a contract for a specified amount of time; cancellation will usually incur a penalty. Both subscriptions and pay-as-you-go are operating expenditures.

16. A. If you need a price quote for a standard set of services, you need an RFQ. An RFP is a more detailed document for more custom solutions. PoC and PoV are two types of cloud evaluations.

17. B. When setting up a pilot, successful completion should not be a selection criteria or the ultimate goal. The goal of the pilot is to learn whether a capability works as it's supposed to. Therefore, usability, data security, and latency are all important things. But failure of a pilot can actually mean success if it helps your company avoid serious losses.

18. C. The RFI is an initial fact-finding request. It should be a high-level request, with clear objectives, processes, timelines, and next steps. A template for the CSP to fill out is also helpful. An SOW is too detailed for an RFI.

19. D. Phased migrations are ones that occur over time. In a rip and replace, software needs to be redeveloped to take advantage of cloud services. The lift and shift, where data and applications are picked up as is and moved to another location, is the quickest and cheapest migration option. A hybrid is a combination of the two, or a migration where some items stay in the original location.

20. A. There are four professional services to be aware of: time to market, skill availability, support, and managed services. Running a PoC is a type of evaluation. Using developers who are skilled in a language is an example of skill availability. Data backups are a form of support, and developing and selling more quickly refers to time to market.

Chapter 5: Management and Technical Operations

1. C. Since the instances are production and required, reserved is the most cost effective. On-demand is the most expensive option. Spot is the cheapest, but is not designed for production instances. Quick is not a type of instance.

2. A. Option A is the only option that satisfies all the requirements. Options B and C use pay-for-use software from Microsoft. Option D uses free-for-use software, but the zones are in two different regions.

3. C. A CDN will offer lower latency around the globe. Immutable infrastructure should be used but does not offer any of the requirements. Synchronous replication cannot be used around the globe. Autoscaling should also be used but does not offer any of the requirements.

4. C. No, because you are performing an in-place upgrade, which goes against the concept of disposable resources. Option A may save costs temporarily but has increased risk with an on-prem upgrade. Option B is not correct because Server 2016 being compatible is not enough. You have not performed any testing. D is not correct because the reason for No is not sufficient; load testing is not testing the upgrade process.

5. A, C. Bootstrapping and golden images are technologies that will speed up the deployment and in a repeatable fashion. API does not address any of the requirements. Tagging should be used to fulfill auditing requirements, but those are not mentioned in the question.

6. A, B. Object storage and network usage will have costs associated with the transfer of the data out of the CSP infrastructure. Compute and block storage transfers will be local to the instance itself. Any transfer of data out from the compute will be counted as network costs.

7. A, B, C. All storage offerings including object, block, and file storage will have a cost associated with the amount of data storage, even if resources are powered off (the data is still being stored). All storage is replicated in some manner in the cloud, but there is no storage offering called replicated.

8. C. Chargebacks is the process of creating the tags needed to provide accurate and detailed billing to be able to bill a third party. Right-sizing deals with the process of moving to the cloud. Maintenance is services that are purchased from third parties. You can set up an alert or monitoring for billing, but that is not specific to the question.

9. A. The new feature is a search function. Searches require increased CPU and memory usage. Load testing will be needed to determine which resources will need to be increased. Regression testing should be done, but since this is a new feature, there are no previous bugs concerning searches that can be performed. Sandbox testing should have already been performed. Penetration testing is important from a security perspective but does not address the requirements in the question.

10. D. Right-sizing is the process of evaluating current on-premises servers for need and sizing before moving to the cloud. Templating is used for provisioning servers. Autoscaling is sizing resources in the cloud. Orchestrating is part of configuration management once already in the cloud.

11. B. Alerts can perform actions when events occur or when thresholds are met. Logging does not perform notifications but can be used to trigger an alert. API can be used to set up alerts. Autoscaling is used for increasing or decreasing resources.

12. C. Continuous integration continuous delivery (CI/CD) is the pipeline that is used in the real world. Continuous integration and continuous deployment are used but not in the real world because of the impact on user experience. Options A and D are not real terms.

13. A. Public clouds, such as Microsoft Azure and Amazon Web Service (AWS), offer the best in scalability, reliability, and cost effectiveness. Private clouds do not offer as much cost effectiveness. Community clouds and hybrid clouds are between public and private in terms of scalability and cost effectiveness.

14. B. Blue/green deployment is used for upgrades and patching. Regression and sandbox testing uses different infrastructure than production. Development uses infrastructure that is separate from production.

15. C. Cloud services should lower the cost of network operations and software use for companies. Cloud characteristics include elastic, self-service, scalability, broad network access, pay-as-you-go, and availability.

16. A. The recovery point objective (RPO) defines the maximum age of files that must be recovered from backups in order to restore normal operations. In this case, the RPO needs to be less than an hour. The recovery time objective (RTO) specifies how long services can be down in the event of a disaster. There is no TSO in disaster recovery plans. The service level agreement (SLA) usually contains a section for the disaster recovery plan.

17. A, B, C. API calls are used to manage cloud resources via the web, CLI, and SDK. SSH is a management software of Linux systems.

18. C. Block storage is the storage type used for all OS boot partitions. File and object storage can be used in an instance, but due to their shared nature, neither one can be used as a boot partition. HDD is a type of block storage, but so is SDD. It might be the underlying technology.

19. B. Orchestration is the combination of separate automation tasks. Automation is what we are trying to combine. Autoscaling can be orchestrated but is specific. Patching should be automated but is also too specific.

20. A, B. Both Linux and Apache are open source and free for use. Windows and Cisco ASA are commercial and pay for use.

Chapter 6: Governance and Risk

1.   C. You have not had time to validate the identity of the requestor and whether they have the authority to revoke someone's account. You also have not had time to validate the request with HR, whom the request should have come from. Disabling a user's account would not fall under change management. While a security policy and/or an access and control policy may be the reasoning for disabling the user account, you have not validated the request yet.

2.   A. Your manager sees the value in the change but is requesting information on the risks (known issues and rollback). Resource management is the management of storage, networking, and compute; this question is about making a change, not managing the networking. Risk avoidance is avoiding the risk entirely; your manager is trying to either accept or mitigate the risk. Asset inventory would only pertain to the firewall itself.

3.   C. Resource management, specifically mobile device management, would be able to offer the requested features. There is a sole vendor, but you can change mobile devices if needed, so no vendor lock-in is necessary. Resource management would be able to provide a start of an asset inventory. Security policies are what are driving the request, but the request is specific to the iPhone and on-call engineer staff.

4.   B. At this point you don't know what has occurred. The CEO's account could have been hacked, or this could just be an email phishing attempt. You don't know what the risk is yet, so you don't know how to mitigate it. Communication policies might apply, but only after a full investigation. Findings will be part of the reporting in the incident response.

5.   A. Even though the request is coming from your manager and he is requesting a list of staff and contractors who report to you, this is not a department-specific policy because it is about access to the building itself. This is an access and control policy because it is between two or more assets. Your manager might be following an SOP in making the request, but the request is a policy. There is no assessment; this is an action.

6.   D. This is a department-specific policy because all the information and requests are specific to the HR department. Communication policies deal with communication to the public, and this is internal. There is no risk transfer in the question. It is unclear from the question with this is a violation of SOP or not.

7.   B. The email is a communication of events and response to events that impacted your clients or third parties; the information would be dictated by communication policies. Findings and incident response would be part of the power outage, but they would have already occurred. The steps taken to prevent future outages might be a risk transfer, but that is not spelled out in the question.

8. C, D. Vendor lock-in and data portability are two risks that must be managed when moving services to the cloud. Change and resource management would be part of the move and would continue afterward, but will not make the decision.

9. A, D. Findings and incident response both include reports that would detail events after a risk event occurred. Risk assessment happens before a risk event or will be assessed again now. Change management may have approved a change that caused the event, but that would be part of the report.

10. D. A risk register contains all assets and an organization's response to the identified risks. Owners will have determined the appropriate risk. Standard operating procedures will not detail specific assets. Security policies would help create the risk register but would not encompass security-related assets.

11. B. You are avoiding the increased risk of flooding by moving the infrastructure to the cloud. You are not transferring the risk to the cloud because the cloud will not have the same risk of flooding. Acceptance and mitigation both will have some risk of the identified flooding risk, but since the infrastructure will be moved away from the flooding, there is no risk.

12. C. The organization is mitigating the risk of employees being harmed crossing the busy intersection by offering convenience to the parking garage. Since the organization is purchasing the shuttle, there is no transfer. There is no acceptance because the risk is lower. There is no avoidance because employees could still park at the closer parking garage.

13. A. The security company is offering a service and will pay for any damages incurred while their services are in place; this is a risk transfer. The store is in the same location, so there is no risk avoidance. You are not willing to pay for the window for every breakage, so there is no risk acceptance. The patrol might mitigate the risk slightly, but since they are paying for all damage, it is a transfer.

14. B. The organization is accepting the risk that the sales personnel will not return the organization's equipment half of the time. The organization is not avoiding, mitigating, or transferring the risk of loss of company assets.

15. C. You are accepting the risk of the firewall upgrade even though the upgrade could fail and the current version will end support soon. There is no mitigation or avoidance; the upgrade could fail. There is no transfer of risk to the firewall vendor.

16. B. Risk classifications are generally broken into five categories. They are usually graded either A, B, C, D, F or 1, 2, 3, 4, 5.

17. A, B. The risk owner and asset owner are responsible for assets and the risk response for any asset. Change manager controls change in an organization, not assets or risks. CEOs do not own individual assets or risks.

18. B. The definition of a risk is the occurrence or realization of a threat. Vulnerability, security breach, and phishing attempt are all examples of threats.

19. B. A threat can cause the decrease in value of an asset. Importance does not measure value. Harm and risk are properties of the threat.

20. B. An asset is an item of value through quantitative or qualitative analysis. Threat and value are properties of a risk assessment on an asset. A policy is applied to an asset.

Chapter 7: Compliance and Security in the Cloud

1. B, C. The question mentions China and Germany, which have data sovereignty laws that govern storing for information (saved chat logs). Additionally, it is a public corporation, and the accounting department is involved, which could trigger SOX compliance. No offices are in the United States, so federal regulations will not apply. There is no mention of a security regulation.

2. A. This is an internal email that applies to all employees; therefore, it should remain internal to the organization. It is not sensitive because it applies to all employees. Since it deals with employees' health benefits, it should not be made public. The email does not include any national security matters, so it is not classified.

3. C. This email would be considered public because it will be sent to potential new clients. These clients would not be covered by any nondisclosure agreements; therefore, you must assume it is public. Even though internal metrics are being pulled (private), they are being shared with the public, so it is no longer private.

4. D. This list contains information about a proposed change to employee compensation. Since it is just a proposal and has not been approved, then only management or privileged individuals should know. Once approved, it could become private but should not be public. There are no national security interests; therefore, it's not classified.

5. B. Encryption is a process of ensuring confidentiality. Integrity is ensuring that the transaction is valid. There is no mention of a system being available. No data is being categorized.

6. A. Network diagrams should be considered sensitive due to the information that can be gleaned from their information. Additionally, the old paper diagrams are being destroyed or sanitized, which is confidentiality.

7. C. You performed no actions to validate or prove the integrity of the email. The email contained links that you clicked; this could have been a phishing attempt. You have not locked the CEO's account, so you did not impact availability. Confidentiality and Categorization do not apply.

8. D. Making a copy of a configuration file before a software update is making a backup. You are trying to ensure the availability of the firewall if the software patch fails or makes the firewall unavailable.

9. B. Storing passwords in clear text would be a vulnerability. A script is not an application, and storing passwords would not be a bug because it was specifically set to store the password in clear text. No penetration testing was done. FISMA is specific to information security when working with the federal government.

10. A, D. Vulnerability and application scanning deal with known threats and bugs in software. There is no assessment that deals with scanning data specifically. Auditing is a trail or log of past events.

11. C. Authorization is the security mechanism that should be maintained in a group instead of individuals. Authorization means properties of an asset, not the access of the asset. Categorization and availability do not apply. Authorization could be a vulnerability, but there is no mention of testing or scanning in the question.

12. A. You have been performing off-site backups; therefore, you should be able to recover their files. Paying the ransom is the last resort if backups are not available. Vulnerability scanning and threat analysis might be useful once access to the files has been restored.

13. C. Vulnerabilities are threats that haven't been mitigated. Threats encompass vulnerabilities; options A and B make threats be part of vulnerabilities.

14. B. The key is a right or permission to enter an asset; that makes it an access. You do not have authorization to make any changes yet. The server room is sensitive, but that is the server room, not the key or you. Audit is a history of access, but that is not mentioned.

15. C. A security event happened. Management is requesting changes that would prevent the same security event from occurring again, which is hardening. Changing authorization is not part of scanning or testing. Auditing is a history of actions.

16. B. Risk classification is generally broken into five categories, either graded A, B, C, D, F or 1, 2, 3, 4, 5.

17. D. Network discovery and the list services provided are part of a penetration test. No vulnerability or application scan is performed. Auditing is the history of past actions.

18. B. Certifications are validated by third parties and prove compliance with regulations. Backups are not proofs or involve third parties. Requirements and benchmarks are part of compliance but not proof.

19. B. Only privileged individuals should know the admin passwords for networking equipment. They should not be made public or even shared internally within an organization.

20. D. Any information about a merger that has not occurred yet would be categorized as sensitive; only senior management should know. This information should not be shared with the public or internally. No national security measures are involved.

Index

C

CA (certificate authority), 42

CaaS (communications as a service), 14

CAF (Cloud Adoption Framework)
  AWS (Amazon Web Services), 83
  Microsoft, 84

CALMS (Culture Automation Lean Measurement), 180–181

capacity on demand, 66, 67

CapEx (capital expenditures), 130–131
  human capital, 135–136

categories, 278–279
  private, 279–280
  public, 279
  sensitive, 280–281

CD (continuous delivery), 185

CDNs (content delivery networks), 68–69, 270
  edge servers, 68
  PoP (point of presence), 68

CEO (chief executive officer), 81

certifications, 269

CFO (chief financial officer), 81

change management, 191–192, 235–237

chargebacks, 199–200

Chef, 182

CI (continuous integration), 185

CICD (continuous integration and continuous delivery), 185–186
  automation, 186
  orchestration, 186
  sandboxing, 186

CIO (chief information officer), 81

circumstances, risk and, 217

CISO (chief information security officer), 81

Citrix XenServer, 6

civil investigations, 228

classification, risk, 223–224

CLI (command-line interface), 165

clients
  thick, 165
  thin, 165

cloud, 2
  connecting to
    direct connect, 47
    HTTPS, 39–40
    RDP (Remote Desktop Protocol), 40–43
    SSH (Secure shell), 43–45
    VPN (virtual private network), 45–47

CLOUD Act, 257

cloud computing, 3–4
  advantages, 4
  availability, 18
  broad network access, 18
  disadvantages, 4
  elasticity, 17–18
  pay-as-you-go, 18
  scalability, 18
  self-service, 18

cloud services
  Google, 12–13
  self-service aspect, 117

cloud-defined storage controller, 58

cloud-native applications, 95

cloudware, 11

CloudWatch, 176

code, definition, 183

cold storage, 60

collaboration, 114–115

collaboration tools, 90

communication policies, 243–244

community cloud, 16

compliance, 216
  industry-based requirements, 260–261
  FERPA, 261
  FINRA, 261–262
  GLBA, 262–263
  HIPAA, 263
  MPAA, 263–264
  SOX, 264
  review questions, answers, 321–322

compression, files, 66

compute resources, 198–199

computing model
  cloud computing, 3–4
  traditional, 3

conditions, risk and, 217

confidentiality
  encryption, 281–284
  sanitization, 285

configuration management
  automation, 189–191
  orchestration
    auditing and, 188
    centralized management and, 188
    pipeline, 188
    runbook, 188, 189
    workflow, 188, 189
  patching, 191–192
  upgrades, 191–192

contacts
  point of contact, 82
  SPOC (single point of contact), 81

containerization, 97

content-based load balancing, 52

contract negotiation, 146
  AUP (acceptable use policy), 148
  egress terms, 149
  mistakes, 149
  privacy and security policy, 148
  SLAs (service level agreements), 148
  terms of service, 147–148

control layer, SDN (software-defined networking), 49

corrective access controls, 241

costs, 129–130
  fixed, 132
  licensing models, 132–133
    BYOL (bring your own license), 134
    subscriptions, 135
  variable, 132

criminal investigations, 228

CRM (customer relationship management), 12

cross-region load balancing, 52

CSP (cloud service provider)
  availability, 24
  disaster recovery, 25
  IaaS and, 10
  PaaS and, 11
  shared responsibility model, 20–21
  virtualization and, 8

CTO (chief technology officer), 81

CVE (Common Vulnerabilities Exposures), 272

Online Test Bank

Register to gain one year of FREE access to the online interactive test bank to help you study for your CompTIA Cloud Essentials+ certification exam—included with your purchase of this book! All of the chapter review questions and the practice tests in this book are included in the online test bank so you can practice in a timed and graded setting.

Register and Access the Online Test Bank

To register your book and get access to the online test bank, follow these steps:

1. Go to bit.ly/SybexTest (this address is case sensitive)!
2. Select your book from the list.
3. Complete the required registration information, including answering the security verification to prove book ownership. You will be emailed a pin code.
4. Follow the directions in the email or go to www.wiley.com/go/sybextestprep.
5. Find your book on that page and click the "Register or Login" link with it. Then enter the pin code you received and click the "Activate PIN" button.
6. On the Create an Account or Login page, enter your username and password, and click Login or, if you don't have an account already, create a new account.
7. At this point, you should be in the test bank site with your new test bank listed at the top of the page. If you do not see it there, please refresh the page or log out and log back in.

A Wiley Brand